Cryptographic Security Solutions for the Internet of Things

Mohammad Tariq Banday
University of Kashmir, India

A volume in the Advances in Information Security, Privacy, and Ethics (AISPE) Book Series

IGI Global
DISSEMINATOR OF KNOWLEDGE

Published in the United States of America by
IGI Global
Information Science Reference (an imprint of IGI Global)
701 E. Chocolate Avenue
Hershey PA, USA 17033
Tel: 717-533-8845
Fax: 717-533-8661
E-mail: cust@igi-global.com
Web site: http://www.igi-global.com

Library of Congress Cataloging-in-Publication Data

Names: Banday, Mohammad Tariq, 1969- editor.
Title: Cryptographic security solutions for the Internet of Things / Mohammad Tariq Banday, editor.
Description: Hershey, PA : Information Science Reference, an imprint of IGI Global, [2019] | Includes bibliographical references and index.
Identifiers: LCCN 2017055701| ISBN 9781522557425 (hardcover) | ISBN 9781522557432 (ebook)
Subjects: LCSH: Internet of things--Security measures. | Cryptography.
Classification: LCC TK5102.94 .C77 2019 | DDC 005.8/24--dc23 LC record available at https://lccn.loc.gov/2017055701

This book is published in the IGI Global book series Advances in Information Security, Privacy, and Ethics (AISPE) (ISSN: 1948-9730; eISSN: 1948-9749)

British Cataloguing in Publication Data
A Cataloguing in Publication record for this book is available from the British Library.

Advances in Information Security, Privacy, and Ethics (AISPE) Book Series

ISSN:1948-9730
EISSN:1948-9749

Editor-in-Chief: Manish Gupta, State University of New York, USA

MISSION

As digital technologies become more pervasive in everyday life and the Internet is utilized in ever increasing ways by both private and public entities, concern over digital threats becomes more prevalent.

The **Advances in Information Security, Privacy, & Ethics (AISPE) Book Series** provides cutting-edge research on the protection and misuse of information and technology across various industries and settings. Comprised of scholarly research on topics such as identity management, cryptography, system security, authentication, and data protection, this book series is ideal for reference by IT professionals, academicians, and upper-level students.

COVERAGE

- Global Privacy Concerns
- Telecommunications Regulations
- Cyberethics
- Privacy Issues of Social Networking
- Access Control
- Electronic Mail Security
- Device Fingerprinting
- Tracking Cookies
- CIA Triad of Information Security
- Computer ethics

IGI Global is currently accepting manuscripts for publication within this series. To submit a proposal for a volume in this series, please contact our Acquisition Editors at Acquisitions@igi-global.com or visit: http://www.igi-global.com/publish/.

The Advances in Information Security, Privacy, and Ethics (AISPE) Book Series (ISSN 1948-9730) is published by IGI Global, 701 E. Chocolate Avenue, Hershey, PA 17033-1240, USA, www.igi-global.com. This series is composed of titles available for purchase individually; each title is edited to be contextually exclusive from any other title within the series. For pricing and ordering information please visit http://www.igi-global.com/book-series/advances-information-security-privacy-ethics/37157. Postmaster: Send all address changes to above address.

Titles in this Series

For a list of additional titles in this series, please visit:
https://www.igi-global.com/book-series/advances-information-security-privacy-ethics/37157

Advanced Methodologies and Technologies in System Security, Information Privacy, and...
Mehdi Khosrow-Pour, D.B.A. (Information Resources Management Association, USA)
Information Science Reference • ©2019 • 417pp • H/C (ISBN: 9781522574927) • US $285.00

Handbook of Research on Information and Cyber Security in the Fourth Industrial Revolution
Ziska Fields (University of KwaZulu-Natal, South Africa)
Information Science Reference • ©2018 • 647pp • H/C (ISBN: 9781522547631) • US $345.00

Security and Privacy in Smart Sensor Networks
Yassine Maleh (University Hassan I, Morocco) Abdellah Ezzati (University Hassan I, Morocco) and Mustapha Belaissaoui (University Hassan I, Morocco)
Information Science Reference • ©2018 • 441pp • H/C (ISBN: 9781522557364) • US $215.00

The Changing Scope of Technoethics in Contemporary Society
Rocci Luppicini (University of Ottawa, Canada)
Information Science Reference • ©2018 • 403pp • H/C (ISBN: 9781522550945) • US $225.00

Handbook of Research on Information Security in Biomedical Signal Processing
Chittaranjan Pradhan (KIIT University, India) Himansu Das (KIIT University, India) Bighnaraj Naik (Veer Surendra Sai University of Technology (VSSUT), India) and Nilanjan Dey (Techno India College of Technology, India)
Information Science Reference • ©2018 • 414pp • H/C (ISBN: 9781522551522) • US $325.00

Handbook of Research on Network Forensics and Analysis Techniques
Gulshan Shrivastava (National Institute of Technology Patna, India) Prabhat Kumar (National Institute of Technology Patna, India) B. B. Gupta (National Institute of Technology Kurukshetra, India) Suman Bala (Orange Labs, France) and Nilanjan Dey (Techno India College of Technology, India)
Information Science Reference • ©2018 • 509pp • H/C (ISBN: 9781522541004) • US $335.00

For an entire list of titles in this series, please visit:
https://www.igi-global.com/book-series/advances-information-security-privacy-ethics/37157

IGI Global
DISSEMINATOR OF KNOWLEDGE

701 East Chocolate Avenue, Hershey, PA 17033, USA
Tel: 717-533-8845 x100 • Fax: 717-533-8661
E-Mail: cust@igi-global.com • www.igi-global.com

Editorial Advisory Board

Table of Contents

Section 3
Security Protocols

Section 4
Social/Legal Issues and Forensics

Detailed Table of Contents

Section 1
Introduction

This section provides an overview of the Internet of Things including its applications, underlying technologies, and security challenges and reviews the literature and potential applications of cryptography to secure the internet of things.

The chapter discusses various security challenges in the design of the internet of things and their possible solutions. After presenting a precise introduction to the internet of things, its applications, and technologies enabling it, the chapter discusses its various architectures and models which follow with an introduction of development kits, boards, platforms, hardware, software, and devices used in the internet of things. A concise explanation and discussion on the internet of things standards and protocols with emphasis on their security is presented. Next, various possible security threats and attacks to the internet of things are presented. The subsequent sections of the chapter discuss identified security challenges at individual layers of various models along with their possible solutions. It further presents cryptographic and lightweight cryptographic primitives for the internet of things, existing use of cryptography in the internet of things protocols, security challenges, and its prospectus.

Section 2
Encryption and Cryptography

This section presents encryption principles and discusses various cryptographic algorithms including lightweight cryptography that are applicable for the security of the Internet of Things.

This chapter explores the encryption techniques used for the internet of things (IoT). The security algorithm used for IoT should follow many constraints of an embedded system. Hence, lightweight cryptography is an optimum security solution for IoT devices. This chapter mainly describes the need for security in IoT, the concept of lightweight cryptography, and various cryptographic algorithms along with their shortcomings given IoT. This chapter also describes the principle of operation of all the above algorithms along with their security analysis. Moreover, based on the algorithm size (i.e., the required number of gate equivalent, block size, key size, throughput, and execution speed of the algorithm), the chapter reports the comparative analysis of their performance. The chapter discusses the merits and demerits of these algorithms along with their use in the IoT system.

There are various emerging areas in which profoundly constrained interconnected devices connect to accomplish specific tasks. Nowadays, internet of things (IoT) enables many low-resource and constrained devices to communicate, do computations, and make smarter decisions within a short period. However, there are many challenges and issues in such devices like power consumption, limited battery, memory space, performance, cost, and security. This chapter presents the security issues in such a constrained environment, where the traditional cryptographic algorithms cannot be used and, thus, discusses various lightweight cryptographic algorithms in detail and present a comparison between these algorithms. Further, the chapter also discusses the power awakening scheme and reference architecture in IoT for constrained device environment with a focus on research challenges, issues, and their solutions.

Section 3
Security Protocols

This section discusses some schemes and protocols for securing Internet of Things. These include physically unclonable functions that promise cryptographic security enablers for resource-constrained IoT devices and hardware primitive-based security protocols. It also discusses gateway discovery protocol using ECC for MANET, scheme for node localization, security framework based on contextual information, and secure computation of private set intersection cardinality with linear complexity.

The spatial ubiquity and the huge number of employed nodes monitoring the surroundings, individuals, and devices makes security a key challenge in IoT. Serious security apprehensions are evolving in terms of data authenticity, integrity, and confidentiality. Consequently, IoT requires security to be assured down to the hardware level, as the authenticity and the integrity need to be guaranteed in terms of the hardware implementation of each IoT node. Physically unclonable functions recreate the keys only while the chip is being powered on, replacing the conventional key storage which requires storing information. Compared to extrinsic key storage, they are able to generate intrinsic keys and are far less susceptible against physical attacks. Physically unclonable functions have drawn considerable attention due to their ability to economically introduce hardware-level security into individual silicon dice. This chapter introduces the notion of physically unclonable functions, their scenarios for hardware security in IoT devices, and their interaction with traditional cryptography.

IoT is the enabling technology for a variety of new exciting services in a wide range of application areas including environmental monitoring, healthcare systems, energy management, transportation, and home and commercial automation. However, the low-cost and straightforward nature of IoT devices producing vast amounts of sensitive data raises many security concerns. Among the cyber threats, hardware-level threats are especially crucial for IoT systems. In particular, IoT devices are not physically protected and can easily be captured by an adversary to launch physical and side-channel attacks. This chapter introduces security protocols for IoT devices based on hardware security primitives called physically unclonable functions (PUFs). The protocols are discussed for the following major security principles: authentication and confidentiality, data provenance, and anonymity. The security analysis shows that security protocols based on hardware security primitives are not only secure against network-level threats but are also resilient against physical and side-channel attacks.

PSI and its variants play a major role when the participants want to perform secret operations on their private data sets. The importance of this chapter is twofold. In the first phase, the author presents a size-hiding PSI-CA protocol followed by its authorized variant, APSI-CA, utilizing Bloom filter. All these constructions are proven to be secure in standard model with linear complexity. In the second phase, the author employs Bloom filter to design an efficient mPSI-CA protocol. It achieves fairness using offline semi-trusted third party (arbiter) unlike the most efficient existing protocols. The arbiter is semi-trusted in the sense that he does not have access to the private information of the entities while he will follow the protocol honestly. Proposed mPSI-CA is proven to be secure against malicious adversaries in the random oracle model (ROM) under the decisional Diffie-Hellman (DDH) assumption. It achieves linear complexity.

Integration procedures are employed to increase and enhance computing networks and their application domain. Extensive studies towards the integration of MANET with the internet have been studied and worked towards addressing various challenges for such integration. Some idyllic mechanisms always fail due to the presence of some nasty node or other problems such as face alteration and eavesdropping. The focus of this chapter is on the design and discovery of secure gateway scheme in MANET employing trust-based security factors such as route trust and load ability. Over these, the elliptic curve cryptography is applied to achieve confidentiality, integrity, and authentication while selecting optimum gateway node that has less bandwidth, key storage space, and faster computational time. Simulation results of the security protocol through SPAN for AVISPA tool have shown encouraging results over two model checkers namely OFMC and CL-AtSe.

This chapter introduces a new security scheme for mobile anchors avoiding the physical layer attacks towards localization in wireless sensor networks (WSNs). In a network, anchors are made location-aware equipping them with GPS (global positioning system) receivers. Direction finding capabilities are also incorporated with smart antennas. The proposed algorithm is based on adaptive beamforming of smart array that always minimizes the probabilities of successful attacks, keeping the adversaries beyond its beam coverage. Particle swarm optimization (PSO) technique is used to compute array excitation coefficients, generating the desired pattern. Thus, anchors remain secured through pattern irregularities, deteriorating the information retrieval process even though chances of occurring adequate RSS (received signal strength)/AoA (angle of arrival) measurements may exist. Moreover, anchors are assumed to send pseudo references towards stationary nodes over private links, preserving data integrity for localization. Simulation results validate its effectiveness over the existing methods.

With the growth of Internet of Things and user demand for personalized applications, context-aware applications are gaining popularity in current IT cyberspace. Personalized content, which can be a notification, recommendation, etc., are generated based on the contextual information such as location, temperature, and nearby objects. Furthermore, contextual information can also play an important role in security management of user or device in real time. When the context of a user or device changes, the security mechanisms should also be updated in real time for better performance and quality of service. Access to a specific resource may also be dependent upon user's/device's current context. In this chapter, the role of contextual information for IoT application security is discussed and a framework is provided which auto-updates security policy of the device based on its current context. Proposed framework makes use of machine learning algorithm to update the security policies based on the current context of the IoT device(s).

Section 4
Social/Legal Issues and Forensics

This section illustrates various concerns regarding the social and legal aspects of the internet of things through a case study. It also discusses the importance of digital forensics for the Internet of Things and its underlying challenges.

The advent of internet represents a revolution for the contemporary era, having brought about a striking series of changes in social, institutional, political, and economic life. This ongoing revolution has spread and absorbed within itself all the problems related to its own development. Objects become recognizable and acquire intelligence in that they are able to communicate data regarding themselves and also access other information aggregated by other devices. They are able to participate in a dialogue and interact among themselves within electronic communication networks without human intervention. All objects can acquire an active role thanks to connection with the web. The associated problems, which can no longer be ignored, draw attention above all to the lack of data control, which is to the vast extent of the data collected and more generally to the security of these data. This chapter has the aim of analyzing the ways in which European legislators, and consequently also Italian representatives, have intervened in order to stem the tide of emerging issues.

The pervasive nature of IoT, envisioned with the characteristics of diversity, heterogeneity, and complexity, is diluting the boundaries between the physical and digital worlds. IoT being widely distributed qualifies it as the breeding ground for cyber-attacks. Although remarkable work is being done to ensure security in IoT infrastructure, security vulnerabilities persist. The IoT infrastructure can either be used as a direct target in a cyber-attack or exploited as a tool to carry a cyber-attack. In either case, the security measures in IoT infrastructure is compromised. The enormous IoT data is sensitive that can act as a gold mine to both the criminals for illicit exploitation or investigators to act as digital witness. IoT forensics help the investigators to acquire intelligence from this smart infrastructure to reconstruct the historical events occurred. However, due to sophisticated IoT architecture,

Foreword

The *Internet of Things* is a term used to refer to programmable devices that have the capacity to connect to the Internet, to interact with other devices, to accept and react to controls and commands and to generate and export data. The users of these devices expect, inter alia, that they will be safe to use, will be reliable, will be secure, will be easy to use and configure at scale, will not accept controls or commands from unauthorized parties, can be updated securely with new software, and will protect their privacy. This book addresses these and other challenges posed by this new genus of Internet-enabled devices. The authors address various aspects of these expectations, applying technology and structural organization as well as good operating practices to improve the likelihood that users will not be disappointed. It is vital that manufacturers of this class of device understand these expectations and meet them. To assure user acceptance, manufacturers will almost certainly be expected to support these devices for the expected lifetime of usage. That could be decades in some cases. That may call for retrofitting with new controls, for example. Moreover, if the manufacturers cease support or go out of business, it should be possible for a third party to get access to the source code for purposes of maintenance. One can readily imagine regulatory regimes that require the escrow of source code to protect against this eventuality. One can imagine an "after market" of support and perhaps augmentation with additional accessories and features.

Failure to meet these expectations can have serious if not catastrophic consequences. Devices in manufacturing plants, residences, office buildings could malfunction, leading to fires, mechanical failures brought about by errant controls, invasion of privacy owing to weak and vulnerable operating systems, loss of privacy owing to penetration of the controls of these devices and a multitude of other harms. That the makers of this class of device have ethical responsibilities should be self-evident. To the degree that this is not recognized, regulation to impose penalties for failure to meet these responsibilities can readily be envisioned and in some cases, laws are already being enacted for that purpose. From the academic perspective, better software tools to expose mistakes that lead to malfunction or vulnerability are desirable. Strong authentication to assure that the devices accept controls only from authorized parties seems an obvious choice. Coping with the configuration and operation of dozens to thousands of devices implies that designers have given serious thought to ease and reliability of installation and use. Continuous monitoring for proper operation and auditing of access are two practices that seem essential to meeting user expectations. As they say, the devil is in the details, so this book is a good introduction to what some of those details are.

Vint Cerf
Google, USA
Woodhurst, December 2018

Preface

The paradigm of Internet of Things (IoT) ranges from small wearables to huge industrial systems affecting almost all domains of human environment and promise to offer better experiences. IoT is being embraced by every sphere of the physical world, hence, increasing its market landscape unexpectedly. The number of connected IoT devices is reported to be around 7 billion (7B) excluding smartphones, laptops, tablets, and other similar gadgets. This unprecedented magnitude of connected devices has a profound impact on consumer and industrial applications leading to a surge in academic and industrial research. Overwhelming advancement in technology has led to the genesis of the era of Internet of Things (IoT) and is making rapid advancements with every passing day. At the heart of IoT is the seamless connectivity between objects over the Internet or some private network that adds to pervasiveness and ubiquity of the Internet by connecting everything in a highly distributed manner.

The very existence of IoT relies on many technologies that include application programming interfaces (APIs), cloud services, connectivity technologies, artificial intelligence (AI), big data management, analytics, etc. The significant connectivity technologies surrounding IoT include traditional cellular, short-range wireless, wired, LPWAN, and WWAN, satellite, etc. Each of these technologies, in turn, uses many sub-technologies to meet different requirements specific to IoT applications.

The deployment of IoT is possible due to various backbone frameworks that are needed to support a large number of IoT applications. IoT architectures cover end-to-end elements that include devices, gateways, cloud platforms, and applications. An IoT ecosystem is characterized by the features of connectivity, sensing, intelligence, dynamicity, heterogeneity, enormous scalability, constrained nature, mobility, context-awareness, etc. This highly distributed nature and global heterogeneity in the underlying network technologies and massive scale of constituent devices/objects/things result in fragmented IoT ecosystems that raise the issues of interoperability, semantic conflicts, security, etc.

The constrained IoT devices have limited resources in terms of processing ability/power, memory, size, battery power, etc. which prevent developers from implementing measures to achieve the primary security objectives of Confidentiality, Integrity, and Authentication (CIA). The cumulative impact of factors leads to security vulnerabilities at different layers of its architecture. The main security concerns in IoT pertain to data encryption, data authentication, side channel attacks, hardware testing of a paramount device range, etc.

The full potential of IoT cannot be realized and harnessed until there is absolute guarantee or trust of security and privacy to end users. Trust can be achieved by securing data not only inherent in IoT devices but to all the data in transit over the network during its journey to cloud data centers and beyond. Although traditional security plays its role, yet IoT has its unique aspects that necessitate much broader and integrated approaches towards security. Among various procedures to ensure security in IoT systems, cryptographic solutions are the most promising and prominent ones. However, to implement cryptography and to add security to IoT systems, the practitioners need a better understanding of the cryptographic context, its underlying protocols, and mechanisms.

Cryptography plays a pivotal role in ensuring security in IoT systems by encrypting data before transmitting it over the network. The conventional cryptographic algorithmic computations are unlikely to happen in low-end IoT devices due to requirements of enormous computing power and resources. The current security protocols used in IoT are dependent on cryptographic algorithms that are resource efficient and consume lesser amount of computing resources usually known as lightweight cryptographic algorithms explicitly designed for the resource-constrained devices. These are lightweight symmetric algorithms (a single encryption key), asymmetric algorithms (two encryption keys, public and private), and cryptographic protocols. Compared to the conventional cryptographic algorithms, lightweight cryptographic algorithms used by IoT systems are more responsive and faster, more efficient in terms of energy and storage (less resource hungry) and are usually powered by crypto-engines. These lightweight algorithms have distinct design criteria tailored perfectly considering the limited resources of IoT infrastructure. However, these algorithms still have to make a trade-off between cost, security, and performance when implemented in practice. The key-length and the number of encryption rounds in the lightweight algorithm will be affected significantly based on the underlying hardware architecture features like chip size and energy consumption and the software architecture features like RAM size and smaller code. Currently, the lightweight cryptographic algorithms are either designed afresh or as some efficient modifications of conventional cryptographic algorithms. The primitives of block ciphers, stream ciphers, hash functions, etc. in lightweight cryptography enhance their performance over traditional cryptography in such resource-constrained IoT systems.

Although there is a dramatic evolution of IoT and remarkable improvement in security techniques, IoT remains open for new vulnerabilities and threats. The increased number of threats, attacks, vulnerabilities, etc. motivates IoT device manufacturers, Cloud Service Providers (CSPs) and researchers in academia and industry to work towards addressing these issues by designing systems with controlled and secure information flow, vulnerability detection capabilities, etc. with a constant improvement in architectural design and adaptive frameworks. The simplified implementation of IoT applications requires to follow a set of standards and protocols. Hence, the current practitioners work towards the development of strategies about standardization of these lightweight IoT algorithms.

While its works is progressing, most of the solutions applied to make IoT ecosystems secure are still in their inception phase and have a long way to go. As the IoT proliferation increases, there is a proportional rise in security issues and concerns as well.

The book explores the strategies towards determining the best security solutions to safeguard the devices, networks, and data in IoT systems. The field of IoT is relatively new; the infrastructure is marketed with existing embedded system security measures. Soon, the IoT systems are expected to be intelligent enough to be adaptive to detect and deal with the security risks and attacks automatically. The security in IoT environments continues to evolve with the evolution of general network security. The security needs to be implemented in a multi-layered manner from basic design to end application. The consideration of secure booting, access control, device authentication, firewalling and IPS, and updates and patches is the spine of security solutions.

This book walks the readers through concepts related to IoT cryptographic solutions that shape the security of concurrent IoT ecosystems. It aims to educate readers, practitioners, and researchers in the critical areas of IoT security, and provide an in-depth understanding of IoT infrastructure, its characteristics, application domain, potential security issues and challenges, the basic principles of cryptography and encryption, etc. A clear description of the concepts underlying IoT ecosystems is provided. The book explores the available cryptographic algorithms exhaustively. A comprehensive study of IoT security protocols required to handle the challenge of building a secure IoT architecture and infrastructure is discussed. Social and legal issues faced in the deployment of IoT environments along with the forensic investigations and challenges in case of security compromise are also provided. A framework for the critical understanding of key elements that uniquely emphasize the IoT security solutions has also been given. The book uses realistic examples to describe and explain the IoT security concepts and has been structured in a way that it allows readers to think of the future context of IoT security. Significant scientific literature has been reviewed thoroughly during the chapter build-up, enhancing the pedagogical value of the book. The book is a perfect balance of theory and practice for the understanding and evaluation of security policies, issues, challenges, and solutions.

The book is intended for academic and professional personnel including engineers, scientists/researchers or students interested in understanding the basics of IoT, its security issues and the associated cryptographic solution. It explains the basic terminology and the technology encountered when dealing with IoT systems. The book, however, assumes that the reader has elementary knowledge of cryptographic algorithms and is quite useful for aspirants eager to learn communication of data within an IoT environment. The book is an endeavor to encourage its readers to dig deeper into the depths of IoT security issues and cryptographic solutions. The functional features of the chapters are better explained and visualized with the help of diagrams and figures that enhance the understanding of readers. The readers of this book will also be exposed to computational and mathematical preliminaries of IoT security solutions that will aid them in limiting the attack possibilities for hackers.

The chapters in this book are the result of a lot of reflection, incisive insight, comments, and suggestions submitted by well-renowned reviewers in the field. The readers are encouraged to follow chapters sequentially to get a thorough understanding of the book.

The content of the book is organized into four major sections that are further sub-divided into constructive chapters. Each section includes chapters based on some specific relationships or similarity between their subject matter. A brief discussion of each chapter is presented below:

Chapter 1 introduces in detail the Internet of Things (IoT), its applications, associated technologies, various available architectural models proceeded by the presentation of various development kits, boards, platforms, hardware, software and devices used to deploy Internet of Things (IoT). Also, the chapter brings forth a healthy discussion of IoT security, standards, and protocols. The chapter highlights the potential security vulnerabilities, threats, and attacks that can compromise an IoT system. An explanation of the various challenges present in IoT environments and solutions to deal with these challenges using lightweight cryptographic solutions is provided. This chapter provides the foundation for the further understanding of the subject matter.

Chapter 2 discusses the requirement of security in IoT systems, various encryption techniques that are employed in Internet of Things (IoT) and argues for the demand of lightweight cryptography that fits the constrained IoT systems. The chapter presents the principle of operation of various algorithms; the security analysis, comparative performance analysis based on different parameters, and application, etc. of these algorithms.

Chapter 3 presents the resource-constrained nature of IoT systems and operations and decision-making capabilities by IoT devices. It discusses various security issues that are intrinsic to constrained IoT environments. The chapter proceeds with a detailed and comparative discussion of various lightweight cryptographic algorithms. The chapter also presents the power of awakening scheme and reference architecture in IoT with an emphasis on research challenges and possible solutions.

Chapter 4 reviews literature concerning the design, prospectus, and challenges of Physically Unclonable Functions (PUFs) for ensuring hardware-level authentication in the Internet of Things. It discusses their working, key generation process, and characteristics that make them promising cryptographic security enablers for resource-constrained IoT devices.

Chapter 5 deals with security concerns on the application of Internet of Things (IoT) that generate and consume huge sensitive data. The focus is on more critical hardware-based security threats leaving the physical devices vulnerable to several attacks. Based on this assumption, the chapter discusses various security protocols based on hardware security primitives called Physically Unclonable Functions (PUFs) for main security principles making them resilient against physical and side-channel attacks.

Chapter 6 introduces the remarkable role of PSI and its variants when secret operations on private datasets are performed between mutually distrustful entities. The chapter is divided into two parts: the first presents a size-hiding PSI-CA protocol followed by its authorized variant, APSI-CA, utilizing the Bloom filter and the second part employs Bloom filter to design an efficient mPSI-CA protocol that uses a semi-trusted arbiter to achieve fairness. The proposed mPSI-CA achieves linear complexity and is proven to be more secure against malicious adversaries in the random oracle model (ROM) under the Decisional Diffie-Hellman (DDH) assumption.

Chapter 7 presents the need for integration of MANET with the Internet to enhance the existing networks and their application domain. The chapter focuses on design and discovery of secure gateway mechanism in MANET using trust-based security factors. The elliptic curve cryptography is applied to ensure the security principles in selecting the best gateway node. The chapter simulates the security protocol and the results shown are encouraging over the model checkers of OFMC and CL-AtSe.

Chapter 8 introduces a new paradigm for security of mobile anchors to avoid physical attacks towards localization in wireless sensor networks (WSNs). Incorporation of location and direction awareness in mobile anchors using Global Positioning System (GPS) and smart antennas respectively is discussed. An algorithm is proposed to minimize the probabilities of successful attacks based on adaptive beamforming. The chapter argues that the irregularities in pattern ensure the security of anchors at the same time preserving data integrity using pseudo references. The simulation results are calculated that validate the effectiveness of the proposed algorithm over existing methods.

Chapter 9 discusses the importance and role of contextual information in security management of a user or device in real-time in IoT ecosystems. The chapter presents the need to update the security mechanisms in real-time whenever the user or device context changes. A framework is proposed which uses a machine learning algorithm to provide a capability to auto-update the device security policy based on its context making it highly adaptive.

Chapter 10 discusses the impact of Internet revolution in all the aspects of human life like social, institutional, political, economic, etc. and the incorporation of intelligence in almost all the objects connected to the network. The chapter highlights the problems associated with the lack of control over the amount of data generated or consumed and the security of this data. The chapter takes up a case study to analyze how, European legislators generally and Italian representatives specifically, intervene legally to tackle these current emerging social and legal issues about the Internet.

Chapter 11 highlights the importance of IoT generated data in digital forensic techniques carried to solve any compromise in IoT environments. It discusses the various challenges investigators face during various phases of the forensic process, forensics at different architectural levels and the digital evidence acquisition and extraction from IoT associated data. The chapter also discusses the requirement of a separate forensic framework and tools for IoT related crimes to cater to the specific needs of IoT regarding its intrinsic characteristics of device and data diversity, heterogeneity, lack of standards, etc.

For the best understanding and experience of concepts, an attempt for an in-depth treatment of topics with a striking balance between the existing issues and their potential solutions are presented. The book is a comprehensive and all-inclusive presentation of the state-of-the-art IoT security issues and challenges that build a base link towards their solution measures.

Acknowledgment

My acknowledgement would be incomplete if I failed to express my gratitude to IGI Global for consenting to the publication of my manuscript. I also extend my thanks to the development, editorial and marketing teams of IGI Global for their sedulous efforts in the absence of which my book would have remained a distant dream.

Praise is due to the authors who contributed to this volume.

I am humbled by the invaluable inputs and suggestions of members of the editorial board and reviewers that helped improve the quality, structural framework and presentation of the chapters.

I thank my colleagues and scholars at the University of Kashmir for their wholehearted support.

My debt to my parents, wife and children remains ineffable. It is too profound to be put into words.

Mohammad Tariq Banday
University of Kashmir, India

Section 1
Introduction

This section provides an overview of the Internet of Things including its applications, underlying technologies, and security challenges and reviews the literature and potential applications of cryptography to secure the internet of things.

Chapter 1
Security in Context of the Internet of Things: A Study

Mohammad Tariq Banday
University of Kashmir, India

ABSTRACT

The chapter discusses various security challenges in the design of the internet of things and their possible solutions. After presenting a precise introduction to the internet of things, its applications, and technologies enabling it, the chapter discusses its various architectures and models which follow with an introduction of development kits, boards, platforms, hardware, software, and devices used in the internet of things. A concise explanation and discussion on the internet of things standards and protocols with emphasis on their security is presented. Next, various possible security threats and attacks to the internet of things are presented. The subsequent sections of the chapter discuss identified security challenges at individual layers of various models along with their possible solutions. It further presents cryptographic and lightweight cryptographic primitives for the internet of things, existing use of cryptography in the internet of things protocols, security challenges, and its prospectus.

DOI: 10.4018/978-1-5225-5742-5.ch001

INTRODUCTION

The Internet of Things (IoT) is a technological revolution in the field of computing and communications due to practical and rapid innovation in many technologies including Internet, computing, artificial intelligence, data processing, communications, sensors, processors, networks, control and many other technologies underlying it. Web of Things, Internet of Objects, Embedded Intelligence, and Connected Devices are some of the aliases used for this technological revolution. It involves a very high prevalence of entities called things which have unique identities on the Internet and communicate to transfer data over it. Several other computing technologies such as Cyber-Physical Systems, Pervasive Computing, Ubiquitous Computing or Calm technology, Machine-to-Machine Interaction, Human-Computer Interaction, and Ambient Intelligence have a very close resemblance with the Internet of Things. Kevin Ashton is believed to have first used the term 'Internet of Things'. Though no uniquely agreed definition of this term has been agreed upon by academicians, researchers, practitioners, innovators, developers, and corporates, however, the definition given by ITU-T Y.2060 is most widely used. The term 'Internet of Things' is defined by ITU-T Y.2060 as: *"a global infrastructure for the information society, enabling advanced services by interconnecting (physical and virtual) things based on existing and evolving interoperable information and communication technologies"*. Further in the context of the Internet of Things, it defines 'Things' as: *'a piece of equipment with the mandatory capabilities of communication and the optional capabilities of sensing, actuation, data capture, data storage, and data processing'*. A significant focus in this definition is on the edge devices. The services offered by or through the cloud such as 'data collection,' 'brokerage and storage,' 'data analytics,' 'inventory and sensor management,' 'visualization and monitoring,' and 'device relationship' play an important a role in the successful implementation of its capabilities. The Internet of Things can be realized as a centralized system, or a distributed system or a combination of both. In the centralized approach, objects, i.e., 'Things' are connected to centralized cloud infrastructures while as in distributed approach 'Things' at the edge of the network collaborate without the requirement of centralized control. All of these approaches create a worldwide network of interconnected objects. These objects range from human beings to everyday objects such as cars, appliances, etc. and specialized tools such as industrial machinery, medical devices, etc. All of these objects can behave as producers and consumers of services, and can also communicate directly or indirectly with each other. Internet of Things may be either cloud-centric or distributed. In a centralized approach of IoT, acquisition networks provide data to the Cloud. The requirements of various IoT applications: from eHealth to retail, from logistics to smart city management can be fulfilled using this approach. In this distributed approach of IoT, multiple entities located at the edge of the network can locally and remotely collaborate without depending on a purely centralized infrastructure.

Applications

Since its inception, Internet of Things has made significant progress in some application areas such as home automation, smart cities, agriculture, livestock management, healthcare, industrial control, transportation, and many other utilities. The active involvement and research of small and large business houses to offering IoT enabled services have increased applications of IoT in almost every sphere of human activity. However, the depth and breadth of this application vary significantly from one region to another due to various factors that include economic, regional, technical and others. Applications of the Internet of Things in different industries offer different services and solutions that benefit its users. As an example, with the application of the Internet of Things, home automation can be made more intelligent, remotely monitored, and more secure. Gadgets such as air conditioners, lights, security systems, etc. can be remotely monitored and controlled from different types of devices having diverse connectivity with the Internet. Another example is its use to make cities smart where the applications of the Internet of Things is very vast. It has potential to monitor and regulate cities intelligently, automatically offer and control services, real-time information sharing among netizens, real-time disaster management, etc. Another example is the use of Internet of Things in the domain of agriculture and livestock management. Alerts and automated processes can be set up for water control, air control, environmental monitoring and control, food safety, crop yield management, etc. Another example is its vast range of applications for healthcare. Internet of Things can be used to effectively and efficiently manage better health care, improve quality and reduce service delivery time and costs. Not only monitoring of health data of patients but treatments can be done remotely using appropriate IoT setups. Internet of things offers various services, solutions and benefits by the use of appropriate setups in different domains of its application. Remote monitoring and diagnosis, remote expert diagnosis in case of failure, production line automation, equipment handling and diagnosis through sensors are some of the services that IoT offers in the manufacturing domain. These services reduce field costs, improve quality, lower energy usage, lower breakdowns, optimize scheduling, improve operational efficiency, and permit anomaly detection. In healthcare domain, it can offer services such as patient care, remote consultation, disease management and at the same time benefit the user by a reduction in cost associated with the care, real-time disease monitoring, and improved healthcare. Real-time vehicle tracking, asset management, logistics optimization, and security and control are some of the services that Internet of Things can offer in the Transportation domain while benefiting its users with improved service levels at reduced costs. Every domain of human activity can offer new services and support by the application of the Internet of Things, thereby benefiting its users by one or more of cost reduction, improved service quality and ease of use. With the availability of easy to use IoT platforms, devices and services, the scale of the Internet of Things applications is growing very fast.

TECHNOLOGIES ENABLING INTERNET OF THINGS

Internet of Things encompasses many underlying technologies that permit it to sense, communicate, analyze, and act or react to people and other machines autonomously. This has been explained by Mark Weiser (Godowsky et al., 2015) through an information value loop which has discrete but connected stages. These are:

- **Create:** Collect information about a physical event or state.
- **Communicate:** Information transfer from one place/device to another place/device.
- **Aggregate:** Collection of information together at different times from multiple sources.
- **Analyze:** Examination of collected information to derive meaning or relationships.
- **Act:** Maintaining, changing or initiating a physical event or state.

Each stage is connected with another stage through a specific set of technologies. These are:

- **Sensors:** Belonging to the broader category of transducers, the sensor (Simpson & Lamb, 2010) is a device that generates an electronic signal from a physical condition or event. Sensors may be active or passive depending upon the requirement of the power source. For acquiring different physical conditions more than one sensor may be required. Even more than one sensor may be combined to create a complex loop. Accuracy, repeatability, range, noise, resolution, and selectivity are general factors that determine the suitability of a particular sensor for a particular application. (Fraden, 2010; Rakocevic, 2004)
- **Networks:** Networks are used to transmit data gathered from sensors to other locations for aggregation, processing, and analysis. Networking devices such as routers, gateways, switches, hubs, etc. may be used in the path between the sensor-driven source and the destination. In the Internet of Things, sensors

are part of a node which comprises of other hardware such as processors, actuators, communication interfaces, etc. and software as well. These nodes have unique addresses on the network for identification and communication. Proprietary or Open network protocols are used for their identification and authorization. Internet Protocol version 6 due to its larger address space has become a de facto standard for most of the IoT technologies. Depending upon the type of the application, geographical spread, and coverage, wireless network technologies are being used in the Internet of Things. Due to the higher power consumption of the conventional wireless technologies in the Internet of Things, emphasis is given on those technologies which have lower power consumption.

- **Standards:** Technology standards and regulatory standards are the two types of standards, relevant for the aggregation of data collected through sensors. Technology standards, in turn, comprise of network protocols, and communication protocols. These have been briefly listed in the above item. In IoT, communication protocols refer to lighter versions of the conventional communication protocols for the device to device communications such as the Constrained Application Protocol (CoAP). Data aggregation standards refer to the protocols that permit data to be collected from diverse formats and make it useful for analytical applications. With the growth of the Internet of Things in recent years, several such tools under the name big-data tools have been developed. Several standards as discussed in detail in later part of this chapter have evolved for the Internet of Things, however, lately, there have been considerable efforts from standardizing bodies such as IEEE and IETF to build a worldwide standard for the Internet of Things (Stephen, 2014).
- **Augmented Intelligence:** It is a set of analytical tools to improve the ability to predict, describe and exploit the relationship among phenomena facilitating cognitive technologies. (Schatsky et al., 2014) These technologies include computer vision, natural language processing, and speech recognition.
- **Augmented Behavior:** It involves carrying out of some action by previous stages of the information value loop, i.e., from sensing to data analysis. A delicate line divides augmented intelligence from the augmented behavior; the former drives information action and the latter is an observable action.

The technologies enabling the Internet of Things have been described by Ala Al-Fuqaha et al. (Al-Fuqaha, 2015) as various elements that are: Semantic, Service, Computation (hardware and software), Communication, Sensing, and Identification. The work has presented examples for each of these elements including standards, protocols, and operating systems that enable the Internet of Things.

Architectures and Protocols

The heterogeneous nature of the Internet of Things, the diverse type of technologies underlying it, and necessities to achieve better interoperability demands an architectural framework that separates services and operations between its layers. Conventional network models and architectures have been the basis for the current IoT architectures. However, various architectures have been put forth to explain the IoT ecosystem, implementation, services, and applications, creating a much more full range of architectures and models that made its standardization difficult. As such, there is no agreed referential architecture for the Internet of Things. The basic referential architecture which was introduced during early stages of research in the area is a '*three-layer architecture*' (Mashal, 2015; Said & Masud, 2013) having a perception layer, a network layer, and an application layer. This architecture defines the basic idea of the Internet of Things from sensing at the perception layer that acts as a physical layer to the delivery of specific service at the application layer through networking devices at the network layer. This architecture is, however, not sufficient for research and therefore, various 5-layer architectures (Mashal, 2015; Said & Masud, 2013; Wu et al., 2010) have been proposed. Apart from the application and perception layers, this architecture includes transport, processing (middleware) and business layers. Also, many other architectures based on human brain (Ning & Wang, 2011), cloud and fog reference architectures (Bonomi et al., 2014; Bonomi et al., 2012; Stojmenovic & Wen 2014) and social (Atzori, Iera & Morabito, 2011) inspirations have also been proposed.

- **Reference Architecture Model for Industrie 4.0 (RAMI4.0):** A reference architecture (Hankel & Rexroth, 2015) for smart industries focusing on to manage vertical integration within the factories and horizontal integration extending beyond individual factories through value networks.
- **Industrial Internet Reference Architecture (IIRA):** A reference architecture (Lin et al., 2017) based on ISO/IEC/IEEE42010:2011 standards focus on the implementation of industrial Internet of Things. The three-tier example of industrial IoT reference architecture (IIRA) consists of an edge tier which collects data from the sensing, actuating and control nodes; platform tier providing services for data analytics and device management and an enterprise tier that implements applications.
- **IoT Architectural Reference Model (IoT-ARM):** A generic architecture (Bassi et al., 2013) focusing on building interoperable vertical applications with common horizontal grounds has several sub-models and is based on technologies, devices, objects and services. These are the domain model, information model, functional model, communication model, IoT trust,

security and privacy model, and IoT reference architecture. All sub-models are based on the underlying dynamic model.

- **IEEE Standard for an Architectural Framework for the Internet of Things (P2413):** This reference architecture covers the definition of basic architectural building blocks and their ability to be integrated into multi-tiered systems. It provides a blueprint for data abstraction, security, and privacy.
- **WSO2 IoT Reference Architecture:** This is a five-layer architecture (Fremantle, 2015) comprising of the device, communication, aggregation/bus, event processing and client/external vertical layers. Also, this architecture has two cross-cutting layers namely device manager and identity and access management layers. This architecture aims to support integration between systems and devices.
- **Internet-of-Everything Reference Model:** This architecture (CISCO, 2014) proposed by Architecture Committee of IoT World Forum hosted by Cisco defines standard terminology and functionality for a better understanding of Internet of Things and its working. It is aimed to explain the process of connecting people, processes, data and things to enable valuable business opportunities by taking its advantage of intelligent interactions between involved entities. It is a 7-layer architecture and divides the Internet of Things in physical devices, connectivity, edge/fog computing, data accumulation, data abstraction, applications, and colorations.
- **Microsoft Azure IoT Reference Architecture:** Build upon Microsoft Azure, this architecture (Microsoft, 2018) comprises of core platform services and application-level components to facilitate device connectivity, data processing, analytics and management, and presentation and business connectivity using Microsoft Azure services.
- **Intel IoT Platform Reference Architecture:** Intel IoT Reference Architecture is a layered model having two versions; one for the legacy and unconnected devices and the other for smart and connected devices. This architecture comprises of communication and connectivity layer, data layer, management layer, control layer, application layer and business layer (Intel, 2014). Also, it includes a vertical security layer for protection and security across all layers.
- **Arrowhead Framework:** This architecture (Arrowhead, 2018) based on service-oriented architecture has been proposed specifically for manufacturing, smart buildings, and infrastructure, electro-mobility, virtual markets and energy production applications of the Internet of Things. The service-oriented architecture uses a service model where every device is associated with one or more set of micro-services, providing leverage of modular service creation and implementing micro-services in a platform-independent manner.

In addition to the above briefly introduced reference architectures, there have been many other proposed referential architectures for the Internet of Things. All proposed architectures have divided the tasks into vertical layers for easy understanding, interoperability, etc. while a few of them gives horizontal layering for other aspects such as security. All architectures have similarities across technical, architectural, quality and key system and business and people perspectives (Breivold, 2017). These referential architectures are highly beneficial for not only understanding of key concepts, technologies, interfaces, applications, hardware, and software involved in it but also to devise software stacks which can have interoperability across diverse systems.

Various Internet of Things technologies uses different protocols for different functionalities at each of the protocol stacks with IPv6 protocol used in most of them due to its benefits such as that include unicast, multicast, mobility support, address scope, and auto configuration. These technologies have been compiled and summarized by Triantafyllou et al. in their recent research work (Triantafyllou, Sarigiannidis & Lagkas, 2018). These are: Bluetooth Low Energy (BLE), ZigBee, Z-Wave, 6LoWPAN, WiFi-ah (HaLow), LTE-A or eMTC (3GPP), 2G (GSM), 3G, 4G, 5G (3GPP), Weightless -N/-W/-P, Thread, NFC, RFID, LoRaWAN, SigFox, Neul, Dash7, WirelessHART, EnOcean, DigiMesh, Ingenu, ANT and ANT+, and NB-IoT (3GPP). The Technologies can use one or more of the following network topologies: star, P2P, multihop mesh, mesh, cluster tree, scatter nets, L2-Mesh, Bus, or MS/TP. Protocols for different operations can be classified as follows:

- **Application or Session Layer Protocols:** MQTT, SMQTT, AMQP, CoAP, XMPP, DDS, XML, HTTP, REST.
- **Transport Layer Protocols:** UDP, TCP, mTP, UDP-LITE.
- **Network Layer Routing Protocols:** RPL, CORPL, CARP, AODV, LOADng, AODv2.
- **Network Layer Encapsulation Protocols:** 6LoWPAN, 6TiSCH, ZigBee IP, IPv6 over G.9959, IPv6 over BLE, IPV6 over NFC, IPv6 over MS/TP-(6LoBAC), IPv6 over DECT/ULE, Ipv6 over 802.11ah.
- **Data Link Layer or Physical Layer Protocols:** IEEE 802.15.4e (TSCH), IEEE 802.11ah -Wi-Fi Hallow, WirelessHART, Z-Wave, INGENU RPMA (IEEE 802.15.4k), BLE, ZigBee Smart Energy, DASH7, HomePlug, G.9959, LoraWAN, Weightless, DECT/ULE.

The above protocol listing is partial and does not include many other protocols in the layers mentioned or other additional layers of various architectures. Since past decade researchers, corporates and standardizing bodies have been carrying significant research towards standardizing Internet of Things and protocols associated with it. However, there are many open challenges for improving reliability, throughput, energy efficiency, and security control. A protocol set used in a particular IoT technology has well-defined usage, based on the supported data rates, mobility, topology, security, and advantages.

Development Kits, Platforms, Hardware and Software

Internet of Things requires hardware components, such as sensors, processors, controllers, communication hardware, local communication buses, and so forth to permit smart, physical objects to connect to the Internet. Embedded microprocessors are core to many IoT-enabled systems. Most makers of embedded microprocessors and other key electronic components offer families of IoT products, such as those from Texas Instruments, Qualcomm, and Freescale, as well as IoT component collections from distributors like Avnet Memec and Arrow Electronics. Comprehensive IoT platforms are built by semiconductor companies on their core hardware component to facilitate the rapid development of IoT Applications. The ARM has built one such platform named IoT Platform which consists of the mBed OS for the ARM processor; mBed Device Server which provides device protocols, device management, and many other services; mBed Tools, a complete web-based IDE; and a set of references applications. Also, there are several hardware prototyping kits/platforms for IoT applications which are quite varied in their capabilities and focus. Many are open source platforms, initially created for educational purposes. Examples include Arduino Uno, Raspberry Pi, BeagleBone Black, mBed LPC1768 and many more. A partial listing of prominent IoT platforms is given hereunder:

- Amazon Web Services (AWS) IoT (http://docs.aws.amazon.com/iot/latest/developerguide/what-is-aws-iot.html)
- Microsoft Azure IoT (https://azure.microsoft.com/en-us/)
- The ThingWorx IoT Technology Platform (https://www.thingworx.com/platforms/)
- IBM Watson (http://www.ibm.com/internet-of-things/)
- Cisco IoT Cloud Connect (http://www.cisco.com/c/en_in/solutions/internet-of-things/overview.html)
- Salesforce IoT Cloud (www.salesforce.com/in/iot-cloud/)
- Carriots (https://www.carriots.com/)
- Oracle Integrated Cloud (https://cloud.oracle.com)
- General Electric's Predix (https://www.predix.io)
- Kaa (www.kaaproject.org)
- Xively (https://xively.com/)

- Qualcomm The IoE Development Platform (https://developer.qualcomm.com/hardware/iot-cellular-dev)
- Calvin (https://www.ericsson.com/research-blog/open-source-calvin/)
- Intel IoT Platform (http://www.intel.in/content/www/in/en/internet-of-things/infographics/iot-platform-infographic.html)
- Google Cloud IoT (https://cloud.google.com/solutions/iot/)
- OpenRemote (http://www.openremote.com/about)
- Telit DeviceWise (http://www.telit.com/)
- Macchina.io (http://macchina.io/)
- Ayla Networks (http://www.aylanetworks.com/)

The platforms vary considerably regarding licensing, pricing, supported languages, API, libraries, supported hardware, applications, and features. Such platforms permit rapid development of IoT applications, as the suite often include applications for controlling, managing and monitoring of remotely connected devices. These platforms permit integration with other third-party systems as well. In addition to these platforms, a vast range of IoT prototyping kits and development boards across semiconductor manufacturers combining sensors, processors, radio transmitter and receivers, and other modules have been developed. There are hundreds of such development boards which include PanStamp (http://www.panstamp.com), TinyDuino (https://tinycircuits.com/products/tinyduino-processor-board), Arduino Uno (https://store.arduino.cc/usa/arduino-uno-rev3), RFduino (http://www.rfduino.com), XinoRF (https://emalliab.wordpress.com/tag/xinorf), Cisco: OpenKontrol Gateway (https://wiki.open energymonitor.org/index.php/Open_Kontrol_Gateway), Pinoccio (https://www.crowdsupply.com/pinoccio/mesh-sensor-network), Raspberry Pi (http://www.rasp berrypi.org/), WeIO (http://www.we-io.net/), OpenPicus Flyport (http://wiki.openpicus.com/index.php/FLYPORTPRO), Hackberry, Libelium Wasmote (http://www.libelium.com/products/waspmote), and OpenMote (http://www.openmote.com). Many of the development boards are Open Source Hardware Development Boards which can be used across diverse IoT platforms. Furthermore, rapid IoT application development is strengthened by the use of various Application Programming Interfaces (API) from third parties such as Indigo Domestics (http://www.indigodomo.com), Muzzley (https://muzzley.com/documentation), Zetta (http://www.zettajs.org), Node-RED (https://nodered.org), ioBroker (http://iobroker.net), and Insteon (https://www.insteon.com/google-home) that include functions for device management and control, account information, etc. Apart from above, both open source and closed source operating systems (Gaur, Padmini & Mohit, 2015; Chandra et al., 2016) which have inbuilt protocol stacks implemented for IoT devices and gateways are available for rapid development of the IoT system. The open source operating systems include Contiki, Raspbian, ARM mbed, RIOT,

Mantis OS, Nano RK, Apache Mynewt, TinyOS, LiteOS, FreeRTOS, Zephyr OS, Yocto, Ubuntu Core 16 (Snappy). The closed operating systems include Mentor Graphics Nucleus RTOS, Windows 10 IoT, Particle, Freescale MQX, Android Things, WindRiver VxWorks, Micrium µC/OS, MicroEJ OS, TI RTOS, Micro Digital SMX RTOS, Express Logic ThreadX, Green Hills Integrity. Due to resource constraints, often some devices use embedded firmware in place of the operating system. This, on the one hand, may make the device faster but on the other hand, it requires a deep understanding of the underlying hardware and devising of protocol stacks from scratch (bare metal development) and it would take more efforts and time to develop an IoT system using this approach.

THREATS AND SECURITY

Threats and Attacks

The use of sophisticated technologies underlying Internet of Things and its perceived large-scale applications for e-governance, socio-economic growth, vast opportunities for business management and benefits, ease of operations and control for masses, as well as its applications for management of critical resources of governments has made it prone to cyber-attacks. IoT devices are computers with varying degree of computation and memory capabilities but can provide billions of points for making attacks on not only other IoT devices but any information system connected to the Internet. Cyber-attacks in the past on Internet of Things or through the Internet of Things have made its stakeholders worrisome about security risks and threats involved therein. These include Stufnet Malware (NYTimes. (2016), Mirai Botnet (Dyn Attack) (Dyn, 2016), Finland DDOS attack (The Register, 2016), and BrickerBot Malware (Radware, 2017). Possible exploitation of vulnerabilities in IoT devices, communication technologies, protocols, software, interconnecting devices, IoT platforms, middleware technologies, etc. necessitates protecting IoT infrastructure from known cyber threats and any perceived security risks due to heterogeneous and constrained nature of IoT devices among which most of them do not have adequate security mechanisms. In public interest, FBI issued an alert (FBI, 2015) (FBI Alert Number I-091015-PSA) in 2015 to educate users of IoT devices about security risks involved in their use along with examples of such incidents and defense recommendations. Symantec in its 2018 Internet security threat report (Symantec, 2018) has reported that there has been a 600% increase in the threats to IoT devices in 2017 as compared to that in 2016. Many other articles (HealthData, 2016; Checkpoint, 2017; Trend Micro, 2018; CNN, 2017) and news (WSJ, 2017; Security Intelligence, 2015; CNET, 2018); Pwnieexpress, 2017; The Register, 2017) have shown concerns on threats to IoT systems. Most of these concerns are due to one or other form of Botnets, man-in-the-middle attacks, data and identity theft, social engineering and Denial of Services attacks. Various research works (Dorsemaine et al., 2016; Babar et al. 2010; Kumar & Patel, 2014; Kajaree & Behera, 2017; Guo & Chen, 2015; Deogirikar, 2017; Ahemd, Shah, & Wahid, 2017) have discussed possible threats and attacks from different perspectives that an IoT system may encounter. A listing of the majority of them extracted from the works of Abdul-Ghani et al. (Abdul-Ghani, Konstantas, Mahyoub, 2017) who have classified them in four attack surfaces namely: attacks on physical objects, attacks on protocols, attacks on data at rest, attacks on IoT Software is given below:

- **Physical-Based Attacks:** These are: Object tempering, Outage attack, Object replication, Camouflage, Side-channel attacks, Tag cloning, Social engineering, Physical damage, Malicious Code Injection, Hardware Trojans, Object jamming, and Tag Tampering.
- **Protocol-Based Attacks:** These are sub-classified as follows:
  - Connectivity Protocols-Based attacks:
    - **RFID:** These are: Killing Tag, Spoofing, Man-in-the-middle, Tracking, Virus, Eavesdropping, Replay, and RFID unauthorized access.
    - **NFC:** These are: Eavesdropping, Data modification, Data corruption, Relay attack, Data injection, and Man-in-the-middle attack.
    - **ZigBee:** These are: Sniffing, Replay attack, ZED Sabotage attack, Obtaining Keys, and Redirected communication.
    - **Bluetooth:** These are: Bluejacking, Bluedebugging, Interception, DoS, Blueshafing, Spoofing, and Hijacking.
    - **Wi-Fi:** These are: FMS, Korek, Chopchop, Fragmentation, PTW, Google replay, Michael, Ohigashi-Morii and Dictionary Attack.
  - Network Protocols-Based attacks:
    - **RPL Network Protocol-Based Attacks:** These are: selective forward attack, sinkhole attack, sybil attack, wormhole attack, version attack, blackhole attack, identity attack, hello flooding attack, and selective forward attack.
    - **6LoWPAN Protocol-Based Attacks:** These are: fragmentation attack, authentication attack, and confidentiality attack.
  - Communication Protocol-based attacks:
    - **TLS:** Padding oracle, TIME, klima03, BEAST, Diffie-Hellman parameters TLS, SSL scripting.

  - **Application Protocols:** XMPP: XMPP bomb, MQTT: authentication attack, XMPP: XMPP daemon attack, XMPP: XMPPloit, CoAP: sniffing, CoAP: pre-shared key attacks, MQTT: buffer overflow, XMPP: authentication attacks, MQTT: Denial of Services.
  - **TCP/UDP:** TCP SUN flood, TCP-UDP fragmentation, UDP flooding, TCP-UDP hijacking, TCP-UDO port scan, TCP-UDP port scan, TCP-UDP hijacking, and UDP flood.
- **Data Attacks:** DOS Exposure, Data loss, Data Scavenging, VM Hopping, Malicious VM Creation, Insecure VM Migration, Account Hijacking, Data Manipulation, VM Escape, Data leakage, DoS, Hash-collision, and Brute-force attacks.
- **Software Attacks:** *Operating Systems*: Virus, Worm Trojan Horse, Backdoor attack, Phishing attacks. Brue-Force Search attack, *Application*: Code injection, Reprogram attack, Cross-state request forgery, DDoS, Misconfiguration exploitation, SQL injection, *Firmware*: Control Hijacking, Eavesdropping, Reverse engineering, Maliciously crafted input, and Malware.

The attacks and threats as given in the research work of Abdul-Ghani et al. (Abdul-Ghani, Konstantas, Mahyoub, 2017) do not include threats on account of various types of connectivity and protocols stacks. Further, all mentioned attacks have different threat levels, severity and therefore require different control measures.

IoT Security Research

Security in the context of the Internet of Things cannot be achieved by merely securing the objects (called things in the IoT context) alone because IoT encompasses a full spectrum of information and communication technologies especially Internet infrastructure that serves as its enabler as well as the consumer. Things in the context of the Internet of Things become part of the global public network (the Internet) or the cyberspace, and therefore, its security falls directly with the domain of cyber security which is defined by ISO as the preservation of confidentiality, integrity, and availability of information in the cyberspace. Therefore, cybercrime, cyber espionage, and cyber warfare are well applicable to the Internet of Things as well. The global nature of cyberspace has facilitated people and communities through its diverse services. However, it has not only increased concerns about the security of infrastructure underlying the cyberspace but has also increased security and privacy threats to information transmitted through it, people using it and organizations/ countries connecting it. Cyber security is multidimensional and a shared responsibility of government, police, researchers, academicians, service providers, members of civil society, and regulatory bodies.

Arsalan and Jha in their recent study (Mohsen-Nia & Jha, 2016) have given a detailed analysis of possible attacks and vulnerabilities at each level of the edge-side layer (edge nodes, communication, and edge computing) along with several attacks and their countermeasures. While discussing various countermeasures for the threats, it was concluded that three types of cryptographic schemes are widely discussed in the literature to address the security attacks against RFID tags: Encryption, Hash-based schemes, and Lightweight cryptographic protocols. However, there are various issues with these techniques requiring either large number of gates for AES encryption, or breaking of most lightweight cryptographic schemes, etc. It was also concluded that there are no promising public key encryption methods that provide enough security for the communication between nodes while meeting lightweight requirements. Qi Jing et al. in their latest research (Jing et al., 2014) on IoT security while emphasizing upon the security of the overall system described a security architecture based on a three-layer IoT model. For a better understanding of challenges in each layer, this three-layer architecture has been divided into various sub-layers. The lower layer of the architecture, i.e., the perception layer is divided into two parts namely i) perception node (sensors or controllers, etc.) and ii) perception network. The first sub-layer is used for data acquisition and control while as the second sub-layer communicates with the transportation network and sends collected data to the gateway or sends a control instruction to the controller. The middle layer of the architecture, i.e., transportation layer is divided into sub-layers namely, i) access control, ii) core network and, iii) local area network. The upper layer, i.e. the application layer is divided into: i) application support layer and IoT application layer. The study has identified various security issues with each sublayer. The study suggests that while there are security issues at every sublayer of the architecture that needs to be addressed but at the same time every unique application of the IoT has its unique security issues and challenges that need to be addressed before its deployment. Ajit Jha & Sunil (Jha, & Sunil, n.d.) have given a defense-in-depth approach emphasizing stage based embedded security. Various security consideration guidelines and risk management strategies including guidelines for devices, gateways, networks, facilitation and applications using the developed security technologies including cryptography have been provided in the whitepaper. Various IoT security issues have been highlighted by Kai Zhao and LinaGe (Zhao, LinaGe, 2013). These include perception layer security issues namely node capture, fake node, attacks (such as denial of service, timing, routing, malicious data, replay, side channel), and mass node authentication problem. The highlighted network layer security issues include traditional security problems such as data confidentiality and integrity, DoS attack, man-in-the-middle attacks, etc.;

compatibility problems such as those due to heterogeneity, interoperability, and coordination; Cluster security problems such as network congestion, authentication, etc.; and privacy disclosures. The discussed application layer security issues include problems in data access permission, identity authentication, data protection, and recovery, problems in dealing with mass-data and application layer software vulnerability. The study proposed the use of chip protection, antenna energy analysis, encryption, cryptography, physical security, secure routing protocols, secret key algorithms and pre-shared keys as security measures at the physical layer. The use of PKI, IPv6 base security control, etc. have been proposed for the network layer. For security at the application layer, the use of cryptography both symmetric and asymmetric, passwords, digital watermarking, biometric authentication, etc. have been suggested. The IoT security requirements have been modeled by Shancang Li et al. (Li, Tryfonas, & Li, 2016) through a four-layer architecture that comprises of sensing, network, service, and application-interface layers. Each layer can provide corresponding security controls, such as access control, device authentication, data integrity and confidentiality in transmission, and availability. The work identified various security threats in sensing layer end-devices, end-nodes, end-gateways) such as unauthorized access, availability, spoofing attack, selfish treat, malicious code, DoS, transmission threats and routing attacks. The possible security threats in network layer include data breach, threats to confidentiality and integrity of data, DoS, compromise of keys, malicious code, routing attacks which can be mitigated through physical protection, introducing transmission security, etc. Likewise, security threats in service and application layers have been discussed. Further, security challenges due to data sharing between various layers and interoperability between them such as identity spoofing have been highlighted and discussed. Jorge Granjal et al. in their work (Granjal, Monteiro, & Sá Silva, 2015) on IoT protocols analyzed and highlighted various open challenges and possible strategies for future research work to improve the security of IoT protocols. Network security, authentication, encryption, public key infrastructure, security analytics, and API security are the fastest growing and researched security technologies among the top most important IoT security technologies (Forrester, 2017). In addition to threats, attacks and addressing of these through devising security technologies, Internet of Things has opened up a new dimension to digital forensics, the IoT forensics. With continuously growing computational and communicational capabilities and resources such as the memory of IoT end-nodes and other devices in the system, forensics of such end-nodes and devices has become necessary. However, this kind of forensics has many challenges (Henry, Williams, & Wright, 2013) associated with it. Zawoad and Hassan (Zawoad, & Hasan, n.d.) have described IoT forensics as a combination of three digital forensics schemes namely device level forensics, network forensics, and cloud forensics. Forensic investigation is performed on the data collected from the local memory of the IoT device, network log is obtained from the networking devices, and data stored in the cloud. Although some research works such as those of Sutherland et al. (Sutherland, Read, & Xynos, 2014) and Ukil et al. (Ukil, Sen, & Koilakonda, 2011), have been carried out toward IoT forensics, but a lot more research needs to be done to make IoT forensics possible.

Institutional Initiatives

Research and development towards securing IoT systems is not only a current topic with the research community, but corporates individually and collectively are making efforts towards devising security standards and policies. These include IBM Open Web Application Security Project (OWASP, 2018), Industrial Internet Consortium (IIC, 2018), Allseen Alliance, Swisscom Group Security (Jungo, 2015) and builditsecure.ly (2018). Also, business houses such as Infineon (2018) are building security solutions and mechanisms and selling them as IoT security products to IoT application and system developers. Testbeds such as IoT-LAB (2018) are highly useful resources for quick scientific experimentation, development, evaluation, and analytics. Such test labs provide remote control of various types of IoT nodes and gateways having different topologies and environment to research and monitor nodes, protocols, etc. for their power consumption, throughput, end-to-end delay, and overheads in varying conditions. In addition to the use of various testbeds, IoT modeling and simulation (and emulation) is typically carried out using various simulation software such as NS2, NetSim, and OPNET before deployment and implementation of the network. A large base of conventional and contemporary test tools have been developed to check any possible vulnerability and security issues in IoT devices and communication within them that include: Wireshark (https://www.wireshark.org), BlueMaho (http://git.kali.org/gitweb/?p=packages/bluemaho.git;a=summary), Bluelog (http://www.digifail.com/software/bluelog.shtml), Crackle (https://github.com/mikeryan/crackle), SecBee (https://github.com/Cognosec/SecBee), KillerBee (http://tools.kali.org/wireless-attacks/killerbee), Scapy-radio (https://bitbucket.org/cybertools/scapy-radio/src), Aircrack-ng (www.aircrack-ng.org), Hardsploit (https://github.com/freaklabs/chibi Arduino), Chibi, HackRF (https://greatscottgadgets.com/hackrf/ and Shikra (http://int3.cc/products/the-shikra).

Universities and Institutions across the Globe have initiated the various application and research-oriented projects. Some of the prominent initiatives are listed hereunder:

- **Georgia Tech:** Center for the Development and Application of Internet of Things Technologies (CDAIT) (http://www.cdait.gatech.edu)
- **Stanford:** Secure Internet of Things Project (http://www.cdait.gatech.edu/)

- **Oregon State University:** IoT Test & Compatibility Lab (http://cass.oregonstate.edu/units/iot-lab/)
- **UMass Dartmouth:** Multidisciplinary Internet of Things Research Lab (http://www.umassd.edu/engineering/ece/research/keyresearchareas/computerengineering/iotresearch)
- **The University of Wisconsin:** Madison Internet of Things Lab (http://www.iotlab.wisc.edu/)
- **The University of Illinois at Urbana-Champaign:** Systems Software Research Group (http://srg.cs.illinois.edu/research/)
- **Carleton:** Sensor Technology for the Internet of Things (http://newsroom.carleton.ca/2015/11/09/carleton-university-establishes-research-chair-to-drive-value-of-internet-of-things/)
- **Frankfurt University of Applied Sciences:** WSN/IoT – Research Group (http://wsn.fb2.frankfurt-university.de/en/)
- **The University of Zurich:** Department of Informatics - Communication Systems Group (http://www.csg.uzh.ch/)
- PETRAS Internet of Things Research Hub (http://www.petrashub.org/index.php/about)
- **University of Southampton:** Agents, Interaction, and Complexity Research Group (http://www.aic.ecs.soton.ac.uk/)
- **University of Surrey:** Semantics and Data Analytics for the Internet of Things - Institute for Communication Systems (ICS) (http://iot.ee.surrey.ac.uk/)
- **Shanghai Institute of Microsystem and Information Technology:** IoT System Technology Laboratory (http://english.sim.cas.cn/rh/kybm/5s/)
- **ETRI:** IoT Convergence Research Department (https://www.etri.re.kr/eng/sub6/sub6_01020101. etri?departCode=19&departInfoCode=70)
- **Sungkyunkwan University:** Internet of Things (IoT) Laboratory (http://cpslab.skku.edu/)
- **Melbourne School of Engineering:** (http://issnip.unimelb.edu.au/research_program/Internet_of_Things)

To undertake research and development in the Internet of Things, a large number of government-funded research projects have been granted in developed countries that include projects aiming to enhance security and privacy of connected devices and data transmitted wirelessly.

- Thales and IoT Security (https://www.thalesgroup.com/en/critical-information-systems-and-cybersecurity/news/safer-internet-things)
- Stanford Secure Internet of Things Project (http://iot.stanford.edu/)

- Web of Things Interest Group (https://www.w3.org/WoT/IG/wiki/Main_Page)
- Microsoft Lab of Things (http://www.lab-of-things.com/)
- iCore (http://www.iot-icore.eu/about-icore)
- **CALIPSO:** Connect All IP-based Smart Objects (http://www.ict-calipso.eu/)
- **CASAGRAS2:** CSA for Global RFID-related Activities and Standardization (http://cordis.europa.eu/project/rcn/95714_en.html)
- **EBBITS:** Enabling business-based Internet of Things and Services (http://www.ebbits-project.eu/news.php)
- **ELLIOT:** Experiential Living Lab for the Internet of Things (http://cordis.europa.eu/project/rcn/95205_en.html)
- **EPoSS:** The European Technology Platform on Smart Systems Integration (http://www.smart-systems-integration.org/public)
- **IERC:** European Research Cluster on the Internet of Things (http://www.internet-of-things-research.eu/)
- **IOT-A:** Internet of Things Architecture (http://www.iot-a.eu/public)
- **SPRINT:** Software Platform for Integration of Engineering and Things (http://www.sprint-iot.eu/)
- SmartSantander Project (http://www.smartsantander.eu/)
- **IOT6:** Universal Integration of the Internet of Things through an IPv6-based Service Oriented Architecture (http://iot6.eu/)
- **IOT@WORK:** Internet of Things at Work (https://www.iot-at-work.eu/)
- **PROACTIVE:** PRedictive reasOning and multi-source fusion empowering AntiCipation of attacks and Terrorist Actions in Urban EnVironmEnts (http://cordis.europa.eu/project/rcn/103500_en.html)
- **IoT-i:** IoT initiative (http://cordis.europa.eu/project/rcn/95102_en.html)
- **AIOTI:** The Alliance for Internet of Things Innovation (https://ec.europa.eu/digital-single-market/alliance-internet-things-innovation-aioti)
- SOCIOTAL (http://www.sociotal.eu/)
- SORBET (http://www.fp7-sorbet.eu/)
- CoherentPaaS (http://coherentpaas.eu/)
- IoT Centre of Excellence, India (http://www.coe-iot.in/overview.php)
- IoT Group of C-DAC, India (http://www.cdac.in/index.aspx?id=pe_iot_Labkit_IOT)

To take the lead in the IoT industry, many universities and corporates throughout the world have initiated research and training programs on the Internet of Things. Some of these are outlined here:

- **University of California, Irvine:** Summer Undergraduate Research Fellowship in the Internet of Things (SURF-IoT) (http://www.urop.uci.edu/surf-it.html)
- **University of Central Florida:** Research Experiences on the Internet of Things (IoT) (http://iotreu.cs. ucf.edu/)
- **University of Minnesota:** Physical Computing and the Internet of Things (http://ias.umn.edu/programs/collaboratives/physical-computing/)
- **IISc:** MSR India Microsoft Research and the Department of Computational & Data Sciences (http://research.microsoft.com/en-us/events/msri_ss_2016/)
- **Microsoft Russia:** Summer School on the Internet of Things (https://www.microsoft.com/en-us/research/event/summer-school-on-the-internet-of-things-2016/?from=http%3A%2F%2Frese arch.microsoft.com%2Fen-us%2Fevents%2Fssiot%2F)
- **Texas State University:** Multidisciplinary Research Experiences for Undergraduates in the Internet of Things (http://reuiot.cs.txstate.edu/)

The security of the "thing" is only as secure as the network in which it resides: this includes the people, processes and technologies involved in its development and delivery. There are many aspects of security to cover in the Internet of Things that include authentication, authorization, auditing, administration, encryption/decryption, key management, and integrity checking. A combination of technologies and processes ensure that the environment remains secure. Devices operate in much less controlled conditions than systems running in a data centre, cloud, or another controlled environment. Each type of IoT system uses specific technologies to offer specific types of services to its consumers, therefore, each such type has specific risks involved in it. Considering comprehensive security measures for each type of system, expertise in designing, analysing, and testing each system is required.

CRYPTOGRAPHY AND ITS APPLICATIONS IN THE INTERNET OF THINGS

The process of keeping information secret by converting it to a non-intelligible form is called Cryptography. The important attributes necessary for cryptography are: a) Confidentiality, which means that the information should not be read by any unauthorized person during communication; b) Integrity, which means protecting information against any changes by unauthorized users during communication; and c) Availability, which means that the information should be available all the time for the authorized users. There are a number of other attributes necessary for cryptography which includes non-repudiation, authentication, access control, etc.

Encryption and Decryption

A message to be transmitted is called plaintext. The process of converting plaintext information to a non-intelligible form, called ciphertext is known as encryption. Encryption is achieved by following a step by step process (i.e., an algorithm) called cipher and the result obtained after encryption is called ciphertext. The inverse process i.e., converting ciphertext back to plaintext is called decryption. The algorithm used for decryption is called decipher. Both of these processes, encryption and decryption are done using a fixed size key. This key is kept secret. Only the sender and receiver have knowledge about the secret key. Depending on the manner the key is used for encryption and decryption, cryptography has two broad areas namely symmetric and asymmetric.

Symmetric Key Cryptography

In symmetric cryptography, the same key is used for both encryption and decryption of the plaintext message. The key used is called the secret key or private key. This process is called secret key cryptography or symmetric key encryption. The algorithm used for symmetric key cryptography is called symmetric algorithm. The algorithm followed for encryption is then reversed for decryption. Symmetric ciphers are classified as Block ciphers or Stream ciphers. Block cipher is an encryption technique which encrypts a block of plaintext using a secret key. Some well-known Block ciphers are DES, 3-DES, AES, BlowFish, TwoFish, IDEA, TEA, RC5, and RC6. A comparison between different block ciphers is given in the Table 1 and their respective merits and demerits in Table 2. AES algorithm is considered more secure and takes less time to execute than other block ciphers.

A stream cipher is an encryption technique which encrypts a bit of plaintext at a time using a secret key. It is used when the length of plaintext is not known. A5/1, Trivium, Grain, RC4, Achterbahn-128/80 are some famous stream ciphers. A comparison between different stream ciphers is given in Table 3 and their respective merits and demerits in Table 4.

Stream ciphers are not frequently used when compared to block ciphers. The only exception being RC4 which is the most popular and most used stream cipher. Stream ciphers require less resource and can be used in a constrained environment.

The algorithms discussed so far are all symmetric algorithms that use only one secret key. This type of cryptosystem is very fast but the problem with this cryptosystem is key distribution. The sender needs to share the key with the recipient before sending the actual message. As electronic communication is insecure, so sending the key without any security mechanism is not possible. Furthermore, the symmetric

Table 1. Comparison between different block ciphers

Algorithm	Block Size (bits)	Key Size (bits)	No of Rounds	Algorithm Structure	Algorithm Strength	Possible Attacks
AES	128	128/192/256	10/12/14	Substitution Permutation Network	Secure	Brute Force
DES	64	56	16	Feistel Network	Secure	Brute Force
Triple DES	64	168	48	Feistel Network	Secure	Meet in the Middle
BlowFish	64	128-448	16	Feistel Network	Highly Secure	Second Order Differential
TwoFish	128	128 /192 /256	16	Feistel Network	Vulnerable	Related Key Attack
IDEA	64	128	8	Feistel Network	Secure	Related Key Attack
TEA	64	128	64	Feistel Network	Vulnerable	Related Key Attack
RC5	32/64/128	0 to 2040	0 to 255	Feistel Network	Conditionally Secure	Differential Attack
RC6	128	128/192/ 256	20	Feistel Network	Considered Vulnerable	Statistical Attack

cryptosystem does not fulfil the constraint of non-repudiation. Thus, a new type of cryptosystem called Asymmetric cryptosystem is used to achieve these properties.

Asymmetric Key Cryptography

In this type of cryptography, two keys are used for encryption and decryption. One is called the public key and the other key is called the private or secret key. The public key is distributed and made public whereas the private key is kept secret and is not shared with anyone. One key is used for encryption and the other key is used for decryption. These keys are made in pairs, that is, for every public key, there is a corresponding private key. This type of cryptography is also known as Public Key Encryption. This encryption scheme can be used to implement encryption as well as digital signature. In the process of encryption, the plaintext information is encoded using a public key and decrypted using a private key. Whereas in the process of Digital signature, the plaintext is encrypted using the private key and decrypted using the public key. The key exchange for symmetric algorithms can also be done using public key encryption. The functioning of encryption and decryption is illustrated in the Figure 1 and the functioning of signing and signature verification is illustrated in Figure 2.

Table 2. Merits and demerits of different block ciphers

Algorithm	Merits	Demerits
AES	• Robust • Widely used • Safe	• Uses simple algebraic structure • Hard to implement in software • Every block is always encrypted in the same way
DES	• Fast in hardware • Hard to break	• Weak keys • Same output can be created by the S-box for two different inputs • Lesser Block Size • Relatively slow in software
Triple DES	• Easy to implement in both hardware and software • It is ubiquitous	• Prone to attacks • Smaller key size compared to AES
BlowFish	• Fastest block cipher except for key changing • Freely available	• Key management is complicated • Can't provide authentication and non-repudiation • Slow decryption
TwoFish	• Ideal for use in both hardware and software • Flexible • Freely available	• Vulnerable • Speed is comparatively less
IDEA	• Twice as fast as DES • No real weakness as such	• Had patent protection • Slow
TEA	• Fast and simple • Small in size	• Vulnerable under related-key attacks • High latency
RC5	• Simple, fast block cipher • Suitable for both hardware and software implementation • Low memory requirements and provides high security	• Slower than RC6 • Timing attack is possible • Patented
RC6	• Fast • Beneficial where high encryption rate is required.	• Complex than RC5

Some of the popular public key encryption algorithms include Diffie-Hellman Key Exchange, ElGamal, RSA, Elliptic Curve Diffie-Hellman, Elliptic Curve ElGamal, Digital Signature Algorithm, RSA Signature, Elliptic Curve Digital Signature Algorithm, etc. A brief comparison between most prominent public key encryption algorithms is given in Table 5 and in Table 6 advantages and disadvantages of each are listed.

Table 3. Comparison between different stream ciphers

Algorithm	Effective Key Size (bits)	Initialization Vector (bits)	Internal State (bits)	Algorithm Structure	Algorithm Strength	Possible Attacks
A5/1	54 or 64	22	64	LFSR Based	Weak	• Known Plaintext Attack
Trivium	80	80	288	Based on the combination of 3 nonlinear feedback shift registers	Secure	• Key Recovery Attack • Cube Attack
Grain	80	64	160	Based on the nonlinear feedback shift register (NFSR), a linear feedback shift register (LFSR), and a nonlinear filtering function	Secure	• Key Derivation Attack
RC4	8 to 2048	Does not have an IV	2064	Is a shared key stream cipher algorithm developed by Ronald Rivest of RSA	Secure	• Known Plaintext Attack
Achterbahn-128/80	80/128	80/128	2967/351	8 binary nonlinear feedback shift registers (NLFSR's)	Secure	• Brute Force Attack • Correlation Attack

Table 4. Merits and demerits of different stream ciphers

Algorithm	Merits	Demerits
A5/1	• Fast in hardware • Provides security on GSM of mobile phones	• Cryptographically Weak
Trivium	• Not patented • Compact • Fast • High throughput	• Vulnerable to Key Recovery Attack and Cube Attack
Grain	• Fast • Simple design • Small area required • High throughput	• Vulnerable to Key Derivation Attack
RC4	• Widely used • Very simple • Works well in hardware and software • Very fast	• Not considered secure • Key can be reconstructed • A particular key can be used only once
Achterbahn-128/80	• Hardware efficient cipher • Simple	• Weakness in the Boolean output function

Figure 1. Procedure for encryption and decryption

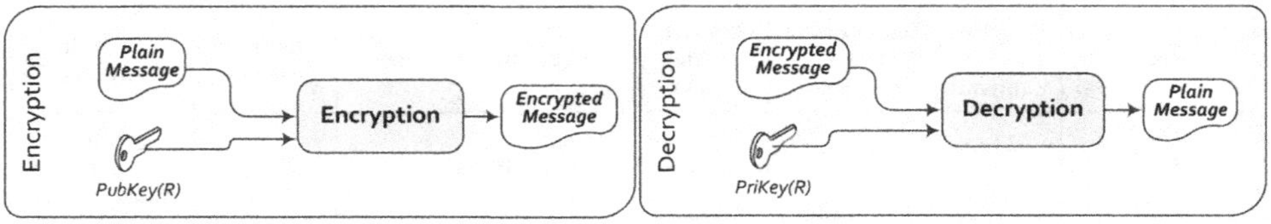

Figure 2. Procedure for signings and signature verification

Table 5. A brief comparison between prominent public key cryptographic algorithms

Algorithm	Key Size (bits)	Public Key System	Dominant Operation	Possible Attacks
Diffie-Hellman	1024	Discrete Logarithm	Integer Multiplication	• Man in the Middle Attack • Clogging Attack • Replay Attack • Subgroup confinement Attack
ElGamal	1024	Discrete Logarithm	Integer Multiplication	• Brute Force Attack • Low-Modulus Attack • Known-plaintext Attack • Man in the Middle Attack
RSA	1024	Integer Factorization	Integer Multiplication	• Factoring Attacks • Timing Attack • Man in the Middle Attack
ECDH and EC ElGamal	163	Elliptic Curve Discrete Logarithm	Polynomial Multiplication	• Generic Attack: ▪ Naive method: Brute Force Attack ▪ Collision search Attack: ▪ Baby-Step-Giant-Step ▪ Pollard's rho ▪ Pollard's lambda ▪ Parallelized Pollard's rho and lambda ▪ Parallel Collision Search • Non-Generic Attack: ▪ Index Calculus Attack ▪ Isomorphism Attack ▪ A grid of Isogeny Classes of EC Attack

Table 6. Advantages and disadvantages of prominent public key cryptographic algorithms

Algorithm	Advantages	Disadvantages
RSA	• Very fast and simple encryption • Easier to implement • Easier to understand • Widely deployed, better industry support	• Very slow key generation • Slow decryption • Large key size • Need more memory and computation power
ECC	• Shorter Key • Faster Encryption/Decryption • Suitable for constrained devices	• New technique – may have new attacks • Too complex to understand
Elgamal	• Based on Discrete Logarithmic Problem (DLP) • Needs less key size than RSA • Asymmetric workload	• The encrypted message is twice the size of the original message • New random needed for every encrypted message
EC Elgamal	• Equal security with small key size • Faster • Reduced processing overhead	• Complex and difficult to understand • Increased size of the encrypted message
Diffie-Hellman	• Communication can take place through an insecure channel • Secret key created only when needed • Exchange requires no pre-existing infrastructure	• Value of private key is smaller which can easily be decoded • No authentication of participants
ECDH	• Based on Discrete Logarithmic Problem (DLP) • Used for key exchange in constrained devices	• The public key of both user and server is not protected • Both server and user need to initialize again for every transaction

Among the above compared asymmetric key cryptographic algorithms, algorithms based on Elliptic Curve Cryptography offer several advantages over the other cryptographic algorithms and therefore, are considered as the most suitable and are thus widely deployed.

Hashing

A hash function is a mathematical function that computes a fixed length bit string from an input message. This string is called a hash or a message digest. To provide security, a hash function must be a one-way function (i.e., it must be computationally impossible to generate input string from the given hash) and collision resistant (i.e., no two inputs should produce the same output) (Awad, 2015). Hash values of any message are always fixed in length and smaller than the message. No two messages can have the same hash values; thus, the hash is used to check the integrity of the message. Some of the best-known hashing algorithms are MD5, MD6, SHA-1,

SHA256, SHA512, and SHA-3. A comparison between them is given in Table 7, and their strengths and weaknesses are given in Table 8.

Digital Signature Certificates

In public key cryptography, the sender uses a hash function to compute message digest and then encrypts the digest using his private key to get message signature. Signing message digest instead of the plain message is performed to ensure faster signing because signing a lengthy plain message can be time consuming. Further, the procedures of hashing wherein message digest is computed from the plain message, and signing, wherein the message digest is encrypted using the private key of the sender, to generate the message signature along with encryption wherein the plain message, the message signature and the public key of the sender is encrypted using the public key of the intended recipient can be used to attain privacy, integrity, authentication and non- repudiation. This procedure is shown in Figure 4 and is called a digital signature.

To overcome the limitations of slow performance of encryption and decryption algorithms using asymmetric keys on long messages, symmetric key encryption is used in the final stage of encryption wherein plain message, the message signature and Public Key of the sender are encrypted. The computed symmetric key is also encrypted and transmitted along with the message. To make this system workable for situations wherein large communicating parties are involved and to make management,

Table 7. A comparison between various hashing algorithms

Algorithm	Message Digest Size (bits)	Message Size (bits)	Block Size (bits)	Word Size (bits)	Number of Rounds	Security
MD5	128	$< 2^{64}$	512	32	64	2^{64}
MD6	224/256/384/512	$< 2^{64}$	4096	64	168	Above 2^{64}
SHA-1	160	$< 2^{64}$	512	32	80	2^{80}
SHA256	256	$< 2^{64}$	512	32	80	2^{128}
SHA512	512	$< 2^{128}$	1024	64	80	2^{256}
SHA-3	224/256/384/512	$< 2^{64}$	1152/1088/832/576	64	24	Upto 2^{512}

Table 8. A comparison between various hashing algorithms

Algorithm	Merits	Demerits
MD5	• Faster	• Less secure • Attacks reported to some extent
MD6	• Arguably secure against known attacks (including differential attacks) • Relatively simple • Highly parallelizable • Reasonably efficient	• Relatively slow
SHA-1	• Requires less computational power • Better performance	• Not that secure
SHA256	• An improved version of SHA-1 • Collision resistant • Secure Hash	• Less secure compared to SHA512 • Prone to many attacks
SHA512	• More bit length • More secure	• Slow compared to SHA256 • Prone to attacks
SHA-3	• An improved version of SHA-2 • More secure compared to SHA-2	• Slower in software

Figure 3. Procedure of signings and verification with hashing

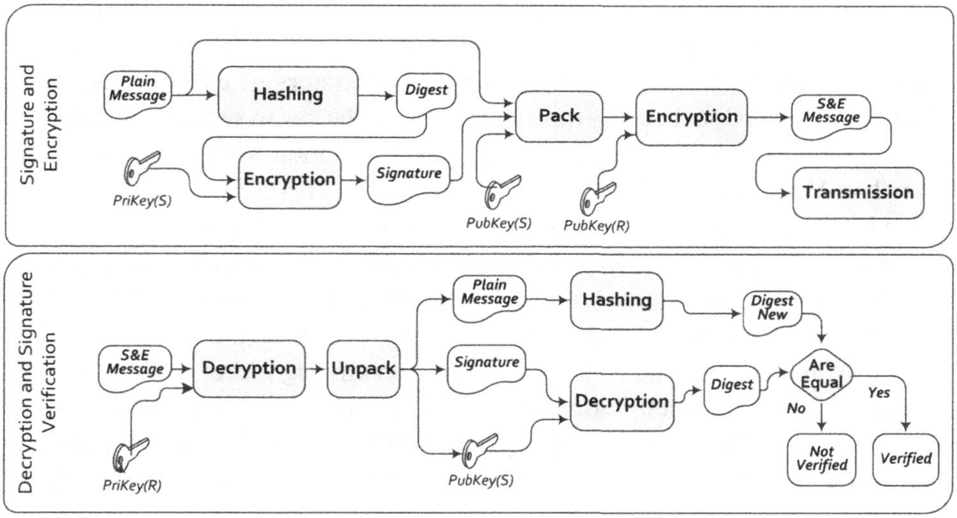

distributions, creation, etc. possible, a full-fledged infrastructure called the Public Key Infrastructure is required wherein digital signatures are made available in the form of digital signature certificates. Digital Signature Certificates are Digital Signatures that have themselves been signed using the Digital Signature of some trusted authority, thus, creating a chain of authentications. A Digital Signature Certificate (DSC) is issued by a certification authority in order to validate the identity of an entity. The supreme certification authority is called the Root Certifying Authority (Root CA). A typical X.509 digital signature certificate contains the information about the certificate serial number, the algorithm used for signing, certificate of the issuer, the validity period of the certificate, name of the entity, public key of the entity, etc. DSC has various types that form a trust chain with root certification authority and are used in various services such as banking, finance, healthcare, business to business. The certificates are issued by governments, or private organizations as commercial products. Digital signature certificates may also permit time stamping. Various protocols such as SSL/TLS, S/MIME use digital signature certificates.

Random Number Generators

In cryptography, the essential requirement for a secure system is the randomness of numbers which are used in generating cryptographic keys. The random numbers used in cryptography are very large and hard to predict, thus, preventing successful brute force attacks. The inputs given to random number generators are called seeds. These seeds need to be random because this randomness is the key to security. If the seeds get compromised, the whole cryptographic implementation will get compromised (Russell, & Van-Duren, 2016).

Random Number Generators (RNGs) are of two types: Deterministic and Non-Deterministic. Deterministic RNG is based on an algorithm which generates same output for a given set of inputs. It is also called pseudo-RNG. Some of the common Deterministic RNGs are linear congruential, lagged Fibonacci, and feedback shift registers. Non-Deterministic RNG is not based on any algorithm and the number generation is totally random based on some different method usually a physical event; thus, the generated output for a given set of inputs is not same every time. It is also known as true-RNG. Some of the Non- Deterministic RNGs are Random.org, Hotbits, lasers, and oscillators.

Light Weight Cryptography

Various light weight cryptographic algorithms have been designed till date that work well on a general-purpose computer. But the use of small-scale computing devices has increased in recent times, which has led to the rise of a new cryptographic field. The traditional cryptographic systems do not fit into the new constrained environment of the small computing devices with limited resources. So, NIST came up with new lightweight cryptographic algorithms, designed especially for resource-limited systems. This has opened up many opportunities for their use in the Internet of Things.

Lightweight Block Ciphers

In order to have a better performance in a constrained environment, a number of lightweight Block ciphers have been proposed. Some of these algorithms are simply a modification of traditional ciphers e.g., DESL (Leander, 2007) is a variant of DES, where improvement is done by reducing the number of S-boxes in the round function. But some algorithms were designed only for lightweight cryptography. Some of these algorithms are PRESENT (Bogdanov, 2007), SIMON and SPECK (Beaulieu, 2013), RC5 (Rivest, 1994), TEA (Wheeler, 1994) and XTEA (Needham, 1997).

Lightweight Stream Ciphers

The stream ciphers are suitable for the constrained environment. All the stream ciphers can be used in lightweight cryptography but the most important algorithms which give better performance are Grain (Hell, 2007), Trivium (De Cannière & Preneel, 2008) and Mickey (Babbage, 2008).

Lightweight Hash Functions

The hash functions that are used in traditional cryptography are not suitable for lightweight cryptography because they require more resources. This has led to the development of lightweight hash functions, such as PHOTON (Guo, 2011), Quark (Aumasson, 2013), SPONGENT (Bogdanov, 2011), and Lesamnta-LW (Hirose, 2010).

Use of Cryptography in the Internet of Things

Understanding the communication between different IoT protocols and the security of these protocols is a major challenge for IoT device designers. The communication protocols usually have a layer of authentication and encryption applied at the link layer. ZigBee, Bluetooth-LE, WirelessHart, 6LoWPAN, and IPSec, are some examples of IoT communication protocols that have an option for confidentiality, authentication and integrity protection by use of one or the other form of a cryptographic algorithm.

- **ZigBee:** ZigBee uses the IEEE 802.15.4 MAC layer security services. The 802.15.4 MAC layer uses the AES-128 algorithm for both encryption/decryption as well as MAC. It is not mandatory for ZigBee to use these security services. It can use other security configurations as well e.g., AES-CBC-MAC-32, AES-CBC-MAC-64, AES-CBC-MAC-128, AES-CTR, AES-CCM-32, AES-CCM-64, AES-CCM-128, etc.
- **Bluetooth-LE (Low Energy):** It is based on the Bluetooth Core Specification Version (4.2). It uses the security concepts of pairing, bonding, authentication, encryption and integrity. The cryptographic algorithms used for these services are AES-128 and P-256 Elliptic Curve, AES-CMC for pairing; AES-CCM for authentication and AES-CCM for encryption (Padgette, 2012).
- **Near Field Communication (NFC):** This protocol supports short-range communication; therefore, it is used to establish pairings for other protocols like Bluetooth. NFC has no in-built cryptographic setup but an endpoint authentication like AES-CCM can be added to the protocol.
- **WirelessHart:** It is a protocol that is used in Wireless Sensor Networks. The security is provided by using encryption and authentication on the Network and Data Link layers. The algorithm used for providing both encryption and authentication is AES-CCM. The limitation of WirelessHart is that it has no provision for Public Key Cryptography, thus, it does not provide services like non-repudiation. It neither provides authorization nor accounting.
- **6LoWPAN:** 6LoWPAN works in a constrained environment with a large number of embedded computing devices. It must offer confidentiality, authentication and integrity. These services are provided by using cryptography while taking the limited resource constraints into consideration. IPSec is used to provide end-to-end security. It also uses Public Key Cryptosystem like RSA and ECC for security. But cryptography alone does not provide the security because it protects the network from external attacks but not from internal attacks. To protect the network from internal attacks, IDS (Intrusion Detection System) is required.
- **IPSec:** This protocol is used for end to end security. It provides security services like confidentiality, integrity, authentication and replay protection. It provides confidentiality and integrity using the cryptographic algorithms like MD5 and SHA. For encryption, it uses DES-CBC, 3DES-CBC and AES algorithms.

A comparison of various protocols wherein some kind of cryptographic algorithm is used to provide security along with the security service provided by each are listed in Table 9.

Table 9. IoT protocols using cryptographic algorithms

Protocol	Function	Security Services	Cryptographic Algorithm
ZigBee and 802.15.4	Used for small-scale projects which require low power and low bandwidth	• Encryption/Decryption • Authentication	• AES-CBC-MAC-32 • AES-CBC-MAC-64 • AES-CBC-MAC-128 • AES-CTR • AES-CCM-32 • AES-CCM-64 • AES-CCM-128
Bluetooth-LE	Small range communication which requires less energy consumption and is cost effective	• Pairing • Bonding • Authentication • Encryption • Integrity	• AES-128 and P-256 Elliptic Curve for pairing • AES-CMC for pairing • AES-CCM for authentication • AES-CCM for encryption
Near Field Communication (NFC)	Supports short-range communication; therefore, used to establish pairings for other protocols	• Authentication	• AES-CCM
WirelessHart	Used in Wireless Sensor Networks	• Encryption • Authentication	• AES-CCM
6LoWPAN	Operates in a constrained environment with a large number of embedded computing devices	• Confidentiality • Authentication • Integrity	• RSA • ECC • IPSec
IPsec	Provides end-to-end security	• Confidentiality • Integrity • Authentication • Replay protection	• MD5 • SHA • DES-CBC • 3DES-CBC • AES

In addition, various messaging protocols such as CoAP, MQTT, and REST support the security protocols that employ one or the other form of a cryptographic algorithm including digital signature certificates for an end-to-end security in the Internet of Things. A report published by one of the rapidly growing and popular architectural frameworks for the Internet of Things that promises interoperability with existing Internet standards is the IEEE P2413 (https://standards.ieee.org/develop/project/2413.html). This architectural framework promises an end-to-end integration and comprises of an application layer, a networking/routing layer, an adaption layer, a MAC and a physical layer. In this section, existing security control mechanisms in protocols operating at various levels of this architecture as discussed by Jorge Granjal et al. (Granjal, Monteiro & Sá Silva, 2015) are enumerated in Table 10.

Table 10. Security mechanisms and challenges in IoT protocol stack

Layer	Security Mechanism	Security Challenges
Application Layer	• DTLS in CoAP: DTLS (Datagram TLS) operates at the transport layer to provide security services to CoAP messages. • CIA Trio: The use of DTLS at transport layer allows achieving confidentiality, integrity, authentication and non-repudiation at the application layer. Replay attacks are also defended by DTLS. The use of DTLS makes each datagram lengthier by 13 bytes which puts further burden on constrained devices. • Cryptography in DTLS: DTLS uses AES/CCM algorithm for providing security. • CoAP Security Modes: Four modes are supported. They are: i) NoSEC (No security) ii) PreSharedKey (Preprogramed Symmetric Cryptographic Keys), iii) RawPublicKey (Authentication is achieved through public keys. PKI device can be reprogramed), and iv) Certificate (Supports PKI and existing X.509 certificates for device authentication). For each mentioned security modes, the CoAP specification has defined a cipher suite.	• No Inherent Securities in CoAP • DTLS Handshake Issues: For resource constrained devices, DTLS handshake for device authentication and the key agreement, particularly the use of ECC public key cryptography is challenging. Retransmission is required for large messages because fragmentation of packets at adaptation (6LoWPAN) layer result in less reliability and more complexity. • Issue with Support for Public Keys and Certificates: Though ECC is a well know crypto for low resource devices, however, for severely constrained sensing platforms it is still not currently consensual among researchers. In addition, no certification verification protocol for the CoAP is yet standardized for online certificate verification of X.509 certificates. • Inability to support multicast communications due to non-availability of group-keying mechanism.
Network Layer	• No Security in 6LoWPAN: Despite several RFCs such as RFC 4944, RFC 4919, RFC 6568, RFC 6606 and RFC 6775 highlighting specific need for addressing various vulnerabilities of 6LoWPAN, no security for 6LoWPAN adaption layer has been defined and standardized. These documents discuss issues with mesh routing mechanisms in IEEE 802.15.4, routing approaches, Neighbor Discovery, etc.	• Difficult IPSec and IKE Adaption: IPSec and IKE used in conventional networks for network layer security cannot be directly used in 6LoWPAN due to resource constraints of devices in these networks. • No Authentication Mechanism: This makes the 6LoWPAN network prone to fragmentation attacks wherein normal functioning of the resource constrained device is under threat due to possible transmission duplicate, overlapping or forged fragments.
Routing Layer	• Security Modes: RPL protocol used for routing permits security modes for transmission of routing control messages. These security modes permit authentication by the use of preinstalled symmetric keys or by obtaining a key from some key server. RPL defines use of AES/CCM at MAC and RSA with SHA-256 for achieving integrity and authentication. Key management can be done either explicitly or implicitly.	• Non-Definition of Threat Model: RPL does not define any application level threat model. • Authentication & Key Retrieval: Use of digital signature certificates and public keys for node authentication is not defined. • No Defense Mechanism against Internal Attacks
Physical and MAC Layers	• At MAC layer, the IEEE 802.15.4 standard permits use of one out of many available security modes, which also motivates hardware accelerated 128-bit AES. For example, confidentiality is achieved using AES-CTR (AES in Counter Mode). Use of AES-CBC-MAC (AES in Cipher Block Chaining Mode) mode permits to achieve data authentication as well as integrity and Confidentiality. To protect message replay attacks auxiliary security headers can be used in MAC layer. As many as 255 entries for access control (ACL) can be stored on 802.15.4 radio chips for access control mechanism.	• No security control is available at the Physical layer in IEEE 802.15.4. • Limitations for network-shared and group keying in the link layer. • Limitations of ACL management for group and network-shared keying.

Forrester (Forrester, 2018) has discussed thirteen (13) most relevant and important IoT security technologies that include cryptographic technologies and listed them across various phases of adoption, business value and success. The report suggests that the most significant IoT security technologies include network security, authentication, encryption, public key infrastructure, security analytics and API security. The report lists IAM, identity store, device hardening, threat detection and device user privacy controls as various IoT security technologies that till date have attained moderate success. The IoT blockchain is listed by the report as the least successful IoT Security technology. The report further suggests that these security technologies face various challenges for their successful adoption in the Internet of Things owing to its unique characteristics. These characteristics include a very wide range of protocols, standards and device capabilities, variety of authentication scenarios, varying hardware profiles and capabilities, and unique attacks and intrusions. Cryptography has a huge scope in securing devices, networks, communication between devices and the data at rest as well as during transmission. However, it is very challenging and therefore, needs substantial research to fine tune the existing cryptographic procedures or to develop new solutions and to standardize them.

CONCLUSION

Cryptographic methods at various layers of the network stack are being applied to conventional networks for information security. However, due to diverse requirements, capabilities and resources of devices in the Internet of Things, direct applications of all such cryptographic methods has not been yet possible. They are thus, being applied with modification and moderation and often with their lightweight versions. Security standards have also been created to secure IoT data exchange across networks by adapting these methods. Applicability of cryptographic security methods for Internet of Things faces several challenges due to various inherent characteristics of Internet of Things which include availability of diverse communication protocols, standards, and device capabilities, varied authentication scenarios and hardware profiles. As such, a huge scope for the design and development of low power, low resource cryptographic security control procedures to improve the efficiency of existing security mechanism, that can help in securing sensors, devices, networks, communication and data in the Internet of Things, persists. This includes development of new standards, protocols, systems for controlling security risks through cryptographic techniques at various layers of the communication stack such as incorporation/strengthening of cryptographic security in existing protocols such as CoAP, MQTT, RPL, 6LoWPAN, etc., optimization of ECC and certificates for IoT devices, online verification of certificates, and lightweight key management.

REFERENCES

Abdul-Ghani, H. A., Konstantas, D., & Mahyoub, M. (2017). Comprehensive IoT Attacks Survey based on a Building-blocked Reference Model. *(IJACSA). International Journal of Advanced Computer Science and Applications*, *9*(3), 2018.

Ahemd, M. M., Shah, M. A., & Wahid, A. (2017). IoT Security: A layered approach for attacks & defenses. *2017 International Conference on Communication Technologies (ComTech)*, 104–110.

Al-Fuqaha, A., Guizani, M., Mohammadi, M., Aledhari, M., & Ayyash, M. (2015). Internet of Things: A Survey on Enabling Technologies, Protocols, and Applications. *IEEE Communications Surveys and Tutorials*, *17*(4), 2015.

All Seen Alliance. (n.d.). Retrieved from https://allseenalliance.org/

Arrowhead. (2018). *Arrowhead Framework*. Retrieved from https://forge.soa4d.org/plugins/ mediawiki/wiki/arrowhead-f/index.php/Main_Page

Atzori, L., Iera, A., & Morabito, G. (2011). SIoT: Giving a social structure to the internet of things. *IEEE Communications Letters*, *15*(11), 1193–1195.

Aumasson, J. P., Henzen, L., Meier, W., & Naya-Plasencia, M. (2013). Quark: A Lightweight Hash. *Journal of Cryptology*, *26*(2), 313–339.

Awad, W. S. (Ed.). (2015). Improving Information Security Practices through Computational Intelligence. IGI Global.

Babar, S., Mahalle, P., Stango, A., Prasad, N., & Prasad, R. (2010). Proposed security model and threat taxonomy for the Internet of Things (IoT). *International Conference on Network Security and Applications*, 89, 420–429.

Babbage, S., & Dodd, M. (2008). The MICKEY Stream Ciphers: 'New Stream Cipher Designs - The eSTREAM Finalists'. *LNCS*, *4986*, 191–209.

Bassi, A. (2013). Enabling things to talk – designing IoT solutions with the IoT architectural reference model. Springer.

Beaulieu, R., Shors, D., Smith, J., Treatman-Clark, S., Weeks, B., & Wingers, L. (2013). *The SIMON and SPECK Families of Lightweight Block Ciphers*. IACR Cryptology ePrint Archive.

Bogdanov, A., Knežević, M., Leander, G., Toz, D., Varıcı, K., & Verbauwhede, I. SPONGENT: A Lightweight Hash Function. *Proc. 13th International Workshop on Cryptographic Hardware and Embedded Systems (CHES 2011)*, 312-325.

Bogdanov, A., Knudsen, L. R., Leander, G., Paar, C., Poschmann, A., Robshaw, M. J. B., ... Vikkelsoe, C. (2007). PRESENT: An Ultra-Lightweight Block Cipher. *Proc. 9th International Workshop on Cryptographic Hardware and Embedded Systems (CHES 2007)*, 450-466.

Bonomi, F., Milito, R., Natarajan, P., & Zhu, J. (2014). *Fog computing: a platform for internet of things and analytics. In Big Data and Internet of Things: A Road Map for Smart Environments* (pp. 169–186). Berlin, Germany: Springer.

Bonomi, F., Milito, R., Zhu, J., & Addepalli, S. (2012). Fog computing and its role in the internet of things. *Proceedings of the 1st ACM MCC Workshop on Mobile Cloud Computing*, 13–16.

Breivold, H. P. (2017). A Survey and Analysis of Reference Architectures for the Internet-of-things. *ICSEA 2017: The Twelfth International Conference on Software Engineering Advances*.

BuildItSecure. Ly. (2018). *BuildItSecure.Ly*. Retrieved from http://builditsecure.ly

Chandra, B. T., Verma, P., & Dwivedi, A. K. (2016). Operating systems for internet of things: A comparative study. *Proceedings of the Second International Conference on Information and Communication Technology for Competitive Strategies*.

Checkpoint. (2017). *A New IoT Botnet Storm is Coming*. Retrieved from https://research.checkpoint.com/new-iot-botnet-storm-coming

CISCO. (2014). *Internet-of-everything Reference Model*. CISCO. Retrieved from http://cdn.iotwf.com/resources/71/IoT_Reference_Model_White_Paper_June_4_2014.pdf on Nov 23, 2018.

CNET. (2018). *IoT attacks are getting worse -- and no one's listening*. CNET. Retrieved from https://www.cnet.com/news/iot-attacks-hacker-kaspersky-are-getting-worse-and-no-one-is-listening on Nov 23, 2018.

CNN. (2017). *FDA confirms that St. Jude's cardiac devices can be hacked*. Retrieved from https://money.cnn.com/2017/01/09/technology/fda-st-jude-cardiac-hack/

De Cannière, C., & Preneel, B. (2008). Trivium: 'New Stream Cipher Designs - The eSTREAM Finalists'. *LNCS*, *4986*, 244–266.

Deogirikar, J. (2017). Security Attacks in IoT: A Survey. *International conference on I-SMAC*, 32–37.

Dorsemaine, B., Gaulier, J. P., Wary, J. P., Kheir, N., & Urien, P. (2016). A new approach to investigate IoT threats based on a four layer model. *IEEE Transactions on Emerging Topics in Computing.*

Dyn. (2016). *Dyn Status Update.* Retrieved from https://www.dynstatus.com / incidents/nlr4yrr162t8

FBI. (2015). *Internet of Things Poses Opportunities for Cyber Crime.* FBI, Alert Number: I-091015-PSA. Retrieved from https://www.ic3.gov/media/2015/150910.aspx

FIT. (2018). IoT experimentation at a larger scale. *FIT IoT Lab.* Retrieved from https://www.iot-lab.info/

Forrester. (2017). *Internet of Things Security Report.* Author.

Forrester. (2018). *Predictions 2019: The Internet of Things.* Retrieved from https://www.forrester.com

Fraden, J. (2010). *Handbook of Modern Sensors: Physics, Design and Applications* (4th ed.). Springer.

Fremantle, P. (2015). *A reference architecture for the Internet of things.* WSO2 white paper, version 0.9.0, 2015.

Gaur, P., & Mohit, P. T. (2015). Operating systems for IoT devices: A critical survey. In *Region 10 Symposium (TENSYMP).* IEEE.

Granjal, J., Monteiro, E., & Sá Silva, J. (2015). Security for the Internet of Things: A Survey of Existing Protocols and Open Research Issues. *IEEE Communications Surveys and Tutorials, 17*(3), 2015.

Guo, J., & Chen, I. R. (2015). A Classification of Trust Computation Models for Service-Oriented Internet of Things Systems. *Proceedings - 2015 IEEE International Conference on Services Computing, SCC 2015,* 324–331.

Guo, J., Peyrin, T., & Poschmann, A. (2011). The PHOTON Family of Lightweight Hash Functions. *Proc. 31st Annual International Cryptology Conference (CRYPTO 2011),* 222-239.

Hankel, M., & Rexroth, B. (2015). *Industrie 4.0: The Reference Architectural Model Industrie 4.0 (RAMI 4.0).* ZVEI - German Electrical and Electronic Manufacturers' Association. Retrieved from https://www.zvei.org

HealthData. (2016). Medical devices pose weak link in preventing cyber-attacks. *Health Data Management*. Retrieved from https://www.healthdatamanagement.com/news/medical-devices-pose-weak-link-in-preventing-cyber-attacks?issue=00000158-7951-dff3-a1db-fb7b29000000

Henry, P., Williams, J., & Wright, B. (2013). The SANS Survey of Digital Forensics and Incident Response. In Tech Rep.

Hirose, S., Ideguchi, K., Kuwakado, H., Owada, T., Preneel, B., & Yoshida, H. (2010). A Lightweight 256-Bit Hash Function for Hardware and Low-End Devices: Lesamnta-LW. *Proc. 13th International Conference on Information Security and Cryptology (ICISC 2010)*, 151-168.

Holdowsky, J., Mahto, M., Raynor, M. E., & Cotteleer, M. (2015). Inside the Internet of Things (IoT): A primer on the technologies building the IoT. *Deloitte Insights*. Retrieved from http://dupress.com/articles/iot-primer-iot-technologies-applications

IIC. (2018). Reference Architecture. *IIC Security Working Group Reference Guide*. Retrieved from http://www. iiconsortium.org/wc-security.htm

Infineon. (2018). The right security for the Internet of Things (IoT). *Infineon*. Retrieved from http://www.infineon.com/cms/en/applications/smart-card-and-security/internet-of-things-security

Intel. (2014). The Intel IoT Platform. *Intel Corporation*. Retrieved from https://www.intel.com/content/dam/www/public/us/en/documents/white-papers/iot-platform-reference-architecture-paper.pdf

Jha, A., & Sunil, M. C. (n.d.). Security considerations for Internet of Things. *L&T Technology Services*.

Jing, Q., Vasilakos, A. V., Wan, J., Lu, J., & Qiu, D. (2014). Security of the Internet of Things: Perspectives and challenges. *Wireless Netw. Springer, 2014*. doi:10.100711276-014-0761-7

Jungo, C. (2015). Integrity and trust in the Internet of Things. *Swisscom Ltd.* Retrieved from https://www.swisscom.ch/content/dam/swisscom/en/about/responsibility/digital-switzerland/ security/documents/integrity-and-trust-in-the-internet-of-things.pdf.res/integrity-and-trust-in-the-internet-of-things.pdf

Kajaree, D., & Behera, R. (2017). A Survey on IoT Security Threats and Solutions. *International Journal of Innovative Research in Computer and Communication Engineering*, *5*(2), 1302–1309.

Kumar, J. S., & Patel, D. R. (2014). A Survey on Internet of Things: Security and Privacy Issues. *International Journal of Computers and Applications*, *90*(11), 20–26.

Leander, G., Paar, C., Poschmann, A., & Schramm, K. (2007). New Lightweight DES Variants. *Proc. 14th International Workshop on Fast Software Encryption (FSE 2007)*, 196-210.

Li, S., Tryfonas, T., & Li, H. (2016). The Internet of Things: A security point of view. *Internet Research*, *26*(2), 337–359.

Lin, S., Miller, B., Durand, J., Bleakley, G., Chigani, A., Martin, R., . . . Crawford, M. (2017). *The Industrial Internet of Things Volume G1: Reference Architecture.* Industrial Internet Consortium, white paper.

Mashal, I., Alsaryrah, O., Chung, T.-Y., Yang, C.-Z., Kuo, W.-H., & Agrawal, D. P. (2015). Choices for interaction with things on Internet and underlying issues. *Ad Hoc Networks*, *28*, 68–90.

Micro, T. (2018). Threats to Voice-Based IoT and IIoT Devices. *Trend Micro*. Retrieved from https://www.trendmicro.com/vinfo/us/security/news/internet-of-things/threats-to-voice-based-iot-and-iiot-devices

Microsoft. (2018). *Microsoft Azure IoT Reference Architecture.* Microsoft Corporation. Retrieved from https://aka.ms/iotrefarchitecture

Mohsen-Nia, A., & Jha, N. K. (2016). A Comprehensive Study of Security of Internet-of-Things. *IEEE Transactions on Emerging Topics in Computing*. doi:10.1109/TETC.2016.2606384

Needham, R. M., & Wheeler, D. J. (1997). Tea extensions. Technical Report, Computer Laboratory, University of Cambridge.

Ning, H., & Wang, Z. (2011). Future internet of things architecture: Like mankind neural system or social organization framework. *IEEE Communications Letters*, *15*(4), 461–463.

NYTimes. (2016). Cyberattacks on Iran — Stuxnet and Flame. *New York Times*. Retrieved from https://www.nytimes.com/2011/01/16/world/middleeast/16stuxnet.html

OWASP. (2018). *Open Web Application Security Project (OWASP) Top 10 IoT Issues, OWASP Internet of Things Project, 11 Nov, 2018*. Retrieved from http://www.owasp.org /index.php/OWASP_Internet_of_Things_Top_Ten_Project

Pwnieexpress. (2017). *The IoT Attacks Everyone Should Know About.* Retrieved from https://www.pwnieexpress.com/blog/the-iot-attacks-everyone-should-know-about

Radware. (2017). *'BrickerBot' Results In PDoS Attack.* Retrieved from https://security.radware.com/ddos-threats-attacks/brickerbot-pdos-permanent-denial-of-service

Rakocevic, G. (2004). *Overview of Sensors for Wireless Sensor Networks.* Internet Journals.

Rivest, R. L. (1994). The RC5 Encryption Algorithm. *Proc. Second International Workshop on Fast Software Encryption (FSE 1994)*, 86-96.

Russell, B., & Van-Duren, D. (2016). Practical internet of things security. *Packt Publishing Ltd.*

Said, O., & Masud, M. (2013). Towards internet of things: Survey and future vision. *International Journal of Computer Networks*, *5*(1), 1–17.

Schatsky, D., Muraskin, C., & Gurumurthy, R. (2014). Demystifying Artificial Intelligence: What business leaders need to know about cognitive technologies. Deloitte University Press.

Security Intelligence. (2015). *Eight Crazy Hacks: The Worst and Weirdest Data Breaches of 2015.* Retrieved from https://securityintelligence.com/eight-crazy-hacks-the-worst-and-weirdest-data-breaches-of-2015

Simpson, L., & Lamb, R. (2010, February 20). IoT: Looking at sensors. Jefferies Equity Research, 4.

Stephen, L. (2014). IEEE standards group wants to bring order to IoT. *Computerworld.* Retrieved from https://www.computerworld.com/article/2686714/networking-hardware/ieee-standards-group-wants-to-bring-order-to-internet-of-things.html

Stojmenovic, I., & Wen, S. (2014). The fog computing paradigm: scenarios and security issues. *Proceedings of the Federated Conference on Computer Science and Information Systems (FedCSIS '14)*, 1–8, IEEE.

Sutherland, I., Read, H., & Xynos, K. (2014). Forensic Analysis of Smart TV: A Current Issue and Call to Arms. *Digital Investigation*, *11*(3), 175–178.

Symantec. (2018). Internet Security Threat Report. *Symantec.* Retrieved from https://www.symantec.com/content/dam/symantec/docs/reports/istr-23-2018-en.pdf

The Register. (2016). Finns chilling as DDoS knocks out building control system. *The Register.* Retrieved from https://www.theregister.co.uk/2016/11/09/finns_chilling_as_ddos_knocks_out_building_ control_ system

The Register. (2017). Reaper IoT botnet ain't so scary, contains fewer than 20,000 drones. *The Register*. Retrieved from https://www.theregister.co.uk/2017/10/27/reaper_iot_botnet_follow_up

Triantafyllou, A., Sarigiannidis, P., & Lagkas, T.D. (2018). Network Protocols, Schemes, and Mechanisms for Internet of Things (IoT): Features, Open Challenges, and Trends. *Wireless Communications and Mobile Computing*. . doi:10.1155/2018/5349894

Ukil, A., Sen, J., & Koilakonda, S. (2011). Embedded Security for Internet of Things. In *2011 2nd National Conference on Emerging Trends and Applications in Computer Science* (pp. 1–6). IEEE.

Wheeler, D. J., & Needham, R. M. (1994). TEA, A Tiny Encryption Algorithm. *Proc. Second International Workshop on Fast Software Encryption (FSE 1994)*, 363-366.

WSJ. (2017). WikiLeaks Dumps Trove of Purported CIA Hacking Tools. *The Wall Street Journal*. Retrieved from https://www.wsj.com/articles/wikileaks-posts-thousands-of-purported-cia-cyberhacking-documents-1488905823 on Nov 23, 2018.

Wu, M., Lu, T.-J., Ling, F.-Y., Sun, J., & Du, H.-Y. (2010). Research on the architecture of internet of things. *Proceedings of the 3rd International Conference on Advanced Computer Theory and Engineering (ICACTE '10)*, 5, V5-484–V5-487.

Zawoad, S., & Hasan, R. (n.d.). FAIoT. *Towards Building a Forensics Aware Eco System for the Internet of Things.*

Zhao, K. & Ge, G. (2013). A Survey on the Internet of Things Security. *2013 Ninth International Conference on Computational Intelligence and Security.*

Section 2

Encryption and Cryptography

This section presents encryption principles and discusses various cryptographic algorithms including lightweight cryptography that are applicable for the security of the Internet of Things.

Chapter 2
Encryption Principles and Techniques for the Internet of Things

Kundankumar Rameshwar Saraf
Dr. D. Y. Patil College of Engineering Lohegaon, India

Malathi P. Jesudason
Dr. D. Y. Patil College of Engineering Akurdi, India

ABSTRACT

This chapter explores the encryption techniques used for the internet of things (IoT). The security algorithm used for IoT should follow many constraints of an embedded system. Hence, lightweight cryptography is an optimum security solution for IoT devices. This chapter mainly describes the need for security in IoT, the concept of lightweight cryptography, and various cryptographic algorithms along with their shortcomings given IoT. This chapter also describes the principle of operation of all the above algorithms along with their security analysis. Moreover, based on the algorithm size (i.e., the required number of gate equivalent, block size, key size, throughput, and execution speed of the algorithm), the chapter reports the comparative analysis of their performance. The chapter discusses the merits and demerits of these algorithms along with their use in the IoT system.

DOI: 10.4018/978-1-5225-5742-5.ch002

INTRODUCTION

By using the Internet of Things, physical objects can communicate with each other over the Internet. Therefore, there is a strong need to define and implement security mechanisms which can ensure security and privacy of data that passes through the Internet of Things. The security algorithm used for IoT should follow many constraints of IoT. Hence, lightweight cryptography is the optimum security solution for securing IoT devices.

Simon, KATAN, and LED are optimized for hardware implementations while as Speck and Scalable Encryption Algorithm (SEA) ciphers are optimized for software implementations. Simon and Speck algorithms have been developed by the National Security Agency (NSA). Canniere et al. designed KATAN, and LED was designed by Guo et al. Low performing small computers can use the TEA encryption algorithm invented by David Wheeler and Roger Needham. PRESENT algorithm, invented by Andrey Bogdanov et al. is compact (occupies only 40% of space as compared to that of AES). Scalable Encryption Algorithm has been designed for software implementations in smart cards, processors, and controllers. This chapter provides a detailed description of all these algorithms along with their benefits and drawbacks and concludes with the comparison of all algorithms based on specific common metrics.

BACKGROUND

Encryption is a method of concealing the sensitive information and substituting it by other numbers, letters or symbols which can hide its meaning and readability. The cipher formed by encryption is used to protect the original word or plaintext from any possible third-party attacks. Cipher is of two subtypes, namely classical and modern. A classical cipher, in turn is of two types namely substitution and transposition ciphers. Substitution cipher may be monoalphabetic or polyalphabetic. Presently, modern ciphers are in practice. Symmetric and asymmetric key are the two types of modern ciphers. Symmetric ciphers are further classified into block and stream ciphers. Various modern cipher encryption algorithms and standards that are prominent include AES, DES, 3DES, RC4, SEAL, RSA, DSA and DH. A partial classification of ciphers is shown in Figure 1.

In the Internet of Things, physical devices embedded with sensors, software and connectivity enable data exchange and communication between devices. To secure communication in such environments, i.e., constrained physical devices, the implementation of new lightweight encryption algorithms which can replace the existing modern unconstrained encryption algorithms becomes highly essential.

Figure 1. Classification of ciphers

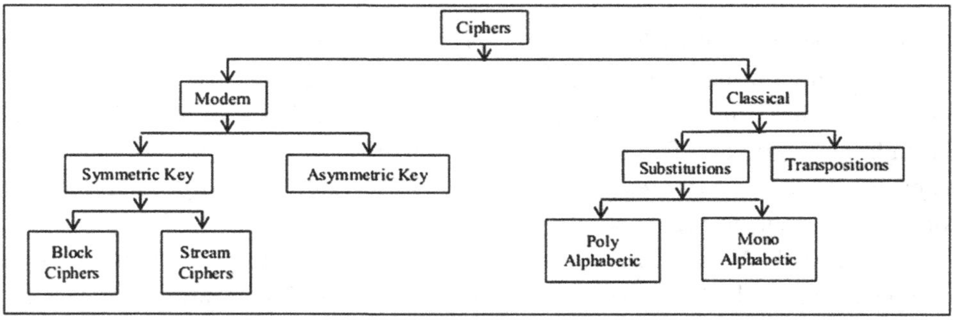

LIGHTWEIGHT CRYPTOGRAPHY

Internet of things (IoT), mostly employed in embedded systems are highly constrained regarding power, size, speed, security, complexity, and cost. The IoT based embedded devices handle storing, processing and transmission of sensitive, private and critical information many times and therefore, the security of data against any possible attack due to some vulnerability is a great challenge. One of the best ways to ensure security is through encryption. However, these methods are not straightforwardly applicable in situations of resource constrained and portable embedded system environments. In such systems, lightweight cryptographic algorithms, which are operable in tight memory and resource constraints are best possible options to use. Embedded systems preferably use Application Specific Integrated Circuit (ASIC) design which resists reprogramming after manufacturing of an IoT device. A hard-embedded system based IoT device can operate in hostile and time-critical environments. In this case, even a slight delay or speed-up can lead to severe damage to life or assets. LWC is an encryption method with a small footprint and low computational complexity. Lightweight cryptography is mainly a trade-off between security and light weight (computational burden) and as such for different IoT applications different implementations of LWC algorithm may be beneficial that target particular embedded hardware or target platform. For example, healthcare devices, sensors, and RFID tags may all use different variations of the same LWC algorithms. This is done to achieve maximum security for given RAM size, energy and software requirements, etc. On low resource hardware and software platforms, LWC is efficient and well suited with high performance compared to standard cryptographic techniques (Manifavas et al., 2014). Some of the essential attributes of LWC are as follows:

- **Size:** LWC must fit into small size of chip area.
- **Cost:** Cost of the device should not increase substantially by the use of LWC.
- **Speed:** Code of LWC should be optimized for faster results.
- **Power Consumption:** LWC should utilize minimum power for its execution. Also, due to faster execution of LWC instructions, module quickly returns into an idle state. This method will reduce power consumption (Nakahara et al., 2009).

The primary design goal of LWC is the reduction in logic gates known as Gate Equivalent (GE) required for materializing the cipher. Along with this, energy consumption is essential for battery operated IoT based embedded devices (Chandramouli et al., 2006). Power constraint is an essential factor in LWC when a device is passive and consumes energy from the host device for its significant operation like RFID tags. To satisfy the software constraints, LWC should occupy minimum memory, and it should provide maximum throughput by saving power (Quedenfeld, 2015).

BASIC OPERATIONS

This section describes the various arithmetic and logical operations and their symbols (used in this chapter) to represent the cipher structure or round function of algorithms.

- **Bitwise XOR ⊕: -** The symbol ⊕ represents the bitwise XOR operation between two parameters. Suppose, $z = x \oplus y$; then the value of z will depend on various values of x and y as given in truth table 1 below.
- **Bitwise AND ⋀: -** The symbol ⋀ or & represents bitwise AND operation between two parameters. Suppose, $z = x \wedge y$; then various values of z are shown in Table 1.
- **Bitwise OR V: -** The symbol **V** represents bitwise OR operation between two parameters. Suppose, z = x **V** y; then various values of z are shown in Table 1.
- **Cyclic right shift inside a word ⋙:** In this operation, the sequence is shifted by n number of positions to the right. Let an 8-bit sequence 11001100 be right shifted by 3 bits cyclically inside the word; the output sequence will be 10011001.
- **Cyclic left shift inside a word ⋘:** In this operation, the sequence is shifted by n number of positions to the left. Let an 8-bit sequence 11001100 be left shifted by 3 bits cyclically inside the word; the output sequence will be 01100110.

Table 1. The truth table of bitwise XOR, bitwise AND and bitwise OR operation

Bitwise XOR operation ⊕			Bitwise AND operation ∧			Bitwise OR operation V		
x	y	z	x	y	z	x	y	z
0	0	0	0	0	0	0	0	0
0	1	1	0	1	0	0	1	1
1	0	1	1	0	0	1	0	1
1	1	0	1	1	1	1	1	1

Any cyclic shift operation can be denoted by letter **r** (both right as well as left cyclic shift inside a word). Word rotation operation is similar to cyclic shift operation and can be denoted by letter **R**.

- **Mod 2^b addition ⊞:** In this operation, the mod 2^b operation will be performed on vector word.

ENCRYPTION TECHNIQUES FOR IOT

This section describes various lightweight encryption techniques preferable for use in the Internet of Things.

Simon

Simon is a lightweight block cipher released by National Security Agency (NSA) in June 2013 (Appel, n.d.). Simon is secure, lightweight, flexible and analyzable. This block cipher offers outstanding performance on hardware (Chen and Wang, 2016). The Simon algorithm is mainly optimized for performance in hardware implementation. Classical Feistel scheme is used for designing the Simon algorithm. In each round, this scheme operates on two n-bit halves. Hence, the block size of Simon is 2n bits. Each Simon round applies non-bijective, non-linear, non-invertible function denoted by $F : (F_2)^n \rightarrow (F_2)^n$ to the left half of state. The function F is given by equation 1 below:

$$F\left(x\right) = \left(\left(x \ll 8\right) \odot \left(x \ll 1\right)\right) \oplus \left(x \ll 2\right) \quad (1)$$

where $x \ll j$ denotes that x is rotated by j number of positions and $\odot$ is binary AND operation.

Simon Cipher

As mentioned earlier the block length of Simon is 2n. The key length of Simon is denoted by 'm'. The value of key length m is multiple of n by factor 2, 3 or 4. For example, Simon cipher is denoted by Simon 32/64 and can be obtained by the formula Simon 2n/mn. Here, 2n = 32, therefore, n = 16. Also, value of nm = 64, as value of n = 16, therefore, value of m = 64/16 = 4. Hence, block length 2n = 16*2 = 32, key length nm = 64 and number of rounds = 32 (Beaulieu, 2015). Simon has ten block ciphers distinctly with a different block and key size combinations. Combinations of block sizes, key sizes, and the number of rounds supported by Simon block cipher are given in Table 2.

The range of parameters supported by the Simon algorithm is shown from low to high-end security scenarios. A 32-bit block size with 64-bit key requires 32 rounds during encryption whereas, 128-bit block size with 256-bit key requires 72 rounds during encryption. A higher degree of security can be achieved by using some key size which is above 80-bits.

Simon Round Function

Simon Cipher mainly performs three operations through (i) Bitwise XOR $\oplus$, (ii) Bitwise AND, and (iii) Left Circular shift S^j, by j bits. As shown in Figure 2, plaintext message 1 (PT1) is circularly shifted to left by 1 bit and circularly shifted to left by 8 bits. The output obtained after both shifting will be logically ANDed (&) to obtain output **q**. The plaintext message 1 is circularly shifted to left by 2 bits and

Table 2. Simon block cipher parameter support

Value of 'n' in bits	Value of 'm' in bits	Block Size '2n' in bits	Key Size 'nm' in bits	Number of Rounds
16	4	32	64	32
24	3	48	72	36
	4		96	36
32	3	64	96	42
	4		128	44
48	2	96	96	52
	3		144	54
64	2	128	128	68
	3		192	69
	4		256	72

XORed with output **q** of the previous operation and thus, output **m** is obtained. The plaintext message 2 is XORed with message **m** from which output **t** is obtained. Key $\mathbf{k}_i$ is XORed with **t.** The ciphertext message 1 will be obtained at the output of XOR operation. The ciphertext message 2 will be obtained from plaintext message 1.

Key Schedule of Simon

Simon key schedule is a function operated on 2, 3 or 4, n-bit word registers which depend on the master key size. It performs two right rotations $x \gg 3$ and $x \gg 1$ and the obtained result is XORed with fixed constant c and a sequence of five constants $(z_j)_i$ which depends on the version. All rounds of Simon Block Cipher are exactly the same except round key. Operation of Simon is flawlessly symmetric with regard to circular shift map on the n-bit word. Simon key schedule is mathematically described as:

$$\boldsymbol{k}_{i+m=c\oplus(z_j)_i\oplus k_i\oplus\left(I+S^{-1}\right)S^{-3}k_{i+1},\, for\ m=2} \tag{2}$$

$$\boldsymbol{k}_{i+m=c\oplus(z_j)_i\oplus k_i\oplus\left(I+S^{-1}\right)S^{-3}k_{i+2},\, for\ m=3} \tag{3}$$

$$\boldsymbol{k}_{i+m=c\oplus(z_j)_i\oplus k_i\oplus\left(I+S^{-1}\right)S^{-3}k_{i+3}\oplus k_{i+1},\, for\ m=4} \tag{4}$$

Figure 2. One round of Simon

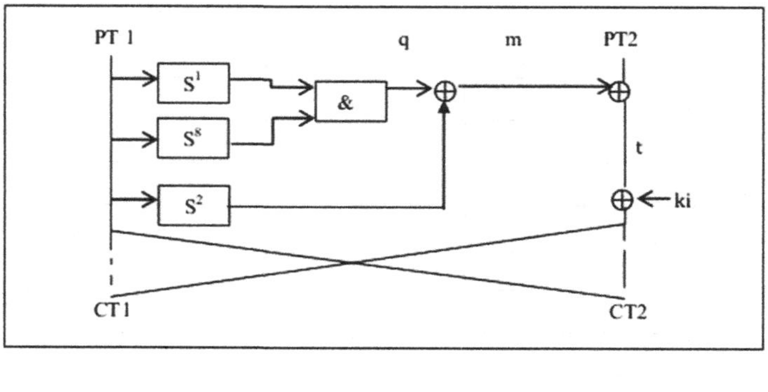

Key schedule of Simon may be imbalanced sometimes. Keyword count m determines the key expansion structure. Keyword expansion contains right shift operation, XOR operation, and sequence of constants denoted by z_x (Degnan and Durgin, 2017).

Advantages of Simon Algorithm

- It is secure and analyzable block cipher.
- It offers outstanding performance when implemented in hardware.
- Due to its flexibility, it can be used for different types of implementations.
- It is possible to analyze Simon using existing techniques.
- It can be used for a full range of lightweight applications.

Disadvantages of Simon Algorithm

- It can be optimized for hardware implementations only, hence, for the software implementations, new algorithms may be required.
- It is affected by the reduced round variety attack, which determines the maximum number of rounds that would be vulnerable to a theoretical attack.
- It is susceptible to linear hull and differential attacks with dynamic key-guessing technique. (AlKhzaimi and Lauridsen, 2013).

Speck

Lightweight block cipher, Speck was released by National Security Agency along with Simon in 2013. It is also known as the sister algorithm of Simon, optimized for mainly software implementations.

Speck Round Function

Speck involves only three operations in its round function (i) Bitwise XOR $\oplus$, (ii) Modulo Addition 2^n, +, and, (iii) Left and right circular shifts S^j, S^{-j}. Therefore, Speck is called Add-Rotate-XOR cipher, i.e., ARX cipher. Speck round function is shown in Figure 3.

Speck Cipher

A vast variety of block and key size combinations are supported by Speck. A Speck block always contains two words. Size of the word may be 16, 24, 32, 48 or 64 bits in size. The corresponding key size for these words will be 2, 3, and 4. Speck round function contains two rotations as shown in Figure 3, rotate 8 bits of first plaintext message to the right side and rotate 3 bits of second plaintext message to the left side (Dinur, 2014). Then the right word will be added to the left word by modulo addition block. The key will then be XORed to the left word. The left word will then be XORed with the right word. The Speck round function is shown in Figure 3.

The number of rounds supported by Speck depend on the parameters selected, as shown in Table 3.

Advantages of Speck Algorithm

- It is a secure and analyzable block cipher.
- It offers outstanding performance when implemented in software.
- Due to its flexibility, it can be used for different types of implementations.
- Round function of Speck can be reused for key scheduling.
- Extremely small code size can be used for its implementation.

Figure 3. Speck Round Function (3 Speck rounds with two-word key schedule) (Abed, 2014)

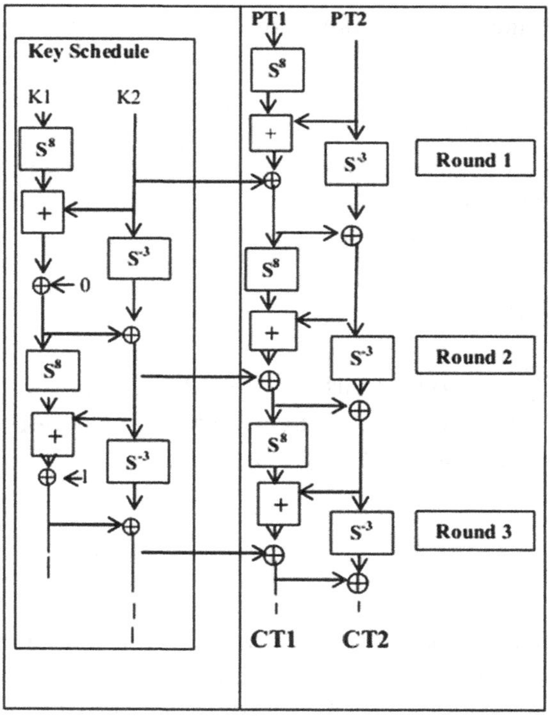

Table 3. Speck block cipher parameter support (Abed et al., 2014)

Block size (bits) Block = 2 words*size of the word in bits	Key size (bits) Key = (2, 3 or 4) words*size of words	Rounds
2 * 16 = 32	4 * 16 = 64	22
2 * 24 = 48	3 * 24 = 72	22
	4 * 24 = 96	23
2 * 32 = 64	3 * 32 = 96	26
	4 * 32 = 128	27
2 * 48 = 96	2 * 48 = 96	28
	3 * 48 = 144	29
2* 64 = 128	2 * 64 = 128	32
	3 * 64 = 192	33
	4 * 64 = 256	34

- According to eBACS: ECRYPT Benchmarking of Cryptographic Systems, Speck is one of the fastest ciphers for both long and short messages.
- Speck can be used for a full range of lightweight applications (Abed et al., 2014).
- To resist slide attack and rotational cryptanalysis attack, Speck Cipher includes round counter in its key schedule.

Disadvantages of Speck Algorithm

- It is only optimized for software implementations.
- It is affected by reduced round variety attack, which determines the maximum number of rounds that would be susceptible to a theoretical attack.
- It is prone to differential cryptanalysis and improved differential cryptanalysis attack (Chen and Wang, 2016; Beaulieu, 2015).
- Speck has a minimal security margin which makes it vulnerable to any future advances in cryptanalysis.

KATAN and KTANTAN Ciphers

KATAN belongs to hardware-oriented block cipher family designed in 2009 by Canniere et al. (De et al., 2009). KATAN family consists of six block ciphers which are further classified into two sets of KTANTAN block ciphers with a block size of 32-bits, 48-bits or 64-bits and three KATAN block ciphers with the same 32-bit,

48-bit and 64-bit block size. KATAN and KTANTAN share the same 80-bit key, and both have the same security level. Low-end devices such as RFID tags are used in many applications with extremely constrained environments. Security in such applications can be incorporated by a highly compact and minimal size algorithm called KATAN. KTANTAN is more compact as compared to KATAN. Differences between KTANTAN and KATAN are given in Table 4.

KATAN Cipher

KATAN ciphers are of three types: KATAN32, KATAN48, and KATAN64. KATAN key schedule accepts the 80-bit key, and it has 254 rounds. All types of KATAN ciphers share same non-linear functions and key schedule.

KATAN32: It has plaintext and ciphertext size of 32-bits. The 13-bit plaintext is loaded in the L_1 register, and 19-bit plaintext is loaded in the L_2 register. Bit number 0 of L_2 register stores least significant bit and bit number 12 of register L_1 stores most significant bit of plaintext message. In each round, L_1 and L_2 are shifted to the left due to which bit i will become i+1 after shifting. The content of register L_1 and L_2 will be updated after shifting. After 254 rounds, the content present in L_1 and L_2 registers will be called as ciphertext. Two non-linear functions used by KATAN 32 in each round are $f_a(\cdot)$ and $f_b(\cdot)$. These are defined by equations given below,

$$f_a\left(L_1\right) = L_1\left[x_1\right] \oplus L_1\left[x_2\right] \oplus \left(L_1\left[x_3\right] \cdot L_1\left[x_4\right]\right) \oplus \left(L_1\left[x_5\right] \cdot IR\right) \oplus k_a \quad (5)$$

Table 4. Comparison between KTANTAN and KATAN

KTANTAN	KATAN
Key of KTANTAN is burnt into the device, and it cannot be changed on a later stage.	Key is not burnt into the device, and it can be changed at a later stage.
Very small block ciphers	Comparatively larger than KTANTAN
More compact in nature	Less compact in nature
It can be used only in cases where a device is initialized with one key	It can be used in other cases also
KTANTAN32 has 462 Gate Equivalent and has 12.5 Kbits/sec encryption speed	KATAN32 has 802 Gate Equivalent and has 12.5 KBit/sec encryption speed
KTANTAN48 is recommended for RFID tags, has 588 Gate Equivalent and has 18.8 KBit/sec encryption speed	KATAN48 has 927 Gate Equivalent and has 18.8 KBit/sec encryption speed
KTANTAN64 has 688 Gate Equivalent and has 25.1 KBit/sec encryption speed	KATAN64 has 1054 GE and has 25.1 KBit/sec encryption speed

$$f_b\left(L_2\right) = L_2\left[y_1\right] \oplus L_2\left[y_2\right] \oplus \left(L_2\left[y_3\right] \cdot L_2\left[y_4\right]\right) \oplus \left(L_2\left[y_5\right] \cdot L_2\left[y_6\right]\right) \oplus k_b \tag{6}$$

where IR is Irregular Update Rule i.e., $L_1\left[x_5\right]$ is XORed in a round where the irregular update is used, k_a and k_b are two sub-key bits, k_a is denoted by $\mathbf{k}_{2i}$ and k_b is denoted by $\mathbf{k}_{2i+1}$ for round number i. x_i and y_i bits for each variant are independently selected, as given in Table 5.

After computation of $f_a(\cdot)$ and $f_b(\cdot)$ non-linear functions, L_1 and L_2 are shifted. In this shifted form, MSB falls into the corresponding non-linear function, and LSB is loaded with the output of the second non-linear function. Hence, after completion of all rounds, the output of f_b will be LSB of L1 and output of f_a will be LSB of L_2. KATAN 32 key schedule loads 80 bit key into LFSR where LSB of the key is loaded to position 0 of LFSR. The outline structure of KATAN 32 is shown in Figure 4 below.

Table 5. x_i and y_i bits defined for KATAN and KTANTAN families of ciphers

Cipher	$\lvert L_1\rvert$	$\lvert L_2\rvert$	x_1	x_2	x_3	x_4	x_5	y_1	y_2	y_3	y_4	y_5	y_6
KATAN32/KTANTAN32	13	19	12	7	8	5	3	18	7	12	10	8	3
KATAN48/KTANTAN48	19	29	18	12	15	7	6	28	19	21	13	15	6
KATAN64/KTANTAN64	25	39	24	15	20	11	9	38	25	33	21	14	9

Figure 4. KATAN/ KTANTAN cipher round outline

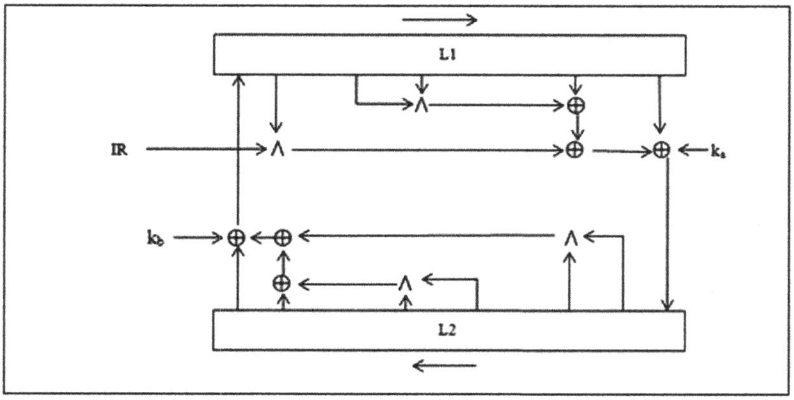

Advantages of KATAN / KTANTAN Algorithm

- It is a very efficient hardware-oriented block cipher algorithm.
- KTANTAN has a compact structure.

Disadvantages of KATAN / KTANTAN Algorithm

- The meet-in-the-middle attack can find the key of KTANTAN32 with a time complexity of 279.
- KATAN is affected by the differential attack, meet-in-the-middle attack, algebraic side channel attack (Fuhr and Minaud 2014; Isobe et al. 2013; Bard 2010).
- Both KATAN / KTANTAN are affected by slide attack which finds two messages that share most of the encryption process.
- Both KATAN / KTANTAN are affected by the related key attack in which attacker searches for two intermediate encryption values as well as keys which develop in the same manner for as many rounds as possible (Bard, 2010).

LED (Light Encryption Device)

LED is lightweight symmetric block cipher that can be efficiently implemented in hardware. LED was published in 2011 by Guo et al. (Shanmugam, 2014). LED has 64-bit block size and 64 or 128-bits of key size. The key length of LED may vary between 64 and 128 bits, for example, a key length of 70 bit in size. In case of 70-bit key size, remaining bits will be padded with a prefix of the key. In LED input, plain text bytes are converted into state matrix of size 4*4. Key of LED is also converted into 4*4 matrix size (Mendel et al., 2012).

LED Round Function

- **Add Constants:** In this function, at each round, six bits (i.e., from rc_5 to rc_0) are shifted one position to the left with the new value to rc_0. It is computed as $rc_5 \oplus rc_4 \oplus 1$. The six bits are updated and initialized to zero before used in a given round.
- **SubCells:** In this operation, each nibble in the array state is replaced by nibble generated after using the present Sbox.
- **ShiftRows:** In this operation, row i of the array STATE is rotated i cell positions to the left, for i = 0, 1, 2, 3.

- **Mix Columns Serial:** In this operation, each column of the array state is viewed as a column vector and replaced by the column vector that results after post-multiplying the vector by the matrix M.

The final value of the state provides the ciphertext with nibbles of the "array" being unpacked in an obvious way (Isobe & Shibutani, 2012).

A single round of LED contains the steps like Add Constants, Sub Cells, Shift Rows and Mix Columns Serial as shown in Figure 5.

Advantages of LED Algorithm

- It is mainly used for compact hardware implementations.
- It offers comparatively smallest footprint of silicon among comparable lightweight block ciphers (Guo et al., 2011).

Disadvantages of LED Algorithm

- LED algorithm is susceptible to the following attacks as shown in Table 6 (Nikolić, 2013).

TEA Cipher

The primary objective of the design of Tiny Encryption Algorithm (TEA) is high performance and less complicated encryption algorithm which can be used for low performance, small computers in the IoT environments. TEA was designed in 1994 by David Wheeler and Roger Needham. TEA operates on two unsigned integers of 32 bits and uses 128-bit length key. TEA has a Feistel structure with 64 rounds (Wheeler and Needham1994). The TEA is implemented in pairs, which is termed as cycles. TEA employs round based encryption method. Two Feistel rounds constitute a single cycle of TEA algorithm as shown in Figure 6. Due to this, in each TEA

Figure 5. An overview of Single Round of LED

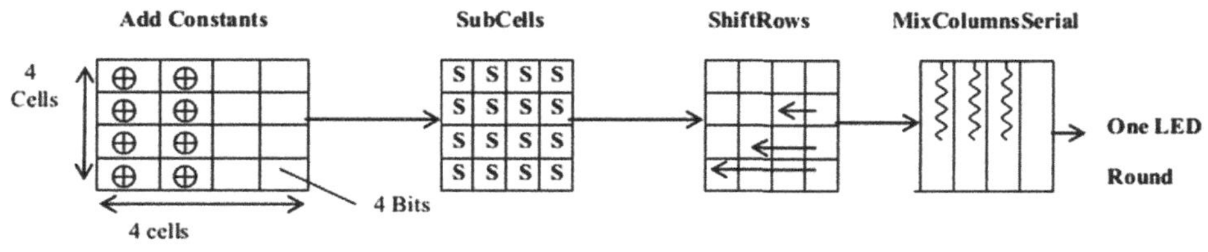

Table 6. Attacks on LED algorithm

Cipher Algorithm Name	Name of the Attack	Round Number where the attack is observed	Reference
LED – 64 (32 rounds)	Meet-in-the-Middle Attack	8	(Mendel et al., 2012)
	Linear / Differential Cryptanalysis Attack	16	(Isobe & Shibutani, 2012)
	Linear / Differential Cryptanalysis Attack	15	(Guo et al., 2011)
	Meet-in-the-Middle Attack / Differential Cryptanalysis Attack	16	(Nikolić, 2013)
	Meet-in-the-Middle Attack / Differential Cryptanalysis Attack	20	(Nikolić, 2013)
LED – 128 (48 rounds)	Meet-in-the-Middle Attack	16	(Mendel et al., 2012)
	Linear / Differential Cryptanalysis Attack	24	(Isobe & Shibutani, 2012)
	Linear / Differential Cryptanalysis Attack	27	(Guo et al., 2011)
	Meet-in-the-Middle Attack / Differential Cryptanalysis Attack	32	(Nikolić, 2013)
	Meet-in-the-Middle Attack / Differential Cryptanalysis Attack	40	(Nikolić, 2013)

round, control variable **i** is increased by the value of 2. Variable **i** denotes the Feistel rounds. Following operation is executed in one TEA round.

$$\boldsymbol{delta}\left[\boldsymbol{i}\right] = \left\{\frac{\boldsymbol{i}+1}{2}\right\} * \boldsymbol{delta} \tag{7}$$

$$\boldsymbol{Left}\left[\boldsymbol{i}+1\right] = \boldsymbol{Right}\left[\boldsymbol{i}\right] \tag{8}$$

$$\boldsymbol{Right}\left[\boldsymbol{i}+1\right] = \boldsymbol{Left}\left[\boldsymbol{i}\right] \boxplus \boldsymbol{F}\left(\boldsymbol{Right}\left[\boldsymbol{i}\right], \boldsymbol{K}\left[0,1\right], \boldsymbol{delta}\left[\boldsymbol{i}\right]\right) \tag{9}$$

$$\boldsymbol{Left}\left[\boldsymbol{i}+2\right] = \boldsymbol{Right}\left[\boldsymbol{i}+1\right] \tag{10}$$

$$\boldsymbol{Right}\left[\boldsymbol{i}+2\right] = \boldsymbol{Left}\left[\boldsymbol{i}+1\right] \boxplus \boldsymbol{F}\left(\boldsymbol{Right}\left[\boldsymbol{i}+1\right], \boldsymbol{K}\left[2,3\right], \boldsymbol{delta}\left[\boldsymbol{i}\right]\right) \tag{11}$$

$$\boldsymbol{F}\left(\boldsymbol{M}, \boldsymbol{K}\left[\boldsymbol{j},\boldsymbol{k}\right], \boldsymbol{delta}\left[\boldsymbol{i}\right]\right) = \left(\left(\boldsymbol{M} \ll 4\right) \boxplus \boldsymbol{K}\left[\boldsymbol{j}\right]\right) \oplus \left(\boldsymbol{M} \boxplus \boldsymbol{delta}\left[\boldsymbol{i}\right]\right) \oplus \left(\left(\boldsymbol{M} \gg 5\right) \boxplus \boldsymbol{K}\left[\boldsymbol{k}\right]\right) \tag{12}$$

The first step of TEA round (equations 8 and 9) is known as the first Feistel round. Equations 10 and 11 show second Feistel round of TEA. Equation 12 represents F() which is a round function, and it covers the major steps of cryptographic operations.

Advantages of TEA Algorithm

- It has high performance and can be used on low performing computers.
- Mathematically, it is less complicated.
- Its performance is better than Data Encryption Standard (DES) algorithm.
- It can be implemented in all the programming languages.
- Encryption strength of TEA can further be increased by increasing the encryption cycles.

Figure 6. Two Feistel rounds one cycle of TEA

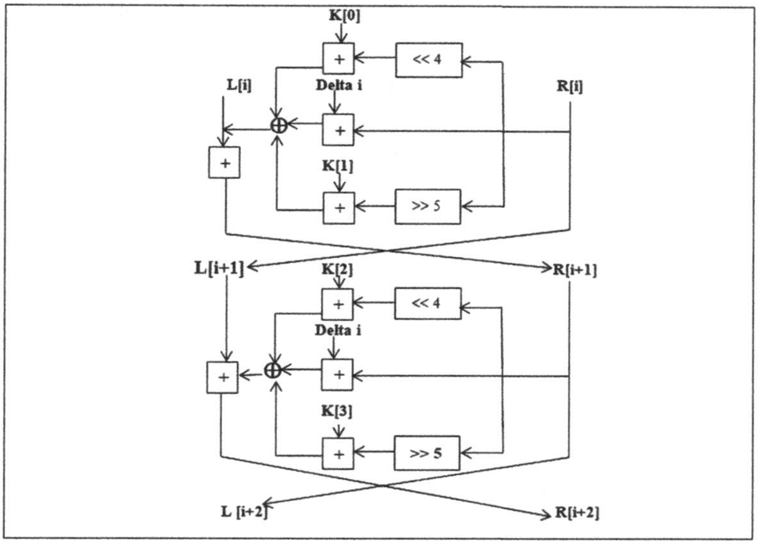

Disadvantages of TEA Algorithm

- With little efforts, it is possible to find the given hash values of X and Y and the input value of X. Therefore, a collision can be calculated in TEA algorithm (Nikolić et al., 2013; Wheeler and Needham, 1994).
- Using Brute Force Attack and a combination of known plaintext-ciphertext pairs, the key of TEA can be easily cracked (Nikolić et al., 2013).
- Due to constructional vulnerability at TEA encryption, every key to decrypt the TEA cipher has three equivalent keys which can also be used to decrypt the same cipher (Nikolić et al., 2013).

PRESENT Cipher

PRESENT (Appel, n.d.) is a lightweight block cipher introduced in 2007 by Orange Labs of Ruhr, University of Denmark. Block size of the PRESENT is 64 bit, and key size is either 80 bit or 128 bits. Single 4-bit S-box is designed by hardware optimization. This S-box acts as a non-linear layer of PRESENT algorithm. PRESENT can be used in applications where low-power consumption and high chip efficiency is required. PRESENT is an algorithm with 31 rounds which uses a classical substitution-permutation network (SPN). Keys are generated in the first 32 rounds of PRESENT. To introduce, a round key K_i for $1 \leq i \leq 31$, the first 31 rounds have an XOR operation. K_{32} is used for post-whitening, which can confuse the structure of linear and non-linear substitution layer of round 31. In all of the 31 rounds, each round has three operations. In the first operation, the current round key is applied to the block which is being encrypted. S-Box is a second operation which holds Shannon's property of confusion. Due to this confusion, each ciphertext character depends on several key parts. A permutation is the third and last step of each round.

Advantages of PRESENT Algorithm

- The main focus is to achieve high security and hardware efficiency.
- Compact hardware implementation of PRESENT needs only 1570 Gate Equivalent.
- PRESENT can be implemented in both hardware and software platforms.

Disadvantages of PRESENT Algorithm

- PRESENT is susceptible to statistical saturation attack.
- PRESENT is also susceptible to linear algebraic cryptanalysis of reduced round variant (Appel, n.d.).

SEA Cipher

It is a low-cost encryption algorithm that can run on limited processing resources (Standaert, 2006). $SEA_{n,b}$ can be run on many different platforms with the same behavior. $SEA_{n,b}$ is represented by the following parameters:

- n = plaintext size, key size
- b = processor size
- nb = n / 2b: number of words per Feistel round
- nr = Number of block cipher rounds

SEA round consists of encryption and decryption procedure as well as the key round function. Figure 7 shows the SEA round function.

Simple Feistel round is used by $SEA_{n,\,b}$ for encryption-decryption as well as for the key round. First portion of Figure 7 shows encryption-decryption round. Plaintext splits into two blocks namely left block L_i of n_b and right block R_i of n_b at the beginning of each round. Left block L_i is rotated and XORed with right block R_i as follows:

$$R_{i+1} = R\left(L_i\right) \oplus r\left\{S\left(R_i \boxplus K_i\right)\right\} \tag{13}$$

$$L_{i+1} = R_i \tag{14}$$

Figure 7. SEA round function

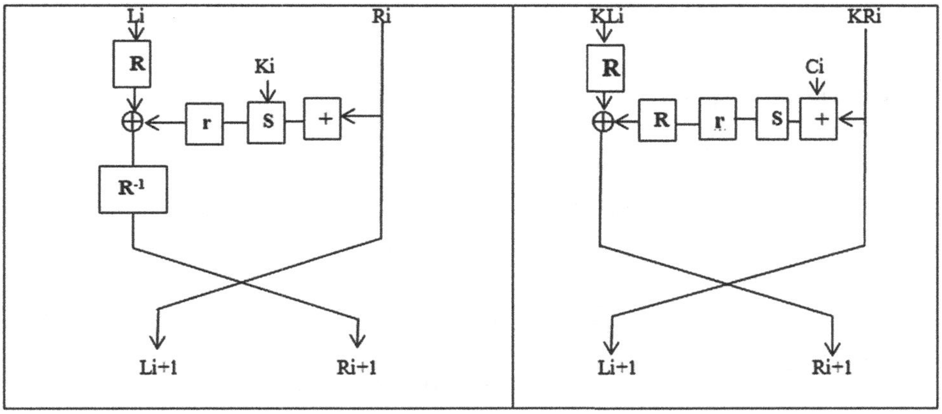

In the process of decryption, left block L_i is not rotated after the XOR operation, the block is rotated inverse of the word rotation as shown in the equation (15) below:

$$R_{i+1} = R^{-1}\left[L_i \oplus r\left\{S\left(R_i \boxplus K_i\right)\right\}\right] \quad (15)$$

$$L_{i+1} = R_i \quad (16)$$

The second portion of Figure 7 shows the key round. The key is first split into KL_i and KR_i blocks of n_b words. The left KL_i block is XORed with the right block as shown in equation 17 below:

$$KR_{i+1} = KL_i \oplus R[r\{S(KR_i \boxplus C_i\}] \quad (17)$$

$$KL_{i+1} = KR_i \quad (18)$$

The key schedule is mainly designed to maintain the same key round during encryption as well as decryption process. To achieve this and to allow a different number of rounds, after $[n_r / 2]$, the KL_i and KR_i will be switched. This switching operation reverses the earlier key derivation and expands the key as shown in the equation (19) below,

$$K_0, K_1 \ldots\ldots\ldots, K_{\left\lceil \frac{nr}{2} \right\rceil}, K_{\left\lceil \frac{nr}{2} \right\rceil - 1}, \ldots\ldots\ldots K_1, K_0 \quad (19)$$

Advantages of SEA Algorithm

- It is a low-cost algorithm.
- It can run using very limited processing resources.
- It has a very small code size; hence, low memory is required for its implementation.
- Very limited instruction sets are required for implementation of SEA algorithm.
- Flexible enough to run on different platforms.

- By performing certain modifications in the SEA, it is resistant to linear cryptanalysis attack, differential cryptanalysis attack, structural attack, outer round improvement of statistical attack, truncated and impossible differential attack.

Disadvantages of SEA Algorithm

- SEA is susceptible to Related-Key Attack or interpolation attack.

COMPARISON OF LIGHTWEIGHT CRYPTOGRAPHIC ALGORITHMS FOR IOT

Software and Hardware Implementations

Performance comparison of all algorithms on hardware and software is shown in Table 7. Mainly Simon, Speck, KATAN, LED, TEA, PRESENT and SEA are designed to be implemented on software platforms and Simon, KATAN, LED and PRESENT are designed to be implemented on hardware platforms. This comparison considers the hardware as ASIC implementation and software implementation uses an 8-bit microcontroller, clock speed is 100 kHz for hardware and 16 MHz for software. The best performance is indicated by number in underlined font and second best performance is indicated by number in dashed underlined font [Ref 5]. Table 7 shows a comparison of the performance of various lightweight cryptographic algorithms on hardware as well as software platform.

Table 7 shows the performance of various LWC algorithms on ASIC implementation. It uses an 8-bit microcontroller for the software simulation of the algorithm. Clock speed for hardware is 100 kHz, and for software, it is 16 MHz. GE means the Gate Equivalent required for hardware implementation. GE is a unit of measure to specify the relative complexity of a circuit. GE represents the number of logic gates interconnected to perform a specific function which is similar to the digital circuit under evaluation. BPS/GE means bits per second required for each gate equivalent execution. It is a unit to measure the speed of algorithm on the hardware.

The speed of each cipher depends on the number of gate equivalents. In Table 7, it can be observed that SIMON is overall best for hardware implementation. SEA has the highest speed 103. 2 kbps but requires more area due to a large number of gate equivalents, i.e., 4313 GE. KATAN 64n and SEA has the highest efficiency about 24 bps/GE. SPECK gives the best performance among software implementations.

Table 7. Performance comparison for hardware and software implementation for LWC algorithms (Appel, n.d.)

(Block/Key) Size	Name of the Algorithm	Hardware			Software		
		Area (GE)	Throughput (kbps)	Efficiency (bps/GE)	Flash (bytes)	SRAM (bytes)	Throughput (kbps)
32/80	KATAN32	802	12.5	16	-	-	-
48/80	KATAN48	927	18.8	20	-	-	-
48/96	SIMON	763	15.0	20	196	0	589
48/96	SPECK	884	12.0	14	134	0	943
64/64	LED	966	5.1	5	-	-	-
64/80	LED	1040	3.4	3	-	-	-
64/80	PRESENT	1030	12.4	12	487	0	96
64/80	Katan64	1054	25.1	24	272	18	14
64/96	SIMON	838	17.8	21	274	0	540
64/96	SPECK	984	14.5	15	182	0	888
64/96	LED	1116	3.4	3	-	-	-
64/128	SIMON	1000	16.7	17	282	0	515
64/128	SPECK	1127	13.8	12	186	0	855
64/128	LED	1265	3.4	3	-	-	-
64/128	TEA	-	-	-	-	0	163.2
64/128	PRESENT	1339	12.1	9	487	0	96
96/96	SIMION	984	14.85	15	454	0	454
96/96	SPECK	1134	13.8	12	276	0	866
96/96	SEA	4313	103.2	24	-	0	1588
128/128	SIMON	1317	22.9	17	732	0	342
128/128	SPECK	1396	12.1	9	396	0	768

CONCLUSION AND FUTURE DIRECTIONS

Lightweight cryptographic (LWC) algorithms are mainly optimized either for hardware or software implementation. Hence, it is desired to invent the new algorithm which gives the best performance on both hardware and software. LWC algorithms are subjected to various attacks such as improved linear hull attack, differential attacks, differential cryptanalysis, improved differential cryptanalysis attack, meet-in-the-middle attack, algebraic side channel attack, slide attack, Brute Force Attack, etc. Hence, a new algorithm should be designed that can resist all these attacks and offer excellent performance in any attack environment. Research can be performed to optimize the area required for the LWC algorithm, to increase the throughput and efficiency of the algorithm.

With the use of the Internet of Things, different electronic devices can communicate with each other. Hence, security of this communication is provided by lightweight cryptographic (LWC) algorithms. The main aim of this chapter is to provide the introduction to various LWC algorithms designed for the resource-constrained environment of the IoT applications. LWC algorithm can be used for privacy protection in surveillance video monitoring (Zhang et al., 2018). Table 7 shows that all LWC algorithms require less area, i.e., gate equivalents for its implementation. Also, LWC algorithms have high throughput and efficiency. LWC algorithm uses small bytes of flash and SRAM memory for its operation. Such extensive analysis of all LWC algorithms is considered essential for researchers to use these algorithms on the newly designed system or for researchers who want to replace their existing cryptographic algorithm on available systems.

REFERENCES

Abed, F., List, E., Lucks, S., & Wenzel, J. (2014, March). Differential cryptanalysis of round-reduced Simon and Speck. In *International Workshop on Fast Software Encryption* (pp. 525-545). Springer.

AlKhzaimi, H., & Lauridsen, M. M. (2013). Cryptanalysis of the SIMON Family of Block Ciphers. *IACR Cryptology ePrint Archive, 2013*, 543.

Bard, G. V., Courtois, N. T., Nakahara, J., Sepehrdad, P., & Zhang, B. (2010, December). Algebraic, AIDA/cube and side channel analysis of KATAN family of block ciphers. In *International Conference on Cryptology in India* (pp. 176-196). Springer. 10.1007/978-3-642-17401-8_14

Beaulieu, R., Treatman-Clark, S., Shors, D., Weeks, B., Smith, J., & Wingers, L. (2015, June). The SIMON and SPECK lightweight block ciphers. In *Design Automation Conference (DAC), 2015 52nd ACM/EDAC/IEEE* (pp. 1-6). IEEE. 10.1145/2744769.2747946

Chandramouli, R., Bapatla, S., Subbalakshmi, K. P., & Uma, R. N. (2006). Battery power-aware encryption. *ACM Transactions on Information and System Security, 9*(2), 162–180. doi:10.1145/1151414.1151417

Chen, H., & Wang, X. (2016, March). Improved linear hull attack on round-reduced Simon with dynamic key-guessing techniques. In *International Conference on Fast Software Encryption* (pp. 428-449). Springer. 10.1007/978-3-662-52993-5_22

De Canniere, C., Dunkelman, O., & Knežević, M. (2009). KATAN and KTANTAN—a family of small and efficient hardware-oriented block ciphers. In *Cryptographic Hardware and Embedded Systems-CHES 2009* (pp. 272–288). Berlin: Springer. doi:10.1007/978-3-642-04138-9_20

Degnan, B., & Durgin, G. D. (2017). *Simontool: Simulation support for the Simon Cipher*. IEEE J. RFID.

Dinur, I. (2014, August). Improved differential cryptanalysis of round-reduced speck. In *International Workshop on Selected Areas in Cryptography* (pp. 147-164). Springer.

Fuhr, T., & Minaud, B. (2014, March). Match box meet-in-the-middle attack against KATAN. In *International Workshop on Fast Software Encryption* (pp. 61-81). Springer.

Guo, J., Thomas, P., Axel, P., & Matt, R. (2011). The led block cipher. *Proceedings of the 13th International Conference on Cryptographic Hardware and Embedded Systems, CHES'11* (pp 326-341). Springer.

Isobe, T., Sasaki, Y., & Chen, J. (2013, July). Related-key boomerang attacks on KATAN32/48/64. In *Australasian Conference on Information Security and Privacy* (pp. 268-285). Springer. 10.1007/978-3-642-39059-3_19

Isobe, T., & Shibutani, K. (2012, July). Security analysis of the lightweight block ciphers XTEA, LED and Piccolo. In *Australasian Conference on Information Security and Privacy* (pp. 71-86). Springer. 10.1007/978-3-642-31448-3_6

Manifavas, C., Hatzivasilis, G., Fysarakis, K., & Rantos, K. (2014). Lightweight cryptography for embedded systems–A comparative analysis. In *Data Privacy Management and Autonomous Spontaneous Security* (pp. 333–349). Berlin: Springer. doi:10.1007/978-3-642-54568-9_21

Mendel, F., Rijmen, V., Toz, D., & Varıcı, K. (2012, December). Differential analysis of the LED block cipher. In *International Conference on the Theory and Application of Cryptology and Information Security* (pp. 190-207). Springer. 10.1007/978-3-642-34961-4_13

Nakahara, J., Sepehrdad, P., Zhang, B., & Wang, M. (2009, December). Linear (hull) and algebraic cryptanalysis of the block cipher PRESENT. In *International Conference on Cryptology and Network Security* (pp. 58-75). Springer. 10.1007/978-3-642-10433-6_5

Nikolić, I., Wang, L., & Wu, S. (2013, March). Cryptanalysis of Round-Reduced $$\mathtt {LED} $$. In *International Workshop on Fast Software Encryption* (pp. 112-129). Springer.

Quedenfeld, F. M. (2015). *Modellbildung in der algebraischen Kryptoanalyse* (Doctoral dissertation). Universitätsbibliothek Kassel.

Shanmugam, D., Selvam, R., & Annadurai, S. (2014, October). Differential power analysis attack on SIMON and LED block ciphers. In *International Conference on Security, Privacy, and Applied Cryptography Engineering* (pp. 110-125). Springer. 10.1007/978-3-319-12060-7_8

Standaert, F. X., Piret, G., Gershenfeld, N., & Quisquater, J. J. (2006, April). SEA: A scalable encryption algorithm for small embedded applications. In *International Conference on Smart Card Research and Advanced Applications* (pp. 222-236). Springer. 10.1007/11733447_16

Wheeler, D. J., & Needham, R. M. (1994, December). TEA, a tiny encryption algorithm. In *International Workshop on Fast Software Encryption* (pp. 363-366). Springer.

Zhang, X., Seo, S. H., & Wang, C. (2018). A Lightweight Encryption Method for Privacy Protection in Surveillance Videos. *IEEE Access: Practical Innovations, Open Solutions*, *6*, 18074–18087. doi:10.1109/ACCESS.2018.2820724

KEY TERMS AND DEFINITIONS

3DES: Triple data encryption standard.

AES: Advanced encryption standard.

Algebraic Side-Channel Attack: This attack represents the physical information leakages and target algorithms in the form of equations to determine the plaintext and key.

DES: Data encryption standard.

DH: Diffie Hellman.

Differential Attacks or Differential Cryptanalysis: This attack compares the variations in the input with variations in the encrypted output to find the desired key or plaintext message.

DSA: Digital signature algorithm.

Dynamic Key-Guessing Technique: This technique exploits the property of and operation to get the desired key.

Improved Linear Hull Attack: This attack is mainly proposed to improve the differential attack.

Linear Cryptanalysis Attack: It finds an affine approximation to the action of a cipher to reveal the key or plaintext message.

Meet-in-the-Middle Attack: This attack targets the cryptographic function and brute force technique is applied to both plaintext and ciphertext block. Then various keys are applied to achieve intermediate ciphertext simultaneously; keys are used to decrypt the ciphertext. If a match of intermediate ciphertext occurs, it is concluded that key used for encryption of plaintext and decryption of ciphertext is derived.

RC4: Rivest cipher 4.

Reduced-Round Variety Attack: Number of rounds susceptible to theoretical attack can be determined by this attack.

RSA: Rivest–Shamir–Adleman.

SEAL: Software-optimized encryption algorithm or simple encryption algorithm.

Slide Attack: It increases the number of rounds in a ciphertext or makes them irrelevant to the cryptographic algorithm to find the plaintext or key.

Theoretical Attack: The strategy of this attack is designed through theory or calculation.

Chapter 3
A Review of Cryptographic Algorithms for the Internet of Things

Issmat Shah Masoodi
University of Kashmir, India

Bisma Javid
University of Kashmir, India

ABSTRACT

There are various emerging areas in which profoundly constrained interconnected devices connect to accomplish specific tasks. Nowadays, internet of things (IoT) enables many low-resource and constrained devices to communicate, do computations, and make smarter decisions within a short period. However, there are many challenges and issues in such devices like power consumption, limited battery, memory space, performance, cost, and security. This chapter presents the security issues in such a constrained environment, where the traditional cryptographic algorithms cannot be used and, thus, discusses various lightweight cryptographic algorithms in detail and present a comparison between these algorithms. Further, the chapter also discusses the power awakening scheme and reference architecture in IoT for constrained device environment with a focus on research challenges, issues, and their solutions.

DOI: 10.4018/978-1-5225-5742-5.ch003

INTRODUCTION

In recent years, the Internet of Things has witnessed rapid growth and is being perceived as hypernym for interconnected technologies, objects, devices, and services. Nevertheless, after years of contribution to this research, there is still no clear and universal definition of the concept. However, still, the application frameworks and opportunities offered in the market by objects are communicating actively far beyond specific horizons. The novel contributions, new applications, and services conceived by innovators and researchers are bewildering and clearly show the high and vast opportunities for our next generations. In the early 2000s, RFID technology was designed and developed mainly across the engineering sector for tracking and tracing goods. At the same time, research was conducted on sensor networks and miniaturized smart systems. The size of sensors was becoming very small and computing power dramatically increased. Nevertheless, innovative solutions were always developed and provided for specific application cases, and there was no absolute interconnectivity and interoperability between different application areas. For example, fields like logistics and manufacturing are well-known as they provide an immediate business benefit regarding asset tracking and supply chain management. However, real solutions cannot be applied to other fields such as demotics, where business synergies can provide services with obvious added-value benefits. As the IoT zone covers such a vast spectrum of application fields, the happening cycles and technologies used can be completely classified. Often, the developments in technology are driven by idealistic, tiny and medium-sized enterprises (SME) that try to meet targets try to catch ongoing trends at a faster pace. However, the target is usually an output within a narrow scope, the solutions are usually non-interoperable, and while successful, they are unable to produce a common abstract infrastructure capable of marking notable progress in the whole field. This holds for large-scale companies that usually develop dedicated solutions for specific business opportunities without implementing applicable concepts. Therefore, current solutions can still be seen as peaceful solutions, that can implement some "INTRAnet of Things" despite "INTERnet of Things." While being logical regarding the point, in the long term, the prevailing situation is unsustainable. Nowadays, we can observe a situation of a similar sort to that in the networking field, where at its infancy many solutions are obtained but were subsequently discarded in favor of a unified communication infrastructure, the TCP/IP protocol suite. We do believe that different classes of devices will always co-exist. Taxonomies are to be created according to various principles, such as critical or non-critical, or distributed or centralized. These classes can promote different profiles as per the specific needs and requirements of domains and applications. By the reference model, we mean an abstract framework that comprises at least a set of unifying concepts and relationships for understanding essential relationships between the entities of an environment. This framework must be able to develop the specific architectures which may constitute different levels of abstraction. The high-level work used drives the realization of a framework for identifying specific reference architectures that subsequently define both essential building blocks as well as choices for the design dealing with different functionality, performance, deployment, and security. The main aim of the IoT-A project was to prove its work on the current state of the art, rather than deploying a clean slate approach. Because of this, common traits came into existence to form the baseline of the IoT Architectural Reference Model (ARM). The primary advantage of enacting this model is its backward compatibility.

BACKGROUND

With the advent of a new era in computation, Internet of Things (IoT) (ITU Internet Report, 2005) has emerged as a building block of ubiquitous computing (Lee et al., 2012). IoT is a smart technology that interconnects every "thing" through a network in one form or another. The term "thing" includes sensors, actuators, hardware, software, and storage, spread over multiple disciplines such as healthcare, industry, transport, and home appliances. The primary objective of IoT is to maximize the communication of hardware objects with the physical world and to convert the data harvested by these objects into useful information without any human aid. IoT consists of three elements namely hardware, middleware, and presentation. The hardware element has battery-powered embedded sensors, actuators, and communication systems. The sensors collect data from the monitoring area, and their communication hardware sends the collected data to the middleware element. An enormous amount of data received by middleware is processed and analyzed by using various data analysis tools to extract interpretable information. The presentation element of IoT is responsible for the visualization of processed data and results in a novel and easily readable form. It also receives user queries and passes them to the middleware element for necessary actions.

Figure 1 shows the elements and data transfer mechanism in IoT systems. The term Internet of Things (IoT) was coined by Kevin Ashton during 1999 (Ashton, 2014), although this concept was discussed in scientific literature well before that. This term tries to define a future Internet, where the growth in the number of devices continues, and almost all electronic devices have Internet connectivity. This extension is not limited to user-controlled devices only, but machine-to-machine (M2M) communication is also included. All of these connected devices are represented on the Internet either in the form of an IP address or some other identifying information. Setting up such an infrastructure has many benefits, including remote monitoring,

Figure 1. Elements of IoT

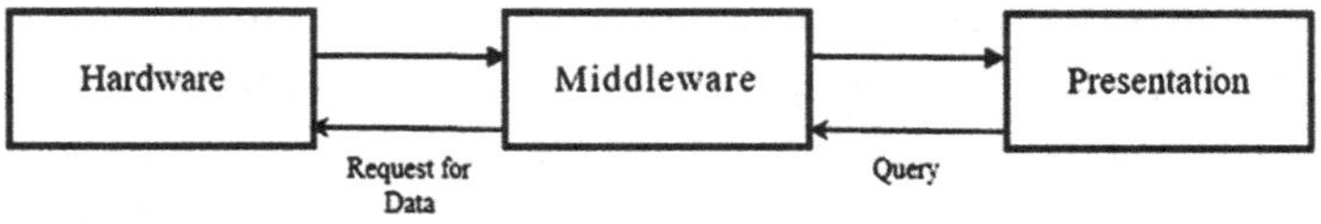

convenient control of devices owned by an individual and increasing numbers of automated systems. Estimates of the number of wireless devices connected to the Internet suggest 30 billion devices by 2020 (ABI Research,2014). Even today, IoT has emerged as an area for research and development. The limited battery power of hardware elements is consumed while collecting and transmitting data. The more is the data collected and analyzed, the more is the accuracy of extracted information, but at the same time, the more is the energy consumed. Due to energy limitations, there is a need to maintain a trade-off between quality of information extracted and energy consumption by IoT systems. Moreover, the lifetime of any resource in IoT depends upon the availability of energy. The loss of energy affects the whole environment under observation. Thus, there is a prominent need to reduce energy consumption for the extended lifetime of resources and the effective operation of IoT systems.

Energy Relevance in IoT

The escalation of the Internet of Things provides various opportunities but may also lead to risks. Previously, the neglected issue in the Internet of Things was a possible increase in power consumption. Since IoT devices remain in the vicinity of other devices at all times, the device itself, or at least its communication module, is consuming electrical energy even when the device is not in use for its primary function. When idle, most devices will enter a sleep state, which consumes a significantly lesser amount of energy. Billions of such low power devices raise concerns towards excessive sleep state energy consumption, even if the particular device has only moderate power needs (Harrington & Nordman, 2014). Worldwide, the computational power consumption of network-enabled devices has already touched 615 TWh in 2013 (Rozite, 2014), overtaking the power consumption of Germany. This demand is predicted to grow to 1,140 TWh by 2025, analogous to 6% of current total global electricity consumption (Rozite, 2014).

These estimates are focused on the expected escalation of "traditional" network-enabled devices, such as desktop and laptop computers, tablets, set-top boxes, game consoles, and smart TVs. Robust IoT devices like sensors, household appliances, personal health gadgets, and RFID tags, are yet to be included fully. Therefore, it is necessary to address the topic of IoT at an early stage to develop guidelines and policies to prevent excessive energy consumption of these novel network-enabled devices. On the other hand, IoT may enable more efficient use of energy, because it has the potential to provide new data collection and control possibilities in many areas of our daily life (Coroama & Hilty, 2009).

Power Awakening Schemes for IoT Nodes

Various power awakening schemes have been proposed for IoT nodes. One among them is a sleepy-awake scheme for energy efficiency of IoT nodes using CoAP protocol. Sleepy approaches are necessary for constrained devices. Many models are designed and implemented towards a sleepy mechanism for supporting a sleepy approach for IoT nodes. One of the approaches includes IoT node, IoT middleware and Web Client that uses HTTP and CoAP for communication between each element in the network. For this scheme, CoAP libraries are used to implement communication that is not only used for sleepy mechanism but also used for delivering data to the web client application. The CoAP is a protocol meant for devices that are constrained regarding memory, processing speed and computational power such as low power small sensors, switches, and valves. It is a web transfer protocol, specialized for constrained devices to communicate over the Internet actively. In CoAP networks, it is expected that there will be a particular portion of nodes that suspend CoAP protocol communication temporarily to conserve energy. The sleepy feature is necessary for a constrained environment. CoAP nodes work on the constrained environment. Therefore, direct discovery of nodes is not practical due to sleepy nodes. There have been several IETF drafts for sleepy nodes in constrained environments which are based on the sleepy mechanism presented in (Cheng et al., 2001). CoRE RD is an entity which hosts descriptions of CoAP nodes held on a server. The server should be based on some power supply (not batteries), which can always allow lookups for retrieving registered information (Dasgupta et al.,2003). In a CoAP based communication network, a CoAP client can search a CoAP node from RD and access it. Before the searching process, the CoAP node needs to register its information to the RD (Dhillon et al., 2003). MQ broker published as a draft in IETF is an extension of the CoRE RD (Dhillon et al., 2003). Functionalities for publish-subscribe communication are incorporated using the broker which enables to store and forward a message from CoAP nodes. A CoAP node can send a data to the MQ broker and can switch into sleep mode. Then a CoAP client can request to MQ broker for getting the data which is sent by the CoAP node before sleep. The data is temporal, that can be updated or removed.

IoT Applications

The Internet of Things (IoT), sometimes referred to as the Internet of Everything, will change everything around us including ourselves. The Internet has changed the system of education, business, government, science, communication, and humanity. The Internet is among the most potent creations in all of human history, and now with the idea of the Internet of Things, the Internet is becoming more favorable to have various smart life aspects. By developing the IoT technology, testing and deploying products, it will be much closer to implementing smart environments by 2020 (Tang et al.,2005). In future, storage and communication services will be convenient and distributed: people, smart objects, machines, surrounding space and wireless/wired sensors, Machine to Machine devices, RFID tags are going to create highly decentralized resources connected by a dynamic network of networks (Cheng et al., 2001). By 2020, around 50 to 100 billion things will be connected electronically by Internet (Gupta et al.2003). Figure 2 shows the growth of the things connected to the Internet from 1988 to forecast 2020. The Internet of Things (IoT) can provide technology to making the means of smart action for machines to communicate with each other and with many different kinds of information (Pan et al.,2003). The success of IoT depends on standardization, which provides interoperability, reliability, compatibility, and effective operations on a global scale (Tang et al.,2005). Nowadays, more than sixty companies from leading technologies, in communications and energy are working with standards, such as IETF, IEEE, and ITU to specify new IP based technologies for the Internet of Things (Vallimayil et al.,2011).

IOT ARCHITECTURE

The Internet of Things will circumscribe a wide range of technologies from highly constrained to unconstrained devices. Therefore, one reference architecture is not enough to be used as a blueprint for all possible valid implementations. Since a reference model can be identified, probably it is expected that various reference architectures will co-exist at the same time in the Internet of Things. Architecture is defined as the specification of physical components of the network and their functional organization in this context. It also includes the procedures and operational principles. For instance, identification architecture based on RFID Tag may be entirely different from the architecture based on sensors, which is highly comparable to the current Internet (Sai et al., 2014).

Figure 2. Number of devices connected (year wise)

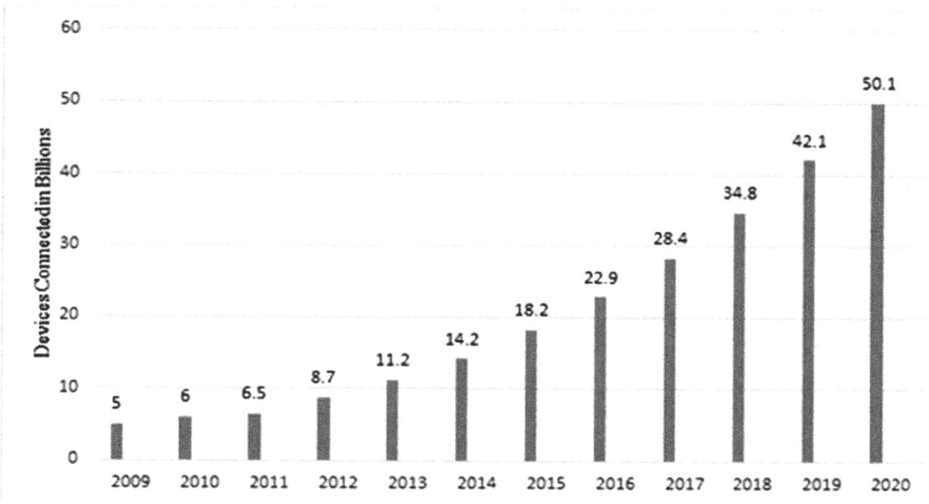

Table 1. Example IoT applications

Application	Edge Devices	Criteria			
		Range	Frequency	Data Rate	Latency
Smart Homes					
Smart Lighting	Smart LED bulb	Low	Low	Low	Low
	Gateways	Low	Low	Low	Low
Home Automation	Sensors	Low	Low	Low	Low
	Actuators	Low	Low	Low	Medium
	Camera	Low	Low	High	Low
	Gateway	Low	Low	Low	Mid
Smart Appliances	Smart Appliances	Low	Low	Low	Low
	Smart Appliances	Low	Low	Low	Low
Smart Mobility					
Smart Roads	Roadside Unit	Medium	High	High	High
Smart Street Lighting	Street Light	Medium	Low	Low	Low
Smart Health					
Smart Health Monitors	Sensors	Low	Low	Low	Low
	Monitors	Medium	High	High	Medium
	Gateway	Low	Low	Low	Medium

Like the Internet, the IoT architecture will grow exponentially from a varsity of separate contributions, rather than from a planned one (Yu et al.,2014). Considering the developments from various organizations like ITU-T by the ITU, Model for Smart Grid by NIST, ETSI with M2M Model or the EU's Reference are factored by the group into future developments of the policy debate in Europe. There exists an area of overlap in between Identification and Architecture. Till now it is not evident that a single model will apply to all application domains of the Internet of Things. There are many valid reasons to have reference architecture for IoT. These include:

- The Inherent connection between IoT devices.
- For the scalability purposes, because already there are billions of connected devices and the number is increasing day by day, and these devices are interacting with each other every time.
- The model that can manage and control the identity for IoT devices and the data they throw and consume is key-dependent.

Requirements for Reference Architecture

Various requirements are applicable only for IoT devices and the IoT environments that support them. Various requirements come from the manufacturing of the IoT devices. The overall requirements are:

- Connectivity and communications
- Data collection, analysis, and actuation
- Device management
- High availability
- Integration
- Scalability
- Predictive analysis
- Security

Connectivity and Communications

Already existing protocols like HTTP is playing a vital role in many devices. Even an 8-bit controller generates a simple GET and POST command request. However, the overhead of the HTTP protocol and other traditional protocols is the issue to be addressed because the IoT devices are memory and power constrained. For that, we need a small and straightforward protocol that meets the conditions mentioned above.

Data Collection, Analysis, and Actuation

In order to manage a vast number of devices, a reference model is designed. If the devices fly the stream of data, i.e., a large amount of data is created, then a highly scalable data storage system is required having a large volume. This action requires real-time analytics as this may happen in real time. In addition to that, analysis of the data is required in order to act upon it. This process may require massive event processing utilizing powerful engines.

Device Management

From past few times, the management has become a challenge which was not necessarily ideal in the past. The trajectory is like and desired for IoT also. Various abilities that are required for device management include the ability to:

- Disconnect a stolen device;
- Update software on a device automatically;
- Update security credentials;
- Disable and enable remotely;
- Destroy the data in the stolen device;
- Reconfigure network parameters remotely.

Scalability

The ideal server-side architecture should be scalable and be able to support billions of devices all constantly transmitting, receiving, and enacting on the data. However, a lot of "high-scalability architectures" that have been implemented came with an equally high price – both in software as well as in hardware and also in complexity. The requirement for this architecture is to be able to support scaling from a small-scale deployment to a very large-scale deployment of devices.

Security

Security is a prime concern in IoT. IoT devices are made to collect highly confidential and personal data. Various attempts already have been made in order to secure the data keeping the computational cost and other constraints in consideration. The proposed work has given a thorough description of attempts using cryptographic measures. Security brings three categories of risks:

- The IoT designer or the product designer may not be aware of the risks inherent in any Internet system.
- Specific risks are unique to IoT devices.
- Safety must be ensured to avoid harmful situations such as misuse of actuators.

Reference Architecture of IoT

The reference architecture constitutes a set of components. We will discuss various options for realizing each component because layers need to be realized by means of specific technologies.

The layers in IoT architecture are:

- Client/external communications - Web/Portal, Dashboard, APIs
- Event processing and analytics
- Aggregation layer
- Relevant transports - /HTTP /CoAP etc.
- Devices
- Device management

Figure 3. Layered IoT protocol architecture

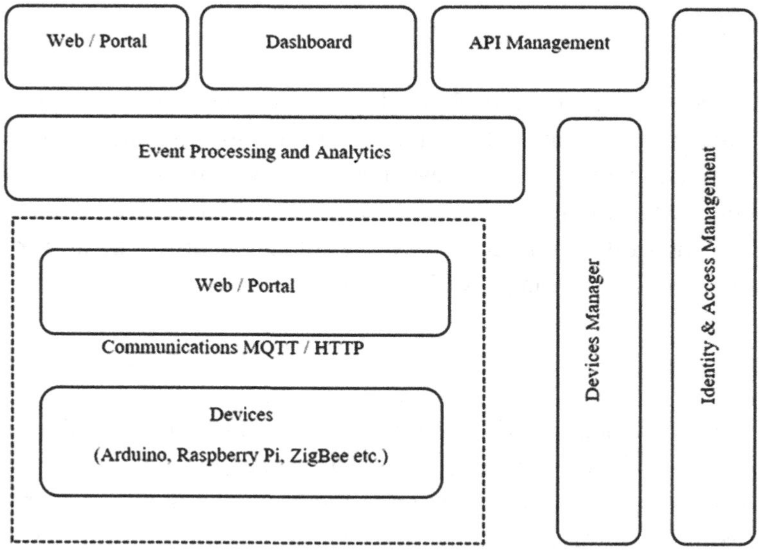

Client / External Communication Layer

This reference architecture has to find a way by which all the devices can communicate with the device-oriented system outside. This includes three main possible approaches. First one is the ability to create web-based front-ends and portals for the interaction with devices and other layers like an event-processing layer — the second one is the ability to create dashboards that present views into analytics and event processing — lastly, the ability to use M2M communication APIs to interact with systems outside.

Event Processing and Analytics Layer

The main operation performed is to store the data in the database. This may occur in three forms. The primary form is the traditional model used to write a server-side application like database backed JAX-RS application. Many approaches can support more agile approaches. The first among these is to use a large data analytics platform. The other approach is to support event processing complex, in which real-time activities and actions performed on data from the devices and rest of the system are to be initiated.

Aggregation / Bus Layer

This layer is of vital importance in the architecture because it is this layer which aggregates and brokers the communications. The importance of this layer is because of the following three reasons:

- This layer can support an HTTP server and also MQTT broker in order to talk to the connected devices.
- This layer provides a facility to aggregate and combine different types of communications among different devices and routes the communication to a gateway.
- This layer serves as a bridge among different protocols.

The aggregation layer is capable of providing such facilities as well as adapt to the legacy protocols.

Communication Layer

The communication layer supports the connectivity of the devices. There are lots of capable protocols for communication between the devices and the cloud. The well-known potential protocols are Constrained Application Protocol (CoAP), HTTPS/HTTP and MQTT 3.1/3.1.1.

Device Layer

At the bottom of the architecture is the device layer. There are various types of device layers, but in order to consider them as IoT devices, the direct or indirect attachment to the Internet must exist for the communication purpose. Few of direct connections at device layer are:

- Arduino with an Ethernet connection.
- Arduino UNO with Wi-Fi connection.
- Raspberry Pi connected via Wi-Fi/ Ethernet.
- Intel Galileo connected via Wi-Fi/ Ethernet.

Device Management

Device management (DM) layer is handled by two components viz., device manager and device management agents. The device manager (server-side system) communicates with devices through various protocols and can provide both bulk and individual control of devices. The software and the applications deployed on the device are managed remotely. Remote access can be used to lock or wipe the data if necessary. Device management agents work in conjunction with the device manager. There are three levels of the device: non-managed, semi-managed and fully managed (NM, SM, FM).

CRYPTOGRAPHIC ALGORITHMS FOR IOT

The future of the Internet is the "Internet of Things" where trillions of physical objects, most of them with low or meager resources, communicate with each other without human intervention. Lightweight cryptography includes cryptographic algorithms specifically meant for extremely constrained resources. They cannot only be applied for encryption but also for hashing as well as authentication under environments that are constrained at large. An overview of various lightweight cryptographic algorithms is presented in this section.

Some of the critical cryptographic algorithms available in the market are Rivest-Shamir-Adleman (RSA), Data Encryption Standard (DES) (which is no longer considered secure), Triple DES (3DES), Advanced Encryption Standard (AES), Blowfish, RC2, and RC6. Although those algorithms are vital in information systems security, they consume a significant amount of computing resources such as CPU time, memory, and battery power. Symmetric key encryption strength depends on the size of key used, for example, RC2 and DES uses a 64-bit key, Triple DES (3DES) uses two 64- bits keys, AES and RC6 use any of 128-, 192- or 256-bit keys and Blowfish uses 32- to 448-bit range keys (default being 128 bits).

Energy consumption of different symmetric algorithms depends on key size, as more energy is required for performing more number of operations. For example, it is found that after only 600 encryptions of 5 MB file using 3DES, 55% of battery power is consumed (Ruangchaijatupon N, 2001). In AES, as the key size is increased by 64-bits, the energy consumption increased by about 8% without any data transfer. In a study to evaluate the performance of encryption algorithms on power consumption for wireless devices, Figure 4 shows the power consumption for encrypting text data with different data block size by calculating the change in battery left for encryption process without data transmission.

Figure 4. Battery consumption by various encryption algorithms

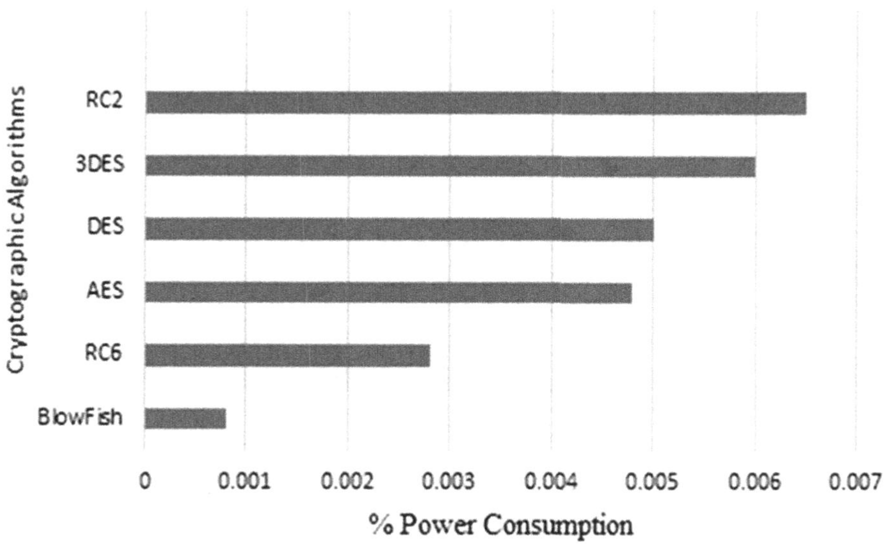

As seen in Figure 4, most of the encryption algorithms consume energy which affects battery power. Due to the slow increasing rate in battery technology than other technologies, we face a "battery gap", so decisions need to be made about energy consumption and security to reduce the consumption of battery powered devices. In an encryption scheme, the throughput is calculated by dividing the total size of plaintext encrypted in megabytes by the total encryption time for each algorithm. As we increase the throughput value, the power consumption and CPU process time of this encryption technique are decreased. CPU Process Time reflects the load of the CPU. This load depends on the CPU time used in the encryption process. Therefore, the more time the CPU will be used in the encryption process, the higher the load of the CPU will be. In Figure 5, it is evident that other than Blowfish algorithm, all other algorithms' throughput is very low and cannot be recommended for low computing systems.

The Internet of Things (IoT) is now one of the essential topics in the industry of technology. It has a significant impact on various aspects of our life including industrial components, customer goods, cars, smartphones, TVs, and many of our daily use objects (''things'') that have unique identities and are being provided with Internet connection in order to make them remotely available. IoT enables highly

Figure 5. The throughput of various encryption algorithms (Megabyte/sec)

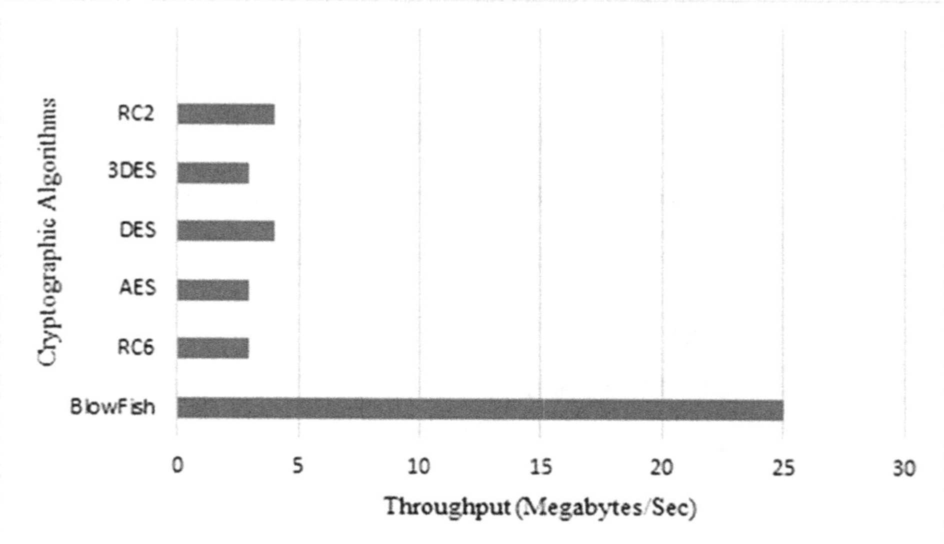

resource-constrained devices which have lower computational power, smaller memory size, lower power consumption, and smaller physical size to communicate with each other. Moreover, the implementation of conventional cryptographic algorithms involves heavy computations and have more substantial memory requirements, and as such is unfit for securing the constrained IoT devices. As discussed above, the commonly used cryptographic algorithms consume a considerable amount of computing resources like CPU time, memory, and battery power, so the primary challenge in IoT is to develop resource-efficient cryptographic algorithms which are lightweight in nature and are energy efficient, storage efficient and are fast and responsive than conventional encryption/decryption algorithms, and are powered by optimized crypto engines.

LIGHTWEIGHT CRYPTOGRAPHY ALGORITHMS

The cryptographic algorithms to be used in extremely low resource devices are different from that of the commonly used ones. For these resource-constrained IoT devices, lightweight cryptographic algorithms are developed having extremely low requirements. Even though no strict criteria are defined for lightweight cryptographic algorithms, the features usually include any one or more of the following:

- Minimum size required for hardware implementation
- The low computational power of microprocessors or microcontrollers
- Low implementation cost
- Good security

There is a trade-off between security, cost, and performance, i.e., to achieve higher security, the larger key size is required, but this may lead to higher power consumption, which is undesired in power-hungry IoT devices.

DESL and DESXL

DESL (Paar et al., 2007) is a lightweight version of classical DES algorithm, and DESXL is a lightweight version of classical DESX algorithm, both use a single S-box (substitution block) instead of 8 S-boxes. As there is only a single S-box, memory is saved. Also, the S-box design criteria make them resistant to most of the common cryptanalytic attacks.

CURUPIRA

Curupira algorithm is based on the Wide Trail strategy by Joan Daemen (Daeman et al.,1995). The following features make this algorithm a lightweight algorithm:

- The data block size is 96-bits and is represented as a 3x4-byte array. The key lengths can be 96-, 144- or 192- bits.
- The number of rounds is determined based on the key length.
- The 8x8-bit S-box is implemented as two 4x4-bit S-boxes. This reduces the space required to store the S-boxes.

KATAN and KTANTAN

KATAN & KTANTAN (Kushwaha et al.,2014) are from a family of hardware-oriented six block ciphers which are divided into three KATAN ciphers: KATAN32, KATAN48, and KATAN64 and three KTANTAN ciphers: KTANTAN32, KTANTAN48,and KTANTAN64. The block size of the algorithm in bits is represented by the number in the algorithm's name. They both use 80-bit key size. The difference is that compactness of KTANTAN is more in hardware where the target device is burnt with the key and cannot be changed. So, KTANTAN ciphers are small block ciphers when compared to KATAN and are used in devices which are initialized with one key. Due to the following features, the resource requirements for KATAN & KTANTAN algorithms are low:

- The size of the internal state is equivalent to the block size of the algorithm. They use the shift registers and feedback functions which are easy to implement in hardware and provides required non-linearity.
- Small blocks of data are processed which may vary from 32- to 64-bits.
- KTANTAN's key schedule is simple.

AES

AES is a preferred choice for many block ciphers (Lu et al.,2002). It can be used to produce a higher level of security and throughput with less area. AES was developed by two scientists Joan and V. Rijmen in 2000. AES is a symmetric block cipher with block size equal to128-bits and key length equal to128-bits, 192-bits, or 256-bits, and accordingly, it is popularly referred to as AES-128, AES-192, or AES-256 respectively. The number of rounds executed in AES-128, AES-192, and AES-256 are respectively 10, 12 and 14. AES involves the following four steps of operation:

- **Sub Byte:** The input data is substituted by bytes, and 8-bit substitution box is used to update each byte in the array. This 8-bit substitution box is called as Rijndael S-box. The multiplicative inverse over GF (2^8) is used to derive S-box, because of its good non-linearity properties.
- **Shift Rows:** Used to rotate the rows of the input matrix circularly upwards.
- **Mix Column:** In this operation, the input matrix is multiplied to data matrix using Modulo Matrix Multiplication.
- **Add Round Key:** The current state block data and the round key are combined using the bitwise XOR transformation.

PRESENT

PRESENT is one of the leanest lightweight algorithms and has obtained the ISO/IEC standard for lightweight cryptography. It is based on the transformation layers of Serpent (Anderson et al.,2016) and DES (FIPS Publications 46-3,1999) that have been analyzed in-depth, especially for security and hardware efficiency. Following features are responsible for it being a leanest algorithm:

- It uses very less gate count and less memory.
- 31 rounds are performed on the 64-bit data block
- It allows using 80- or 128-bit keys.
- The most compact hardware implementation of PRESENT needs 1570 (GE) and is, therefore, competitive with leading compact stream ciphers, which need 1300-2600 GE.

PRESENT was designed for attaining hardware performance but can also be implemented in software. The main application of the PRESENT algorithm is for encrypting small or reasonable amount of data.

Hummingbird

Hummingbird (Collard et al., 2016) is a hybrid algorithm, comprising of both block and stream ciphers. It has the following features:

- It encrypts 16-bit blocks of data.
- It uses a 256-bit key.
- It has 80-bit internal state.
- It uses simple logic and arithmetic operations.

Because it uses a small block size, it has a minimum response time and power consumption requirements and is suitable for RFID tags or wireless sensors without any modification of the current standard. Even though Hummingbird performs operations on small 16-bit block size, but when compared to PRESENT, it has higher latency and requires more execution time. So, it has less encryption speed and is less efficient for authentication mechanisms. Later, Hummingbird-2 was designed, which can optionally produce an authentication tag for each message. In comparison to its predecessor,

- It operates on 16-bit blocks.
- The key size is 128-bit.
- Its internal state, with size=128-bit, is initialized using a 64-bit initialization vector.

To authenticate any associated data that travels with ciphertext, Hummingbird-2 uses a method called Authenticated Encryption with Associated Data. Processing of associated data happens only after the processing of entire encrypted payload. For messages with size less than 16-bits, it is better to communicate without message expansion. The advantage of Hummingbird-2 is its low power consumption and higher processing speed.

TEA

The Tiny Encryption Algorithm (TEA) (Engels et al.,2017) was developed with the objective to be used on low performing small computers. This block cipher is based on high performance but mathematically simple encryption algorithm, which is a variant of Feistel Cipher.

- TEA encrypts 64-bit blocks which are divided into two 32-bit blocks.
- It uses a 128-bit length key.
- TEA is a round based encryption method. The number of the used rounds are variable, but 32 Tea cycles are recommended.
- It is developed based on the assumption that security can be enhanced by increasing the number of iterations.

Even though TEA has 32 rounds, it is faster than DES with 16 rounds, and all modes of DES apply to it. It can be implemented in all programming languages. The XTEA (eXtended TEA) algorithm is a further development of TEA. It works with:

- 64-bit blocks.
- 128-bit key length.
- 64 encryption rounds.

When compared to TEA, XTEA has a more complex key management and involves a change of the Shift, XOR and addition operations. Along with XTEA, Block TEA was also released, which differs only on the part that it does not require a fixed block size but can work with blocks of any size. Block TEA does not need an operation mode to ensure confidentiality and authenticity and can be applied directly to the entire message.

TWINE

TWINE, proposed by Tomoyasu (Suzaki et al.,2017), is based on a GFS (Generalized Feistel Structure), which enables small implementations on hardware and software. The implementation is done on hardware with 1.5K Gates and low-end micro-controllers. This drawback is recovered employing TWINE as an improved variant of Generalized Feistel Structure which results in making it an ultra-lightweight while keeping sufficient speed. TWINE is generalized Feistel Type-2 with following features:

- Block size is 64-bits.
- 36 rounds.
- TWINE has two types - TWINE-80 and TWINE-128 where the key size is 80-bits and 128- bits respectively.

Other Algorithms

Skipjack (NIST,1998) is a lightweight block encryption technique based on an unbalanced Feistel network designed by U.S. NSA for embedded applications. For the operation, we use 64-bit block length with the 80-bit key.

NOEKEON is another block cipher, designed for hardware by Daemen et al.(Daemen et al.,2000). HIGHT was designed by Hong et al.(Hong et al., 2006) which is a generalized Feistel-like cipher as it possesses 64-bit block length and 128-bit key length to be suitable for low-cost, low-power, and ultralight implementation and it undergoes 32-round iterative structure.

Lightweight block cipher KeeLoq was proposed by Bogdanov in 2007, with 32-bit block size and 64-bit key size. Despite its small key size, it is widely used in remote keyless entry systems and various other wireless authentication applications.

It has been noticed that block ciphers such as DESL, HIGHT, and PRESENT are more suitable for resource-constrained environments when compared to stream ciphers. KATAN, LED, SIMON and PRESENT ciphers are optimized for performance on hardware devices and SPECK, SEA, and TEA ciphers for performance in software.

COMPARISON OF LIGHTWEIGHT CRYPTOGRAPHIC ALGORITHMS

The lightweight cryptographic algorithms are designed taking AES as standard because it is standardized by NIST. It is a symmetric block cipher, works on the block length of 128-bits with variable key sizes of 128-, 192- and 256-bits. It is based on a substitution-permutation network (SPN) and works on 4x4 matrixes. Each byte undergoes four operations viz., sub-bytes, shift rows, Mixed Columns and Add Round Key. Various other algorithms are proposed in order to increase the security in constrained devices. Table 2 depicts the pros and cons of lightweight algorithms and the layers where these algorithms can be implemented.

For security purposes, we try to increase the code length to reduce the number of rounds. The increase in code length will bring in complexity resulting in better security, but on the other hand, it will increase the utilization of computational power. In the resource-constrained environment, we cannot afford energy inefficient algorithms. Many attempts have been made to increase the efficiency of the network. Figures 6 and 7 show the code length and number of rounds of various lightweight algorithms used in resource-constrained atmosphere. There is a trade-off between code length and a number of rounds. Larger the code length, lesser the number of rounds needed. AES provides a better solution to this problem.

The key size is defined merely by the number of bits in the key. The key size directly relates to the strength of the key or algorithm. Larger the key size, more secure is the algorithm. For AES, the internal key schedule and the number of rounds are different for each key size. The related key attacks on AES-256 but not on AES-128 or AES-192 are due to the difference in key schedule. 10, 12 or 14 are the number of rounds for 128-, 192-, and 256-bit key sizes respectively. The number of bits or bytes that can be transformed by the block cipher is called the block size. The block size for AES is 128-bits or 16-bytes. So a plaintext from the set of 21282128 possible plaintexts is permuted to a single ciphertext from the set of 21282128 possible ciphertexts. It is also called PRP (pseudo-random permutation) as there is no relation between the plaintext and the ciphertext. Of course, it is only *pseudo*-random as the same plaintext will always permute to the same ciphertext, as long as the key does not change. Figure 8 shows the key size and block size of various lightweight cryptographic algorithms.

Table 2. Comparison table of various cryptographic algorithms

Algorithm	Implementation Layer/s	Pros	Cons
AES	Data link layer Presentation layer Application layer Adaption layer Network layer	A robust security protocol, implemented in hardware as well as software. It uses higher length key sizes such as 128-, 192- and 256-bits for encryption. For 128-bit, about 2128 attempts are needed to break the key. Number of the rounds are less.	It uses a straightforward algebraic structure. Every block is always encrypted in the same way. AES in counter mode is complex to implement in software, taking both performance and security into consideration.
HIGHT	Presentation layer Adaption layer	Consumes less energy. limited number of line of code A limited number of lines of code.	Vulnerable to Saturation attacks.
TEA	Presentation layer	Requires less RAM. Less vulnerable to attacks on the integrity.	No. of rounds are 32. Consumes more power. Prone to key related attacks.
RC5	Transport layer	Small key size.	Lesser no. of combinations. Susceptible to differential attacks.
SIT (Secure IoT)	Session layer	Least complexity. Lesser no. of rounds.	Integrity under threat. Prone to square attacks.
SKIPJACK	Session layer Presentation layer	Small key size. Lesser complexity.	Requires large RAM. Code size is large. Prone to key related attacks.
KLEIN	Transport layer	A small key size A small amount of RAM required	Large no rounds = 254. Energy inefficient.
KATAN	Transport layer	A small key size. A small amount of RAM required.	Large no rounds = 254. Energy inefficient.
ECC	Transport layer Network layer Adaption layer	A small key size. Fast processing speed. Requires less memory.	Timing attack vulnerabilities. Large code length.

CONCLUSION AND FUTURE WORK

This work provides an overview of lightweight cryptographic algorithms and the power awakening scheme. Since low-resource devices perform computations in an IoT environment, these devices are resource constrained with regards to memory, battery life, power consumption, and computations. IoT devices also face the challenges of security and privacy as well as the issue of how to maintain trust between users. Furthermore, the summary of different kinds of lightweight cryptographic

Figure 6. Code length of various cryptographic algorithms

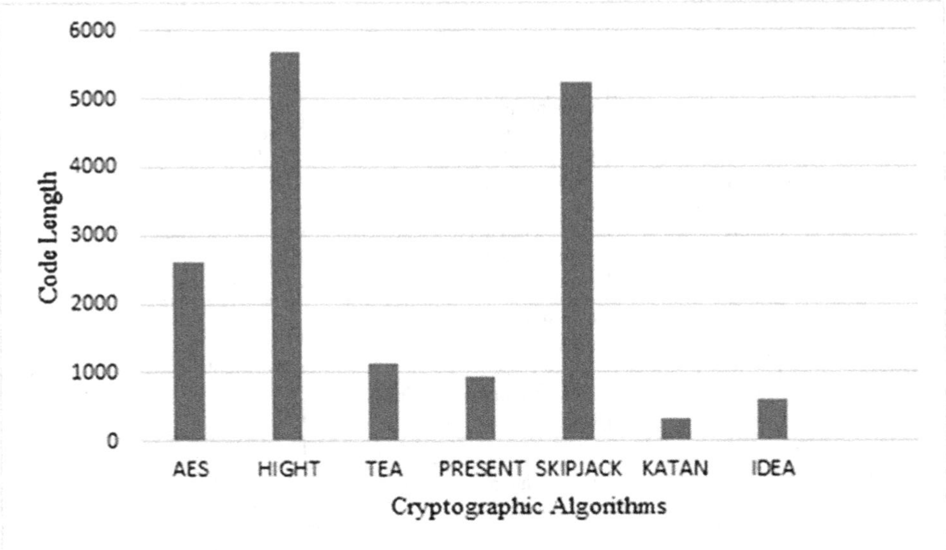

Figure 7. Number of rounds required in various cryptographic algorithms

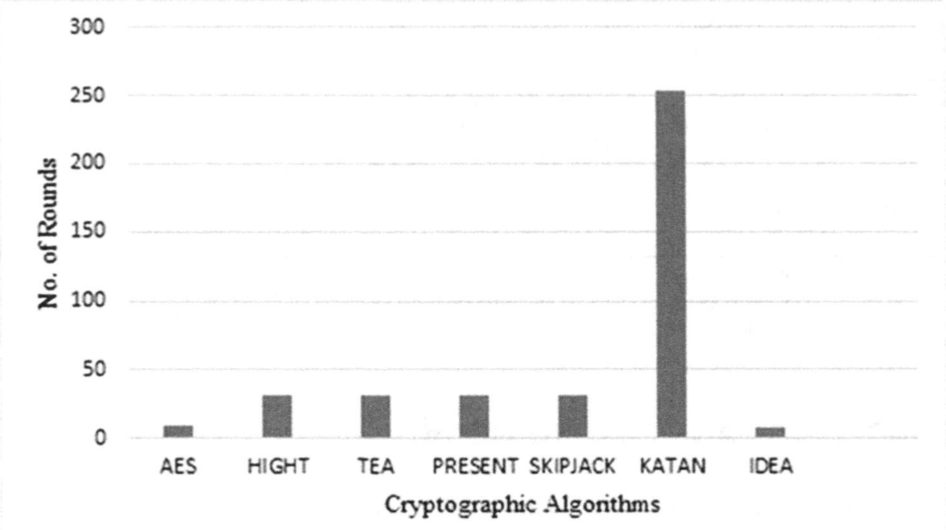

Figure 8. Key size and block size of various cryptographic algorithms

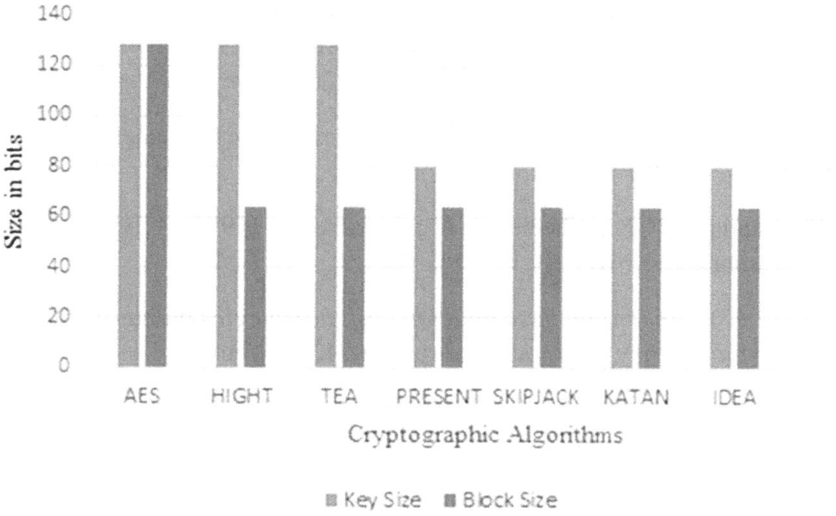

algorithms which are easy to implement in software as well as hardware has been provided. Also, a brief idea of the importance of developing more secure and lightweight encryption algorithms that must have faster processing, smaller key size, and require less computation power has been discussed. In the present work, open issues regarding block size, key size, cipher structure, implementation, pros and cons, new attacks, and security metrics for the algorithms used are discussed and compared with each other.

REFERENCES

ABI Research. (2013). *More Than 30 Billion Devices Will Wirelessly Connect to the Internet of Everything in 2020.* ABI Research Press Release. Retrieved from https:// www.abiresearch. com/press/more-than-30-billion-devices-willwirelessly-conne

Anderson, R. J., Biham, E., & Knudsen, L. R. (2000). *Serpent: A Proposal for the Advanced Encryption Standard.* Retrieved from https://www.cl.cam.ac.uk/~rja14/ Papers/serpent.pdf

Ashton, K. (2009). That "Internet of Things" Thing. *RFID Journal.* Retrieved from: http://www.rfidjournal.com/articles/view?4986

Bari, A. (2005). Relay Nodes in Wireless Sensor Networks: A Survey. University of Windsor.

Cheng, P., Chuah, C. & Liu, X. (2004). Energy-aware Node Placement in Wireless Sensor Networks. *IEEE Communications Society, Globecom 2004*.

Cheng, X., Du, D. Z., Wang. L. & Xu, B. (2001). Relay Sensor Placement in Wireless Sensor Networks. *IEEE Transactions on Computers*.

Collard, B., Standaert, F.-X., Wheeler, D. J., & Needham, J. (1995). *A Tiny Encryption Algorithm*. Cambridge University.

Daemen, J. (1995). *Cipher and hash function design strategies based on linear and differential cryptanalysis* (Doctoral Dissertation). K. U. Leuven.

Daemen, J., Peeters, M., Assche, G. V. & Rijmen, V. (2000). The Noekeon block cipher. *The NESSIE Proposal*.

Dasgupta, K., Kukreja, M., & Kalpakis, K. (2003). Topology-Aware Placement and Role Assignment for Energy-Efficient Information Gathering in Sensor Networks. *Proceedings of the Eighth IEEE International Symposium on Computers and Communication (ISCC'03)*. 10.1109/ISCC.2003.1214143

Dhillon, S. S., & Chakrabarty, K. (2003). Sensor Placement for Effective Coverage and Surveillance in Distributed Sensor Networks. IEEE.

Engels, D., Fan, X., Gong, G., Hu, H., & Smith, E. M. (2010). Hummingbird: Ultra-Lightweight Cryptography for Resource-Constrained Devices. In FC 2010 Workshops, LNCS 6054, (pp. 3–18). IFCA/Springer-Verlag Berlin Heidelberg.

Ergen, S. C. & Varaiya, P. (2006). Optimal Placement of Relay Nodes for Energy Efficiency in Sensor Networks. *IEEE ICC*.

Fang, S., Xu, L. I., Zhu, Y., Ahati, J., Pei, H., Yan, J., & Liu, Z. (2014). An integrated system for regional environmental monitoring and management based on Internet of things. *IEEE Transactions on Industrial Informatics*, *10*(2), 1596–1605. doi:10.1109/TII.2014.2302638

Farooq, H. & Jung, L. T. (2013). Energy, Traffic Load, and Link Quality Aware Ad Hoc Routing Protocol for Wireless Sensor Network, Based Smart Metering Infrastructure. *International Journal of Distributed Sensor Networks*.

FIPS. (1999). *FIPS Publication 46-3. Data Encryption Standard (DES)*. U. S. Department of Commerce / National Institute of Standards and Technology. *Reaffirmed, 1999*.

Gupta, G., & Younis, M. (2003). Performance Evaluation of Load Balanced Clustering of Wireless Sensor Networks. IEEE.

Hong, D., Sung, J., Hong, S., Lim, J., Lee, S., Koo, B., ... Chee, S. (2006). HIGHT: A new block cipher suitable for low-resource device. In L. Goubin & M. Matsui (Eds.), *Cryptographic Hardware and Embedded Systems – CHES 2006, Vol. LNCS 4249* (pp. 46–59). Springer. doi:10.1007/11894063_4

ITU. (2015, November). *The Internet of Things.* ITU Internet Reports.

Jia, J., Zhang, G., Wu, X., Chen, J., Wang, X., & Yan, X. (2013). On the Problem of Energy Balanced Relay Sensor Placement in Wireless Sensor Networks. *International Journal of Distributed Sensor Networks.*

Kulau, U., Busching, F., & Wolf, L. (2015). Undervolting in WSNs—Theory and practice. *IEEE Internet Things J.*, *2*(3), 190–198. doi:10.1109/JIOT.2014.2384207

Kushwaha, P., Singh, M., & Kumar, P. (2014, June). A Survey on Lightweight Block Ciphers. *International Journal of Computers and Applications.*

Leander, G., Paar, C., Poschmann, A., & Schramm, K. (2007). New lightweight des variants. In *Fast Software Encryption* (pp. 196–210). Springer. doi:10.1007/978-3-540-74619-5_13

Lin, K., Rodrigues, J., Ge, H., Xiong, N., & Liang, X. (2011). Energy efficiency QoS assurance routing in wireless multimedia sensor networks. *IEEE Systems Journal*, *5*(4), 495–505. doi:10.1109/JSYST.2011.2165599

Lloyd, E. L., & Xue, G. (2007). Relay Node Placement in Wireless Sensor Networks. *IEEE Transactions on Computers*, *56*(1), 134–138. doi:10.1109/TC.2007.250629

Lu, C. C., & Tseng, S. Y. (2002). Integrated design of AES (Advanced Encryption Standard) encrypter and decrypter. *Application-Specific Systems, Architectures and Processors, 2002. Proceedings. The IEEE International Conference*, 277-285.

Myoung, G. L., Park, J., Kong, N., Crespi, N., & Chong, Y. (2012). *The Internet of Things - Concept and Problem Statement.* Internet Research Task Force.

NIST. (1998). *Skipjack and kea algorithm specifications (version 2.0).* National Institute of Standards and Technology. Retrieved from http://csrc.nist.gov/groups/ST/toolkit/documents/ skipjack/s kipjack.pdf

NS. (n.d.). *Network Simulator-2.* Retrieved from http://www.isi.edu/nsnamlnsl

Pan, J., Hou, T., Cai, L., Shi, Y. & Shen, S. X. (2003). Topology Control for Wireless Sensor Networks. *MobiCom'03.*

Patel, M., Chandrasekaran, R., & Venkatesan, S. (2005). Energy Efficient Sensor, Relay and Base Station Placements for Coverage, Connectivity and Routing. IEEE.

Paula, M., Durand, F. R., & Abrao, T. (2016). WDM/OCDM energy-efficient networks based on heuristic ant colony optimization. *IEEE Systems Journal.*

Ruangchaijatupon, N., & Krishnamurthy, P. (2001). Encryption and Power Consumption in Wireless LANs-N. *Third IEEE workshop on wireless LANS 2001*, 148-152.

Sai, V., & Mickle, M. H. (2014). Exploring energy efficient architectures in passive wireless nodes for IoT applications. IEEE Circuits Syst. Mag., 14(2), 48–54.

Silberschatz, A., Galvin, P. B., & Gagne, G. (2009). *Operating System Concepts* (8th ed.). New Delhi, India: Wiley.

Sun, G., Anand, V., Liao, D., Lu, C., Zhang, X., & Bao, N. (2015, June). Power-Efficient Provisioning for Online Virtual Network Requests in Cloud-Based Data Centers. *IEEE Systems Journal*, *9*(2), 427–441. doi:10.1109/JSYST.2013.2289584

Suzaki, T., Minematsu, K., Morioka, S., & Kobayashi, E. (2012). TWINE: A Lightweight, Versatile Block Cipher. *Pre-proceeding of SAC 2012.*

Tang, J., Hao, B., & Sen, A. (2005). Relay node placement in large scale wireless sensor networks. In Computer Communications. Elsevier.

Tang, J., Hao, B., & Sen, A. (2005). Relay node placement in large scale wireless sensor networks. *Computer Communications.*

Tao, F., Zuo, Y., Xu, L. D., & Zhang, L. (2014). IoT-based intelligent perception and access of manufacturing resource toward cloud manufacturing. *IEEE Transactions on Industrial Informatics*, *10*(2), 1547–1557. doi:10.1109/TII.2014.2306397

Vallimayil, A., Karthick, R. K. M., Sarmam V. R. D., & Chandrasekaran, R. M. (2011). *Role of Relay Node in Wireless Sensor Network: A Survey.* IEEE.

Yu, C., Yao, D., Yang, L. T., & Jin, H. (2017). Energy Conservation in Progressive Decentralized Single-Hop Wireless Sensor Networks for Pervasive Computing Environment. *IEEE Systems Journal*, *11*(2), 823–834. doi:10.1109/JSYST.2014.2339311

Zhang, D., Yang, L. T., Chen, M., Zhao, S., Guo, M., & Zhang, Y. (2014). Real-time locating systems using active RFID for Internet of things. *IEEE Systems Journal.* doi:10.1109/JSYST.2014.2346625

Zheng, Y., Matsumoto, T., & Imai, H. (1990). On the construction of block ciphers provably secure and not relying on any unproved hypotheses. Advances in Cryptology CRYPTO 89 Proceedings, 461–480.

Zoyama, A. Y. (Ed.). (2008). Algorithms and Protocols for Wireless Sensor Networks. Wiley-IEEE Press.

Section 3
Security Protocols

This section discusses some schemes and protocols for securing Internet of Things. These include physically unclonable functions that promise cryptographic security enablers for resource-constrained IoT devices and hardware primitive-based security protocols. It also discusses gateway discovery protocol using ECC for MANET, scheme for node localization, security framework based on contextual information, and secure computation of private set intersection cardinality with linear complexity.

Chapter 4
Addressing Security Issues of the Internet of Things Using Physically Unclonable Functions

Ishfaq Sultan
University of Kashmir, India

Mohammad Tariq Banday
University of Kashmir, India

ABSTRACT

The spatial ubiquity and the huge number of employed nodes monitoring the surroundings, individuals, and devices makes security a key challenge in IoT. Serious security apprehensions are evolving in terms of data authenticity, integrity, and confidentiality. Consequently, IoT requires security to be assured down to the hardware level, as the authenticity and the integrity need to be guaranteed in terms of the hardware implementation of each IoT node. Physically unclonable functions recreate the keys only while the chip is being powered on, replacing the conventional key storage which requires storing information. Compared to extrinsic key storage, they are able to generate intrinsic keys and are far less susceptible against physical attacks. Physically unclonable functions have drawn considerable attention due to their ability to economically introduce hardware-level security into individual silicon dice. This chapter introduces the notion of physically unclonable functions, their scenarios for hardware security in IoT devices, and their interaction with traditional cryptography.

DOI: 10.4018/978-1-5225-5742-5.ch004

INTRODUCTION

The Internet of Things (IoT) exemplifies the interconnection of a vast number of 'Things' (uniquely identifiable physical objects) through the Internet, with sensing, communication and actuation capabilities (Dragomir et al., 2016). Internet of Things (IoT) domain is an appealing target of numerous cyber-attacks because IoT devices generate, process, and exchange massive sums of privacy-sensitive information, and security-critical data (Dorri et al., 2017). There are many constraints and restrictions in IoT devices in terms of power and computational resources, and the heterogeneous and ubiquitous nature of IoT initiate additional apprehensions concerning security establishment (Sain et al., 2017). IoT security needs to be part of the design at physical, network, and application levels. The IoT device itself needs to be designed using security principles. This covers the sensors that capture data, the data storage mechanism, and the micro-controller or actuator capable of controlling the device behavior, processing data and establishing a network connection (Wurm et al., 2016). Traditional security structures, such as public key cryptography, are not viable in IoT devices due to strict cost and power requirements. Physical and network attacks are common in the IoT domain due to backdoors created by a large number of IoT devices and the ensuing scale of IoT network. Software attacks, device cloning, eavesdropping, and data-stealing are also possible in IoT devices due to their always-connected feature (Mahalle & Railkar, 2015). The limited amount of energy accessibility of IoT devices can make them susceptible to resource enervation and denial of service attacks. Firmware and Software updates are inevitable due to the long life of IoT devices and hence, requires robust authentication procedures to evaluate the reliability and authenticity of any updates and patches, considering the tight power budget of IoT devices.

IoT needs security at the hardware level to ensure authenticity and integrity of hardware implementation of each node. Physically unclonable functions (PUFs) have been developed in the recent past as a potentially lightweight and secure solution for assuring security down to the hardware level. PUFs sometimes denoted as silicon biometrics (unique for each chip) are functions that map an *input digital challenge* with an *output digital response* repeatedly in an unpredictable manner, taking benefit from random process variations of the chip. In PUFs the key is naturally generated and embedded into the chip at the time of manufacturing, eliminating the need to store the key. PUFs are primarily utilized for device identification and authentication (Alvarez et al., 2015), lightweight encryption and secure key storage (Mathew et al., 2014), hardware entangled cryptography (Sadeghi & Naccache, 2010) and detection of malicious hardware (Maes, 2013). PUFs are very favorable primitives because of their randomness and unclonable feature, and hence, are extremely difficult to compute without the possession of PUF hardware. Although PUFs are established on measurements of the vast diversity of physical parameters, the ones obtained from measurements of integrated circuits are predominantly convenient because the output is easily integrated into computational operations. In traditional encryption schemes, data is usually encrypted using an externally stored key, or a key that is stored in an on-chip non-volatile memory for the transmission security. Storing the key in an on-chip non-volatile memory or off chip enables the retrieval of the key by intruders. Since non-volatile memory is easy to read and prone to attacks, PUFs can be used to replace the traditional key storage offering better robustness against intrusive attacks. This is possible because PUFs do not store data rather they restore the keys only when the chip is being powered on.

In literature, PUFs have been proposed for use in remote attestation (Schulz et al., 2011), protecting intellectual property (Alkabani et al., 2007), random number generators (Maiti et al., 2009) and authentication (Hamlet et al., 2014). The effectiveness of PUFs for the applications mentioned above is governed by the credibility of the randomness of the PUF output. Statistical tests can be employed to access random number generators. Although not all the tests are utilized to the comparatively short binary strings generated by PUFs, the applicable tests can be applied to boost conviction in the randomness of PUF responses. Determining the number of unique output variants per specific PUF design is a relevant query. Although it may not be achievable to determine the number of unique output variants of a PUF that is physically possible, we can approximate the quantity. We can compare the response from the PUFs in two ICs by observing the fractional Hamming distance between their responses if a collection of distinct ICs is given containing technically identical PUF circuits. PUFs can also be manipulated to authenticate ICs for anti-counterfeiting security. Considering the output of IC PUF as a device-specific arbitrary binary string with a low occurrence of a collision, we can assume that PUF is suitable as an identifier. This kind of identifier is inherent to the structure of device, rather than shown on the surface of device as a serial number. It is easy to spoof serial numbers as they are extrinsic attributes created by methods like screen printing. On the other hand, PUF outputs are hard to spoof or clone because they are an indirect measurement of hysterical variability of the fabrication procedures used for manufacturing ICs. This is the primary reason that PUFs are used beyond authentication and identification purposes.

PUF ATTRIBUTES AND METRICS

The chip-specific keys produced by PUFs are unpredictable, repeatable, and are not directly accessible and quantifiable externally. Weak PUFs and strong PUFs are two main types of PUFs. Weak PUFs permit only a limited number of challenge-response pairs, which makes them equivalent to random key generators that are usually used for encryption and decryption. Strong PUFs provide a huge number of challenge-response pairs. PUFs having a massive number of challenge-response pairs consume more area, and hence, are very costly and typically infeasible for the long lifespan necessary for IoT applications. Table 1 illustrates an example of the cost for a PUF having the 256-bit key in 65nm, whose cost perpetually surpasses the overall cost of the node (Alwarez et al. 2015; Alwarez et al. 2016). Numerous metrics have been initiated to enumerate the quality of PUFs in consideration with the fundamental PUF properties, such as repeatability, uniqueness, stability, and randomness. PUF output should not usually change under unpredictable environmental conditions such as pressure, voltage, or temperature. However, the real PUFs are not capable enough to provide entirely stable outputs due to incompetency in rejection of noise and environmental fluctuations. Stability is evaluated by calculating all the unstable bits across repeated PUF estimations and environmental conditions, within specified temperature and voltage of operation.

Repeatability and uniqueness are calculated from the Hamming distance through numerous measurements of PUF Keys. Those measurements are then compared to a reference key (golden key) that is chosen as the first measurement under nominal conditions. Repeatability refers to the average intra-PUF Hamming distance measured under different environmental conditions between the golden key and numerous key assessments, with the challenge and the chip being same. On the other hand, uniqueness can be considered as the average inter-PUF Hamming distance between key assessments and golden key from various chips in the same PUF input. The ideal inter-PUF Hamming distance of a 256-bit key is 128, that means the inter-PUF Hamming distance should be ideally equal to the half of the length of PUF key. Fractional Hamming distance, in which the Hamming distance is calculated as a percentage of key length, or the number of bits in a PUF key, can be used alternatively to compute uniqueness and reproducibility (Maes, 2012). The ideal value of inter-PUF Fractional Hamming distance can be 50%. Identifiability, which is roughly taken as the ratio between the inter-PUF and the intra-PUF Hamming distance, computes the dissimilarity of a PUF occurrence to other occurrences (Yang et al., 2015).

The randomness in PUF responses is one more important property of PUFs, which is used to ensure the unpredictability of the PUF responses. Randomness is typically calculated by the statistical representation in terms of 0/1 bits (i.e., the probability of having 1 in a PUF output bit) (Yu et al., 2012), the entropy, and more comprehensively by the NIST randomness tests (Rukhin et al., 2010). The autocorrelation function is consistently used to identify repeating or interrelated patterns among varying responses, and to compute the randomness of PUF responses among different positions of PUF bit-cell within the same die. The correlation among

PUF output bits is normally due to arrangement dependent variations (Li & Seok, 2015]. The NIST statistical test suite is a set of tests used to calculate the randomness of a bit stream. The test suite comprises of 15 tests, each of them employing one property to test the randomness. The frequency test, being the simplest of the 15 tests calculates the 0/1 ratio of the entire bitstream. Specific parameters need to be necessarily set for each of the tests, like the length of bitstream n, block size M, etc. Table 2 shows the list of the NIST statistical test suite with a description of each test and stream length.

Energy consumption of PUFs is another significant metric because the IoT devices are energy and power constrained, operating either on a battery or harvested energy. Energy per bit, acquired by dividing the average energy per access by the number of bits within the key is the most frequently approved metric to extract the energy from the PUF organization and size. Due to the strict cost and area requirements in IoT devices, effective area per bit is another important metric of PUFs and is acquired by considering the actual quantity of accessible PUF bits attained after eliminating the unstable bits and incorporating the area cost of the circuitry. Accelerated aging tests are used to assess the chip lifetime and robustness to aging (Selimis et al., 2011).

PUF CIRCUIT DESIGNS

The work on the use of physical variations for authentication has been done from 1980s. The initial systems recommended that the stochastic physical arrangement of tiny optical fibers within a device (e.g., currency), could be used to substantiate that device. The first electronic circuit designs meant to exploit the manufacturing variations in electronics emerged nearly twenty years later and hence instigating an immense interest in PUFs. The mostly prevailing silicon PUFs can be categorized as either memory-based or delay-based PUFs. As far as delay based PUFs are concerned, bits are produced by equating the delay of two technically identical paths, and a sign of the random delay difference between them determines the output bit.

Table 1. Example of PUF silicon cost (SRAM PUF)

Data Transmitted (Time)	PUF Area (mm^2)	PUF Capacity (MB)	Silicon Cost (US$)
1 hour	24	5	1.2
10 minutes	147	32	7.4
1 minute	1478	320	7.4

Table 2. NIST statistical test suite

NIST Test	Description	Stream Length (n)
Frequency Test	The ratio of the sum of 0's and 1's	10^2
DFT	Detect periodic features	10^3
Runs Test	Relative oscillation of bits	10^2
Longest Run of Ones	Measurement of longest consecutive 1's within a block	128
Binary Matrix Run	Disjoint sub-matrix rank	38
Universal Statistical Test	Number of bits among matching patterns	387840
Overlapping Template	Detect existence of patterns (including overlaps)	10^6
Non-overlapping Template	Detect existence of patterns	10^6
Serial Test	Identify frequency of overlapping patterns	-
Approximate Entropy	Identify frequency of overlapping patterns	-
Linear Complexity Test	The distance of equivalent LFSR	10^6
Random Excursions Test	Random walk cycle	10^6
Random Excursions Variant Test	Variations from a random walk	10^6
Cumulative Sums	Random walk	10^2

Arbiter PUFs and ring oscillator PUFs are the two unique electronic PUF designs, exploiting unique variations in the propagation delays through logic gates and interconnects. The arbiter PUF includes two symmetrically laid out paths as illustrated in Figure 1. A rising edge is given as input simultaneously to two paths, to measure the response bit from the arbiter. The latch at the output identifies which path disseminated the input signal faster, as the input signal races through the circuit. A bitstream of 0s and 1s can be generated by comparing several delay paths. For example, if A and B are two parallel circuits and if A is faster than B, then a bit 0 is assigned, and if B is faster than A, then a bit 1 is assigned. The arbiter PUF circuit in Figure 1 demonstrates a multiplexed circuit that optimizes area efficacy through an arbiter that is compiled with stages. For each stage Si, there is an input challenge bit c[Si] which determines whether the signal paths cross. Hence 2n different structures of the circuit are achievable, permitting 2n bits to be extracted from the circuit. The two paths of the arbiter PUF should be symmetric, which is possible in integrated circuits with manual placement and routing. It is challenging to implement the arbiter PUF in FPGAs (field programmable gate arrays) due to the lack of fine control over circuit layout.

Another broadly studied and one of the earliest PUF design is the ring oscillator PUF (ROPUF) shown in Figure 2. Ring oscillator PUF is although larger and more suitable for FPGAs than the arbiter PUF, but both of them exploit disparities in

Figure 1. Arbiter PUF

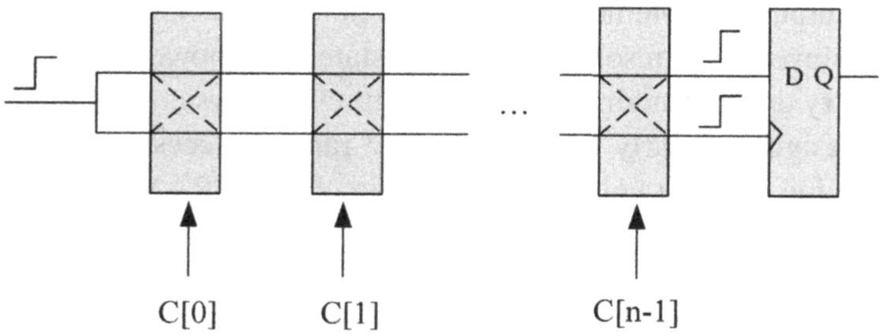

propagation delays to produce response bits. In ROPUF, delay variations are evident as differences between the oscillation frequencies of identically arranged ring oscillators. By comparing the frequencies from two oscillators, one PUF bit can be generated. A challenge can be given input to the multiplexer which helps it to select the two oscillators for comparison. As shown in Figure 2, the ROPUF challenge selects two of the available ring oscillators, and ultimately the corresponding response depends on whether the frequency of the first chosen oscillator is more than the second or not. Several methods have been initiated to upgrade the high native instability rate and insignificant statistical quality of the pair-wise comparison in ROPUFs, as these ring oscillators are very susceptible to environmental conditions. The above mentioned delay-based PUFs are intrinsically susceptible to PUF modeling attacks, which have the capability of capturing and cloning the content of the whole PUF with little effort. Although each stage of delay in delay-based PUFs is unpredictable, however, due to their fixed nature, the recognition of all stage delays from PUF output analysis requires only a linear complexity and hence, makes the PUF easy to clone (Rührmair et al., 2010).

Figure 2. Ring oscillator PUF

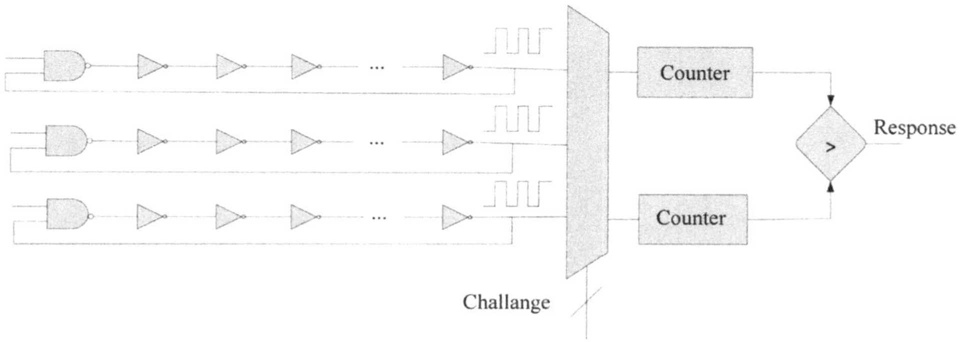

Memory-based PUFs use a bi-stable arrangement of two cross-coupled inverters to create the output bits. Memory-based PUFs hold on the normal tendency of the cross-coupled inverters to resolve to a favored state at the power-up, as governed by their asymmetry due to random variations. Figure 3, shows an important memory-based PUF design popularly known as static random-access memory (SRAM) PUF. By applying an input voltage V_{in} to the circuit, the SRAM PUF is forced into a stable state. With no input voltage applied (i.e., $V_a = V_b = 0$), the PUF cell is in an unstable state. The PUF cell transitions to a stable state when power is applied, with either V_a or V_b (but not both) at logical 0. The power-on value of the PUF cell can subsequently be applied as a PUF bit. In this way, any SRAM with symmetric cells can be used provided that the SRAM should be powered on in an uninitialized state. The butterfly PUF as shown in Figure 4 (Kumar et al., 2008), is analogous to the SRAM PUF and follows the same perception of leveraging on the unstable state of cross-coupled inverters. As illustrated in Figure 4, the butterfly PUF utilizes the available cross-coupled latches in place of inverters and is recommended for implementation in an FPGA. The procedure of the circuit starts by triggering the excitation signal, thereby driving the PUF to be in an unstable state. The signal is then released and subsequently after a few clock cycles, the out-signal sinks to its natural stable state established by the random variations in the related logic gates.

The experimental description and the existing literature on memory-based PUFs shows that these PUFs usually have poor stability (Schrijen & Van Der Leest, 2012), and are extremely susceptible to semi-invasive attacks such as electrical and optical probing (Nedospasov et al., 2014). The same susceptibility to semi-invasive attacks can be discovered in other PUFs as well, such as sense amps (Bhargava & Mai, 2014) relying on the same principle. For this kind of PUFs, practical stages of stability are

Figure 3. SRAM Based PUF

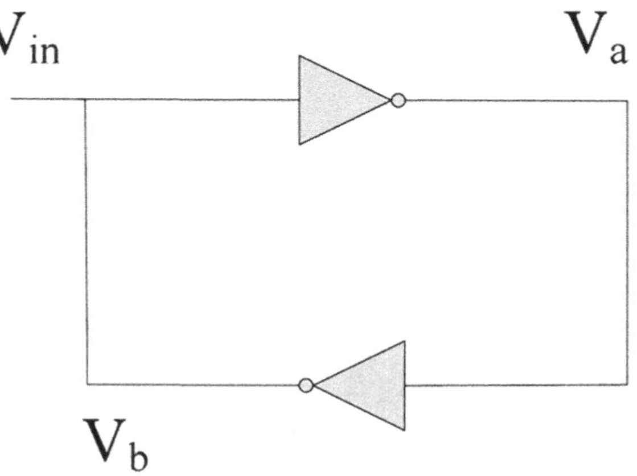

Figure 4. Butterfly PUF (Kumar et al., 2008)

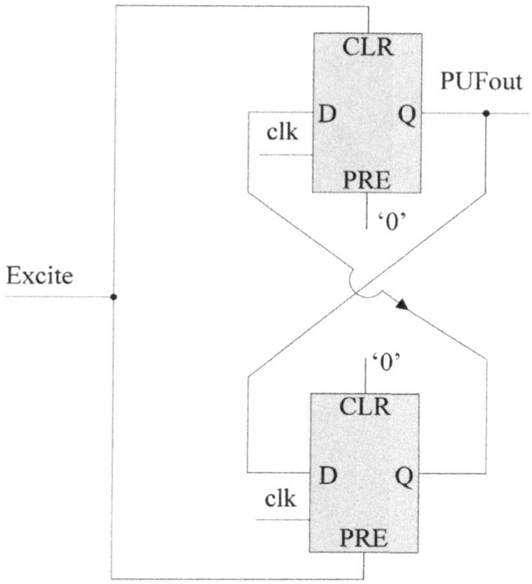

characteristically accomplished through extensive temporal redundancy at the cost of energy utilization (Helinski et al., 2009). A hybrid PUF amalgamating delay and metastability as bases of randomness was proposed in (Mathew et al., 2016). The metastability based PUF bit-cell is shown in Figure 5, where bi-stability is enforced through already charged transistors controlled by clk0 and clk1. The clock skew between the clk0 and clk1 gives rise to randomness in a delay in the PUF bit-cell. Li et al. 2015 have proposed a PTAT (proportional-to-absolute-temperature) as a PUF bit-cell in order to accomplish acceptable innate stability despite temperature and voltage variations. The output of the PTAT based PUF bit-cell is determined by the sign of difference between the inputs, which are independent of temperature and voltage. Another remarkable feature of the PTAT-based PUF is its good area proficiency apart from the high resiliency against voltage and temperature fluctuations. Table 3 shows a comparison of PUFs in terms of various applicable and studied metrics that have been recently proposed.

GENERATION OF PUF RESPONSES

Generally, PUFs can be classified into two categories: those having a large and preferably exponential area of input challenges, and those that have only a single challenge. Delay-based PUF designs have huge challenge spaces in comparison to

Figure 5. Metastability-based PUF (Mathew et al., 2016)

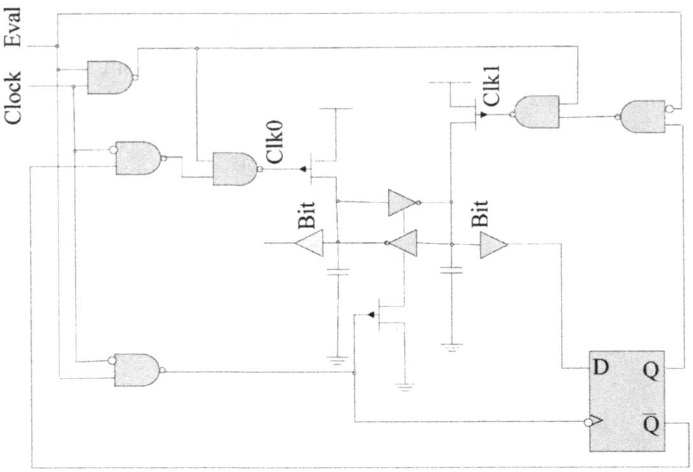

Table 3. A comparison of different PUFs

PUF	ROPUF (Alvarez et al., 2016)	Arbiter PUF (Lim et al., 2005)	PTAT-based PUF (Li et al. 2015)	SRAM PUF (Alvarez et al., 2016)	Mathew et al. (2015)	Yang et al. (2015)
Technology	65 nm	0.18 μm	65 nm	65 nm	22 nm	40 nm
V-T variation	0.4–0.5 V	1.8 V ±2%, 27–70° C	-	0.6–1 V	0.7–0.9 V	0.7–0.9 V
Energy (pJ/bit)	0.4748	0.17125	1.1	1.1	0.19	17.75
Stability (Unstable bits %)	18.16	9.8	7.1	16.66	30	12..5
Area (F^2/bit)	39,000	708,403	727	306	9628	2062
Uniqueness (mean inter-PUF FHD)	0.4738	0.3800	0.5001	0.3321	0.5100	0.5007
Randomness (bias = Probability of 1)	0.5023	-	0.4928	0.6141	0.4805	-
Repeatability (mean intra-PUF FHD)	0.0458	-	0.0057	0.0602	0.0268	0.0101
Identifiability (inter-PUF/ intra-PUF FHD)	10	88	-	6	19	50
Percent error with V-T variation	53.9	4.82	-	55.73	30	12.5
NIST test	-	-	PASS	-	PASS	PASS
Entropy	0.0884	-	0.9998	0.9903	0.9997	-

memory-based PUFs, which have a single and fixed challenge. Key generation is the typical application for a PUF with a small input space. In this scenario, PUF's response to a fixed input challenge is used as a cryptographic key or as a beginning for key generation algorithm. Applying PUF responses for a key generation often necessitates the use of a fuzzy extractor (which merges error correction with hash-based entropy amplification), as the PUF responses can contain noise and vary with environmental conditions. The resultant key can be used in any of the applications that requires cryptography. PUFs having larger input spaces are often anticipated for use in inter-active challenge-response protocols. The user should choose a subset of the PUF's input space and measure the responses to each of the challenge, during an enrolment phase. The challenges and the subsequent responses are then saved for later use. A challenge is chosen from the saved database and presented to the PUF for the verification of device containing PUF. The device is considered authentic if the saved response is close enough to the PUF's response. The challenges should be employed only once to avoid replay attacks.

The manufacturer can store the PUF-originated public key and serial number coupled with the device to alleviate the security concerns associated using the PUFs in a method that necessitates storing information in a database maintained by the device manufacturer. The purchaser can then query the manufacturer to ascertain the legitimacy of a purchased product, and then re-enroll the PUF to authenticate a new signature of the device. In this way, the relationship between the PUF and the manufacturer breaks, thereby inhibiting the manufacturer from tracing the device and also preventing the purchaser from using the PUF to verify the device as genuinely manufactured after the re-enrollment. In case of PUFs with a substantial input space, the user can simply ascertain a new set of challenge-response pairs which are unknown to the manufacturer. In both of the discussed scenarios, the PUF eradicates the compulsion to store the secrets on the chip in non-volatile memory. In case of PUFs with small input space, the secret never leaves the chip. The challenge-response pairs computed during enrolment must be locked as secrets, but they do not need to be saved on the chip. The secrets can be computed from the PUF when they are required, and then can be deleted from volatile memory in both of the scenarios. This can significantly decrease the key's exposure to attackers and is a substantial development in hardware security.

VULNERABILITY ANALYSIS IN PUFs: CHALLENGES AND OPPORTUNITIES

Practically only a few PUFs are available in market, as the existing PUFs suffer from many imperfections that have hampered their implementation in actual products.

For example, metastability- and delay-based PUFs are very much vulnerable to temperature and voltage deviations, noise and aging, and very stiff to authenticate at design time as far as output statistics and randomness are concerned. Therefore, this kind of PUF typically necessitates several silicon runs to consistently assess a given design. The glitch based PUFs, which are still not much mature are well recognized as unstable and complicated. Leakage-based PUFs are vulnerable to environmental deviations and require additional circuitry (for current and voltage biasing) which adds the budget in terms of energy, area, and design. Memory-based PUFs are not technology-convenient because these kind of PUFs are strongly technology dependent. DRAM error maps are known to have apparent co-relation between different responses, thereby significantly reducing the unpredictability of responses (Rosenblatt et al., 2013). Supply network-based and delay-based PUFs are extremely vulnerable to modeling attacks (Rührmair et al., 2013).

There have been some effective modeling and cloning attacks against PUFs, despite being called as unclonable functions (Helfmeier et al., 2013). Simulated arbiter PUFs and ROPUFs can be modeled by machine-learning techniques with precisions surpassing the experimental steadiness of those designs. These models presume that the attacker can access numerous challenge-response pairs, which can be attained via measurement of a device under the attacker's influence or by thieving the list produced during enrolment for instructing the models. The models can then help to envisage the responses to new challenges. However, it is essential to mention that an effective attack on a PUF compromises only the particular instantiation of the PUF. This process must be reiterated by the attacker to study the response of next instantiation of the PUF. However, those PUFs are not vulnerable to modeling attacks which do not utilize cooperative challenge-response mechanism. The fuzzy extractors characteristically used in such PUFs are prone to side-channel and template attacks (Karakoyunlu et al., 2010). SRAM PUFs can be physically cloned by applying near-infrared emissions to depict the response of one PUF cell, followed by focused ion beam (FIB) circuit edits which helps to produce the same PUF response in a second circuit. In the ring oscillators, the propagation delays can also be regulated with FIB circuit edits. Hence, delay-based PUFs are possibly also vulnerable to cloning attacks if the attacker can adequately portray the device to be cloned (Schlangen et al., 2009). Keeping in consideration the vulnerabilities, the researchers should continue developing PUFs that are resilient to cloning and modeling attacks. The attempt to model or clone newly projected designs will preferably help the customers to converge on favored PUF designs. The trend in the literature to eradicate the necessity for error correction obfuscates side channel attacks (Bhargava & Mai, 2013), (Aarestad et al., 2013), resulting in modeling-resistant PUFs (Kumar & Burleson, 2014), (Yu et al., 2014). Accelerated aging experiments and long-term reliability tests are required to be executed on a huge number of chips to illustrate the sustainability of PUFs for deployment.

The reliability of a PUF is determined by its opposition to attacks that try to impersonate, reproduce or retrieve portions of the PUF bits. These attacks can be categorized as active (inserting defects into the design) or passive (merely observing), invasive (involving de-packing the chip to see the design or investigate the internal signals) or non-invasive. The modeling attacks which are non-invasive and passive includes only the examination of transmitted data and consecutive trails to imitate the device by taking advantage of the searched PUF keyspace or poor randomness, or by copying and reusing earlier challenge-response pairs. For identification, a robust PUF with numerous challenge-response pairs is required to reduce the efficacy of the man-in-the-middle cryptanalytic attacks, but unfortunately, all possible robust PUFs are very susceptible to modeling attacks. The main intention of side-channel attacks is to recognize the PUF key utilized by the chip through its relationship with the measured power consumption, e.g., differential power analysis (DPA) (Kocher et al., 1999), electromagnetic emissions (Mangard et al., 2007), leakage power analysis (Alioto et al., 2014), or correlation attacks (Brier et al., 2004). These kinds of attacks are accomplished on the implementation of the cryptographic algorithm which manipulates the key that the attacker is aiming to retrieve. In differential power analysis, the cipher key is recovered by using divide and capture method in which the sections of the key are predicted, thus, splitting the exponential difficulty of deciphering the key and decreasing the number of requisite trials. The same kind of technique is employed to specific processes in the algorithm in order to assist in identifying whether the initially anticipated key is correct or not. In (Alioto et al., 2010b) a power model for DPA attacks on symmetric-key cryptographic algorithms executed using static logic was proposed. In this model, the success of DPA attacks and the circumstances for which the circuit becomes susceptible to these attacks are predicted. One way to thwart the DPA attacks is to mask the power consumption of different processes, as these attacks target the cryptographic core rather than the PUF. The goal of the semi-invasive attacks is to intervene the circuit operation by initiating glitches and inserting faults, thereby exposing the data that would otherwise be securely processed. At the cost of additional runtime and area, consistency checking can be exploited to avoid fault injection and timing attacks. Secure coprocessors can be utilized to counteract the invasive attacks that target the device by physically monitoring the chip and modifying its physical implementation (Smith & Weingart, 1999). However, the disadvantage of these coprocessors is that they need to be powered-on at all times, and hence are very costly both in terms of area and energy. In (Wan et al., 2015) a technique is proposed to thwart invasive attacks by placing metal wires above transmission lines to switch capacitor circuitry.

This changes the capacitance of the sampling capacitor during invasive attacks, and hence make the PUF output fallacious.

There are also infrastructure challenges for a company selling millions of ICs per year. The company will need an authentication infrastructure capable of supporting millions of devices if every chip is provided with a PUF for anti-counterfeiting and authentication. Although there are already existing public-key infrastructures supporting a large number of devices (Red Hat & August Schell, 2007), developing, installing and maintaining such a huge-scale infrastructure is a big challenge for IC manufacturers. Effective methodologies are also required for "rekeying" PUFs, e.g., an IC manufacturer can quantify some challenge-response pairs from a PUF, and the user could use one of these to authenticate the legitimacy of a newly purchased IC. The user can generate a new set of challenge-response pairs that are unknown to the manufacturer, which may require modifying the PUF in some way. The user can have an option to repeat the enrolment process (for generating a new key unknown to the manufacturer) in case of a fixed challenge PUF with a fuzzy extractor. Another challenge faced by the PUFs is to ensure the stability of output with time, as it is expected that PUF responses will vary over time as a consequence of aging effects such as temperature instability, negative bias, etc. (Maiti et al., 2011). The aging effects can be fixed with fuzzy extractors provided that the impact is less, and it should be able to discover and mitigate higher aging-induced changes (Kirkpatrick & Bertino, 2010).

The aimed degree of trustworthiness explains a suitable set of attacks that must be counteracted in a PUF design, although till this time only discrete and fragmented methods have been recommended. A thorough set of procedures would be required to endure a certain level of trustworthiness, with each being assigned to the suitable level of abstraction to achieve targeted security at low cost. There are also opportunities to develop standardized security procedures around PUF. As far as authentication and key generation is concerned, industry standards can be established for facilitating large implementation of PUFs. Such standards would advocate the adoption of technology and would accelerate common interfaces and efficiencies for allowing customers to validate the authenticity of their devices. This would assist to decrease the abundance of counterfeit electronics in critical infrastructure and military systems (Kazmierski, 2011).

PUF-ENHANCED CRYPTOGRAPHY

Physically uncloned functions have made a very restricted impression on real applications due to various challenges that hamper PUF trustworthiness. PUF responses could be unstable requiring huge cost in terms of testing, area, and energy overhead. Post-processing circuits become a portion of the PUF itself and create additional backdoors to it, hence making it more susceptible to physical attacks like side channel and probing. At the time of design and verification of the PUF there is no existing procedure to certify a level of security and trustworthiness thoroughly. This exceptionally extends the design cycle and time to market and requires repeated silicon runs to converge to a targeted and provable security level. Existing solutions aim to target only a specific kind of security threat and level of abstraction. Hence, they are not able to tackle the security challenges impersonated by different types of attacks. The PUFs are primarily designed by a manual procedure, prohibiting design automation and technology portability, and requiring very little design productivity. IoT devices necessitate continuous data transmission and node-to-node communications. Hence, they need regular authentication. This means that they will require a huge sum of challenge-response pairs and PUF capacity, which is not possible through conventional cryptographic techniques.

PUFs are simply considered as secure random key generators primarily used for chip identification through traditional challenge-response pairs, as depicted in Figure 6 (a). A more promising method is shown in Figure 6 (b), where a PUF is used through a crypto-core by employing the PUF key as an encryption key, and then treating input/output as challenge-response pairs. In (Zhao et al., 2015), AES design is proposed explicitly for IoT applications where the power consumption of AES is below 1μW, and the area cost is decreased by almost three times, hence, becomes very reasonable for exponential growth in challenge-response pairs. Moreover, the notion of merging a PUF with a crypto-core can be utilized to decrease the energy requirement and circuit complexity for authentication in IoT node-to-node communications, thus, decreasing the expected PUF capacity at an approved level of security. An exciting implication of PUF-enhanced cryptography is its capability to significantly improve the safety of a crypto-core against cryptanalytic attacks, by properly implanting a PUF into it (Alvarez & Alioto, 2017). PUF-enhanced cryptography enables to expand the crypto-key in contrast to the size levied by crypto-algorithm, which is beyond the conventional method of secure storage of a single crypto-key, hence, increasing its resistance against cryptanalytic attacks. The conventionally key expansion is not possible as the length of the key is determined by encryption standard, however, in PUF-enhanced cryptography, repeatable and unpredictable new keys are joined with the traditional user key by the PUF with a capacity higher than the key to produce fixed length enhanced key employed by the on-chip crypto-core. The key-enhancer shown in Figure 7 is used for this purpose to dynamically combine and compress the user and PUF keys to a fixed length. The key enhancer in Figure 7 is indicated to be exterior to the crypto-core, although it can also stretch to the interior of the core and operate through many chunks of plaintext. The key enhancer could generally be a finite state machine generating time-varying challenges to a PUF, or to a lightweight cipher (Shiozaki et al., 2015). The PUF-enhanced cryptography uses a bigger set of keys, whose quantity is primarily restricted by the required PUF capacity as compared to the conventional system that uses a single private key.

In traditional cryptographic schemes, the prediction of private key by an attacker necessitates an effort that is exponentially described by the size of single key. In contrast to that, the search space of the crypto-key is amplified by the volume of PUF in PUF-enhanced cryptography, hence, making the key search impossible even under extremely powerful equipment. Practically PUF-enhanced cryptography aims to significantly increase the security of a prevailing algorithm with reduced area cost and no throughput penalty. The ability of the key to change itself with time is a powerful tool to enhance the intensity of PUF-enhanced cryptography against cryptanalytic attacks. Since IoT devices mostly depend on batteries and energy harvesting, altering keys becomes a compulsion as governed by the availability of the supply. In (Aysu & Schaumont, 2016) key generation is distributed into numerous phases, precomputation is done and in-between results are stored which can be used in the next phase.

Figure 6. (a) PUF shown as a key generator, (b) Crypto-core based PUF

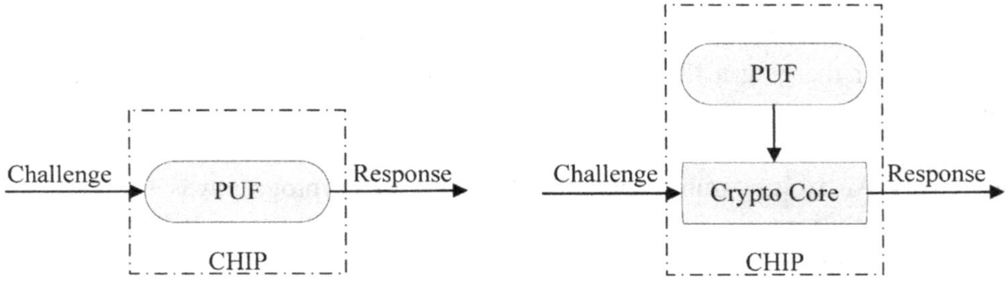

Figure 7. PUF-enhanced cryptography

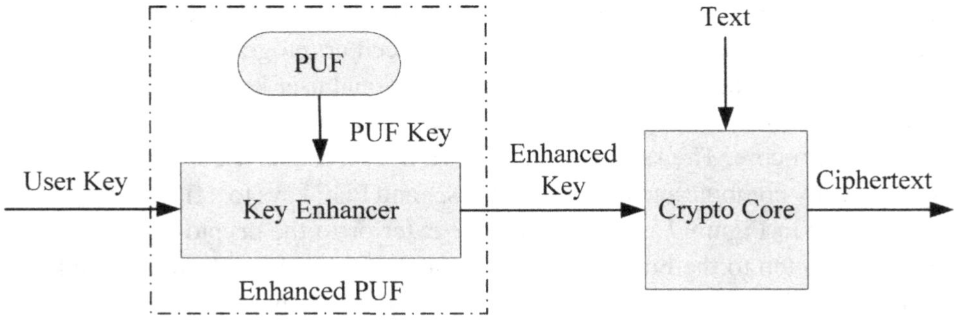

Instead of having a single fixed key, PUF-enhanced cryptography produces time-varying crypto-keys which considerably improve the security of the crypto-core by taking advantage of its synergy with a PUF. In addition to that, the implementation of such PUF to improve the crypto-algorithm also allows to increase the level of required security easily. The level of security indeed specifies the number of desirable PUF words, and hence it only influences the periodicity of the key enhancer for a particular PUF capacity. The PUF explicitly authenticates the chip on which the crypto-core runs. The energy and area overheads dictated by a PUF on a crypto-core are very less in magnitude (e.g. the energy/bit of a PUF usually is two to three orders less in magnitude as compared to crypto-core). In the case of the IoT domain, these characteristics are exceptionally interesting, as they make crypto-cores and crypto-algorithms inexpensive in terms of area and energy, thus, permitting uninterrupted and pervasive security. If the level of required security is much higher, the PUF-enhanced cryptography can facilitate the desired security level at a quiet low area and energy cost.

CONCLUSION

One of the critical challenges faced by IoT practitioners and developers is to ensure the physical security of IoT nodes that store the keys locally. Although there are myriad number of conventional or traditional primitives and solutions available, however, they are not suitable for IoT systems. PUF technology is ready to be developed into a foundational aspect for next-generation hardware-oriented security systems. PUFs offer a method to produce unique keys that do not need to be stored in non-volatile memory, and they suggest rousing prospects for authentication, privacy, data integrity, access control, etc. in IoT devices. The identification of entropy sources in addition to noise reduction and deterministic influences employing PUFs is emerging as a substantially potential and new field. Since IoT systems demand pervasive security, the hardware root of trust is required at device level to protect the sensitive data. The design and development of tamper-sensing IoT nodes is not feasible considering the constrained computational power and low-cost requirements. PUFs, due to their unique features, are suitable to provide energy efficient and cost-effective hardware level security solution to IoT systems. These characteristics of PUFs have been refined over time to make them suitable for such constrained environments in an economical manner, the best example being the PUF-enhanced cryptography. PUF-enhanced cryptography permits new tactics to switch crypto-keys over an insecure channel without employing the traditional energy and area hungry public cryptography schemes.

REFERENCES

Aarestad, J., Plusquellic, J., & Acharyya, D. (2013). Error-Tolerant Bit Generation Techniques for Use with a Hardware-Embedded Path Delay PUF. *IEEE Int'l Symp. Hardware- Oriented Security and Trust (HOST 13)*, 151–158. 10.1109/HST.2013.6581581

Alioto, M., Bongiovanni, S., Djukanovic, M., Scotti, G., & Trifiletti, A. (2014). Effectiveness of leakage power analysis attacks on DPA-resistant logic styles under process variations. *IEEE Transactions on Circuits and Systems. I, Regular Papers*, *61*(2), 429–442. doi:10.1109/TCSI.2013.2278350

Alioto, M., Poli, M., & Rocchi, S. (2010b). Differential power analysis attacks to pre charged buses: A general analysis for symmetric-key cryptographic algorithms. *IEEE Transactions on Dependable and Secure Computing*, *7*(3), 226–239. doi:10.1109/TDSC.2009.1

Alkabani, Y., Koushanfar, F., & Potkonjak, M. (2007). Remote activation of ICs for piracy prevention and digital right management. *Proc. IEEE/ACM Int'l Conf. Computer- Aided Design (ICCAD 07)*, 674–677. 10.1109/ICCAD.2007.4397343

Alvarez, A., & Alioto, M. (2017). Security Down to the Hardware Level. In M. Alioto (Ed.), *Enabling the Internet of Things: From Integrated Circuits to Integrated Systems* (pp. 247–270). Singapore: Springer. doi:10.1007/978-3-319-51482-6_8

Alvarez, A., Zhao, W., & Alioto, M. (2015). 15 fJ/bit static physically unclonable functions for secure chip identification with <2% native bit instability and 140x inter/intra PUF hamming distance separation in 65 nm. *IEEE Int. Solid-State Circuits Conf. 5*, 256–258.

Alvarez, A. B., Zhao, W., & Alioto, M. (2016). Static physically unclonable functions for secure chip identification with 1.9–5.8% native bit instability at 0.6–1 V and 15fJ/bit in 65 nm. *IEEE Journal of Solid-State Circuits*, *60*(5), 1–4.

Aysu, A., & Schaumont, P. (2016). Precomputation methods for hash-based signatures on energy-harvesting platforms. *IEEE Transactions on Computers*, *65*(9), 2925–2931. doi:10.1109/TC.2015.2500570

Bhargava, M., & Mai, K. (2013). A high reliability PUF using hot carrier injection based response reinforcement. *Proc. 15th Int'l Workshop Cryptographic Hardware and Embedded Systems (CHES 13)*, 90–106. 10.1007/978-3-642-40349-1_6

Bhargava, M., & Mai, K. (2014). An efficient reliable PUF-based cryptographic key generator in 65 nm CMOS. *Design Autom. Test Europe Conf. Exhibition*, *1*, 1–6.

Brier, E., Clavier, C., & Olivier, F. (2004). Correlation power analysis with a leakage model. *Cryptographic Hardware and Embedded Systems*, 16–29.

Dorri, A., Kanhere, S. S., Jurdak, R., & Gauravaram, P. (2017). Blockchain for IoT security and privacy: the case study of a smart home. *2017 IEEE International Conference on Pervasive Computing and Communications Workshops (PerCom Workshops)*, 618-623.

Dragomir, D., Gheorghe, L., Costeal, S., & Radovici, A. (2016). A survey on secure communication protocols for IoT systems. *International Workshop on Secure Internet of Things*, 47-62. 10.1109/SIoT.2016.012

Hamlet, J. R., Bauer, T. M., & Pierson, L. G. (2014). *Deterrence of device counterfeiting, cloning, and subversion by substitution using hardware fingerprinting*. US patent 8,848,905, Sandia Corporation.

Helfmeier, C., Boit, C., Nedospasov, D., & Seifert, J. P. (2013). Cloning Physically Unclonable Functions. *IEEE Int'l Symp. Hardware-Oriented Security and Trust (HOST 13)*, 1–6.

Helinski, R., Acharyya, D., & Plusquellic, J. (2009). A physical unclonable function defined using power distribution system equivalent resistance variations. *ACM/IEEE Design Automation Conference*, 676–681. 10.1145/1629911.1630089

Karakoyunlu, D., & Sunar, B. (2010). Differential template attacks on PUF enabled cryptographic devices. *IEEE Int'l Workshop Information Forensics and Security (WIFS 10)*, 1–6. 10.1109/WIFS.2010.5711445

Kazmierski. C. (2011). *SIA president testifies at Senate Armed Services Committee on dangers of counterfeit chips*. Retrieved from www.semiconductors.org/news/2011/11/08/news_2011/ sia_president_testifies_at_senate_armed_services_committee_on_dangers_of_counterfeit_chips

Kirkpatrick. M. S, & Bertino. E. (2010). Software techniques to combat drift in PUF-based authentication systems. *Secure Component and System Identification (SECSI 10)*.

Kocher, P., Ja, J., & Jun, B. (1999). Differential power analysis. *Lecture Notes in Computer Science*, *1666*, 388–397. doi:10.1007/3-540-48405-1_25

Kumar, R., & Burleson, W. (2014). On design of a highly secure PUF based on non-linear current mirrors. *IEEE Int'l Symp. Hardware-Oriented Security and Trust (HOST 14)*, 38–43. 10.1109/HST.2014.6855565

Kumar, S. S., Guajardo, J., Maes, R., Schrijen, G., & Tuyls, P. (2008). The butterfly PUF protecting IP on every FPGA. *IEEE International Workshop on Hardware-Oriented Security and Trust (HOST)*, 67–70.

Li, J., & Seok, M. (2015). A 3.07 μm^2/bitcell physically Unclonable function with 3.5% and 1% bit-instability across 0 to 80 _C and 0.6 to 1.2 V in a 65 nm CMOS. *IEEE Symposium on VLSI Circuits, Digest of Technical Papers*, 250–251.

Maes, R. (2012). *Physically unclonable functions: Constructions, properties and applications*. Leuven: Katholieke Universiteit.

Maes, R. (2013). *Physically Unclonable Functions: Construction, properties and applications*. London: Springer. doi:10.1007/978-3-642-41395-7

Mahalle, N., & Railkar, P. N. (2015). *Identity management for Internet of Things*. Rivers Publishers.

Maiti, A., McDougall, L., & Schaumont, P. (2011). The impact of aging on an FPGA-based Physical Unclonable Function. *Int'l Conf. Field Programmable Logic and Applications (FPL 11)*, 151–156. 10.1109/FPL.2011.35

Maiti, A., Nagesh, R., Reddy, A., & Schaumont, P. (2009). Physical Unclonable Function and True Random Number Generator: A compact and scalable implementation. *Proc. ACM Great Lakes Symp. VLSI (GLSVLSI 09)*, 425–428. 10.1145/1531542.1531639

Mangard, S., Oswald, E., & Popp, T. (2007). *Power analysis attacks: Revealing the Secrets of smart cards*. New York: Springer.

Mathew, S., Satpathy, S., Suresh, S., Anders, M., Kaul, H., Agarwal, A., ... De, V. (2016). A 4fJ/bit delay-hardened Physically unclonable function circuit with selective bit destabilization in 14 nm trti-gate CMOS. *Symposium on VLSI Circuits*, 248–249.

Mathew. S. K, Satpathy. S. K, Anders. M. A, Kaul. H, Hsu. S. K, Agarwal. A, … De. V. (2014). A 0.19pJ/b PVT-variation- tolerant hybrid physically unclonable function circuit for 100% stable secure key generation in 22 nm CMOS. *Digest Tech. Pap. - IEEE Int. Solid-State Circuits Conf., 2*, 278 280.

Nedospasov, D., Seifert, J. P., Helfmeier, C., & Boit, C. (2014). Invasive PUF analysis. *Workshop on Fault Diagnosis and Tolerance in Cryptography (FDTC)*, 30–38.

Red Hat and August Schell run world's largest PKI installation on Red Hat Enterprise Linux. Red Hat government team. (2007). Retrieved from www.redhat.com/ about/ news/archive/2007/6/red-hat-and-august-schell-run -worlds-largest-pki-installation-on -red-hat-enterprise-linux

Rosenblatt, S., Fainstein, D., Cestero, A., Safran, J., Robson, N., Kirihata, T., & Iyer, S. S. (2013). Field tolerant dynamic intrinsic chip ID using 32 nm high-K/metal gate SOI embedded DRAM. *IEEE Journal of Solid-State Circuits*, *48*(4), 940–947. doi:10.1109/JSSC.2013.2239134

Rührmair, U., Sehnke, F., S€olter, J., Dror, G., Devadas, S., & Ürgen Schmidhuber, J. (2010). Modeling attacks on physical unclonable functions. *Proceedings of ACM Conference on Computer and Communications Security*, 237–249.

Rührmair, U., S€olter, J., Sehnke, F., Xu, X., Mahmoud, A., Stoyanova, V., ... Devadas, S. (2013). PUF modeling attacks on simulated and silicon data. *IEEE Trans. Inf. Forensics Secur.*, *8*(11), 1876–1891.

Rukhin, A., Soto, J., Nechvatal, J., Smid, M., Barker, E., Leigh, S., ... Vo, S. (2010). A statistical test suite for random and pseudorandom number generators for cryptographic applications. *Natl. Inst. Stand. Technol. 800–22(Rev 1a)*, 131.

Sadeghi, A. R., & Naccache, D. (2010). *Towards hardware-intrinsic security: Foundations and practice*. Berlin: Springer. doi:10.1007/978-3-642-14452-3

Sain, M., Kang, Y. J., & Lee, H. J. (2017). Survey on Security in Internet of things: state of the art and challenges. *2017 19th International Conference on Advanced Communication Technology (ICACT)*, 699-704.

Schlangen, R., Rainer, L., Lundquist, T. R., Egger, P., & Boit, C. (2009). RF performance increase allowing IC timing adjustments by use of backside FIB processing. *IEEE Int'l Symp. Physical and Failure Analysis of Integrated Circuits (IPFA 09)*, 33–36. 10.1109/IPFA.2009.5232703

Schrijen. G. J, & Van Der Leest. V. (2012). Comparative analysis of SRAM memories used as PUF primitives. *Design, Automation & Test in Europe Conference & Exhibition (DATE)*, 1319–1324.

Schulz, S., Sadeghi, A. R., & Wachsmann, C. (2011). Short paper: Lightweight remote attestation using physical functions. *Proc. ACM Conf. Wireless Network Security (ACM WiSec)*, 109–114. 10.1145/1998412.1998432

Selimis, G., Konijnenburg, M., Ashouei, M., Huisken, J., De Groot, H., Van Der Leest, V., ... Tuyls, P. (2011). Evaluation of 90nm 6T-SRAM as physical unclonable function for secure key generation in wireless sensor nodes. *Proceedings of IEEE International Symposium on Circuits Systems*, 567–570. 10.1109/ISCAS.2011.5937628

Shiozaki, M., Kubota, T., Nakai, T., Takeuchi, A., Nishimura, T., & Fujino, T. (2015). Tamper-resistant authentication system with side-channel attack resistant AES and PUF using MDR-ROM. *IEEE International Symposium on Circuits and Systems (ISCAS)*, 1462–1465. 10.1109/ISCAS.2015.7168920

Smith, S. W., & Weingart, S. (1999). Building a high-performance, programmable secure coprocessor. *Computer Networks*, *31*(8), 831–860. doi:10.1016/S1389-1286(98)00019-X

Wan, M., He, Z., Han, S., Dai, K., & Zou, X. (2015). An invasive attack- resistant PUF based on switched-capacitor circuit. *IEEE Trans. Circuits Syst. I*, *62*(8), 2024–2034. doi:10.1109/TCSI.2015.2440739

Wurm, J., Hoang, K., Arias, A., Sadeghi, A. R., & Jin, Y. (2016). Security analysis on consumer and industrial IoT devices. *2016 21st Asia and South Pacific Design Automation Conference (ASP-DAC)*, 519-524.

Yang, K., Dong, Q., Blaauw, D., & Sylvester, D. (2015). A physically unclonable function with BER < 10^-8 for robust chip authentication using oscillator collapse in 40 nm CMOS. *IEEE International Solid-State Circuits Conference (ISSCC)*, 254–256.

Yu, M., M'Raïhi, D., Verbauwhede, I., & Devadas, S. (2014). A noise bifurcation architecture for linear additive physical functions. *IEEE Int'l Symp. Hardware-Oriented Security and Trust (HOST 14)*, 124–129.

Yu, M. M., Sowell, R., Singh, A., Raihi, D. M., & Devadas, S. (2012). Performance metrics and empirical results of a PUF cryptographic key generation ASIC. *IEEE International Symposium on Hardware-Oriented Security and Trust (HOST)*, 108–115.

Zhao, W., Ha, Y., & Alioto, M. (2015). Novel self-body-biasing and statistical design for near-threshold circuits with ultra-energy-efficient AES as case study. *IEEE Trans. VLSI Systems*, *23*(8), 1390–1401. doi:10.1109/TVLSI.2014.2342932

Chapter 5
Hardware Primitives-Based Security Protocols for the Internet of Things

Muhammad Naveed Aman
National University of Singapore, Singapore

Kee Chaing Chua
National University of Singapore, Singapore

Biplab Sikdar
National University of Singapore, Singapore

ABSTRACT

IoT is the enabling technology for a variety of new exciting services in a wide range of application areas including environmental monitoring, healthcare systems, energy management, transportation, and home and commercial automation. However, the low-cost and straightforward nature of IoT devices producing vast amounts of sensitive data raises many security concerns. Among the cyber threats, hardware-level threats are especially crucial for IoT systems. In particular, IoT devices are not physically protected and can easily be captured by an adversary to launch physical and side-channel attacks. This chapter introduces security protocols for IoT devices based on hardware security primitives called physically unclonable functions (PUFs). The protocols are discussed for the following major security principles: authentication and confidentiality, data provenance, and anonymity. The security analysis shows that security protocols based on hardware security primitives are not only secure against network-level threats but are also resilient against physical and side-channel attacks.

DOI: 10.4018/978-1-5225-5742-5.ch005

INTRODUCTION

The Internet of Things can be included in the list of the most important emerging technologies of the present era. The number of new things or devices being added to the system every day is over five million. The number of IoT devices connected to the Internet in 2016 crossed six billion (Gartner, 2015) and is expected to reach over 20 billion by 2020 (Intel). This considerable number of connected objects presents an excellent opportunity for the use of an extended knowledge base, e.g., healthcare, industrial control, smart cities, transportation systems, and the smart power grid. However, IoT security and privacy are deemed to be the most critical and essential aspect that has to be addressed for the future growth of IoT. A survey report released by HP shows that IoT enabled devices suffer from at least 25 security flaws (HP, 2014).

Virtually any device that is connected to the Internet or other devices poses a threat to the user. For example, an attacker may try to sabotage equipment or even cause human injuries by gaining unauthorized access to the IoT devices monitoring and controlling the manufacturing equipment in a factory. Wearable IoT devices are used to monitor patients, collect vital health data, and wirelessly convey this data to health professionals to make treatment decisions. An attacker may try to eavesdrop or even change this data resulting in wrong treatment. Similarly, IoT sensors onboard vehicles may monitor the engine temperature, and the condition of transmission fluid, brakes, and tire pressure, etc. Moreover, the use of driving aid systems such as ESC (electronic stability control) and ACC (adaptive cruise control) allow even greater control to electronic components. In this case, it is essential to isolate the vehicle's automotive control network from an IoT connected navigation or multimedia system to minimize the risk of cyber-attacks.

Some of the high-profile cases from the hacking of IoT devices include the following. A passenger onboard a commercial airline flight allegedly gained access to the jet's thrust management system by connecting through the in-flight entertainment (IFE) systems (Moyer, 2015). Similarly, two security researchers successfully hacked into a jeep mile away and were able to interfere with the vehicle's entertainment system, engine, and brakes (Greenberg, 2015). In another incident in Germany, attackers used a spear-phishing attack to gain access to a steel mill's control system through the plant's business network causing significant damage (Zetter, 2015). In another high-profile incident in Ukraine in December 2015, attackers were successful in gaining access to the power grid and cutting power to over 200,000 people (Zetter, 2016). Realizing the risk of cyber-attacks on devices in IoT, the US security agency had disabled the wireless capabilities of the monitoring and smart apparatus of his embedded medical device when the former vice president of USA Mr. Dick Cheney was hospitalized (Grau, 2015). These are some of the examples which highlight the importance of protecting IoT from diverse forms of cyber-attacks. Note that IoT security becomes a core requirement when these devices are involved in the monitoring and control of systems that can cause widespread human or infrastructure damage.

The unique characteristics of IoT devices that make them unsuitable for traditional security approaches and make the task of designing security protocols more challenging are as follows:

1. **Small Size:** It is difficult to add security modules or components to the small-sized IoT devices which limits the hardware and its capabilities.
2. **Simple and Low Cost:** The low-cost and straightforward IoT devices are usually designed to carry out a specific task, resulting in limited computational capabilities. Therefore, running a complex security algorithm may not be feasible.
3. **Limited Power:** IoT devices may have limited power and may even need to harvest power for their usage. Therefore, any security module (whether software or hardware) needs to be energy efficient.
4. **Headless:** IoT devices usually have to operate independently without the involvement of any human. This, combined with the long usage life requirement, can result in (apart from other problems) an outdated device that may no longer be secure after a few years.
5. **No Physical Protection:** Contemporary security protocols make the underlying assumption of physically protected devices. Although this assumption may be valid for desktops and PCs, however, IoT devices are usually deployed in locations where an adversary can quickly gain access, e.g., traffic signals, street lights, and smart grid field controllers, etc. Therefore, with the increase in physical security threats, any protocol designed for IoT needs to be robust against hardware level attacks.
6. **IP Protection:** User accessible devices such as the IoT, are vulnerable to intellectual property (IP) theft. Therefore, IoT device needs to be protected against not only network threats but also against IP theft, tampering, cloning, and reverse engineering.

Security Issues in IoT

IoT security can be divided into two major categories, i.e., Network level threats and Hardware level threats, as described in the following sections.

Network Level Threats

Network level threats include eavesdropping, impersonation, man-in-the-middle attacks, replay attacks, unauthorized access, hacking, etc. For example, using malware, an attacker may gather sensitive information such as passwords or credit card numbers, etc. To mitigate these types of threats, computers may use firewalls, up-to-date software, and update their virus databases on a regular basis. To protect IoT devices against these types of attacks, the cryptographic primitives not only need to be strong but should have low computational complexity and high energy efficiency. Most of the traditional work on security covers network level threats.

Hardware Level Threats

Hardware has traditionally been seen as an abstract layer responsible for running instructions and is well protected. Most of the existing work at the hardware level has been focused on the optimization of cryptographic operations by implementing them on a particular type of hardware, and the integrated circuit supply chain is assumed to be well protected. However, there is a lack of sufficient research on the topic of how to make the hardware itself secure. The increase in cost and complexity of modern system-on-chip (SOC) designs has led to a distributed system for VLSI fabrication including third-party fabrication and IP cores. Although this approach has reduced the cost, workload, and time-to-market (TTM), it has also made the IC supply chain insecure. For example, hardware trojans may be maliciously inserted into ICs, or attackers may exploit malicious soft/hard IP cores after the IP cores are used in a SOC platform. The main threat, in this case, was identified as the untrusted third-party fabrication facilities.

The term hardware security was initially coined for hardware trojan detection, categorization, and isolation. A hardware trojan can be defined as a malicious circuit or the malicious modification of hardware during the design or fabrication process of an IC (Chakraborty, Narasimhan and Bhunia, 2009). Thus, hardware trojans may result in information leakage or malfunction of the SOC. Some of the techniques used to detect hardware trojans include current integration technique (Wang, Salmani, Tehranipoor and Plusquellic, 2008), path delay testing (Jin and Makris, 2008), temperature analysis and power based analysis (Tehranipoor et al., 2011).

Hardware security research has recently moved towards the construction of a root-of-trust using trustworthy hardware. A root of trust can be considered the starting point for implementing hardware security. If the root-of-trust device is secure against physical/hardware attacks, then the rest of the system built around it can employ the root-of-trust to protect against hardware level threats. A famous example of a device used to provide a root-of-trust is the development of physically unclonable functions

(PUFs). PUFs have emerged as a hot topic in the domain of hardware security and leading to a large number of published results. A PUF has been defined by (Suh and Devadas 2007) as "A Physically Unclonable Function (PUF) is a function that maps a set of challenges to a set of responses based on an intractably complex physical system". PUFs take advantage of the inherent device process variation to obtain unique chip-specific fingerprints in the form of challenge-response pairs (CRPs).

Security Principles

This part focuses on the following main areas of concern in the context of IoT devices. The core objectives for IoT security include authentication and confidentiality, data provenance, and anonymity described as follows.

Authentication and Confidentiality

An IoT device/user should be able to verify that the data received from another device/user is indeed, sent by the stated sensor. In most of the cases, it is desirable that the data be sent securely (e.g., using encryption) without being exposed to anyone else. Therefore, authentication is the first step towards establishing a session after a secure boot of the IoT device. However, this authentication must be done securely and efficiently, by making sure that the secrets (e.g., keys) of an IoT device are secure against physical attacks. This chapter considers the problem of mutual authentication between an IoT device and a server. Techniques and protocols based on hardware security primitives that may be used to provide authentication in IoT and at the same time are safe against physical attacks are discussed in this chapter.

Data Provenance

Data provenance establishes trust in the origin and creation processes of data, i.e., the data is indeed collected by the specific IoT device at the stated location and time. Self-trust or data provenance is critical to the correct operation of IoT. This chapter discusses the impact of physical attacks on data provenance and describes some PUF based techniques and protocols that may be used to provide physically secure data provenance for IoT devices.

Anonymity

Given the critical nature of data produced by some IoT devices, it is desirable that an attacker be unable to determine the identity of the source of a packet or message. In some application scenarios, IoT devices may query other IoT devices to get relevant information. An attacker passively eavesdropping the traffic may try to seek information regarding the identity of the IoT device that generated or responded to a query. Moreover, an attacker may try to impersonate an IoT device after obtaining information about its identity. This chapter discusses techniques that may be used by IoT devices to achieve anonymity with hardware security.

Benefits of Hardware Security

Hardware security can be used to provide the following desirable features, especially for IoT devices that require the highest level of authentication, confidentiality, data provenance and anonymity.

- Tamper-resistant and robust storage of secrets such as cryptographic keys.
- Protection against physical and cloning attacks.
- Protection against side channel attacks.
- Produce secure hardware elements that are ultra-fast, have low energy consumption, and have minimal silicon footprint.

INTRODUCTION TO PUFs

The use of random physical features for the identification of people and objects is not new. The field of biometrics to identify humans such as fingerprints dates back to the eighties of the twentieth century, and more recently, the advent of facial and iris recognition is gaining more popularity. Similarly, the use of unique patterns and visual effects in currency notes are quite common. The concept behind PUFs emerged initially as one-way physical functions (Pappu et al., 2002), random physical functions (Gassend et al., 2002), and finally as physically unclonable functions (Maes, 2013).

PUFs exploit the intrinsic variability in the random physical microstructure of ICs to produce a unique output in the form of a response to an input called the challenge. A PUF is characterized by a challenge-response pair (CRP). Using PUFs for IoT security have the following notable benefits:

1. PUFs require a physical basis and therefore, cannot be reproduced using cryptographic primitives.
2. Producing a physical clone of a PUF is extremely hard or even impossible (Bohma, n.d.; Hofer, 2013).
3. Provide physical security by hiding the secrets within a complex microstructure of an IC without actually storing them.

4. PUFs can support ultra-low energy and silicon footprints while maintaining ultra-high throughput.
5. PUFs do not require unique manufacturing, programming or testing processes resulting in a low-cost and straightforward process.

The output for a set of instantiations of a particular PUF is affected by environmental variation (e.g., temperature) and on-chip noise as described as follows.

Effect of Environment and Noise

Although given the same challenge to a PUF multiple times results in the same response each time with high probability, however, the PUF may produce slightly different outputs each time. To use PUFs for security purposes such as secure key generation for cryptography, the output of a PUF must be perfectly stable. To reduce the bit error rate (BER) of PUF outputs, error correcting codes are usually introduced. Simple and inexpensive techniques such as temporal and spatial majority voting can reduce the BERs by orders of magnitude (Maes, 2013).

Unique Response

Giving the same challenge to a different PUF produces responses far apart with high probability. This is due to the physical randomness introduced in the PUF hardware during the fabrication process of ICs. This feature of a PUF establishes the uniqueness of each PUF output. This also forms the basis of tamper resistant and robust storage for secrets using PUFs. This shows that PUFs can be used as a useful tool to establish the root-of-trust and provide secure hardware authentication in the IoT.

PUFs can be realized by leveraging variations in circuit timing and delay such as the delay-based PUFs, or exploiting the random process variations leading to random natural states of memory cells at the power-up. PUFs are used in various ways in cryptographic constructions, and some of the use cases for PUFs in literature are as follows (Frikken, Blanton and Atallah, 2009):

1. **Simple Authentication:** This is the most common use case for PUFs found in the literature. A server initially obtains a number of CRPs from each device's PUF and stores them in a database. Each time a device needs to be authenticated, the server selects one of the CRPs stored in its database for that respective device and sends the corresponding challenge to the device. The device responds by sending back a response generated from the device's PUF and the challenge. If the response stored with the server matches the response

sent by the device, the device is successfully authenticated. Each time a CRP is used, it is deleted from the database.

2. **PUF as a Computable Function:** (Hammouri and Sunar, 2008) proposed a delay based PUF that can be modeled using a linear inequality. The advantage of this scheme is that the server does not need to store a large number of CRPs for each device. The authors assumed that the behavior of the function could not be predicted by an attacker without physical access to it. This exposes the proposed protocol to physical attacks.
3. **PUF as an Identity:** PUFs have been used to extend known identification protocols by providing the desired resilience against physical attacks. (Tuyls and Batina, 2006) employed PUFs in the Schnorr's identification protocol. Similarly, (Batina et al., 2008) used PUFs with the Okamoto identification protocol.

PUF BASED SECURITY PROTOCOLS FOR THE IOT

Authentication Protocols

The physical un-clonability property of PUFs makes them a prime candidate for identification and authentication in IoT systems. A PUF response can be used as a biometric fingerprint for ICs.

One of the initial protocols for authentication and secret key generation using PUFs was proposed by (Suh and Devadas, 2007). The proposed protocol requires a trusted server to store a large number of CRPs for each device during an enrollment phase. If a device requires authentication, the trusted server selects one of the stored CRPs which has not been used previously and inputs the selected challenge to the device's PUF to get a response. The trusted server then compares the response obtained from the PUF to the response stored in its database. If the verification succeeds, the server accepts the identity and authenticity of the device. A CRP is not reused to protect against man-in-the-middle attacks.

Another protocol proposed by (Frikken et al., 2009) uses PUFs and the ZKPK technique for authentication. A trusted server selects a group G_q (and its generator g) of prime order q, for a hard-discrete logarithm problem. Moreover, G_q may be a subgroup of the multiplicative group Z_p^* for a prime p. The proposed protocol uses fuzzy logic extractors for error correction and produces stable outputs from a PUF. Two procedures Gen and Rep are used to stabilize the PUF output using helper bits. The proposed protocol is described as follows:

1. Enrollment Phase:
   a. The server selects a challenge *c* and sends *c* along with <G_q> denoting the description of the group G_q (including a prime pair (*p*,*q*) and the generator *g*).
   b. The user sends H(*c*|| *pwd*), <G_q>, and *g* to the device.
   c. The device calculates a challenge d = H(H(c||pwd), <G_q>,*g*) and runs the Gen function on this value to obtain response *r* (from the PUF), and *P* (helper bits). The device then sends (g^r,*P*) to the user.
   d. The user sends (g^r,*P*) to the server.
   e. The server stores (g^r,*P*) along with *c*, *g*, and <G_q>.
2. Authentication Phase:
   a. The server sends *c*, *g*, *P*, <G_q> and a random nonce *N* to the user.
   b. The user sends (H(*c*||*pwd*), <G_q>,*g*,*P*,*N*) to the device for the Rep function.
   c. The device applies the Rep function to obtain the response *r*. The device then generates a random value $v \epsilon \mathbf{Z}_q$ and calculates

$$t = g^v,$$

$$c' = H\left(g, g^r, t', N\right),$$

$$w = v - c'r \bmod q$$

The device then sends c' and w to the user, who forwards them to the server.

   d. The server calculates $t' = g^w g^{rc'}$ and the authentication is completed if

$$c' = H\left(g, g^r, t', N\right)$$

and otherwise, it is rejected.

The reader is referred to (Frikken et al., 2009) for further details on the Gen and Rep functions.

A recent protocol proposed by (Aman et al., 2017) uses PUFs for mutual authentication and forming of a secure session between an IoT device and the server. The authors show that the proposed protocol has low computation complexity and is suitable for resource-constrained devices such as the IoT. The protocol flow is shown in Figure 1.

Figure 1. Mutual authentication protocol proposed by (M. Aman et al., 2017)

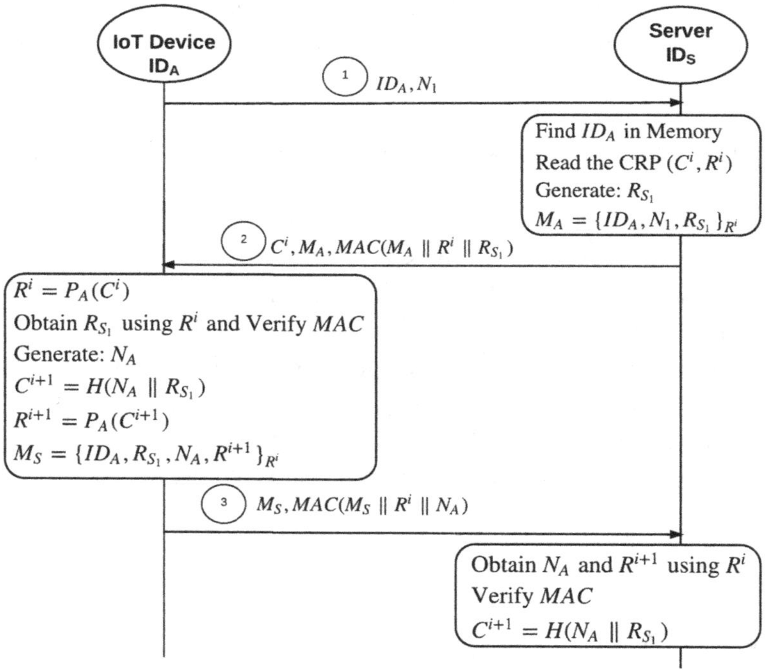

The proposed protocol uses secret keys generated using a PUF to identify and exchange a session key between an IoT device and a server. The server obtains the initial CRP using a one-time password authentication approach with the help of an operator when the IoT device is deployed in the field for the first time. The steps of the protocol are as follows:

1. The IoT device sends its identity (ID_A) and a random nonce (N_1) to the server requesting authentication.
2. The server tries to locate ID_A in its memory and if the search fails, the authentication request is rejected. Otherwise, the server uses the response (R^i) from the stored CRP to form an encrypted message, $M_A = \left\{ID_A, N_1, R_{S_1}\right\}_{R^i}$ and sends the challenge C^i, M_A and the corresponding message authentication code (MAC) to the IoT device.
3. The IoT device uses its PUF to generate R^i and decrypt M_A. The IoT device then calculates a new challenge as $C^{i+1} = H(N_A \| R_{S_1})$ and obtains a new response R^{i+1} using this challenge. The IoT device then uses R^i to form an

encrypted message $M_S = \left\{ID_A, R_{S_1}, N_A, R^{i+1}\right\}_{R^i}$. The IoT device then sends M_S and the corresponding MAC to the server.

4. The server decrypts MS using R^i to obtain N_A and R^{i+1}. The server then verifies the MAC received in the message and if the verification fails, the authentication request is rejected. Otherwise, the server calculates the new challenge $C^{i+1} = H(N_A \,||\, R_{S_1})$ and replaces the old CRP with a new CRP for this device and the authentication is complete.

Once the protocol is completed, the IoT device and the server can use N_A and R_{S1} to establish a session key such as $H\left(R_{S_1}\right) \oplus H(N_A)$.

Another protocol by (Xie et al., 2017) uses PUFs to establish mutual authentication among sensor nodes in Body Area Networks (BAN). The proposed protocol uses PUFs to establish secret shared keys between sensor nodes. The system model consists of a BAN network with *n* sensors and one control unit *cu*. The sensors are attached to the patient's body to measure physiological data. Each sensor is equipped with a PUF. The sensor nodes are assumed to have the capability of computing secure hash functions but do not support symmetric or asymmetric encryption functions.

The sensors initially share some CRPs with the control unit *cu,* i.e., cu stores m CRPs $(c_{i,1}, r_{i,1})$, $(c_{i,2}, r_{i,2})$, …, $(c_{i,m}, r_{i,m})$ for each sensor s_i. The control unit also stores an additional CRP $(s_i, F_i(s_i))$ for each sensor s_i, where $F_i()$ represents the PUF function for sensor s_i. Let us consider the scenario where the control unit learns that sensor s_2 wants to communicate with sensor s_1. The steps of the protocol are as follows:

1. $s_1 \rightarrow cu$: random number y_1, $H\left(F_1\left(S_1\right), y_1\right)$
2. $cu \rightarrow s_1$: $s_1, c_{1,1}, y_2, H\left(F_1\left(s_1\right), y_1, y_2, s_2, c_{1,1}\right)$
3. $s_1 \rightarrow cu$: $H\left(r_{1,1}\right) \oplus F_1\left(s_2\right), H\left(F_1\left(s_1\right), y_1, y_2, F_1\left(s_2\right)\right)$
4. $cu \rightarrow s2$: random number $y_3, c_{2,1}, H\left(F_2\left(s_2\right), y_3, c_{2,1}\right)$
5. $s2 \rightarrow cu$: $y_4, H\left(F_2\left(s_2\right), y_3, y_4, s_1, c_{2,1}\right)$
6. $cu \rightarrow s2$: $H\left(r_{2,1}\right) \oplus F_1\left(s_2\right), H\left(F_2\left(s_2\right), y_3, y_4, F_1\left(s_2\right)\right)$

Thus, in the end, s_1 can use $F_1\left(s_2\right)$ as the secret key while s_2 can use $F_2\left(s_1\right)$ as the secret key for the session between s_1 and s_2.

In another work by (Chatterjee, Chakraborty and Mukhopadhyay, 2017) for authentication and key sharing, the system model consists of several mobile data nodes ($Node_1$, $Node_2$, …, $Node_m$) which generate and receive information. Multiple server nodes are used to connect the data nodes to the Internet cloud. The server nodes and data nodes are instantiated with their own PUFs. The proposed protocol starts with an enrollment phase in which each server node generates a CRP database for each data node in its area using a secure and trusted environment. The server nodes obtain *k* CRPs for each node using the challenge-response mechanism of a PUF.

Let us consider the scenario where $Node_1$ wants to initiate a session with $Node_2$. The steps of the protocol are as follows:

1. $Node_1$ requests the server to supervise its communication with $Node_2$.
2. The server chooses two CRPs C_1 and C_2 for $Node_1$ and C_3 and C_4 for $Node_2$ from their respective databases. It then performs the following computations using a time stamp TS:

$$\Delta_1 = H_1\left(R_1 \| R_2 \| TS\right)$$

$$\Delta_2 = H_1\left(R_3 \| R_4 \| TS\right)$$

$$TS_1^{'} = TS \oplus (R_1 \,||\, R_2)$$

$$TS_2^{'} = TS \oplus (R_3 \,||\, R_4)$$

where R_1, R_2 are the PUF responses for $Node_1$ with C_1 and C_2, while R_3 and R_4 are the PUF responses for $Node_2$ with C_3 and C_4. The server then sends $\left(C_1, C_2, TS_1^{'}\right)$ to $Node_1$ and $\left(Node_1, C_3, C_4, TS_2^{'}\right)$ to $Node_2$.

3. After receiving the message from the server, Node1 calculates:

$$TS = TS_1^{'} \oplus (PUF_1\left(C_1\right) \,||\, PUF_2\left(C_2\right))$$

$$ID_1 = H_1\left(PUF_1\left(C_1\right) \| PUF_1\left(C_2\right) \| TS\right)$$

$$P_1 = H_1\left(C_1 \oplus C_2\right)$$

If $ID_1 = \Delta_1$, $Node_1$ choose a random value t and computes

$$K1_{PUB} = t \cdot P_1$$

$$K1_{PRV} = t \cdot ID_1$$

$$d_1 = H_4(PUF_1(C_1) \oplus PUF_1(C_2) \oplus ID_1 \oplus P_1 \oplus K1_{PUB} \oplus TS$$

where $K1_{PUB}$ and $K1_{PRV}$ act as the public and private key for $Node_1$. $Node_1$ then sends $(ID_1, P_1, K1_{PUB}, d_1)$ to the server. Node2 repeats a similar process using Δ_2 and TS_2' and sends $(ID_2, P_2, K2_{PUB}, d_2)$ to the server.

4. The server node establishes authentication and the integrity of the messages from $Node_1$ and $Node_2$ using the Δ_1, Δ_2, d_1, and d_2. The server then calculates

$$d_3 = H_4(R_1 \oplus R_2 \oplus ID_2 \oplus P_2 \oplus K2_{PUB})$$

$$d_4 = H_4(R_3 \oplus R_4 \oplus ID_1 \oplus P_1 \oplus K1_{PUB})$$

and sends $(ID_2, P_2, K2_{PUB}, d_3)$ to $Node_1$ and $(ID_1, P_1, K1_{PUB}, d_4)$ to $Node_2$.

5. $Node_1$ and $Node_2$ after receiving the message from the server verify the integrity of the message using the hash function and accept the public keys.

After completion of the protocol, the two parties use the Weil pairing with the respective public keys for secure communication. For further details on the secure communication phase, readers are referred to (Chatterjee et al., 2017).

Data Provenance Protocols

Unlike authentication, the amount of work on using hardware security primitives for data provenance in IoT systems is very limited, especially when it comes to protocols that use PUFs.

A protocol for data provenance in body area networks was proposed by (Ali, Sivaraman, Ostry, & Jha, 2013). The proposed protocol uses wireless channel characteristics to generate link fingerprints. Experimental results show that the protocol can be successfully used to produce unique and almost perfectly matching link fingerprints. The proposed protocol exploits the fact that wireless channel characteristics are symmetric for a transmitter and receiver, and highly sensitive to spatial-temporal changes. If, for instance, a user Alice is sending some data to Bob, the protocol works as follows:

1. After sending some data to Bob, Alice sends a hash digest of the data, session identifiers (e.g., counter value, timestamp, and identity, etc.), and an encrypted link fingerprint (using a symmetric key shared with the trusted server) in the form of a bundle to a trusted server. The bundled session record is also digitally signed by Alice using her public key before sending it to the server.
2. After receiving data from Alice, Bob similarly generates a session record as Alice and sends it to the trusted server after digitally signing it.
3. The trusted server can now verify the provenance of the said data using the session records. The server verifies the digital signatures and session identifiers for the data in question. The server then uses the individual symmetric key that it shares with Alice and Bob to decrypt the corresponding link fingerprints. If the link fingerprints are highly correlated, the fact that Alice and Bob communicated the particular data item using the wireless link between them is established and verified.

(Rosenfeld, Gavas & Karri, 2010) proposed the sensor PUF. Unlike normal PUFs, the response of a sensor PUF is based on a challenge as well as a sensed quantity. Thus, a sensor PUF is characterized by a challenge-quantity-response instead of a CRP and provides authentication, un-clonability, and verification of a sensed value. The sensor PUF was proposed to solve the problem of spoofed measurements in which an attacker tampers with the analog signals that go from the sensor element to the embedded microcontroller. Therefore, sensor PUFs can be used to verify the integrity and establish data provenance for a specific sensor.

In another protocol proposed by (Aman et al., 2017), PUFs are used to establish data provenance in IoT systems. The proposed protocol consists of two phases – a setup phase and the data transfer phase. The setup phase of the proposed protocol is shown in Figure 2.

Figure 2 shows that in the setup phase, the IoT device authenticates itself with the server and sends a list of link fingerprints L_i to the server. L_i is generated by inputting the challenge $H(W_i \,||\, N_A)$ for the different possible RSSI values (denoted by W_i) for the wireless link between the IoT device and the server. After successful completion of the setup phase, the two parties can proceed towards the data transfer phase. The data transfer phase is shown in Figure 3.

Figure 2. Setup phase for protocol proposed by (M. N. Aman et al., 2017)

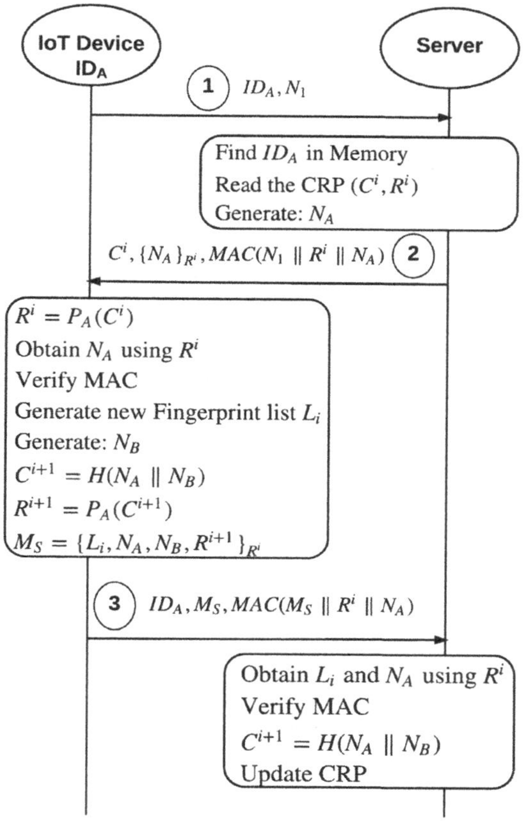

During the data transfer phase, the IoT device generates a link fingerprint F_j and encrypts the data using this fingerprint. The resulting encrypted message is then sent to the server with the corresponding MAC. The link fingerprints used to establish data provenance in this protocol are generated using two separate interfaces: firstly, the wireless link characteristics and secondly the IoT device's PUF. The authors show that the proposed protocol has low computation overhead and is suitable for IoT devices.

Anonymity

IoT applications frequently include the collection of sensitive data from users. Thus, it is essential to protect the identity of IoT devices to preserve user privacy and protect users against illegal profiling. An adversary should not be able to determine the identity of a device, and nor should it be able to trace different devices (Juels,

Figure 3. Data transfer phase for protocol proposed by (M. N. Aman et al., 2017)

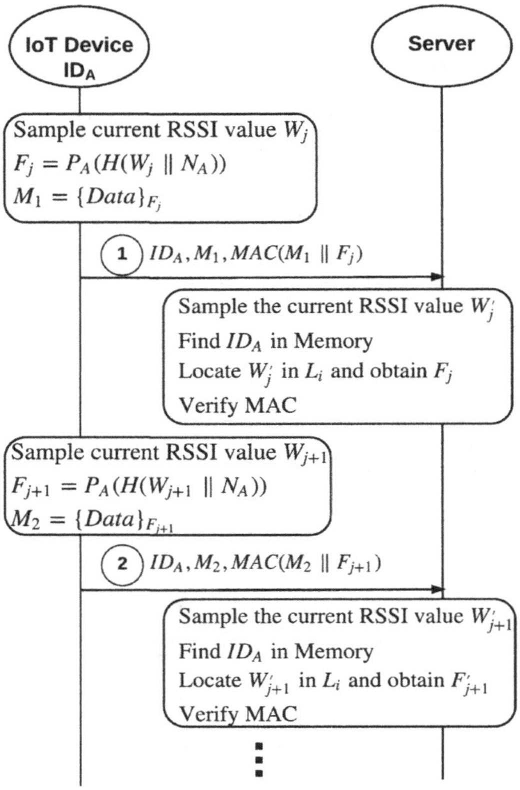

2006). For example, tracking an IoT device may lead to a detailed movement profile, leaking sensitive information such as interest, personal habits, and whereabouts of the user. Most of the work in existing literature for anonymity is related to RFID (radio frequency identification) systems.

The authors of (Sadeghi, Visconti and Wachsmann, 2010) propose a protocol based on PUFs to improve the privacy of existing RFID systems. The proposed protocol does not send the identity of an RFID tag to the reader. Instead, it sends a string using a pseudorandom function with inputs from the tag's PUF and a random nonce. Each RFID tag is equipped with a PUF, and the reader saves the tuple (*ID*, *K*) for each tag, where *ID* is the identity of a tag and *K* is the secret key shared between the tag and the reader. The protocol works as follows:

1. The reader sends a random challenge *a* to the tag.

2. The tag uses a random internal state S as an input to its PUF to get a secret key *K*.
3. The tag generates a random value *b* and uses a pseudorandom function *F* with key *K* to calculate $c = F_K(a, b)$.
4. The tag sends *b* and *c* to the reader.
5. The reader also computes $F_K(a, b)$ for each entry in its database. If a match is found, the reader returns the identity of the tag otherwise, the tag is rejected.

(Jung & Jung, 2013), proposed a protocol for mutual authentication with anonymity using HMAC (hash-based MAC) and PUFs. The security goals of the proposed protocol include protection against tracking ID, cloning attacks, and spoofing attacks. The proposed protocol uses the output of a PUF as the secret key for the HMAC. The authors use a random number generator at the output of the PUF to produce a key longer than the response of the PUF. The protocol steps are as follows:

1. Setup Phase
   a. A back-end server sends a challenge (C_t^0) to a tag *t*.
   b. The tag *t* inputs C_t^0 to its PUF and receives a response (R_t^0). The tag sends R_t^0 back to the server.
   c. The server saves a tuple $\langle ID_t, ID_t \oplus C_t^0, R_t^0 \rangle$ in the database.
2. Authentication Phase
   a. A reader sends its ID (ID_r) to the tag.
   b. The tag sends $ID_t \oplus C_t^0, \alpha = HMAC_{R_t^0}(T_t, ID_t, ID_r), T_t$ to the reader, where T_t is the timestamp of the tag and R_t^0 is a response against C_t^0.
   c. The reader forwards $ID_r, ID_t \oplus C_t^0, \alpha, T_t$ to the back-end server.
   d. The back-end server locates $\langle ID_t, ID_t \oplus C_t^0, R_t^0 \rangle$ in its database using $ID_t \oplus C_t^0$ and computes $\alpha' = HMAC_{R_t^0}(T_t, ID_t, ID_r)$. If α and α' match, the tag is authenticated.

(Aysu et al., 2015) propose an authentication protocol with an end-end design for privacy preservation for constrained devices. The proposed protocol uses a PUF for identification and authentication. The proposed protocol works as follows:

1. Secure Initialization Phase
   a. The server initializes the device with a secret key *sk* and applies a random challenge y_1 to obtain a response z_1.

b. The server saves a tuple $\langle z_1, sk, z_{old}, sk_{old} \rangle$, the server keeps two copies of secret information in its database for resynchronization, where z_{old}, sk_{old} are the credentials used in the previous round of authentication.

c. The device saves *sk* and y_1.

2. Authentication Phase

a. The server sends a random nonce to the device.

b. The device uses its PUF and saved challenge y_1 to produce an output $z_1^{'}$. The device then uses a reverse fuzzy extractor to generate the response r_1, helper data *hd*, and calculates $c = \{hd\}_{sk}$, where *hd* is encrypted using *sk*. The device then generates a new random challenge y_2 and gets a new PUF output $z_2^{'}$. The device then calculates the authentication parameters using a pseudorandom function and encrypts $z_2^{'}$ using these parameters.

c. The device sends the authentication parameters and the encrypted new PUF output to the server along with a MAC for data integrity.

d. The server decrypts *c* to obtain *hd* and the response r_1. The server then uses the same pseudorandom function as the device to obtain the authentication parameters using r_1 and tries to complete the authentication by carrying out an exhaustive search in its database to find a valid index. If the search fails, the server uses the previous PUF outputs (i.e., z_{old}, sk_{old}) to perform the same search. If both searches fail, the authentication request is rejected. Otherwise, the server sends an acknowledgement to the device after updating its database with the new PUF outputs.

e. After receiving the acknowledgment of completion from the server, the device updates its key tuple with new PUF outputs in its non-volatile memory.

SECURITY ANALYSIS AND DISCUSSION

The low-cost and straightforward nature of IoT device exposes them to various security threats. This section discusses why PUFs can be used as a useful tool against various threats.

Physical and Cloning Attacks

An attacker tries to masquerade an authentic IoT device by impersonating another device. There are two ways by which an adversary may succeed in these types of attacks. Firstly, an attacker may extract secrets from a captured device by exposing the device to different types of physical attacks. However, the use of PUFs for managing secrets solves this problem by generating secrets, when needed, instead of saving them in a memory. The second way to clone an IoT device is by creating an exact copy of the device. However, to clone an IoT device equipped with a PUF, an adversary also needs to create a physical clone of the device's PUF. It has been shown that creating a physical clone of a PUF is extremely hard or even impossible. This shows that PUFs are a useful tool for hardware obfuscation and can protect IoT devices against physical and cloning attacks.

Side Channel Attacks

An adversary may gain easy access to IoT devices making them vulnerable to side channel attacks (Delvaux and Verbauwhede, 2013; Mahmoud et al., 2013; Ruhrmair et al., 2014). The most common attacks in the category include the following:

1. **Timing Attacks:** In these types of attacks, an adversary uses statistical analysis of the time delay in performing cryptographic operations by a CPU to extract the secret key. The use of a challenge-*response* mechanism, the fact that accurately measuring the timing delays of an IC may not be feasible, and the isochronous nature of PUFs make them secure against timing attacks.
2. **Power Analysis Attacks:** An adversary monitors the power usage during security operations to extract secrets from a device. It has been shown that by using a data analysis algorithm with the power *side* channel information, the number of zeros and ones stored in an arbiter PUF can be extracted (Mahmoud et al., 2013). However, this attack can be avoided by having an equal number of zeros and ones stored in the latches of an arbiter PUF.
3. **Electromagnetic Attacks:** An adversary monitors the electromagnetic field variations of a circuit to obtain information related to secrets. However, performing an electromagnetic attack is orders of *magnitude* more complex than power monitoring attacks. A PUF can be made secure against these types of attacks by reducing the fluctuations in the current drawn by the circuit.
4. **Differential Fault Analysis:** In these attacks, an adversary produces abnormal environmental conditions to introduce faults into the security hardware. The adversary aims to generate physical data corruption inside the cryptographic hardware which may, in turn, result in leakage of the *internal* state. A fault injection attack on an arbiter PUF is described in (Delvaux and Verbauwhede, 2014). Although the external environment such as variations in temperature and voltage can disturb the output of some PUFs, PUFs do not have any physical data stored inside them and adopting various countermeasures at the device level can help in protecting PUF based protocol from such attacks.

Trust Management

Trust management in IoT systems is a challenging task because of the nature of the IoT devices and the sensitive nature of data related to the human component. To ensure trustworthiness and maintain a chain of trust, it is essential to have a root-of-trust at the hardware level. PUFs can be used to provide a secure and effective root-of-trust at the hardware level. The inherent random variations introduced at the microscopic level by the IC manufacturing/fabrication process (Gassend et al., 2002; Lee et al., 2004; Maes, 2013) make PUFs a unique and promising tool for providing root-of-trust in IoT systems.

Identity Management

The large number of nodes in IoT make the administration of individual identities a challenging and daunting task. Every IoT device should have a unique, easily verifiable and unforgeable identity (Kanuparthi, Karri and Addepalli, 2013). A malicious device may try to fake its identity as that of another authentic device and send malicious commands. For example, in a vehicular network, a malicious node may attempt to propagate false information regarding traffic, speed, and traffic signals, etc. Each PUF produces a unique response to the same challenge which makes it a prime candidate to neutralize the threat of fake identities. Therefore, the IoT device equipped with PUFs can maintain their own unique identity.

Limited Energy and Simple Nature

The resource-constrained nature of IoT devices makes the task of designing security protocols for them even more challenging. Any cryptographic algorithm or security operation carried out by an IoT device needs to be ultra-efficient regarding energy usage. Moreover, the simple IoT devices may not be able to run complex security algorithms. The energy consumption of hardware security primitives is usually lower than security operations implemented in software. Similarly, PUFs consume ultra-low energy making them a suitable choice for IoT systems.

User Convenience

The diverse nature of IoT devices and the disparity in the nature of applications related to IoT necessitates the development of a complete, scalable security architecture. For example, an IoT device or sensor collecting non-critical data such as temperature measurements at home may not require as much security as an IoT device responsible for maintaining a certain temperature or pressure in a nuclear power plant. The level of security may be defined as the effort and time required to break a cryptographic/ security related operation. A tradeoff exists between the convenience provided by any solution and the level of security offered. The security level across different tasks depend on the environment, use case, and application (Embedded Hardware Security for IoT Applications, 2016). For example, a significant fraction of IoT devices may not be able to carry out even a simple cryptographic operation. Therefore, it is essential to find a proper balance between the required security level, cost, and feasibility of implementation.

CONCLUSION

The Internet of Things will be pervasive in our daily lives shortly and will play an essential part in our personal as well as professional spheres. While the IoT promises many benefits, one of the main hurdles in its widespread adoption is the threat of cyber-attacks. The existing work on security protocols is inapplicable to a wide range of IoT devices due to their unique characteristics and hardware limitations, i.e., these protocols focus on network level threats while ignoring hardware level threats. Protection against hardware level threats is crucial to the correct operation of IoT based systems. Consequently, new security protocols that are based on hardware primitives have emerged as an attractive alternative. This chapter introduced security protocols for the IoT that are based on the use of PUFs as hardware-level security primitives. Protocols were presented for authentication, data provenance, and anonymity in IoT. The properties of PUFs that allow them to provide the security objectives of confidentiality, authentication, and integrity, as well as protection against physical, cloning, and side-channel attacks were presented. The security analysis showed that security protocols based on hardware security primitives are not only secure against network level threats but are also resilient against physical and side-channel attacks.

REFERENCES

Ali, S. T., Sivaraman, V., Ostry, D., & Jha, S. (2013). Securing data provenance in body area networks using lightweight wireless link fingerprints. *Proceedings of the 3rd international workshop on Trustworthy embedded devices*. 10.1145/2517300.2517303

Aman, M., Chua, K. C., & Sikdar, B. (2017). Mutual Authentication in IoT Systems using Physical Unclonable Functions. *IEEE Internet of Things Journal*, *4*(5), 1327–1340. doi:10.1109/JIOT.2017.2703088

Aman, M. N., Chua, K. C., & Sikdar, B. (2017). Secure Data Provenance for the Internet of Things. *Proceedings of the 3rd ACM International Workshop on IoT Privacy, Trust, and Security*. 10.1145/3055245.3055255

Aysu, A., Gulcan, E., Moriyama, D., Schaumont, P., & Yung, M. (2015). End-To-End Design of a PUF-Based Privacy Preserving Authentication Protocol. In T. Güneysu & H. Handschuh (Eds.), *Cryptographic Hardware and Embedded Systems -- CHES 2015: 17th International Workshop, Saint-Malo, France, September 13-16, 2015, Proceedings* (pp. 556-576). Berlin: Springer Berlin Heidelberg. 10.1007/978-3-662-48324-4_28

Batina, L., Guajardo, J., Preneel, B., Tuyls, P., & Verbauwhede, I. (2008). Public-Key Cryptography for RFID Tags and Applications. In P. Kitsos & Y. Zhang (Eds.), *RFID Security: Techniques, Protocols and System-on-Chip Design* (pp. 317–348). Boston, MA: Springer US. doi:10.1007/978-0-387-76481-8_13

Bohm, C., & Hofer, M. (2013). *Physical Unclonable Functions in Theory and Practice: Springer*. Chakraborty. doi:10.1007/978-1-4614-5040-5

Chatterjee, U., Chakraborty, R. S., & Mukhopadhyay, D. (2017). A PUF-Based Secure Communication Protocol for IoT. *ACM Transactions on Embedded Computing Systems*, *16*(3), 1–25. doi:10.1145/3005715

Delvaux, J., & Verbauwhede, I. (2013). Side channel modeling attacks on 65nm arbiter PUFs exploiting CMOS device noise. In IEEE International Symposium on Hardware-Oriented Security and Trust. HOST. http://ieeexplore.ieee.org/document/6581579/

Delvaux, J., & Verbauwhede, I. (2014). Fault Injection Modeling Attacks on 65nm Arbiter and RO Sum PUFs via Environmental Changes. *IEEE Transactions on Circuits and Systems*, *61*(6), 13.

Frikken, K. B., Blanton, M., & Atallah, M. J. (2009). Robust Authentication Using Physically Unclonable Functions. *Proceedings of the 12th International Conference on Information Security*.

Gartner. (2015). *Gartner Says 6.4 Billion Connected "Things" Will Be in Use in 2016, Up 30 Percent From 2015* [Press release]. Retrieved from http://www.gartner.com/newsroom/id/3165317

Gassend, B., Clarke, D., Dijk, M. v., & Devadas, S. (2002). Silicon physical random functions. *Proceedings of the 9th ACM conference on Computer and communications security*.

Grau, A. (2015). Can you trust your fridge? *IEEE Spectrum, 52*(3), 7. doi:10.1109/MSPEC.2015.7049440

Greenberg, A. (2015). *Hackers Remotely Kill a Jeep on the Highway—With Me in It.* Retrieved from https://www.wired.com/2015/07/hackers-remotely-kill-jeep-highway/

Hammouri, G., & Sunar, B. (2008). PUF-HB: A Tamper-Resilient HB Based Authentication Protocol. In S. M. Bellovin, R. Gennaro, A. Keromytis, & M. Yung (Eds.), *Applied Cryptography and Network Security: 6th International Conference, ACNS 2008, New York, NY, USA, June 3-6, 2008. Proceedings* (pp. 346-365). Berlin: Springer Berlin Heidelberg. 10.1007/978-3-540-68914-0_21

HP. (2014). *Internet of Things Research Study.* Retrieved from https://www.intel.com/content/www/us/en/internet-of-things/infographics/guide-to-iot.html

IoTSC-16001. (2016). *Embedded Hardware Security for IoT Applications.* Retrieved from https://www.securetechalliance.org/downloads/Embedded-HW-Security-for-IoT-WP-FINAL-December-2016.pdf

Jin, Y., & Makris, Y. (2008). Hardware Trojan detection using path delay fingerprint. *IEEE International Workshop on Hardware-Oriented Security and Trust.*

Juels, A. (2006). RFID security and privacy: A research survey. *IEEE Journal on Selected Areas in Communications, 24*(2), 14. doi:10.1109/JSAC.2005.861395

Jung, S. W., & Jung, S. (2013). *HRP: A HMAC-based RFID mutual authentication protocol using PUF.* Paper presented at the International Conference on Information Networking. Retrieved from http://ieeexplore.ieee.org/document/6496690/

Kanuparthi, A., Karri, R., & Addepalli, S. (2013). Hardware and embedded security in the context of internet of things. *Proceedings of the 2013 ACM workshop on Security, privacy & dependability for cyber vehicles.* 10.1145/2517968.2517976

Lee, J. W., Lim, D., Gassend, B., Suh, G. E., Dijk, M. v., & Devadas, S. (2004). *A Technique to Build a Secret Key in Integrated Circuits for Identification and Authentication Applications.* Academic Press.

Maes, R. (2013). *Physically Unclonable Functions - Constructions, Properties and Roel Maes.* Springer. doi:10.1007/978-3-642-41395-7

Mahmoud, A., Rührmair, U., Majzoobi, M., & Koushanfar, F. (2013). Combined Modeling and Side Channel Attacks on Strong PUFs. *IACR Cryptology ePrint Archive, 2013*, 632.

Moyer, J. W. (2015). Hacker Chris Roberts told FBI he took control of United plane, FBI claims. *Washington Post*. Retrieved from https://www.washingtonpost.com/news/morning-mix/wp/2015/05/18/hacker-chris-roberts-told-fbi-he-took-control-of-united-plane-fbi-claims/

Narasimhan, S., & Bhunia, S. (2009). Hardware Trojan: Threats and emerging solutions. *IEEE High Level Design Validation and Test Workshop*.

Pappu, R., Recht, B., Taylor, J., & Gershenfeld, N. (2002). Physical one-way functions. *Science*, *297*(5589), 2026–2030. doi:10.1126cience.1074376 PMID:12242435

Rosenfeld, K., Gavas, E., & Karri, R. (2010). Sensor physical unclonable functions. IEEE International Symposium on Hardware-Oriented Security and Trust. HOST. http://ieeexplore.ieee.org/document/5513103/

Ruhrmair, U., Xu, X., Solter, J., Mahmoud, A., Majzoobi, M., Koushanfar, F., & Burleson, W. (2014). Efficient Power and Timing Side Channels for Physical Unclonable Functions. *Proceedings of the 16th International Workshop on Cryptographic Hardware and Embedded Systems, 8731*. 10.1007/978-3-662-44709-3_26

Sadeghi, A.-R., Visconti, I., & Wachsmann, C. (2010). Enhancing RFID Security and Privacy by Physically Unclonable Functions. In A.-R. Sadeghi & D. Naccache (Eds.), *Towards Hardware-Intrinsic Security: Foundations and Practice* (pp. 281–305). Berlin: Springer Berlin Heidelberg. doi:10.1007/978-3-642-14452-3_13

Suh, G. E., & Devadas, S. (2007). *Pysical Unclonable Functions for Device Authentication and Secret Key Generation.* Paper presented at the IEEE/ACM DAC.

Tehranipoor, M., Salmani, H., Zhang, Z., Wang, M., Karri, R., Rajendran, J., & Rosenfeld, K. (2011). Trustworthy Hardware: Trojan Detection and Design-for-Trust Challenges. *IEEE Computer*, *44*(7), 9. doi:10.1109/MC.2010.369

Tuyls, P., & Batina, L. (2006). RFID-Tags for Anti-counterfeiting. In D. Pointcheval (Ed.), *Topics in Cryptology – CT-RSA 2006: The Cryptographers' Track at the RSA Conference 2006, San Jose, CA, USA, February 13-17, 2005. Proceedings* (pp. 115-131). Berlin: Springer Berlin Heidelberg.

Wang, X., Salmani, H., Tehranipoor, M., & Plusquellic, J. (2008). *Hardware Trojan Detection and Isolation Using Current Integration and Localized Current Analysis - IEEE Conference Publication.* Paper presented at the IEEE International Symposium on Defect and Fault Tolerance of VLSI Systems.

Xie, L., Wang, W., Shi, X., & Qin, T. (2017). *Lightweight mutual authentication among sensors in body area networks through Physical Unclonable Functions.* Paper presented at the 2017 IEEE International Conference on Communications (ICC), Paris, France. 10.1109/ICC.2017.7996735

Zetter, K. (2015). *A Cyberattack Has Caused Confirmed Physical Damage for the Second Time Ever.* Retrieved from https://www.wired.com/2015/01/german-steel-mill-hack-destruction/

Zetter, K. (2016). *Everything We Know About Ukraine's Power Plant Hack.* Retrieved from https://www.wired.com/2016/01/everything-we-know-about-ukraines-power-plant-hack/

Chapter 6
Secure Computation of Private Set Intersection Cardinality With Linear Complexity

Sumit Kumar Debnath
National Institute of Technology Jamshedpur, India

ABSTRACT

PSI and its variants play a major role when the participants want to perform secret operations on their private data sets. The importance of this chapter is twofold. In the first phase, the author presents a size-hiding PSI-CA protocol followed by its authorized variant, APSI-CA, utilizing Bloom filter. All these constructions are proven to be secure in standard model with linear complexity. In the second phase, the author employs Bloom filter to design an efficient mPSI-CA protocol. It achieves fairness using offline semi-trusted third party (arbiter) unlike the most efficient existing protocols. The arbiter is semi-trusted in the sense that he does not have access to the private information of the entities while he will follow the protocol honestly. Proposed mPSI-CA is proven to be secure against malicious adversaries in the random oracle model (ROM) under the decisional Diffie-Hellman (DDH) assumption. It achieves linear complexity.

INTRODUCTION

At present, sharing of electronic information among mutually unreliable entities increases rapidly. Consequently, there is a strong need of cryptographically secure techniques, that allows sharing of electronic information. Private Set Intersection (PSI) is one such technique that allows two parties to secretly determine the

DOI: 10.4018/978-1-5225-5742-5.ch006

intersection of their respective private sets without revealing any additional information. Depending on the functionality, PSI is of two kinds: (i) one-way PSI which enables either of the two parties to receive the output (intersection), while the other does not get any information and (ii) two-way PSI or mutual PSI (mPSI), whereby both the parties receive the intersection. In DNA matching, two entities may wish to determine private computation of Hamming Distance between two strings on an arbitrarily large alphabet by considering each symbol in the alphabet along with its position in the string as a unique set element. Private Set Intersection Cardinality (PSI-CA) is an appropriate cryptographic technique for this kind of real-life scenarios as it allows the entities to execute the cardinality, instead of any content of the intersection. Similar to PSI, PSI-CA is of two kinds: one-way PSI-CA and two-way PSI-CA or mutual PSI-CA (mPSI-CA). Another variant of PSI or PSI-CA, where the client's set needs to be authorized by a certifying authority before the communications between client and server, is known as Authorized PSI (APSI) or Authorized PSI-CA (APSI-CA). In the recent research community, PSI and its variants have gained considerable attention due to their broad applications. Privacy preserving data mining, location-based services, social networks, testing of fully sequenced human genomes, are a few to name. Let us consider some real-life scenarios where private data needs to be shared:

1. Program chairs of a conference want to make sure that none of the submitted manuscripts are also under review in any other journal or conference, while they have to preserve the privacy of the contents of the submitted manuscript.
2. A social network user, say Bob would like to discover a nearby match from a group of users by determining the number of standard connections.
3. Two NGOs may wish to determine the total number of ordinary villagers, affected by a disease in a village. While none of them are allowed to reveal their list of suspects as revealing that list may create an impact on a patient's mind.

In any real-life application of PSI-CA or its variants, the user's privacy can be preserved using the Internet of things (IoT). For instance, in the case of the aforementioned social networking example, Bob cannot reveal its privacy as that may cause a threat to him. Thus, user's privacy needs to be preserved in PSI-CA and its variants, and in order to do that IoT is required.

Results

In this chapter, the author is mainly interested to design PSI-CA, APSI-CA and $mPSI$ -CA protocols utilizing the Bloom filter. The importance of the work is twofold. In the first phase, the author constructs PSI-CA and APSI-CA protocols. These are secure in the standard model. Both of them achieve linear complexity overheads and independency of the client's set's size. Based on the literature, there is no classical PSI-CA and no APSI-CA with the aforementioned characteristics. The proposed PSI-CA achieves security in the semi-honest environment, whilst the APSI-CA achieves security against the semi-honest server and malicious client. The underlying assumption for both the constructions is the Quadratic Residuosity (QR) assumption. The client is not required to disclose its private set's size to the server, rather only an upper bound is revealed. In other words, these schemes are independent of the client's set's size. In APSI-CA, the client's set needs to be authorized by a certifying authority who is assumed to be trusted. This authorization is required in order to prevent a malicious client from submitting an arbitrary set to the protocol execution to steal server's element. Till date, the most efficient classical (A)PSI-CA constructions are the (A)PSI-CA of (De Cristofaro et al., 2012). However, these schemes achieve security in the random oracle model (ROM) under the non-standard cryptographic assumption. While, the proposed designs achieve security without random oracles under QR assumption. ROM is an oracle (a theoretical black box) that responds to every query with a (truly) random response chosen uniformly from its output domain, except that for any specific query, it responds the same way every time it receives that query. The author emphasizes that the proposed PSI-CA requires only $O\left(v+w\right)$ modular multiplications as opposed to the PSI-CA of (De Cristofaro et al., 2012) that requires $O\left(v+w\right)$ modular exponentiations. In addition to $O\left(v+w\right)$ modular multiplications, proposed APSI-CA requires $O\left(w\right)$ many signature verifications. Efficient PSI constructions of Dong et al. (2013a) and Pinkas et al. (2014) are based on the garbled Bloom filter GBF. However, it seems to be non-trivial to extend these PSI to PSI-CA. The PSI-CA of (Shi et al., 2016) is based on quantum computation and it is more efficient than proposed PSI-CA in terms of communication overhead. The comparative summary of proposed PSI-CA and APSI-CA over prior works are given in Tables 1 and 2.

In the second phase, the author's goal is to construct fair and efficient $mPSI$ -CA protocol utilizing Bloom filter as its building blocks. In order to build the $mPSI$ -CA, the author integrates Cramer-Shoup cryptosystem (Cramer & Shoup, 1998), distributed ElGamal encryption (Brandt, 2006), and blends zero-knowledge argument for shuffle along with zero-knowledge proofs for discrete logarithm. Security of the scheme is to be proven in the ROM (Bellare & Rogaway. 1993) in the malicious environment under the DDH assumption. It attains linear complexity overheads. Fairness is an important feature of $mPSI$ -CA as it ensures that either both the parties will receive the output (intersection) or neither of them. The author emphasizes that fairness is achieved in a proposed scheme in an optimistic way i.e., by involving

Table 1. Comparative summary of classical PSI-CA protocols

Protocol	Security Model	Adversary Model	Security Assumption	Communication Cost	Computational Cost	Size Hiding	Based on
[Sch. 1] (De Cristofaro et al., 2102)	ROM	SH	DDH and GOMDH	$O(w+v)$	$O(w+v)$	No	DLP
[Sch. 2] (De Cristofaro et al., 2012)	ROM	MS, SHC	GOMDH	$O(w+v)$	$O(w+v)$	No	DLP
(Freedman et al., 2016)	Std	SH	DDH	$O(w+v)$	$O(w+v)$	No	*OPE*
Proposed	Std	SH	QR	$O(w+v)$	$O(w+v)$	Yes	*BF*

ROM= Random Oracle Model, SH=Semi-honest, DDH=Decisional Diffie-Hellman, GOMDH=Gap-One-More-Diffie-Hellman, DLP= Discrete Logarithm Problem, MS=Malicious Server, SHC=Semi-honest Client, Std=Standard, OPE=Oblivious Polynomial Evaluation, QR= Quadratic Residuosity, BF= Bloom Filter, $v =$

Table 2. Comparative summary of APSI-CA protocols

Protocol	Security Model	Adversary Model	Security Assumption	Communication Cost	Computational Cost	Size Hiding	Based on
(Camenisch & Zaverucha, 2009)	Std	Mal	Strong RSA	$O(wv)$	$O(wv)$	No	OPE
(De Cristofaro et al., 2012)	ROM	SH	GOMDH	$O(w+v)$	$O(w+v)$	No	DLP
Proposed	Std	MC, SHS	QR	$O(w+v)$	$O(w+v)$	Yes	*BF*

Std=Standard, Mal=Malicious, OPE=Oblivious Polynomial Evaluation, ROM= Random Oracle Model, SH=Semi-honest, GOMDH=Gap-One-More-Diffie-Hellman, DLP= Discrete Logarithm Problem, MC= Malicious Client, SHS=Semi-honest Server, QR= Quadratic Residuosity, BF= Bloom Filter, $v = Size\, of\, Server's\, set, w =$ Size of Client's set,

Size of Server's set, $w =$ Size of Client's set.

an off-line third party, called arbiter. The arbiter is assumed to be semi-trusted in the sense that it has to follow the protocol honestly, although it cannot get access to the secret information of the entities. Till now, there is only one fair $mPSI$ -CA (Debnath and Dutta 2016) with linear complexity over prime order group. When the participants behave maliciously, their scheme does not remain secure. Moreover, the $mPSI$ -CA of (Debnath and Dutta 2016) requires 5 rounds whilst the proposed protocol requires only 4 rounds. Apart from Debnath and Dutta (2016), there are two more existing $mPSI$ -CAs of (Camenisch & Zaverucha, 2009) and (Kissner & D. Song, 2005). Underlying group for both the constructions is of composite order.

Their schemes attain quadratic computation complexity. The scheme of (Kissner & D. Song, 2005) has not considered fairness. The authors of (Camenisch & Zaverucha, 2009) pointed out that their scheme can be modified to achieve fairness using a trusted third party who certifies the input sets. However, they have not provided any such construction. Moreover, in real life applications, if the input sets are not certified by a trusted authority, then their approach towards achieving fairness does not work. The comparison of proposed $mPSI$ -CA from prior works is summarized in Table 3.

BACKGROUND

In the rest of the chapter, κ will be used to denote "security parameter", $a \leftarrow A$ will stand for "a is the output of the procedure A", and $x \in_R X$ will denote "variable x is chosen uniformly at random from set X". Negligible function $\varepsilon(\kappa)$ of κ is a function $\varepsilon : \mathbb{N} \rightarrow \mathbb{R}$ such that $\varepsilon(\kappa) = o(\kappa^{-c})$, for each constant $c > 0$ and for all sufficiently large κ.

- **Definition 2.1 Functionality:** *Let protocol* Π *be executed between two parties* A *with input* X_A *and* B *with input* X_B. *Then the functionality of* Π *is denoted by* $\mathcal{F}_\Pi$ *and defined as* $\mathcal{F}_\Pi : X_A \times X_B \rightarrow Y_A \times Y_B$, *where* Y_A *and* Y_B *represent respectively the outputs of* A *and* B.

Table 3. Comparative summary of $mPSI$ *-CA protocols*

$mPSI$ -CA Protocol	Adversary Model	Security Assumption	Communication Cost	Computational Cost	Fairness	Optimistic	Group Order	Arbiter
(Camenisch & Zaverucha, 2009)	Mal	AHE	$O(v)$	$O(v^2)$	No	No	Composite	No
(Camenisch & Zaverucha, 2009)	Mal	Strong RSA	$O(w+v)$	$O(wv)$	Yes	Yes	Composite	FT
(Debnath & Dutta, 2016)	SH	DDH	$O(w+v)$	$O(w+v)$	Yes	Yes	Prime	ST
Proposed	Mal	DDH	$O(w+v)$	$O(w+v)$	Yes	Yes	Prime	ST

Mal=Malicious, AHE=Additively Homomorphic Encryption, FT=Fully Trusted, SH=Semi-honest, DDH=Decisional Diffie-Hellman, ST= Semi-Trusted, v, w are the sizes of input sets.

- **Definition 2.2 Probabilistic Polynomial Time (PPT) Algorithm:** *It is an algorithm that runs in polynomial time and may use (true) randomness to produce (possibly) non-deterministic results.*
- **Definition 2.3 Quadratic Residuosity (QR) Assumption** (Goldwasser & Micali, 1984)**:** *Let the algorithm $\mathcal{R}Gen$ generates an RSA modulus n on input 1^{κ}, where $n = PQ$ and P, Q are distinct primes. Also let, X be the subgroup of $\mathbb{Z}_n^*$ containing the elements with Jacobi symbol equal to 1. The QR assumption states that, given an RSA modulus n (without its factorization), it is hard to distinguish a random element u of $X \subseteq \mathbb{Z}_n^*$ from an element of the subgroup $\{x^2 \mid x \in \mathbb{Z}_n^*\}$ i.e., there is no PPT algorithm $\mathcal{A}$ such that $\left|Prob\left[\mathcal{A}\left(n, x^2\right) = 1\right] - Prob\left[\mathcal{A}\left(n, u\right) = 1\right]\right|$ is a non-negligible function of κ.*
- **Definition 2.4 Decisional Diffie-Hellman (DDH) Assumption** (Boneh 1998)**:** *On the input 1^{κ}, l et the algorithm $gGen$ generates a modulus n and a generator g of a multiplicative group $\mathbb{G}$ of order n. Also, let $a, b, c \in_R \mathbb{Z}_n$. The DDH assumption states that it is hard to distinguish the distribution $\langle g^a, g^b, g^{ab}\rangle$ from $\langle g^a, g^b, g^c\rangle$ i.e., there is no PPT algorithm $\mathcal{A}$ such that $\mathcal{A}\left|Prob\left[\mathcal{A}\left(g, g^a, g^b, g^{ab}\right) = 1\right] - Prob\left[\mathcal{A}\left(g, g^a, g^b, g^c\right) = 1\right]\right|$ is non-negligible function of κ.*

Security Model for Semi-Honest Adversary (Goldreich, 2009)

A two-party protocol, Π is a random process that computes a function f from a pair of inputs (one per party) to another pair of outputs i.e., $f = \left(f_1, f_2\right) : \{0,1\}^* \times \{0,1\}^* \rightarrow \{0,1\}^* \times \{0,1\}^*$.

Let $x, y \in \{0,1\}^*$ be the inputs of parties P_1, P_2 respectively. Then the outputs of the parties P_1, P_2 are $f_1\left(x, y\right), f_2\left(x, y\right)$ respectively. A protocol Π is said to be secure in the semi-honest model if whatever can be computed by a party after participating in the protocol, it could be obtained from its input and output only. This is formalized using the simulation paradigm. On the input pair $\left(x, y\right)$, view of theparty P_i duringanexecutionof Π isdenotedby $View_i^{\Pi}\left(x, y\right) = \left(w, r^{(i)}, m_1^{(i)}, \ldots, m_t^{(i)}\right)$, where $w \in \left\{x, y\right\}$ represents the input of the party P_i, $r^{(i)}$ is the outcome of P_i's internal coin tosses, and $m_j^{(i)}$ $\left(j = 1, 2, \ldots, t\right)$ represents the j-th message which has been received by P_i during the execution of Π.

- **Definition 2.5:** *Let* $f = (f_1, f_2)$ *be a deterministic function. Then the protocol* Π *securely computes* f *if there exists PPT adversaries, denoted by* S_1 *and* S_2*, controlling* P_1 *and* P_2 *respectively, such that:* S_1*'s view* $\{S_1(x, f_1(x,y))\}_{x,y\in\{0,1\}^*}$ *(given input* x*, output* $f_1(x,y)$*) is indistinguishable from* P_1*'s view* $View_1^{\Pi}(x,y)_{x,y\in\{0,1\}^*}$ *and* S_2*'s view* $\{S_2(y, f_2(x,y))\}_{x,y\in\{0,1\}^*}$ *(given input* y*, output* $f_2(x,y)$*) is indistinguishable from* P_2*'s view* $View_2^{\Pi}(x,y)_{x,y\in\{0,1\}^*}$.

Security Model for *mPSI*-CA (Goldreich, 2009)

The security framework of mPSI-CA is formally described below (Dong et al. 2013a):

- **The real world:** The protocol is mainly executed between two parties A with private input set X and B with private input set Y. It involves another semi-trusted third party, called arbiter Ar with input $\in \{\circ, \perp\}$, where $\perp$ stands for "nothing". Let C be the real world adversary who can corrupt upto two parties in the protocol and can behave arbitrarily. Denote the joint output of A, B, Ar, C in the real world as $REAL_{mPSI-CA,C}(X,Y)$, where an honest party's output is that whatever prescribed in the protocol, a corrupted party's output is nothing, and an adversary's output is its view consisting of the transcripts available to it.
- **The ideal process:** Let the parties $\bar{A}$ with input X, $\bar{B}$ with input Y and $\bar{A}r$ with input $\in \{\circ, \perp\}$ be involved in the ideal process. Also, let T be an incorruptible trusted party who can compute the ideal functionality $\mathcal{F}_{mPSI-CA}$. Then the interaction is as follows:
    - $\bar{A}$ and $\bar{B}$ send respectively $\bar{X}$ and $\bar{Y}$ to T, following it $\bar{A}r$ sends b_A, b_B to T, where $b_A \in (\{\circ, \perp\} \cup X_A)$, $b_B \in (\{\circ, \perp\} \cup Y_B)$ with $X_A = Y_B = \mathbb{N} \cup \{0\}$, set of non-negative integers. Note that if the party behaves maliciously, then $\bar{X}$ and $\bar{Y}$ may be different from X and Y respectively.
    - The response of T to $\bar{A}$(*resp.* $\bar{B}$) depends on b_A(*resp.* b_B) which is given below:
        - If $\bar{X} \neq \perp$, $\bar{Y} \neq \perp$, and b_A(*resp.* b_B) $= \circ$, then T sends $|\bar{X} \cap \bar{Y}|$ to $\bar{A}$(*resp.* $\bar{B}$).

- If $\bar{X} = \perp$ or $\bar{Y} = \perp$, and $b_A\left(resp.\ b_B\right) = \circ$, then T sends $\perp$ to $\bar{A}\left(resp.\ \bar{B}\right)$.
- If $b_A\left(resp.\ b_B\right) \neq \circ$, then T sends $b_A\left(resp.\ b_B\right)$ to $\bar{A}\left(resp.\ \bar{B}\right)$.

On the other hand, if $\bar{A}$, $\bar{B}$ and $\bar{A}r$ are honest then $\bar{A}$ and $\bar{B}$ send their inputs to T and $\bar{A}r$ sends $b_A = \circ$ and $b_B = \circ$ to T. The ideal process simulator $\mathcal{SIM}$ receives the inputs of the corrupted parties and gets T's response to corrupted parties. Denote the joint output of $\bar{A}, \bar{B}, \bar{A}r, \mathcal{SIM}$ in the ideal process by $IDEAL_{\mathcal{F}_{mPSI-CA}, \mathcal{SIM}}\left(X, Y\right)$. The security definition in terms of simulatability is:

- **Definition 2.6 Simulatability:** *Denote the functionality for $mPSI - CA$ protocol as $\mathcal{F}_{mPSI-CA} : \left(\left(X, \left|Y\right|\right), \left(Y, \left|X\right|\right)\right) \to \left(\left|X \cap Y\right|, \left|X \cap Y\right|\right)$. The protocol $mPSI$ -CA securely computes $\mathcal{F}_{mPSI-CA}$ in the malicious model, if for every real world adversary $\mathcal{C}$, there exists an ideal world adversary $\mathcal{SIM}$ such that the joint distribution of all outputs of the ideal world is computationally indistinguishable from the outputs in the real world, i.e., $IDEAL_{\mathcal{F}_{mPSI-CA}, \mathcal{SIM}}\left(X, Y\right) \equiv^c REAL_{mPSI-CA, \mathcal{C}}\left(X, Y\right)$.*

Goldwasser-Micali Encryption (Goldwasser & Micali, 1984)

The Goldwasser-Micali (GM) encryption $\mathcal{GM} = \left(\mathcal{GM}.KGen, \mathcal{GM}.Enc, \mathcal{GM}.Dec\right)$ works as follows:

$\mathcal{GM}$**.KGen**$\left(1^{\kappa}\right) \to \left(\boldsymbol{pk}, \boldsymbol{sk}\right)$**.** This algorithm takes as input 1^{κ} and outputs secret key as $sk = \left(P, Q\right)$, public key as $pk = \left(n, u\right)$, where $n = PQ$ is an RSA modulus, P, Q are distinct primes, u is a pseudo quadratic residue i.e., $L\left(\frac{u}{P}\right) = -1$ and $L\left(\frac{u}{Q}\right) = -1$ but $J\left(\frac{u}{n}\right) = 1$, where L and J denote respectively the Legendre symbol and Jacobi symbol.

$\mathcal{GM}$**.Enc**$\left(\boldsymbol{m}, \boldsymbol{pk}\right) \to \mathbf{c}$**.** Given a message $m \in \left\{0, 1\right\}$, encryptor picks $r \in_R \mathbb{Z}_n$ and outputs the ciphertext c as:

$$c = Enc_{pk}\left(x\right) = \begin{cases} r^2 \ mod\ n\ if \ \ m = 0 \\ ur^2\ mod\ n\ if\ \ m = 1 \end{cases}$$

$\mathcal{GM}$.**Dec**$(\boldsymbol{c}, \boldsymbol{sk}) \to \mathbf{m}$. Given a ciphertext c, decryptor computes $L\left(\frac{c}{P}\right)$ and outputs the message m as 0 if $L\left(\frac{c}{P}\right) = 1$. Otherwise, it outputs the message m as 1.

This encryption scheme is semantically secure under the hardness of QR assumption. It satisfies homomorphic property under the binary operations, exclusive-or $\oplus$ on the message space and modulo multiplication on the ciphertext space, i.e., $Enc_{pk}(x \oplus y) = Enc_{pk}(x) \cdot Enc_{pk}(y)$.

Distributed ElGamal Encryption (Brandt, 2006)

The distributed ElGamal encryption scheme $\mathcal{DEL}$ consists of four algorithms ($\mathcal{DEL}.Setup$, $\mathcal{DEL}.KGen$, $\mathcal{DEL}.Enc$, $\mathcal{DEL}.Dec$) and works as follows between two parties P_1 and P_2:

$\mathcal{EL}$.**Setup**$(1^{\kappa}) \to (\boldsymbol{par})$. This algorithm takes as input 1^{κ} and generates public parameter $par = (p, q, g)$, where p, q are primes with the property that q divides $p - 1$ and g is a generator of the unique cyclic subgroup $\mathbb{G}$ of $\mathbb{Z}_p^*$ of order q.

$\mathcal{DEL}$.**KGen**$(\boldsymbol{par}) \to (\boldsymbol{pk}, \boldsymbol{sk})$. For $i = 1, 2$, P_i chooses $a_i \in_R \mathbb{Z}_q$, makes $y_{P_i} = g^{a_i}$ public. Then the public key for the $\mathcal{DEL}$ is $pk = h = g^{a_1 + a_2}$. Note that $sk = a_1 + a_2$ is not known to anyone.

$\mathcal{DEL}$.**Enc**$(\boldsymbol{m}, \boldsymbol{pk}, \boldsymbol{par}, \boldsymbol{r}) \to (\boldsymbol{dE}_{\boldsymbol{pk}}(\boldsymbol{m}))$. Given a message $m \in \mathbb{G}$, encryptor computes the ciphertext as $dE_{pk}(m) = (\alpha, \beta) = (g^r, mh^r)$, where $r \in_R \mathbb{Z}_q$.

$\mathcal{DEL}$.**Dec**$(\boldsymbol{dE}_{\boldsymbol{pk}}(\boldsymbol{m}), \boldsymbol{a}_1, \boldsymbol{a}_2) \to (\boldsymbol{m} \vee \perp)$. Given $dE_{pk}(m) = (\alpha, \beta) = (g^r, mh^r)$, each of P_i makes $\alpha_i = \alpha^{a_i}$ public and proves the correctness of the proof $PoK\{a_i \mid y_{P_i} = g^{a_i} \wedge \alpha_i = \alpha^{a_i}\}$ to P_j, for $i, j \in \{1, 2\}$ and $i \neq j$. If both the proofs are valid, then each of P_1, P_2 can recover the message m by computing $\frac{\beta}{\alpha_1 \alpha_2} = \frac{\beta}{(\alpha)^{(a_1 + a_2)}} = \frac{mh^r}{g^{r(a_1 + a_2)}} = \frac{mh^r}{h^r} = m$; otherwise they output $\perp$.

The encryption scheme is *multiplicatively* homomorphic and semantically secure under the hardness of DDH assumption.

Verifiable Encryption (Camenisch & Shoup, 2003)

The verifiable encryption scheme $\mathcal{VE} = (\mathcal{VE}.Setup, \mathcal{VE}.KGen, \mathcal{VE}.Enc, \mathcal{VE}.Dec)$ works as follows:

$\boldsymbol{\mathcal{VE}.Setup}\left(1^{\kappa}\right) \to \left(\boldsymbol{ppar}\right)$. This algorithm takes as input 1^{κ} and outputs public parameter $ppar = \left(par, \hat{g}, \mathcal{H}\right)$, where $par = \left(p, q, g\right)$, p, q are primes with the property that q divides $p-1$ and $g, \hat{g}$ are generators of the unique cyclic subgroup $\mathbb{G}$ of $\mathbb{Z}_p^*$ of order q, $\mathcal{H} : \{0,1\}^* \to \mathbb{Z}_q$ is a cryptographically secure one-way hash function.

$\boldsymbol{\mathcal{VE}.KGen}\left(\boldsymbol{par}, \hat{\boldsymbol{g}}, \boldsymbol{U}\right) \to \left(\boldsymbol{vpk}_U, \boldsymbol{vsk}_U\right)$. A user U selects $u_1, u_2, v_1, v_2, w_1 \in_R \mathbb{Z}_q$, makes $vpk_U = \left(a, b, c\right)$ public after computing $a = g^{u_1}\hat{g}^{u_2}, b = g^{v_1}\hat{g}^{v_2}$, $c = g^{w_1}$ and keeps $vsk_U = \left(u_1, u_2, v_1, v_2, w_1\right)$ secret to the user itself.

$\boldsymbol{\mathcal{VE}.Enc}\left(\boldsymbol{m}, \boldsymbol{vpk}_U, \boldsymbol{ppar}, \boldsymbol{z}, \boldsymbol{L}, \boldsymbol{\mathcal{H}}\right) \to \left(\boldsymbol{vE}_{\boldsymbol{vpk}_U}\left(\boldsymbol{m}\right)\right)$. Given a message $m \in \mathbb{G}$, encryptor picks $z \in_R \mathbb{Z}_q$, computes $e_1 = g^z, e_2 = \hat{g}^z, e_3 = c^z m$, $e_4 = a^z b^{z\rho}$, where $\rho = \mathcal{H}\left(e_1, e_2, e_3, L\right)$ and $L \in \{0,1\}^*$ is a label which is computed using some information that are available to both encryptor and decryptor. Finally outputs the ciphertext $vE_{vpk_U}\left(m\right) = \left(e_1, e_2, e_3, e_4\right)$.

$\boldsymbol{\mathcal{VE}.Dec}\left(\boldsymbol{vE}_{\boldsymbol{vpk}_U}\left(\boldsymbol{m}\right), \boldsymbol{vsk}_U, \boldsymbol{L}, \boldsymbol{\mathcal{H}}\right) \to \left(\boldsymbol{m} \vee \perp\right)$. Given ciphertext $vE_{vpk_U}\left(m\right) = \left(e_1, e_2, e_3, e_4\right)$, decryptor U generates $\rho = \mathcal{H}\left(e_1, e_2, e_3, L\right)$ and then verifies the relation $e_1^{u_1} e_2^{u_2} (e_1^{v_1} e_2^{v_2})^{\rho} = e_4$ utilizing secret key $vsk_U = \left(u_1, u_2, v_1, v_2, w_1\right)$. If the verification succeeds, then it computes $e_3 / (e_1)^{w_1} = c^z m / g^{zw_1} = g^{zw_1} m / g^{zw_1} = m$ in order to recover the message m; otherwise outputs $\perp$.

The encryption scheme is CCA2-secure, and it is a variant of Cramer-Shoup cryptosystem (Cramer and Shoup, 1998) over prime order group (Dong et al., 2013a).

Bloom Filter (Bloom, 1970)

Bloom filter (BF) is a space efficient data structure. It is used to represent a set X by an array of size m. In order to insert or check the presence of an element into BF, k independent hash functions $H = \left\{h_1, \ldots, h_k\right\}$ with $h_i : \{0,1\}^* \to \left\{1, \ldots, m\right\}$ for $i = 1, \ldots, k$ are required. Bloom filter of X is denoted by $BF_X \in \{0,1\}^m$ and

$BF_X[i]$ is used to represent the i-th entry in BF_X. A variant of Bloom filter (Bloom, 1970) performs the following three operations- Initialization, Add and Check.

- **Initialization:** Set 1 to all the entries of an array of size m. This is said to be empty Bloom filter.
- ***Add(x)*:** Compute $h_1(x),\ldots,h_k(x)$ and set 0 to the indices $h_1(x),\ldots,\ h_k(x)$ of the Bloom filter. In this way, all the elements $x \in X$ can be added to the Bloom to get $BF_X \in \{0,1\}^m$.
- **Check(*y*):** To check the presence of y in X, one has to compute $h_1(\mathrm{y}),\ldots,h_k(\mathrm{y})$. Now, if at least one of $BF_X[h_1(\mathrm{y})],\ \ldots,BF_X[h_k(\mathrm{y})]$ is 1 then y is not in X, otherwise y is *probably* in X.

Bloom filter attains false positive, i.e.; an element can mistakenly pass the check step even though it was not inserted in the Bloom filter. However, it never allows false negative since an element that has been inserted in the filter will always pass the check test.

- **Theorem 2.7** (Dong et al., 2013b) *If the desired maximum false positive rate of a Bloom filter with* v *elements is* $\frac{1}{2^k}$, *then the optimal size* m *of the Bloom filter is* $m = \frac{vk}{ln2}$.

Zero-Knowledge Proof of Knowledge (Bellare & Goldreich, 1993)

Zero-Knowledge proof is a two-party protocol, where one party (prover) wants to convince the other (verifier) about the truth of some claim, and the verifier wants to check that the claim is valid. The prover can prove to the verifier that the claim is true without conveying any additional information apart from the fact that the claim is indeed valid. It satisfies the following three properties:

- **Completeness:** An honest prover can always convenience a verifier that he knows the secret.
- **Soundness:** A dishonest prover, who does not know the secret, can construct the correct proof with negligible probability.
- **Zero-knowledge:** A dishonest verifier cannot get any useful information about the secret of the prover.

Zero-Knowledge Proof for Discrete Logarithm

The notations introduced by Camenisch and Zaverucha (2009) are to be used. General construction of zero-knowledge proof for discrete logarithm is denoted by

$$PoK\{(\theta_1,\ldots,\theta_t) \mid \bigwedge_{i=1}^{\eta} X_i = f_i(\theta_1,\ldots,\theta_t)\}, \tag{2.1}$$

where the prover P wants to prove the knowledge of $(\theta_1,\ldots,\theta_t)$ to the verifier V by sending the commitments of $X_i = f_i(\theta_1,\ldots,\theta_t), i = 1,\ldots,\eta$. See Dong et al. (2013) for the verification process.

Zero-Knowledge Argument for Shuffle (Furukawa, 2005)

The zero-knowledge argument for the shuffle of Furukawa (2005) is used in the construction of proposed $mPSI$ -CA. A general construction of the zero-knowledge argument for shuffle for the distributed ElGamal encryption $\mathcal{DEL}$ presented in the above section, is denoted by

$$PoK\{(\phi \in £_v, \rho_1,\ldots,\rho_v \in \mathbb{Z}_q) \mid \left\{C_i' = C_{\phi^{-1}(i)} \mathcal{DEL}.Enc(g^0, pk, par, \rho_i)\}_{i=1}^{v}\right\}, \tag{2.2}$$

where ciphertexts $\{C_i = (g_i, m_i)\}_{i=1}^{v}$ are shuffled to $\{C_i' = (g_i', m_i')\}_{i=1}^{v}$ using the permutation ϕ. See Debnath and Dutta (2016) for verification process.

RELATED WORKS

One-Way PSI-CA

The first PSI-CA dates back to the work of Agrawal et al. (Agrawal et al. 2003). Security of this scheme is in the semi-honest environment under the Decisional Diffie-Hellman (DDH) assumption. The work of Hohenberger and Weis (2006) constructed an efficient PSI-CA based on OPE (Oblivious Polynomial Evaluation) that offers better performance over the PSI-CA that could be extracted by extending the PSI scheme of (Freedman et al. 2004). Later, (De Cristofaro et al., 2012) constructed a PSI-CA with linear communication and computation overhead. Recently, (Debnath and Dutta 2015) proposed two PSI-CA protocols achieving linear complexity against malicious adversaries. Very recently, Freedman et al. modified their work of (Freedman et al. 2016) to construct a PSI-CA with linear communication and computation overhead. The scheme is secure against semi-honest parties without random oracles. Lastly, (Shi et al. 2016) constructed a PSI-CA protocol utilizing quantum computation that achieves linear complexity. More recently, (Dong & Loukides, 2017) developed an approximate PSI-CA protocol based on the Flajolet-Martin (FM) sketch (1985) with logarithmic complexity.

APSI-CA

The first APSI-CA attaining quadratic complexity was proposed in works of (Camenisch & Zaverucha, 2009). Their scheme is proven to be secure in a malicious setting without ROM. Later, (De Cristofaro et al., 2012) designed an APSI-CA with linear communication and computation overhead in the ROM.

mPSI-CA

The concept of $mPSI$ -CA was introduced in (Kissner and Song 2005). Their scheme relies on OPE and works for $n\left(\geq 2\right)$ players. However, they have not considered fairness in their construction. In the following, Camenisch and Zaverucha (2009) designed fair $mPSI$ -CA protocol utilizing OPE. They used certified sets in their design. Recently, (Debnath and Dutta 2016) constructed the first fair $mPSI$ -CA protocol attaining linear complexity over prime order group.

ONE-WAY PSI-CA AND APSI-CA PROTOCOLS

Protocol Requirements

Each of one-way PSI-CA and APSI-CA is executed between a client C with private input set $Y=\left\{c_1,\ldots,c_w\right\}$ and a server S with private input set $X=\left\{s_1,\ldots,s_v\right\}$ for $w\leq v$. In the rest of this chapter, {m, k, H } stands for optimal Bloom filter parameters, pk_C / sk_C denotes public/secret key for GM encryption, Enc_{pk_C} / Dec_{sk_C} represents Encryption/Decryption function for GM under pk_C / sk_C and $\overline{s}_{i,j}$ stands for the j-th bit of the element $\overline{s}_i\in\{0,1\}^k$ with $j=1,\ldots,k$. Set $E\left(\overline{s}_i\right)=\left\{Enc_{pk_C}\left(\overline{s}_{i,1}\right),\ldots,Enc_{pk_C}\left(\overline{s}_{i,k}\right)\right\}$ and

$$D\left(E\left(\overline{s}_i\right)\right) = \{Dec_{sk_C}\left(Enc_{pk_C}\left(\overline{s}_{i,1}\right)\right), \ldots, Dec_{sk_C}(Enc_{pk_C}\left(\overline{s}_{i,k}\right)\}) = \left\{\overline{s}_{i,1}, \ldots, \overline{s}_{i,k}\right\} = \overline{s}_i$$

as decryption of $E\left(\overline{s}_i\right)$. The auxiliary inputs include the maximum set size v, security parameter κ and optimal Bloom filter parameters.

The PSI-CA

Let the client C has the private set $Y = \left\{c_1, \ldots, c_w\right\} \subseteq \{0,1\}^*$ and the server S has the private set $X = \left\{s_1, \ldots, s_v\right\} \subseteq \{0,1\}^*$. Then they proceed as follows:

- The client C generates a key pair $pk_C = \left(n, u\right)$ and $sk_C = \left(P, Q\right)$ for GM encryption using $\mathcal{GM}.KGen$ and executes the following steps:
    - Constructs a Bloom filter $BF_Y = \left(BF_Y\left[1\right], \ldots, BF_Y\left[m\right]\right) \in \{0,1\}^m$ of Y,
    - Encrypts $BF_Y\left[i\right]$ to get $b_i = Enc_{pk_C}\left(BF_Y\left[i\right]\right) \in \mathbb{Z}_n$ for $i = 1, \ldots, m$,
    - Sends $\overline{Y} = \left\{b_1, \ldots, b_m\right\}$ and pk_C to S.
- On receiving $\overline{(Y, pk_C)}$, the server S executes the following steps:
    - For $i = 1, \ldots, v$,
        - Determines $h_1\left(s_i\right), \ldots, h_k\left(s_i\right) \in \left\{1, \ldots, m\right\}$;
        - Extracts $b_{h_1\left(s_i\right)}, \ldots, b_{h_k\left(s_i\right)} \in \mathbb{Z}_n$ from $\overline{Y}$; and
        - Selects $r_{i,1}, \ldots, r_{i,k} \in_R \mathbb{Z}_n$ and sets $E\left(\overline{s}_i\right) = \left\{b_{h_1\left(s_i\right)} \cdot r_{i,1}^2 \ mod\ n, \ldots, b_{h_k\left(s_i\right)} \cdot r_{i,k}^2 \ mod\ n\right\} \in \mathbb{Z}_n^k$.
    - Finally sends $\overline{X} = \left\{E\left(\overline{s}_1\right), \ldots, E\left(\overline{s}_v\right)\right\} \subseteq \mathbb{Z}_n^k$ to C.
- The client C, on receiving $\overline{X}$ from S, sets $card = 0$ and does the following for $i = 1, \ldots, v$,
    - Extracts $\overline{s}_i \in \{0,1\}^k$ by decrypting $E\left(\overline{s}_i\right)$; and
    - Sets $card = card + 1$ only if $\overline{s}_i \in \{0,1\}^k$ is all-zero string.

Finally, the client C outputs the variable $card$ as $\left|X \cap Y\right|$, the cardinality of $X \cap Y$.

The APSI-CA

Similar to PSI-CA, proposed APSI-CA is executed between a client C with input $Y = \{c_1, \ldots, c_w\} \subseteq \{0,1\}^*$ and a server S with input $X = \{s_1, \ldots, s_v\} \subseteq \{0,1\}^*$. Additionally, a mutually trusted certifying authority CA is required in APSI-CA in order to certify C's private set Y. It completes in two phases: off-line phase and online phase.

Off-line Phase:

1. The client C runs the algorithm $\mathcal{GM}.KGen$ to generate a key pair $pk_C = (n, u)$ and $sk_C = (P, Q)$. It then sends (Y, pk_C) to CA.
2. On receiving $(Y, pk_C = (n, u))$ from C, the certifying authority CA, constructs a Bloom filter $BF_Y \in \{0,1\}^m$ and generates a key pair (pk_{DSig}, sk_{DSig}) for some digital signature scheme $DSig$ over $\mathbb{Z}_n$. For each $i = 1, \ldots, m$, the certifying authority CA does the following:
    a. Encrypts $BF_Y[i]$ to get $b_i = Enc_{pk_C}(BF_Y[i]) \in \mathbb{Z}_n$;
    b. Computes $\bar{h}(b_i)$ for some hash function $\bar{h} : \{0,1\}^* \to \mathbb{Z}_n$; and
    c. Uses the secret key sk_{DSig} to generate a signature $Sig(\bar{h}(b_1), \ldots, \bar{h}(b_m))$ on $Y' = \{\bar{h}(b_1), \ldots, \bar{h}(b_m)\}$.

Finally, CA, sends $(\bar{Y}, Sig(\bar{h}(b_1), \ldots, \bar{h}(b_m)), pk_{DSig})$ to C and pk_{DSig} to S.

Online Phase:

1. On receiving $(\bar{Y}, Sig(\bar{h}(b_1), \ldots, \bar{h}(b_m)))$ from CA in the off-line phase, the client C forwards it along with pk_C to S.
2. The server S then verifies the validity of signature $Sig(\bar{h}(b_1), \ldots, \bar{h}(b_m))$ using pk_{DSig} and aborts if verification fails. Otherwise, S generates $\bar{X} = \{E(\bar{s}_1), \ldots, E(\bar{s}_v)\} \subseteq \mathbb{Z}_n^k$ and sends it to C, similar to PSI-CA.

In the following, C determines $|X \cap Y|$ utilizing the similar approach as of PSI-CA.

Security

- **Theorem 4.1** *If the QR assumption holds, then proposed PSI-CA protocol is secure for the functionality* $\mathcal{F}_{PSI-CA} : (Y, X) \rightarrow (|X \cap Y|, \perp)$ *against the semi-honest server and semi-honest client except with negligible probability* $\varepsilon = \frac{1}{2^k}$, *where* $|Y| = w$ *and* $|X| = v$ *with* $w \leq v$.

Proof. Consider the following two cases: Case I (Sever is corrupted) and Case II (Client is corrupted)

Case I (Server S is Corrupted): Let the simulator $\mathcal{SIM}$ has access to the S's private input X and output $\perp$. Then the simulator $\mathcal{SIM}$ selects $\delta_1, \ldots, \delta_m \in_R \mathbb{Z}_n$ and outputs the simulated view as $(X; \delta_1, \ldots, \delta_m)$.

Note that the real view is (X; $b_1, \ldots, b_m$). Therefore, the input set X is same in both the views. Again, by the semantic security of GM encryption, the distribution of $\{b_1, \ldots, b_m\} \in \mathbb{Z}_n^m$ is computationally indistinguishable from the distribution of $\{\delta_1, \ldots, \delta_m\} \in \mathbb{Z}_n^m$. Thus, the simulated view is indistinguishable from the real view.

Case II (Client C is Corrupted): Let the simulator $\mathcal{SIM}$ has access to the client's input Y and output $|X \cap Y|$. Then $\mathcal{SIM}$ selects $|X \cap Y|$ many all-zero strings (ϑ_i's) and $v - |X \cap Y|$ many non-zero strings (ϑ_i's) of length k each. Finally, outputs the simulated view as $(Y, \vartheta_1, \ldots, \vartheta_v)$.

Note that the input set in real view is Y, same as of simulated view. Moreover, similar to simulated view, the real view contains $|X \cap Y|$ many all-zero strings and $v - |X \cap Y|$ many non-zero strings of length k each, except with a negligible probability ε. Therefore, the simulated view is indistinguishable from the real view except with negligible probability ε.

- **Theorem 4.2** *If the QR assumption holds, then proposed APSI-CA protocol is secure for the functionality* $\mathcal{F}_{APSI-CA} : (Y, X) \rightarrow (|X \cap Y|, \perp)$ *against the semi-honest server and malicious client except with negligible probability* $\varepsilon = \frac{1}{2^k}$, *where* $|Y| = w$ *and* $|X| = v$ *with* $w \leq v$.

Proof. **Case I (Server S is Corrupted):** Exactly same as the case I in the proof of the Theorem 4.1.

Case II (Client C is Corrupted): Let $\mathcal{A}$ be the real world adversary that corrupts C and $\mathcal{SIM}$ be the corresponding ideal world adversary who has oracle access to $\mathcal{A}$. An incorruptible trusted third party, say T is also involved in the ideal process. Simulator $\mathcal{SIM}$ does the following in order to simulate S in the ideal process:

- $\mathcal{SIM}$ calls $\mathcal{A}$ with the input Y. It then generates $\left(pk_{DSig}, sk_{DSig}\right)$ for the digital signature scheme used by CA in the real world.
- $\mathcal{SIM}$, on receiving $\left(Y, pk_C\right)$ from $\mathcal{A}$, plays the role of CA by constructing a Bloom filter BF_Y, generating $\overline{Y} = \{b_1,\ldots,b_m\} = \left\{Enc_{pk_C}\left(BF_Y[1]\right),\ldots,Enc_{pk_C}\left(BF_Y[m]\right)\right\}$ using pk_C and $Sig\left(\overline{h}\left(b_1\right),\ldots,\overline{h}\left(b_m\right)\right)$ using sk_{DSig}, and sending $\left(\overline{Y}, Sig\left(\overline{h}\left(b_1\right),\ldots,\overline{h}\left(b_m\right)\right), pk_{DSig}\right)$ to $\mathcal{A}$.
- On receiving $\left(\overline{Y}, Sig\left(\overline{h}\left(b_1\right),\ldots,\overline{h}\left(b_m\right)\right), pk_C = (n,u)\right)$ from $\mathcal{A}$, $\mathcal{SIM}$ plays the role of real world server by verifying the validity of the signature $Sig\left(\overline{h}\left(b_1\right),\ldots,\overline{h}\left(b_m\right)\right)$ using pk_{DSig}. If the verification does not succeed, then $\mathcal{SIM}$ aborts. Otherwise, $\mathcal{SIM}$ sends Y to T, whereas the ideal world server sends X to T who in turn computes $X \cap Y$ and sends it to $\mathcal{SIM}$.
- $\mathcal{SIM}$ chooses $|X \cap Y|$ many all-zero strings ($\overline{s}_i$'s) and the remaining $v - |X \cap Y|$ many non-zero strings ($\overline{s}_i$'s), each of length k. $\mathcal{SIM}$ constructs $\overline{X} = \left\{E\left(\overline{s}_1\right),\ldots,E\left(\overline{s}_v\right)\right\}$ by encrypting each $\overline{s}_i$ for $i = 1,\ldots,v$ and sends $\overline{X}$ to $\mathcal{A}$. Simulator $\mathcal{SIM}$ then outputs whatever $\mathcal{A}$ outputs and terminates.

Note that the honest party has no output. Thus, it is sufficient to show that $\mathcal{A}$'s view in the ideal process is indistinguishable from its view in the real world. The input set Y is same in both the real world and ideal process. Moreover, the number of encrypted all-zero strings and non-zero strings in $\overline{X}$ are respectively $|X \cap Y|$ and $v - |X \cap Y|$ in both the real world and ideal process, except with negligible probability ε. Therefore, $\mathcal{A}$'s views in the real world and ideal process are indistinguishable, except with negligible probability ε.

MPSI-CA PROTOCOL

Construction

The $mPSI$ -CA protocol consists of the following three algorithms: (I) $Setup$, (II) procedure $mPSI$ -CA and (III) procedure $DisputeResolution$. This protocol involves three participants: party A , party B and an arbiter Ar . During the $Setup$ phase, a trusted third party (TTP) generates the global parameter for the protocol and each of A , B, and Ar generate their respective public key-secret key pair. The procedure $mPSI$ -CAisrunbetweentheparty A withinputset $X = \left\{x_1, \ldots, x_v\right\} \subset \{0,1\}^*$ and the party B with input set $Y = \left\{y_1, \ldots, y_w\right\} \subset \{0,1\}^*$ in order to execute the cardinality of the set intersection, i.e., $\left|X \cap Y\right|$. Finally, the arbiter Ar takes part in the procedure $DisputeResolution$ in order to resolve the dispute only if a corrupted player prematurely aborts the procedure $mPSI$ -CA. Note that the arbiter does not have access to the private information of the parties A and B .

Setup $\left(1^{\kappa}\right)$

The distributed ElGamal encryption $\mathcal{DEL}$ and the verifiable encryption $\mathcal{VE}$ over prime order group are used.

- A TTP generates public parameter $par = \left(par, \hat{g}, \mathcal{H}\right)$ using $\mathcal{VE}.Setup\left(1^{\kappa}\right)$, with $par = \left(p, q, g\right)$, chooses Bloom filter parameters $\left\{m, k, H\right\}$, selects $\tau_i, \iota_j \pm \mathbb{G}$ for $i = -4, \ldots, m; j = -4, \ldots, w$, where $\mathbb{G} = \left\langle g \right\rangle$ is the cyclic subgroup of $\mathbb{Z}_p^*$ of order q . It then sets global parameter $gpar = (ppar, m, k, H, \{\tau_i\}_{i=-4}^{m}, \{\iota_j\}_{j=-4}^{w})$ and makes it public. Note that the elements $\{\tau_i\}_{i=-4}^{m}, \{\iota_j\}_{j=-4}^{w}$ will be used in zero-knowledge arguments for shuffle during the procedure $mPSI$ -CA.
- Each of A , B generates

$$\left(epk_A, esk_A\right) \leftarrow \mathcal{EL}.KGen\left(par\right), \ where \ a_1 \in_R \mathbb{Z}_q, epk_A = y_A = g^{a_1}, esk_A = a_1$$

and

$$\left(epk_B, esk_B\right) \leftarrow \mathcal{EL}.KGen\left(par\right), \ where \ a_2 \in_R \mathbb{Z}_q, epk_B = y_B = g^{a_2}, esk_B = a_2.$$

Then they make y_A, y_B public through the TTP (who works as the certifying authority in this case) and keeps esk_A, esk_B the secret to themselves.

- The arbiter Ar generates

$$\left(vpk_{Ar} = (a,b,c), vsk_{Ar} = (u_1, u_2, v_1, v_2, w_1)\right) \leftarrow \mathcal{VE}.KGen(par, \hat{g}),$$

$$with\ u_1, u_2, v_1, v_2, w_1 \in_R \mathbb{Z}_q\ and\ a = g^{u_1}\hat{g}^{u_2}, b = g^{v_1}\hat{g}^{v_2},\ c = g^{w_1}$$

and makes vpk_{Ar} public through the TTP who acts as the certifying authority in this case also.

- Suppose $pk = h = (epk_A)(epk_B) = g^{a_1+a_2}$ and $sk = a_1 + a_2$. Then (pk, sk) works as the public key-secret key pair for $\mathcal{DEL}$, where the secret key $sk = a_1 + a_2$ is not known to anyone. However, anyone can compute the public key pk using epk_A and epk_B.

The scheme uses the multiplicatively homomorphic property of $\mathcal{DEL}$ i.e.,

$$\left(dE_{pk}(m_1)\right)\left(dE_{pk}(m_2)\right) = dE_{pk}(m_1 m_2), (dE_{pk}(m))^k = dE_{pk}(m^k),\ where\ k \in \mathbb{Z}_q.$$

A session identity sid is agreed by all the participants at the start of the procedure $mPSI$-CA.

Procedure *mPSI*-CA

This procedure completes in four rounds. The parties A and B execute the following steps:

Step 1: The party A

- Generates a Bloom filer BF_X for the set X; for each $i = 1,\ldots,m$, encrypts $g^{\bar{b}_i} = g^{BF_X[i]}$ using the public key pk to get

$$C_i = (c_i, d_i) \leftarrow \mathcal{DEL}.Enc\left(g^{\bar{b}_i}, pk, par, r_{\bar{b}_i}\right),\quad where\ c_i = g^{r_{\bar{b}_i}}, d_i = g^{\bar{b}_i}h^{r_{\bar{b}_i}}\ ;$$

- Constructs a zero-knowledge proof π_1 as $\pi_1 = PoK\{r_{b_1},\ldots,r_{b_m} \mid \bigwedge_{i=1}^{m}\left(c_i = g^{r_{b_i}}\right)\}; and$
- Sends $R_1 =< \{C_i\}_{i=1}^{m}, \pi_1 >$ to the party B.

Step 2: The party B checks the validity of the proof π_1, on receiving $R_1 =< \{C_i\}_{i=1}^{m}, \pi_1 >$ from A. It aborts if the verification does not succeed. Otherwise, proceeds as follows:

- Selects a random permutation ϕ from the set $£_m$ of all possible permutations over the set $\{1,\ldots,m\}$, chooses $\alpha_1,\ldots,\alpha_m \in_R \mathbb{Z}_q$ and for each $i = 1,\ldots,m$, computes

$$\bar{C}_i = C_{\phi^{-1}(i)}\mathcal{DEL}.Enc\left(g^0, pk, par, \alpha_i\right) = \left(c_{\phi^{-1}(i)}, d_{\phi^{-1}(i)}\right)\left(g^{\alpha_i}, g^0 h^{\alpha_i}\right) = \left(c'_i, d'_i\right),$$

where $c'_i = c_{\phi^{-1}(i)} g^{\alpha_i}, d'_i = d_{\phi^{-1}(i)} h^{\alpha_i}$;

- Corresponding to each $y_j \in Y$, constructs an m-bit string s_j whose i-th bit $s_j^{(i)}$ is defined as follows $s_j^{(i)} = \begin{cases} 1, & if\ i \in \left\{\phi\left(h_1\left(y_j\right)\right),\ldots,\phi\left(h_k\left(y_j\right)\right)\right\} \\ 0, & elsewhere; \end{cases}$
- Selects $k_1,\ldots,k_w \in_R \mathbb{Z}_q$ and utilizes $\{s_1,\ldots,s_w\}$ to compute for $j = 1,\ldots,w$

$$\nu_j = \prod_{i=1}^{m}(\bar{C}_i)^{s_j^{(i)}} = \left(\lambda_j, \delta_j\right), where \lambda_j = \prod_{i=1}^{m}(c'_i)^{s_j^{(i)}}, \delta_j = \prod_{i=1}^{m}(d'_i)^{s_j^{(i)}},$$

$$\bar{y}_j = (\nu_j)^r = \left(\bar{c}_j, \bar{d}_j\right),\ where\ \bar{c}_j = (\lambda_j)^{k_j}, \bar{d}_j = (\delta_j)^{k_j};$$

- Using a session ID sid which has been agreed by all parities beforehand and the hash of past communication, generates a label $L \in \{0,1\}^*$;
- Chooses $r_1,\ldots,r_w, z_1,\ldots,z_w \in_R \mathbb{Z}_q$, for $j = 1,\ldots,w$ computes $T_j = (\bar{c}_j)^{a_2} g^{r_j}$, and

$$vE_{vpk_{Ar}}\left(g^{r_j}\right) = \left(t_{1j}, t_{2j}, t_{3j}, t_{4j}\right) \leftarrow \mathcal{VE}.Enc\left(g^{r_j}, vpk_{Ar}, ppar, z_j, L, \mathcal{H}\right),$$

where

$$t_{1j} = g^{z_j}, t_{2j} = (\hat{g})^{z_j}, t_{3j} = c^{z_j} g^{r_j}, t_{4j} = a^{z_j} b^{z_j \rho_j}, \rho_j = \mathcal{H}\left(t_{1j}, t_{2j}, t_{3j}, L\right)$$

and $vpk_{Ar} = \left(a, b, c\right)$ is the public key of Ar;

- Generates the proofs $\pi_2, \hat{\pi}_2$ as:

$$\pi_2 = PoK\{\left(a_2, r_1, \ldots, r_w, z_1, \ldots, z_w, k_1, \ldots, k_w\right) \mid \left(y_B = g^{a_2}\right) \bigwedge_{j=1}^{w} \left(t_{1j} = g^{z_j}\right)\left(t_{2j} = \left(\hat{g}\right)^{z_j}\right)$$

$$\bigwedge_{j=1}^{w} \left(t_{3j} = c^{z_j} g^{r_j}\right)\left(t_{4j} = a^{z_j} b^{z_j \rho_j}\right)\left(\overline{c}_j = \left(\lambda_j\right)^{k_j}\right)\left(\overline{d}_j = \left(\delta_j\right)^{k_j}\right)\left(T_j = \left(\overline{c}_j\right)^{a_2} g^{r_j}\right)\},$$

$$\hat{\pi}_2 = PoKArg\{\left(\phi \in \pounds_m, \alpha_1, \ldots., \alpha_m\right) \mid \left\{\overline{C}_i = C_{\phi^{-1}(i)} \mathcal{DEL}.Enc\left(g^0, pk, par, \alpha_i\right)\}_{i=1}^{m}\right\};$$

- Sends $R_2 =< \{\overline{C}_i\}_{i=1}^{m}, \{\overline{y}_j, s_j, T_j, vE_{vpk_{Ar}}\left(g^{r_j}\right)\}_{j=1}^{w}, \pi_2, \hat{\pi}_2 >$ to A.

Note that each element of the set $\left\{g^{r_1}, \ldots, g^{r_w}\right\}$ is encrypted under the public key of Ar to make sure that if B aborts prematurely, then A will receive the correct output by involving in the procedure $DisputeResolution$.

Step 3: On receiving $R_2 =< \{\overline{C}_i\}_{i=1}^{m}, \{\overline{y}_j, s_j, T_j, vE_{vpk_{Ar}}\left(g^{r_j}\right)\}_{j=1}^{w}, \pi_2, \hat{\pi}_2 >$ from B, the party A computes $\nu_j = \prod_{i=1}^{m}(\overline{C}_i)^{s_j^{(i)}} = \left(\lambda_j, \delta_j\right)$ for $j = 1, \ldots, w$. It then verifies the validity of the proofs $\pi_2, \hat{\pi}_2$, and aborts if verification of at least one of $\pi_2, \hat{\pi}_2$ does not succeed; otherwise proceeds as follows:

- Selects a random permutation ψ from the set $\pounds_w$ of all possible permutations over the set $\left\{1, \ldots, w\right\}$, selects $\beta_1, \ldots, \beta_w \in \mathbb{Z}_q$ and does the following for each $j = 1, \ldots, w$,

$$\mu_j = \nu_{\psi^{-1}(j)} \mathcal{DEL}.Enc\left(g^0, pk, par, \beta_j\right) = \left(\lambda_{\psi^{-1}(j)}, \delta_{\psi^{-1}(j)}\right)\left(g^{\beta_j}, g^0 h^{\beta_j}\right) = \left(e_j, f_j\right),$$

$$\overline{e}_j = (e_j)^{a_1}, \ where \ e_j = \lambda_{\psi^{-1}(j)} g^{\beta_j}, f_j = \delta_{\psi^{-1}(j)} h^{\beta_j};$$

- Constructs the proofs $\pi_3, \hat{\pi}_3$ as $\pi_3 = PoK\{(a_1) \mid \left(y_A = g^{a_1}\right) \bigwedge_{j=1}^{w} (\overline{e}_j = \left(e_j\right)^{a_1}\right),$

$$\hat{\pi}_3 = PoKArg\{\left(\psi \in \pounds_w, \beta_1, \ldots, \beta_w\right) \mid \left\{\mu_j = \nu_{\phi^{-1}(j)} \mathcal{DEL}.Enc\left(g^0, pk, par, \beta_j\right)\}_{j=1}^{w}\right\};$$

- Sends $R_3 =< \{\mu_j, \left(\overline{e}_j\right)\}_{j=1}^{w}, \pi_3, \hat{\pi}_3 >$ to B.

Step 4: The party B, on receiving $R_3 =< \{\mu_j, \left(\overline{e}_j\right)\}_{j=1}^{w}, \pi_3, \hat{\pi}_3 >$ from A, checks the validity of the proofs $\pi_3, \hat{\pi}_3$. If verification of at least one of $\pi_3, \hat{\pi}_3$ does not succeed then B aborts, otherwise, proceeds as follows:

- Sets $card = 0$ and for $j = 1, \ldots, w$,
  - Extracts $e_j, f_j, \overline{e}_j = (e_j)^{a_1}$ from $R_3 =< \{\mu_j = \left(e_j, f_j\right), \left(\overline{e}_j\right)\}_{j=1}^{w}, \pi_3, \hat{\pi}_3 >$, received from A in *Step* 3,
  - Computes $(e_j)^{a_2}$ using secret key $esk_B = a_2$ and utilizes $(e_j)^{a_2}$ to compute $l_j = \dfrac{f_j}{\left(\overline{e}_j\right)(e_j)^{a_2}} = \dfrac{f_j}{(e_j)^{a_1}(e_j)^{a_2}}$,
  - Sets $card = card + 1$ if $l_j = 1$;
- Constructs a zero-knowledge proof π_5 as

$$\pi_4 = PoK\{\left(z_1, \ldots, z_w\right) \mid \wedge_{j=1}^{w} \left(t_{1j} = g^{z_j}\right)\left(t_{2j} = \hat{g}^{z_j}\right)\left(t_{3j} = c^{z_j} g^{r_j}\right)\left(t_{4j} = a^{z_j} b^{z_j \rho_j}\right)\};$$

- Sends $R_4 =< \{g^{r_j}\}_{j=1}^{w}, \pi_4 >$ to A and outputs $card$ as the cardinality of $X \cap Y$.

Note that the proof π_4 is generated by B in order to prove that $g^{r_j} \in R_4$ was encrypted in *Step* 2 to generate $vE_{vpk_{Ar}}\left(g^{r_j}\right)$ for $j = 1,\ldots, w$ utilizing Ar's public key.

Step 5: The party A, on receiving $R_4 =< \{g^{r_j}\}_{j=1}^{w}, \pi_4 >$ from B, verifies the validity of the proof π_4. If the verification of the proof succeeds then A executes the following steps:

- Sets $card = 0$ and for $j = 1,.., w$,
  - Extracts $T_j, \bar{c}_j, \bar{d}_j$ from $R_2 =< \{\bar{C}_i\}_{i=1}^{m}, \{\bar{y}_j = \left(\bar{c}_j, \bar{d}_j\right), s_j, T_j, vE_{vpk_{Ar}}\left(g^{r_j}\right)\}_{j=1}^{w}, \pi_2, \hat{\pi}_2 >$, received from B in *Step* 2,
  - Computes $\frac{T_j}{g^{r_j}} = \frac{(\bar{c}_j)^{a_2} g^{r_j}}{g^{r_j}} = (\bar{c}_j)^{a_2}$ and utilizes $(\bar{c}_j)^{a_2}$ to compute $\ell_j = \frac{\bar{d}_j}{(\bar{c}_j)^{a_1}(\bar{c}_j)^{a_2}}$, where $esk_A = a_1$ is A's secret key,
  - Sets $card = card + 1$ if $\ell_j = 1$;
- Finally, outputs $card$ as $|X \cap Y|$.

If the correctness of the proof π_4 fails or B does not send $\left\{g^{r_1},\ldots g^{r_w}\right\}$ to A (i.e., B prematurely aborts) then A sends a dispute resolution request to the arbiter Ar.

Procedure Dispute Resolution

The arbiter Ar, on receiving a dispute resolution request from A, interacts with A and B as follows:

Step 1: Party A sends all the messages sent and received in *Step* 1-2 of the procedure $mPSI$ -CA to Ar. As the session ID sid is known to Ar, on receiving the messages from A, the arbiter Ar generates the label L and checks the consistency between messages and the label L. If the verification does not succeed or if the transcript ends before the end of *Step* 2 of the $mPSI$ -CA protocol, then Ar aborts so that none of A and B gets any advantage. Otherwise, Ar continues with the following steps.

Step 2: As in *Step* 3 of the $mPSI$ -CA protocol, A sends $R_3 =< \{\mu_j, (\overline{e}_j)\}_{j=1}^{w}, \pi_3, \hat{\pi}_3 >$ to Ar.

Step 3: The arbiter Ar, on receiving $R_3 =< \{\mu_j, (\overline{e}_j)\}_{j=1}^{w}, \pi_3, \hat{\pi}_3 >$ from B, verifies the correctness of the proofs $\pi_3, \hat{\pi}_3$. If the verification of at least one of the proofs does not succeed then Ar aborts so that none of A and B gets any advantage. Otherwise, Ar decrypts each member of $\{vE_{vpk_{Ar}}(g^{r_j})\}_{j=1}^{w}$ using its secret key vsk_{Ar} and sends $\{g^{r_j}\}_{j=1}^{w}$ to A who in turn executes $|X \cap Y|$ using the similar procedure as described in *Step* 5 of the procedure $mPSI$ -CA. On the other hand, the arbiter Ar forwards $< \{\mu_j, (\overline{e}_j)\}_{j=1}^{w} >$ to B, thereby B can evaluate $|X \cap Y|$ using the similar procedure as explained in *Step* 4 of the procedure $mPSI$ -CA.

Security

In order to prove the security of $mPSI$ -CA, the following two cases are considered: Case I, when the adversary corrupts two of the three participants and Case II, when the adversary corrupts only one of the three participants.

- **Theorem 5.1** *Suppose the encryption schemes $\mathcal{EL}$, $\mathcal{DEL}$ and $\mathcal{VE}$ are semantically secure, the associated proof protocols are zero knowledge proofs and zero-knowledge argument of proofs for the shuffle. Then proposed $mPSI$ -CA is a secure computation protocol in ROM for the functionality $\mathcal{F}_{mPSI-CA} : (X, Y) \rightarrow (|X \cap Y|, |X \cap Y|)$ against malicious participants except with negligible probability ε, where ε is the false positive rate of the Bloom filter BF_X.*

Proof. Let the real world adversary $\mathcal{C}$ breaks the security of $mPSI$ -CA protocol executed among the party A with input X and the party B with input Y; and an arbiter Ar with no input. In the ideal process, suppose there be an incorruptible trusted party T, parties $\overline{A}, \overline{B}$, $\overline{Ar}$ and simulator $\mathcal{SIM}$. In the real world, a trusted party generates $gpar = (ppar, m, k, H, \{\tau_i\}_{i=-4}^{m}, \{\iota_j\}_{j=-4}^{w})$ and certifies the public keys pk_A, pk_B, pk_{Ar} of A, B, Ar respectively. On the other hand, simulator $\mathcal{SIM}$ performs these works in the ideal process. Let us denote $REAL_{mPSI-CA,\mathcal{C}}(X, Y)$ as the joint output of $A, B, Ar, \mathcal{C}$ in the real world and $IDEAL_{\mathcal{F}_{mPSI-CA}, \mathcal{SIM}}\left(X, Y\right)$ as the joint output of $\overline{A}, \overline{B}, \overline{Ar}, \mathcal{SIM}$ in the ideal process.

Case I (When the Adversary $\mathcal{C}$ Corrupts Two Parties)

There are three subcases – either (I) A and Ar are corrupted or (II) B and Ar are corrupted or (III) A and B are corrupted. Each of these subcases is analyzed below.

Subcase I (A and Ar Are Corrupted)

Let $\mathcal{Z}$ be a distinguisher that distinguishes the real world from the ideal world. The distinguisher $\mathcal{Z}$ controls $\mathcal{C}$, feeds the input of the honest party B and observes B's output. To prove indistinguishability of $\mathcal{Z}$'s views in the real world and in the ideal world, a sequence of games $Game_0, \ldots, Game_4$ is presented. The view of the real world adversary $\mathcal{C}$ together with B's output constitutes $\mathcal{Z}$'s view in the real world. On the other hand, the view of the ideal world simulator $\mathcal{SIM}$ along with the output of $\overline{B}$ forms $\mathcal{Z}$'s view in the ideal world. Here a view of an entity means the transcripts available to it. Argument is that $\mathcal{Z}$'s views in any two neighbouring game are indistinguishable. Let S_i be the simulator in $Game_i$ that simulates the honest party B and, $\mathcal{Z}$ distinguishes the view of $Game_i$ from the view of the real protocol with the probability $Prob\left[Game_i\right]$ for $i = 0, \ldots, 4$.

$Game_0$: This game corresponds to the real protocol, where the simulator S_0. has the full knowledge of B and interacts with $\mathcal{C}$. Hence, $Prob\left[REAL_{mPSI-CA, \mathcal{C}}\left(X, Y\right)\right] = Prob\left[Game_0\right]$.

$Game_1$: This game is the same as $Game_0$ except the following:

- The simulator S_1 maintains a list X' and records all queries the adversary made to the random oracles, such as $h_1, \ldots, h_k$. Without loss of generality, assume the adversary makes no more than $poly\left(\kappa\right)$ queries and stops at some point, where κ is a security parameter.
- If the proof π_1 is valid then the simulator S_1 runs the extractor algorithm for π_1 with $\mathcal{C}$ to extract the exponents $\left\{r_{b_1}, \ldots, r_{b_m}\right\}$. These exponents $r_{\bar{b}_i}$ for $i = 1, \ldots, m$ are utilized by the simulator S_1 to compute $g^{b_i} = \frac{d_i}{h^{r_{b_i}}}$, where $d_i = g^{b_i} h^{r_{b_i}}$ is extracted from $C_i = \left(c_i, d_i\right)$ the first round message

$R_1 = \left\langle \left\{C_1,...,C_m\right\}, \pi_1 \right\rangle$ sent by the party A (i.e., $\mathcal{C}$) to B (i.e., S_1) and S_1) and $h = epk_A \cdot epk_B = g^{a_1+a_2}$. Note that $C_i = \left(c_i, d_i\right)$ is the encryption of $BF_X\left[i\right]$ using distributed ElGamal encryption scheme under pk using randomness r_{b_i}. The simulator S_1 then extracts Bloom filter $BF_X = \left\{b_1,...,b_m\right\}$ for the set X by setting for $i = 1,...,m$ $BF_X\left[i\right] = \begin{cases} 0, & if\ g^{\bar{b}_i} = 1 \\ 1, & otherwise; \end{cases}$

- The simulator S_1 runs the check step of Bloom filter presented in section 2.7 for membership check of each element in X' against BF_X. If the check is valid, then the corresponding element is put in a set X''. Note that the set X'' is identical to the set X except with negligible probability ε.

The views of $\mathcal{Z}$ are indistinguishable in $Game_0$ and $Game_1$ by the simulation soundness property of the proof π_1. Therefore,

$$\left|Prob\left[Game_1\right] - Prob\left[Game_0\right]\right| \leq \varepsilon_1\left(\kappa\right),\ where\ \varepsilon_1\left(\kappa\right)\ is\ a\ negligible\ function.$$

$Game_2$: Note that in this game the simulator S_2 has the knowledge of A's input set $X = \left\{x_1,...,x_v\right\}$ extracted as in $Game_1$, B's input set $Y = \left\{y_1,...,y_w\right\}$ and secret key $esk_B = a_2$ of B. $Game_2$ is exactly same as $Game_1$ except the following:

- If the verifications of both the proofs $\pi_3, \hat{\pi}_3$ succeed, then S_2 outputs $\left|X \cap Y\right|$ as the final output of B using Y and the above extracted set X.
- If the verification of at least one of the proofs $\pi_3, \hat{\pi}_3$ fails or $\mathcal{C}$ aborts prematurely in the procedure $mPSI$-CA, then the following cases arise:
    - If $\mathcal{C}$ sends $\{\mu_j = \left(e_j, f_j\right), \bar{e}_j\}_{j=1}^{w}$ to S_2 in the procedure $DisputeResolution$, then S_2 first sets $card = 0$. For $j = 1,..,w$, the simulator S_2 computes $(e_j)^{a_2}$ and utilizes it to compute $l_j = \dfrac{f_j}{\left(\bar{e}_j\right)(e_j)^{a_2}}$. The simulator S_2 increases $card$ by 1 if $l_j = 1$, for $j = 1,...,w$ and outputs $card$ as the final output of B.
    - If $\mathcal{C}$ aborts in the procedure $DisputeResolution$ then, S_2 outputs $\perp$ as the final output of B.

Clearly, $\mathcal{Z}$'s views in $Game_2$ and $Game_3$ are indistinguishable. Hence,

$$\left|Prob\left[Game_2\right]-Prob\left[Game_1\right]\right| \leq \varepsilon_2\left(\kappa\right), \ where \ \varepsilon_2\left(\kappa\right) \ is \ a \ negligible \ function.$$

$Game_3$: This game is identical to $Game_2$ except that S_3 simulating the honest party B does the following after extracting $X = \left\{x_1, ..., x_v\right\}$ as in $Game_1$:

- Computes $\left|X \cap Y\right|$ using the input set $Y = \left\{y_1, ..., y_w\right\}$ of B and constructs a set $Y' = \left\{y'_1, ..., y'_w\right\}$ by including $\left|X \cap Y\right|$ many random elements of X together with $w - \left|X \cap Y\right|$ many random elements chosen from $\{0,1\}^* \setminus X$.
- Chooses a random permutation $\phi \in £_m$ over the set $\left\{1, ..., m\right\}$, selects $\alpha_1, ..., \alpha_m \in_R \mathbb{Z}_q$ and computes for each $i = 1, ..., m$,

$$\bar{C}_i = C_{\phi^{-1}(i)}\mathcal{DEL}.Enc\left(g^0, pk, par, \alpha_i\right) = \left(c_{\phi^{-1}(i)}, d_{\phi^{-1}(i)}\right)\left(g^{\alpha_i}, g^0 h^{\alpha_i}\right) = \left(c'_i, d'_i\right), \text{ whe}$$

$c'_i = c_{\phi^{-1}(i)} g^{\alpha_i}, d'_i = d_{\phi^{-1}(i)} h^{\alpha_i}$.

- For each $j = 1, ..., w$, constructs an m-bit string s_j whose i-th bit $s_j^{(i)}$ is defined as $s_j^{(i)} = \begin{cases} 1, & if \ i \in \left\{\phi\left(h_1\left(y'_j\right)\right), ..., \phi\left(h_k\left(y'_j\right)\right)\right\} \\ 0, & otherwise, \end{cases}$
- Selects $k_j \in_R \mathbb{Z}_q$, computes $\nu_j = \prod_{i=1}^{m} (\bar{C}_i)^{s_j^{(i)}} = \left(\lambda_j, \delta_j\right)$ and $\bar{y}_j = \left(\bar{c}_j, \bar{d}_j\right)$, where $\bar{c}_j = (\lambda_j)^{k_j}, \bar{d}_j = (\delta_j)^{k_j}$ for $j = 1, .., w$.
- Generates a label $L \in \{0,1\}^*$ using a session ID which has been agreed by all parities beforehand and the hash of past communication, chooses $r_1, ..., r_w, z_1, ..., z_w \in_R \mathbb{Z}_q$ and computes $T_j = (\bar{c}_j)^{a_2} g^{r_j}$ and $vE_{vpk_{Ar}}\left(g^{r_j}\right) = \left(t_{1j}, t_{2j}, t_{3j}, t_{4j}\right)$ for $j = 1, ..., w$ by running the algorithm $\mathcal{VE}.Enc$ on input g^{r_j}.
- Finally, sends $< \{\bar{C}_i\}_{i=1}^m, \{\bar{y}_j, s_j, T_j, vE_{vpk_{Ar}}\left(g^{r_j}\right)\}_{j=1}^w >$ to $\mathcal{C}$ and simulates the proofs $\pi_2, \hat{\pi}_2$.

As the encryption schemes $\mathcal{DEL}$ and $\mathcal{VE}$ are semantically secure, the tuple $<\{\bar{C}_i\}_{i=1}^{m}, \{\bar{y}_j, s_j, T_j, vE_{vpk_{Ar}}\left(g^{r_j}\right)\}_{j=1}^{w}>$ is identically distributed in $Game_3$ and $Game_2$. The zero-knowledge (simulatability) of $\pi_2, \hat{\pi}_2$ and indistinguishability of the tuple $<\{\bar{C}_i\}_{i=1}^{m}, \{\bar{y}_j, s_j, T_j, vE_{vpk_{Ar}}\left(g^{r_j}\right)\}_{j=1}^{w}>$ make the views of $\mathcal{Z}$ in $Game_2$ and $Game_3$ indistinguishable. Therefore, there exists a negligible function $\varepsilon_3(\kappa)$ such that $\left|Prob\left[Game_3\right]-Prob\left[Game_2\right]\right| \leq \varepsilon_3(\kappa)$.

$Game_4$: This game is analogous to $Game_3$ except that during the setup phase, the simulator S_4 in simulating B chooses $a_2 \pm \mathbb{Z}_q$ and simulates π_4 as in *Step* 4. By the zero-knowledge (simulatability) of π_4, the views of $\mathcal{Z}$. in $Game_3$ and $Game_4$ are indistinguishable. Consequently,

$$\left|Prob\left[Game_4\right]-Prob\left[Game_3\right]\right| \leq \varepsilon_4(\kappa), \; where \; \varepsilon_4(\kappa) \; is \; a \; negligible \; function.$$

Construct the ideal world simulator $\mathcal{SIM}$ that uses $\mathcal{C}$ as a subroutine, simulates the honest party B and controls $\bar{A}, \overline{Ar}$ and incorporates all steps from $Game_4$.

- First, $\mathcal{SIM}$ plays the role of the trusted party and generates the global parameter $gpar = (ppar, m, k, H, \{\tau_i\}_{i=-4}^{m}, \{\iota_j\}_{j=-4}^{w})$, where $ppar = \left(par, \hat{g}, \mathcal{H}\right)$. It then plays the role of honest party B by choosing $\bar{a}_2 \in_R \mathbb{Z}_q$ and publishing $g^{\bar{a}_2}$ as the public key $epk_B = y_B$. It also acts as a certifying authority to obtain respective public keys epk_A, vpk_{Ar} of A, Ar. Finally, $\mathcal{SIM}$ invokes $\mathcal{C}$.
- $\mathcal{SIM}$ keeps records for all $poly(\kappa)$ queries the adversary made to the random oracles in a list X', where κ is security parameter.
- On receiving $R_1 =<\{C_i\}_{i=1}^{m}, \pi_1>$ from $\mathcal{C}$, $\mathcal{SIM}$ verifies the proof π_1. If the verification fails, $\mathcal{SIM}$ instructs $\bar{A}$ to send $\perp$ to T, $\overline{Ar}$ to send $b_B = \text{o}$ to T and terminates the execution; otherwise, runs the extractor algorithm for π_1 with $\mathcal{C}$ to extract the exponents $\left\{r_{b_1}, \ldots, r_{b_m}\right\}$ and extracts the Bloom filter BF_X for the set X exactly in the same way as described in $Game_1$. Similar to $Game_1$, $\mathcal{SIM}$ queries each element in X' against BF_X construct a set X'' which is essentially X except with negligible probability ε. $\mathcal{SIM}$

then instructs $\bar{A}$ to send X to T, $\overline{Ar}$ to send $b_A = \circ$ to T and receives $|X \cap Y|$ from T.

- As in $Game_3$, $\mathcal{SIM}$ constructs a set $Y' = \{y'_1, ..., y'_w\}$, computes

$$\bar{C}_i = \left(c'_i = c_{\phi^{-1}(i)} g^{\alpha_i}, d'_i = d_{\phi^{-1}(i)} h^{\alpha_i}\right), i = 1, ..., m$$

$$\nu_j = \prod_{i=1}^{m} (\bar{C}_i)^{s_j^{(i)}} = (\lambda_j, \delta_j) \ \ and \ \ \bar{y}_j = (\bar{c}_j, \bar{d}_j) = ((\lambda_j)^{k_j}, (\delta_j)^{k_j}), j = 1, .., w$$

$$T_j = (\bar{c}_j)^{\bar{a}_2} g^{r_j} \ \ and \ \ vE_{vpk_{Ar}}\left(g^{r_j}\right) = (t_{1j}, t_{2j}, t_{3j}, t_{4j}), j = 1, .., w,$$

$$where \ s_j^{(i)} = \begin{cases} 1, & if \ i \in \left\{\phi\left(h_1\left(y'_j\right)\right), ..., \phi\left(h_k\left(y'_j\right)\right)\right\} \\ 0, & otherwise, \end{cases}$$

$\phi \in_R £_m$ and $\alpha_1, ..., \alpha_m, \bar{k}_1, ..., \bar{k}_w, r_1, ..., r_w \in_R \mathbb{Z}_q$. It also simulates the proofs $\pi_2, \hat{\pi}_2$ and sends $< \{\bar{C}_i\}_{i=1}^{m}, \{\bar{y}_j, s_j, T_j, vE_{vpk_{Ar}}\left(g^{r_j}\right)\}_{j=1}^{w} >$ to $\mathcal{C}$. $\mathcal{SIM}$ then executes the following steps according to $\mathcal{C}$'s reply.

- If $\mathcal{C}$ structs A to send $< \{\mu_j, (\bar{e}_j)\}_{j=1}^{w}, \pi_3, \hat{\pi}_3 >$, then $\mathcal{SIM}$ verifies the validity of each of the proofs $\pi_3, \hat{\pi}_3$. If the verifications of both the proofs succeed, then $\mathcal{SIM}$ instructs $\overline{Ar}$ to send $b_B = \circ$. If verification of at least one of the proofs fails or $\mathcal{C}$ instructs A to abort in the procedure $mPSI$-CA then the following cases arise:
    - If $\mathcal{C}$ instructs Ar to send $\{\mu_j = (e_j, f_j), \bar{e}_j\}_{j=1}^{w}$ in the procedure $DisputeResolution$, then as in $Game_2$, $\mathcal{SIM}$ first computes $(e_j)^{a_2}$, then utilizes it to compute $l_j = \dfrac{f_j}{(\bar{e}_j)(e_j)^{\bar{a}_2}}$ and sets $card = card + 1$ if $l_j = 1$ for $j = 1, ..., w$, where $card$ is a count variable which is set 0 initially. Finally, $\mathcal{SIM}$ instructs $\overline{Ar}$ to send $b_B = card$ to T, outputs whatever $\mathcal{C}$ outputs and terminates.

 - If $\mathcal{C}$ instructs Ar to abort in the procedure $DisputeResolution$, $\mathcal{SIM}$ instructs $\overline{Ar}$ to send $b_B = \perp$ to T, outputs whatever $\mathcal{C}$ outputs and terminates.
- If $\mathcal{C}$ instructs both A and Ar to abort, then $\mathcal{SIM}$ instructs $\overline{Ar}$ to send $b_B = \perp$ to T, outputs whatever $\mathcal{C}$ outputs and terminates.

Note that the ideal world simulator $\mathcal{SIM}$ provides the real world adversary $\mathcal{C}$ exactly the same simulation as the simulator S_4 in $Game_4$. Therefore,

$$Prob\left[IDEAL_{\mathcal{F}_{mPSI-CA},\mathcal{SIM}}\left(X,Y\right)\right] = Prob\left[Game_4\right];$$

yielding

$$\left|Prob\left[IDEAL_{\mathcal{F}_{mPSI-CA},\mathcal{SIM}}\left(X,Y\right)\right] - Prob\left[REAL_{mPSI-CA,\mathcal{C}}\left(X,Y\right)\right]\right|$$

$$= \left|Prob\left[Game_4\right] - Prob\left[Game_0\right]\right|$$

$$\leq £_{i=1}^{4}\left|Prob\left[Game_i\right] - Prob\left[Game_{i-1}\right]\right|$$

$$\leq £_{i=1}^{4}\varepsilon_i\left(\kappa\right) = \rho\left(\kappa\right),\ where\ \rho\left(\kappa\right)\ \ is\ a\ negligible\ function.$$

Consequently,

$$IDEAL_{\mathcal{F}_{mPSI-CA},\mathcal{SIM}}\left(X,Y\right) \equiv^c REAL_{mPSI-CA,\mathcal{C}}\left(X,Y\right).$$

Subcase II (B and Ar Are Corrupted)

Consider $\mathcal{Z}$ as a distinguisher that controls $\mathcal{C}$, feeds the input of the honest party A and also sees the output of B. Now, the argument is that $\mathcal{Z}$'s view in the real world ($\mathcal{C}$'s view + A's output) and its view in the ideal world ($\mathcal{SIM}$'s view + $\overline{A}$'s output) are indistinguishable, where the view of an entity consists of the transcripts available to it. To prove that a sequence of games $Game_0, \ldots, Game_5$, where each $Game_{i+1}$ modifies $Game_i$ slightly, such that $\mathcal{Z}$'s views in $Game_i$ and $Game_{i+1}$

remain indistinguishable, for $i = 0,..,4$. The probability that $\mathcal{Z}$ distinguishes the view of $Game_i$ from the view of the real protocol is denoted by $Prob\left[Game_i\right]$ and S_i. as the simulator that simulates the honest party B in $Game_i$ for $i = 0,...,5$.

$Game_0$: This game is similar to the real protocol, where the simulator S_0 has the full knowledge of A and interacts with $\mathcal{C}$. Hence, $Prob\left[REAL_{mPSI-CA,\mathcal{C}}\left(X,Y\right)\right] = Prob\left[Game_0\right]$.

$Game_1$: This game is the same as $Game_0$ except that S_1 simulates π_1. $\mathcal{Z}$'s views in $Game_0$ and $Game_1$ are indistinguishable because of zero-knowledge (simulatability) of the proof π_1. Therefore, there exists a negligible function $\varepsilon_1\left(\kappa\right)$ such that $\left|Prob\left[Game_1\right] - Prob\left[Game_0\right]\right| \le \varepsilon_1\left(\kappa\right)$.

$Game_2$: This game corresponds to $Game_2$ cept the following:

- The simulator S_2 maintains a list Y' and records all $poly\left(\kappa\right)$ queries the adversary made to the random oracles such as $h_1,...,h_k$, where κ is a security parameter.
- If the verifications of both the proofs $\pi_2, \hat{\pi}_2$ succeed, then the simulator S_2 runs the extractor algorithm for $\hat{\pi}_2$ with $\mathcal{C}$ to extract the permutation $\phi \in £_m$. For each $y' \in Y'$, the simulator S_2 constructs an m-bit string s whose i-th bit $s^{(i)}$ is defined as follows $s^{(i)} = \begin{cases} 1, & if\ i \in \left\{\phi\left(h_1\left(y'\right)\right),...,\phi\left(h_k\left(y'\right)\right)\right\} \\ 0, & otherwise, \end{cases}$

  computes $\nu = \prod_{i=1}^{m}\left(\left(\bar{C}_i\right)^{s^{(i)}}\right)$ and checks that s is in $\left\{s_1,...,s_w\right\}$ or not, where the set $\left\{s_1,...,s_w\right\}$ is extracted from the second round message $R_2 =< \{\bar{C}_i\}_{i=1}^m, \{\bar{y}_j = \left(\bar{c}_j, \bar{d}_j\right), s_j, T_j, vE_{vpk_{Ar}}\left(g^{r_j}\right)\}_{j=1}^{w}, \pi_2, \hat{\pi}_2 >$ sent by the party B (i.e., $\mathcal{C}$) to the party A (i.e., S_2). If the check is valid then S_2 includes y' in Y''. Note that the extracted set Y'' is essentially Y except with negligible probability Ɛ.

The simulation soundness of the proof $\hat{\pi}_2$ makes $\mathcal{Z}$'s views in $Game_1$ and $Game_2$ indistinguishable. Consequently,

$$\left|Prob\left[Game_2\right] - Prob\left[Game_1\right]\right| \le \varepsilon_2\left(\kappa\right), \text{ where } \varepsilon_2\left(\kappa\right) \text{ is a negligible function.}$$

$Game_3$: Note that in this game, the simulator S_3 has the knowledge of A 's input set $X = \{x_1, ..., x_v\}$, secret key $esk_A = a_1$ of A and B 's input set, $Y = \{y_1, ..., y_w\}$ extracted as in $Game_2$. This game is identical to $Game_2$ except that

- If the verification of the proof π_4 succeeds then S_3 outputs $|X \cap Y|$ as the final output of A making use of the extracted set Y,
- If the verification of the proof π_4 fails or C aborts in the procedure $mPSI$ -CA, then the following cases arise:
  - If C sends $\{g_1, ..., g_w\}$ to S_3 in the procedure $DisputeResolution$, then S_3 first sets $card = 0$. For $j = 1, \ldots, w$, the simulator S_3 extracts $T_j, \bar{c}_j, \bar{d}_j$ from $R_2 =< \{\bar{C}_i\}_{i=1}^{m}$,
  - $\{\bar{y}_j = (\bar{c}_j, \bar{d}_j), s_j, T_j, vE_{vpk_{Ar}}(g^{r_j})\}_{j=1}^{w}, \pi_2, \hat{\pi}_2 >$, computes $\hat{e}_j = \frac{T_j}{g_j}$ and uses $\hat{e}_j$ to compute $\ell_j = \frac{\bar{d}_j}{(\bar{c}_j)^{a_1} \hat{e}_j}$. The simulator S_3 then increases the count variable $card$ by 1 if $\ell_j = 0$ for $j = 1, ..., w$ and outputs $card$ as the final output of A.
  - if C aborts in the procedure $DisputeResolution$, then S_3 outputs $\perp$ as the final output of A.

Clearly, $\mathcal{Z}$'s views in $Game_2$ and $Game_3$ are indistinguishable. Therefore, there exists a negligible function $\varepsilon_3(\kappa)$ such that $|Prob[Game_3] - Prob[Game_2]| \leq \varepsilon_3(\kappa)$.

$Game_4$: This game is analogous to $Game_3$ except that S_4 does the following after extracting $Y = \{y_1, ... y_w\}$:

- Computes $|X \cap Y|$ utilizing B 's input set $X = \{x_1, ..., x_v\}$ and constructs a set $\tilde{Y} = \{\tilde{y}_1, ..., \tilde{y}_w\}$ by including $|X \cap Y|$ many ciphertexts of the form $dE_{pk}(0)$ together with $v - |X \cap Y|$ many random ciphertexts as $dE_{pk}(r)$, where $r \in_R \mathbb{Z}_q$ and $r \neq 0$. Let $\tilde{y}_j = (\bar{\lambda}_j, \bar{\delta}_j)$ for $j = 1, ..., w$.
- Chooses a random permutation $\psi \in £_w$ over the set $\{1, ..., w\}$, selects $\beta_1, ..., \beta_w \in_R \mathbb{Z}_q$ and computes for each $j = 1, ..., w$,

$$\mu_j = \tilde{y}_{\psi^{-1}(j)} \mathcal{DEL}.Enc\left(g^0, pk, par, \beta_j\right) = \left(\overline{\lambda}_{\psi^{-1}(j)}, \overline{\delta}_{\psi^{-1}(j)}\right)\left(g^{\beta_j}, g^0 h^{\beta_j}\right) = \left(e_j, f_j\right),$$

$$\overline{e}_j = (e_j)^{a_1}, \ where\ e_j = \overline{\lambda}_{\psi^{-1}(j)} g^{\beta_j}, f_j = f\overline{\delta}_{\psi^{-1}(j)} h^{\beta_j}.$$

- Simulates the proofs $\pi_3, \hat{\pi}_3$ and sends $< \{\mu_j = \left(e_j, f_j\right), \left(\overline{e}_j\right)\}_{j=1}^{w} >$ to $\mathcal{C}$.

As the associated encryption scheme $\mathcal{DEL}$ is semantically secure, the tuple $< \{\mu_j = \left(e_j, f_j\right), \left(\overline{e}_j\right)\}_{j=1}^{w} >$ is identically distributed in $Game_4$ and $Game_3$. Indistinguishability of $< \{\mu_j = \left(e_j, f_j\right), \left(\overline{e}_j\right)\}_{j=1}^{w} >$ and the zero-knowledge (simulatability) of $\pi_3, \hat{\pi}_3$ make the views of $\mathcal{Z}$ in $Game_3$ and $Game_4$ indistinguishable. Hence,

$$\left|Prob\left[Game_4\right] - Prob\left[Game_3\right]\right| \leq \varepsilon_4\left(\kappa\right), \ where\ \varepsilon_4\left(\kappa\right)\ is\ a\ negligible\ function.$$

$Game_5$: This game is similar to $Game_4$ except that during the setup phase, the simulator S_5 in simulating A chooses $a_1 \in_R \mathbb{Z}_q$. Consequently, the views of $\mathcal{Z}$ in $Game_4$ and $Game_5$ are indistinguishable. Therefore, there exists a negligible function $\varepsilon_5\left(\kappa\right)$ such that $\left|Prob\left[Game_5\right] - Prob\left[Game_4\right]\right| \leq \varepsilon_5\left(\kappa\right)$. Construct the ideal world simulator $\mathcal{SIM}$ that uses $\mathcal{C}$ as a subroutine, simulates the honest party A and controls $\overline{B, Ar}$ and incorporates all steps from $Game_5$.

- $\mathcal{SIM}$ first plays the role of the trusted party by generating the global parameter $gpar = (ppar, m, k, H, \{\tau_i\}_{i=-4}^{m}, \{\iota_j\}_{j=-4}^{w})$, where $ppar = \left(par, \hat{g}, \mathcal{H}\right)$. It then simulates the honest party A by choosing $\overline{a}_1 \in_R \mathbb{Z}_q$ and publishing $g^{\overline{a}_1}$ as the public key $epk_A = y_A$. It also acts as a certifying authority to obtain public keys epk_B, vpk_{Ar} of B, Ar. $\mathcal{SIM}$ then invokes $\mathcal{C}$.
- $\mathcal{SIM}$ constructs a Bloom filter BF_X whose all entries are set as 0 and encrypts each of $g^{\overline{b}_i} = g^{BF_X[i]} = g^0$ using public key $pk = epk_A \cdot epk_B$ to get the ciphertext $C_i \leftarrow \mathcal{DEL}.Enc\left(g^{b_i}, pk, par, r_{b_i}\right)$ for $i = 1, ..., m$. $\mathcal{SIM}$ then simulates the proof π_1 and sends $\left\{C_1, ..., C_m\right\}$ to $\mathcal{C}$.

- The simulator $\mathcal{SIM}$ maintains a list Y' by recording all the $poly(\kappa)$ queries the adversary made to the random oracles.
- On receiving $R_2 =< \{\bar{C}_i\}_{i=1}^{m}, \{\bar{y}_j, s_j, T_j, vE_{vpk_{Ar}}(g^{r_j})\}_{j=1}^{w}, \pi_2, \hat{\pi}_2 >$ from C, $\mathcal{SIM}$ verifies each of the proofs $\pi_2, \hat{\pi}_2$. If the verifications of at least one of the proofs does not succeed then $\mathcal{SIM}$ instructs $\bar{B}$ to send $\perp$ to T, $\overline{Ar}$ to send $b_A = \circ$ to T and terminates the execution; otherwise, $\mathcal{SIM}$ runs the extractor algorithm for $\hat{\pi}_2$ with C to extract the permutation $\phi \in £_m$. For each $y' \in Y'$, the simulator $\mathcal{SIM}$ constructs an m-bit string s whose i-th bit $s^{(i)}$ is defined as follows:

$$s^{(i)} = \begin{cases} 1, & if\ i \in \{\phi(h_1(y')), \ldots, \phi(h_k(y'))\} \\ 0, & otherwise, \end{cases}$$

and checks that s is in $\{s_1, \ldots, s_w\}$ or not. If the check is valid, then it includes y' in Y''. Note that the extracted set Y'' is identical to the set Y except with negligible probability ε. $\mathcal{SIM}$ then instructs $\bar{B}$ to send Y to T, $\overline{Ar}$ to send $b_B = \circ$ to T and receives $|X \cap Y|$ from T.

- Similar to $Game_4$, $\mathcal{SIM}$ constructs a set $\tilde{Y} = \{\tilde{y}_1, \ldots, \tilde{y}_w\}$ with $\tilde{y}_j = (\bar{\lambda}_j, \bar{\delta}_j)$, chooses a random permutation $\psi \in £_w$ over the set $\{1, \ldots, w\}$, selects $\beta_1, \ldots, \beta_w \in_R \mathbb{Z}_q$ and computes for each $j = 1, \ldots, w$,

$$\mu_j = \tilde{y}_{\psi^{-1}(j)} \mathcal{DEL}.Enc(g^0, pk, par, \beta_j) = (\bar{\lambda}_{\psi^{-1}(j)}, \bar{\delta}_{\psi^{-1}(j)})(g^{\beta_j}, g^0 h^{\beta_j}) = (e_j, f_j),$$

$$\bar{e}_j = (e_j)^{\bar{a}_1}\ where\ e_j = \bar{\lambda}_{\psi^{-1}(j)} g^{\beta_j}, f_j = f\bar{\delta}_{\psi^{-1}(j)} h^{\beta_j}.$$

$\mathcal{SIM}$ then simulates $\pi_3, \hat{\pi}_3$ and sends $< \{\mu_j = (e_j, f_j), (\bar{e}_j)\}_{j=1}^{w} >$ to C.. $\mathcal{SIM}$ executes following steps according to C's reply.

- If C instructs B to send $< \{g^{r_j}\}_{j=1}^{w}, \pi_4 >$, then $\mathcal{SIM}$ checks the validity of the proof π_4. If the verification succeeds then $\mathcal{SIM}$ instructs $\overline{Ar}$ to send

$b_A = \circ$ to T. If verification fails or $\mathcal{C}$ instructs B to abort the procedure $mPSI$-CA, then the following cases arise:

- ◦ If $\mathcal{C}$ instructs Ar to send $\{g_1, \ldots, g_w\}$ in the procedure $DisputeResolution$, then the simulator $\mathcal{SIM}$ extracts $T_j, \overline{c}_j, \overline{d}_j$ from $R_2 =< \{\overline{C}_i\}_{i=1}^m, \{\overline{y}_j = (\overline{c}_j, \overline{d}_j), s_j, T_j,$ computes $\hat{e}_j = \frac{T_j}{g_j}$ and uses $\hat{e}_j$ to compute $l_j = \frac{\overline{d}_j}{(\overline{c}_j)^{\overline{a}_1} \hat{e}_j}$ for $j = 1, \ldots, w$. The simulator $\mathcal{SIM}$ then increases $card$ by 1 if $l_j = 1$ for $j = 1, \ldots, w$, where the count variable $card$ is initially set as 0. Finally, $\mathcal{SIM}$ instructs $\overline{Ar}$ to send $b_A = card$ to T, outputs whatever $\mathcal{C}$ outputs and terminates.
- ◦ If $\mathcal{C}$ instructs Ar to abort in dispute resolution protocol, then $\mathcal{SIM}$ instructs $\overline{Ar}$ to send $b_A = \perp$ to T. $\mathcal{SIM}$ then outputs whatever $\mathcal{C}$ outputs and terminates.
- If $\mathcal{C}$ instructs both B and Ar to abort, then $\mathcal{SIM}$ instructs $\overline{Ar}$ to send $b_A = \perp$ to T. Then outputs whatever $\mathcal{C}$ outputs and terminates.

Consequently, the ideal world simulator $\mathcal{SIM}$ provides the real world adversary $\mathcal{C}$ exactly the same simulation as the simulator S_5 as in $Game_5$. Hence

$$Prob\left[IDEAL_{\mathcal{F}_{mPSI-CA}, \mathcal{SIM}}(X,Y)\right]$$

$$= Prob\left[Game_5\right] \text{ and}$$

$$\left|Prob\left[IDEAL_{\mathcal{F}_{mPSI-CA}, \mathcal{SIM}}(X,Y)\right] - Prob\left[REAL_{mPSI-CA,C}(X,Y)\right]\right|$$

$$= \left|Prob\left[Game_5\right] - Prob\left[Game_0\right]\right|$$

$$\leq £_{i=1}^{5} \left|Prob\left[Game_i\right] - Prob\left[Game_{i-1}\right]\right|.$$

$$\leq £_{i=1}^{5} \varepsilon_i(\kappa) = \rho(\kappa), \textit{ where } \rho(\kappa) \textit{ is a negligible function.}$$

Thus,

$$IDEAL_{\mathcal{F}_{mPSI-CA},\mathcal{SIM}}\left(X,Y\right)\equiv^{c} REAL_{mPSI-CA,\mathcal{C}}\left(X,Y\right).$$

Subcase III (A and B Are Corrupted)

This case is trivial as $\mathcal{C}$, has full knowledge of X and Y and the encryption scheme used by Ar is semantically secure. Therefore, a simulator can always be constructed.

Case II (When the Adversary $\mathcal{C}$ Corrupts Only One Party)

If only the arbiter Ar is corrupted, then Ar is not involved in the protocol as A and B are honest. Thus, it is trivial to construct a simulator in this case. If only A or B is corrupted, then the simulator can be constructed as in steps (i)-(v) of the case when both A and Ar are corrupted or in steps (i)-(v) of the case when both B and Ar are corrupted. The only change in these cases is that $\overline{Ar}$ is honest and always sends $\circ$ to T.

CONCLUSION

In this work, the author utilized Bloom filter to design PSI-CA and APSI-CA, where GM encryption is used as homomorphic encryption. Each of these constructions achieves linear complexity and satisfies the size-hiding property. In particular, proposed PSI-CA and APSI-CA are the *first* classical size-hiding constructions achieving security in the standard model with linear complexity. In addition to that, the author has designed a *fair* optimistic Bloom filter based $mPSI$ -CA protocol attaining linear complexity overhead. Security of this scheme is provided in the malicious environment under the DDH assumption with random oracles. To preserve fairness, the author has used an off-line semi-trusted arbiter. Particularly, proposed $mPSI$ -CA is more efficient than existing $mPSI$ -CA protocols and it is the *first* $mPSI$ -CA based on *Bloom filter.*

REFERENCES

Agrawal, R., Evfimievski, A., & Srikant, R. (2003). Information sharing across private databases. *Proceedings of the 2003 ACM SIGMOD international conference on Management of data*, 86-97. 10.1145/872757.872771

Bellare, M., & Goldreich, O. (1993). *On defining proofs of knowledge. In Advances in Cryptology CRYPTO92* (pp. 390–420). Springer.

Bellare, M., & Rogaway, P. (1993). Random oracles are practical: A paradigm for designing efficient protocols. *Proceedings of the 1st ACM Conference on Computer and Communications Security*, 62-73.

Bloom, B. H. (1970). Space/time trade-offs in hash coding with allowable error. *Communications of the ACM, 13*(7), 422–426. doi:10.1145/362686.362692

Boneh, D. (1998). *The decision diffie-hellman problem. In Algorithmic number theory* (pp. 48–63). Springer.

Brandt, F. (2006). *Efficient cryptographic protocol design based on distributed elgamal encryption. In Information Security and Cryptology-ICISC 2005* (pp. 32–47). Springer. doi:10.1007/11734727_5

Camenisch, J., & Shoup, V. (2003). Practical verifiable encryption and decryption of discrete logarithms. *Annual International Cryptology Conference*, 126-144. 10.1007/978-3-540-45146-4_8

Camenisch, J., & Stadler, M. (1997). *Efficient group signature schemes for large groups. In Advances in Cryptology CRYPTO '97* (pp. 410–424). Springer. doi:10.1007/BFb0052252

Camenisch, J., & Zaverucha, G. (2009). Private intersection of certified sets. *International Conference on Financial Cryptography and Data Security*, 108-127. 10.1007/978-3-642-03549-4_7

Cramer, R., & Shoup, V. (1998). *A practical public key cryptosystem provably secure against adaptive chosen ciphertext attack. In Advances in Cryptology CRYPTO '98* (pp. 13–25). Springer.

De Cristofaro, E., Gasti, P., & Tsudik, G. (2012). *Fast and private computation of cardinality of set intersection and union. In Cryptology and Network Security* (pp. 218–231). Springer.

Debnath, S. K., & Dutta, R. (2015). Efficient private set intersection cardinality in the presence of malicious adversaries. *International Conference on Provable Security*, 326–339. 10.1007/978-3-319-26059-4_18

Debnath, S. K. & Dutta, R. (2016). Fair mpsi and mpsi-ca: Efficient constructions in prime order groups with security in the standard model against malicious adversary. *IACR Cryptology ePrint Archive*.

Dong, C., Chen, L., Camenisch, J., & Russello, G. (2013a). *Fair private set intersection with a semi-trusted arbiter, Data and Applications Security and Privacy*. Springer.

Dong, C., Chen, L., & Wen, Z. (2013b). When private set intersection meets big data: An efficient and scalable protocol. *Proceedings of the 2013 ACM SIGSAC conference on Computer & communications security*, 789–800. 10.1145/2508859.2516701

Dong, C., & Loukides, G. (2017). Approximating private set union/intersection cardinality with logarithmic complexity. *IEEE Transactions on Information Forensics and Security*, *12*(11), 2792–2806. doi:10.1109/TIFS.2017.2721360

Flajolet, P., & Martin, G. N. (1985). Probabilistic counting algorithms for data base Applications. *Journal of Computer and System Sciences*, *31*(2), 182–209. doi:10.1016/0022-0000(85)90041-8

Freedman, M. J., Hazay, C., Nissim, K., & Pinkas, B. (2016). Efficient set intersection with simulation-based security. *Journal of Cryptology*, *29*(1), 115–155. doi:10.100700145-014-9190-0

Freedman, M. J., Nissim, K., & Pinkas, B. (2004). *Efficient private matching and set intersection. In Advances in Cryptology-EUROCRYPT 2004* (pp. 1–19). Springer.

Furukawa, J. (2005). Efficient and verifiable shuffling and shuffle-decryption. *IEICE Transactions on Fundamentals of Electronics, Communications and Computer Science*, *88*(1), 172–188. doi:10.1093/ietfec/E88-A.1.172

Goldreich, O. (2009). Foundations of cryptography: Volume 2, basic applications. Cambridge University Press.

Goldwasser, S., & Micali, S. (1984). Probabilistic encryption. *Journal of Computer and System Sciences*, *28*(2), 270–299. doi:10.1016/0022-0000(84)90070-9

Hohenberger, S., & Weis, S. A. (2006). *Honest-verifier private disjointness testing without random oracles. In Privacy Enhancing Technologies* (pp. 277–294). Springer.

Kissner, L., & Song, D. (2005). *Privacy-preserving set operations. In Advances in Cryptology–CRYPTO 2005* (pp. 241–257). Springer. doi:10.1007/11535218_15

Pinkas, B., Schneider, T., & Zohner, M. (2014). Faster private set intersection based on ot extension. *USENIX Security*, *14*, 797–812.

Shi, R., Mu, Y., Zhong, H., Zhang, S., & Cui, J. (2016). Quantum private set intersection cardinality and its application to anonymous authentication. *Information Sciences*, *370*, 147–158. doi:10.1016/j.ins.2016.07.071

Chapter 7
A Secure Gateway Discovery Protocol Using Elliptic Curve Cryptography for Internet-Integrated MANET

Pooja Verma
Madan Mohan Malaviya University of Technology, India

ABSTRACT

Integration procedures are employed to increase and enhance computing networks and their application domain. Extensive studies towards the integration of MANET with the internet have been studied and worked towards addressing various challenges for such integration. Some idyllic mechanisms always fail due to the presence of some nasty node or other problems such as face alteration and eavesdropping. The focus of this chapter is on the design and discovery of secure gateway scheme in MANET employing trust-based security factors such as route trust and load ability. Over these, the elliptic curve cryptography is applied to achieve confidentiality, integrity, and authentication while selecting optimum gateway node that has less bandwidth, key storage space, and faster computational time. Simulation results of the security protocol through SPAN for AVISPA tool have shown encouraging results over two model checkers namely OFMC and CL-AtSe.

DOI: 10.4018/978-1-5225-5742-5.ch007

INTRODUCTION

Mobile Ad hoc network is an autonomous stand-alone structureless network without any need of centralized authority. MANET is a galaxy of mobile nodes which can communicate via wireless links. These nodes are free to move and change their location anytime, and anywhere. A type of an interface called a gateway is required to connect a MANET architecture with the Internet. This integrated architecture results in a kind of wireless access network wherein gateway advertises its information regarding its availability along with consumption of resources of the network, however, various challenges arise during this process. Due to mobility of end nodes, they receive several advertisement messages from different gateways. Consequently, the decision-making process regarding the selection of the most efficient gateway out of various available gateways becomes challenging. Being a key towards successful integration of MANET with the Internet, several gateway discovery procedures have been developed, however, a procedure which is both efficient as well as able to transmit and receive packets securely is highly desired. Design of such a gateway discovery procedure requires a clear understanding of the security concept of MANET, various security algorithms and security parameters to have a safer data delivery and a highly efficient integration of MANET with the Internet.

Figure 1, illustrates the integration of MANET with the Internet, where mobile nodes MN1, MN2, MN3, MN4, and MN5 belong to proactive zone and all other mobile nodes belong to the reactive zone. This architecture comprises of two gateway nodes GW1 and GW2 which are used for its integration with Internet. It has three fixed node points to which MN intends to communicate (Gupta, Kumar and Gupta, 2014).

Several strategies for selection of optimum gateway based on 'route trust', 'load capacity of a node', 'path' and 'node trust values', have been proposed. However, these have found to be inadequate to prevent the malicious node activities.

In this chapter, a *gateway discovery scheme* which is efficient, trustworthy and secure is presented. The security is achieved by the use of secure parameters as 'route trust level', 'node trust', 'hop count' and 'residual path load capacity'. To prevent possible malicious activity by some node, an authentication scheme based on elliptic curve cryptographic scheme is used in the proposed method. The proposed scheme also improves the delivery ratio, decreases the packet drop rate with cost lower in comparison to other gateway selection mechanisms. It also requires less bandwidth and storage space, thereby resulting in the fastest computation. The use of elliptic curve cryptography ensures secure integration with the Internet.

Figure 1. Basic architecture of Internet integration with MANET

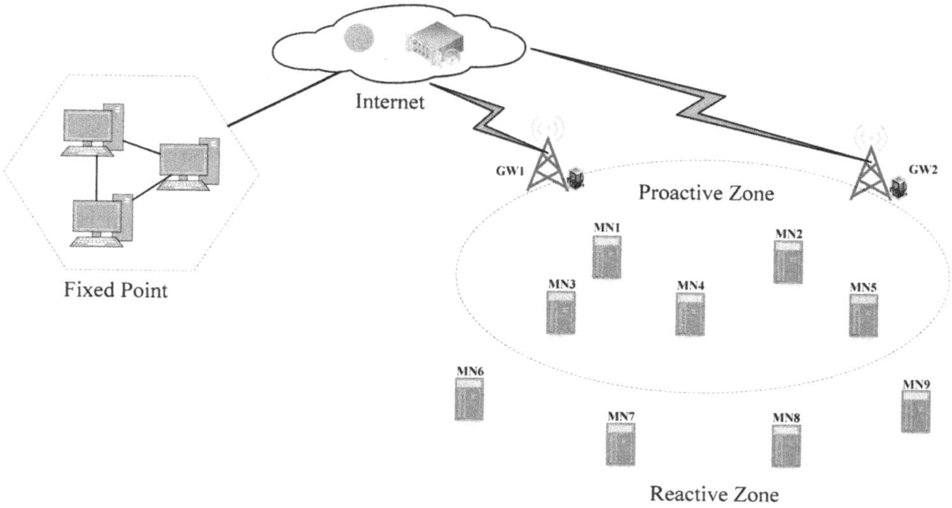

Vulnerability Points in MANET

The prominent features of MANET such as dynamic topology, boundary-less network, fast and easy set up makes it popular primarily for military applications and disaster management. However, these features raise a lot of challenges including its integration with the Internet, management of topologies, security and energy issues, etc. (Dorriet al., 2015). Various vulnerable points in MANETs are given here under:

- **Unprotected Boundary:** Mobile nodes of this network are free to move outside the network range automatically, however, a node can communicate only if it is present in its radio range. Because of the absence of boundaries in MANET, it becomes vulnerable to many active as well as passive attacks including dropping of transmitted data, false responses or alteration of integrity.
- **Negotiable Nodes:** For an attacker to get a full control of the node, the attacks must be carried from within the network. The prevention of such attacks becomes tough because of the self-governing nature of mobile nodes in the network.
- **Absence of Central Administration:** MANET is a self-configurable system in which communication among mobile nodes is possible without the need of any central authority. The forwarding and receiving operation of packets should be performed by nodes that act as routers themselves. Because of

this, the detection and prevention of attack will become the most critical task in MANET. All other communication activities which are based on Blind Mutual Trust should be performed in the absence of central authority.

- **Scalable Network:** Traditional Network establishment is completely wired and requires each machine to be connected to this wired network. At any phase of networking operation, the number of machines which are connected should be counted as the number of connected nodes and must be defined in the starting phase. However, the contemporary MANET is different because in this network architecture all nodes are freely mobile and the prediction at any time about the number of nodes is not possible. All the new services provided by MANET must adapt to this scalable nature.

Security Concepts in MANET

The main goal of security primitives is to make a strong and robust network, concerning the services it provides, to ensure it cannot be defeated or compromised by any malicious node. However, the implicit features of MANET raise certain issues when these security primitives are set. During the process of designing and implementing a secure MANET, certain trade-offs are to be made in the security parameters otherwise the assigned security to the system shall fail in practice, (Sarika et al., 2016). This procedure is completely dependent on the network application, and it is necessary that each primitive be set in a way that guarantees all services. This section defines five security primitives and their underlying challenges:

- **Authentication:** For a genuine communication between nodes, some authentication procedure which verifies the identity of a user is required. For example, with the public key scheme, the public key of nodes which want to communicate with each other must be shared.
- **Confidentiality:** This security primitive ensures that the transmitted information is only readable by the intended recipient. Hence, accessing of information is limited to an authorized person only.
- **Integrity:** This primitive confirms that no change to data occurs during its transmission between nodes. Integrity can be achieved by creating a hash value of the data.
- **Non-Repudiation:** Having this primitive, the sender and receiver cannot deny sending or receiving of data.
- **Availability:** As the name implies, this primitive makes sure that all the required information or services or resources are available to a node at any time for the completion of a procedure. This availability will be affected or denied by attacks such as denial of services (DoS) or selfish node attack.

ARITHMETIC BACKGROUND OF ECC

Authors Koblitz (Koblitz, 1987) and Miller (Miller, 1998) introduced a cryptosystem, called Elliptic Curve Cryptography which uses a smaller key size but provides the same level of security as other popular algorithms like RSA, Diffie Hellman, etc., making it one of the fastest algorithms in execution and saving extra requirement of bandwidth. Therefore, ECC is being used in many areas like mobile devices with limited storage capacity and minimum computational power and time requirements.

The elliptic curves are plane algebraic curves defined over fields which can be finite, polynomial, real, complex, etc. We use finite fields to apply this algorithm which is based on cryptographic action. The equation below is known as *Weierstrass* equations for obtaining *affine* coordinates.

$$E : y^2 + a_1 xy + a_2 y = x^3 + a_2 x^2 + a_4 x + a_6$$

The work mainly considered elliptic curve primitives such as key exchange, encryption, and decryption. These functions are implemented using the concept of points and the arithmetic of points over the selected field. These points form the solution for the respective elliptic curve. As ECC is analogue of Dlog. problem such as its security level is estimated based on a discrete logarithm that is always defined as a hard problem for computation. First, we should be aware of the nomenclature used by ECC, such as:

- **Scalar:** The element which belongs to field GF (P) or GF (2^k) is known as a scalar. Usually, we use lowercase for its representation such as r, p, q, e. These fields are known as finite and polynomial fields respectively.
- **Scalar Addition:** The resultant of Scalar Addition of two elements of a field on which the elliptic curve is defined is also an element of the respective field. For example, for $r = p + q$, if p and q belong to field GF (P) or GF (2^k), then r also belongs to field GF (P) or GF (2^k).
- **Scalar Multiplication:** The multiplication of two elements must be an element which belongs to the respective field. It is demonstrated as follows: $= p.q$, where e, p, and q belong to the finite or polynomial field.
- **Scalar Inverse:**
  - Multiplicative inverse of an element is computed as follows:

$$e.e^{-1} = 1$$

  - The additive inverse of an element is computed as follows:

$$e + e^{-1} = 0$$

where 0 is known as infinity point which has been briefed below.

e^{-1} is computed by using the extended Euclidian algorithm.

- **Point:** To satisfy the elliptic curve equation, a pair of scalars is computed. This is known as a point over the curve and is represented with the help of x and y coordinates which is a scalar of field (either finite or polynomials). Points are demonstrated by using uppercases alphabets like P, Q, R, etc.

Point P can behold two coordinates x and y as P (x, y) which can be written as (x_p, y_p) or (P_x, P_y). Similarly, another point is written as (x_q, y_q) or (Q_x, Q_y).

- **Addition of Points:** By this operation, a third point is found after performing the addition operation over two points present over the curve. Notation '+' is used to denote this operation. If P and Q are two distinct points over the curve, the result of the addition operation is generation of R which is shown as follows:

$$P + Q = R$$

Coordinates of Resultant Point R are calculated as follows:

$$\Delta = {(Q_y - P_y)}\Big/{(Q_x - P_x)}$$

$$R_x = \Delta^2 - P_x - Q_x$$

$$R_y = -P_y + \Delta(P_x - R_x)$$

where Δ is the slope and R must be some another point on a defined curve, when the addition is performed over two distinct points P and Q.

- **Doubling of Point:** When the addition action is performed over same points, the resultant value is known as doubling of points shown as follows:

$$P + P = 2P$$

- **Multiplication of Point:** By using the doubling concept, the multiplication operation performed over two points P and Q is as follows:

$$P.Q = P + P + P + P \ldots\ldots P, Q\, times$$

- **Infinity Point:** For two points P and Q having the same x coordinates, their addition operation yields a vertical line, and the addition result R does not exist. In this case, the infinity point is defined by P+Q. It has several properties like

$$P + e = P$$

$$P.e = e$$

where e is Infinity Point over the elliptic curve.

Elliptic Curve Cryptography Key Exchange Protocol

A selected form of Elliptic Curve is $y^2 = x^3 + ax + b$, which is defined over a prime field. Several domain parameters have been used for this curve with the help of which we calculate y using a given value for a, b, G and prime modulo number P. The curve generated from a series of points (x,y) is symmetric with respect to the x-axis (y=0).

Domain Parameter: (a, b, G, n, P) which are as follows:

P: Field (modulo P)

a, b: These define the curve

G: Generating points

n: Prime order of G = Ord(G)

For the current work, a shared secret key which can be used to provide authentication to nodes (then called authorized nodes) is required. The procedure adopted for exchanging this secret key between the source and destination nodes using elliptic curve cryptography is given in Table 1.

Initially, both nodes send their public key over the channel without any protection. After this step, both the nodes simultaneously compute the shared key by multiplying the received public keys with their own private key, thereby resulting in both sides generating the same shared key. Out of this key, x- coordinate is being used for encryption of transmitted data and decryption of ciphertext, like $K_{S.x}$ is being used to encrypt data and $K_{D.x}$ is used to decrypt the encrypted data.

Table 1. Procedure for shared secret key exchange

SOURCE	DESTINATION
• Private Key (select a random number) $1 < \alpha < n$ • Generate the Public key: $Q_S = \alpha * G$ • Send Q_S • Receive Q_D • Compute Key: $K_S = \alpha * Q_D$ $= \alpha * \beta * G$ • Shared Secret Key: x-coordinate of K_S: $K_{S.x}$	• Private Key (select a random number) $1 < \beta < n$ • Generate the Public key: $Q_D = \beta * G$ • Receive Q_S • Send Q_D • Compute Key: $K_D = \beta * Q_S$ $= \alpha * \beta * G$ • Shared Secret Key: x-coordinate of K_D: $K_{D.x}$

ECC Encryption/ Decryption

This cryptographic algorithm is used for the secure transmission of data over the public channel. Here, the sender sends the encrypted message with a shared key and receiver decrypts the received ciphertext by using its private key. This scheme is mainly used to preserve the confidentiality security primitive.

- **At Sender End**
  a. The first sender uses the public key which is publicly available over the channel.
  b. The sender then uses his own private key and encrypts the data M which it wants to share such as: $(\alpha.G, M + \alpha.Q_D)$. Ciphertext C being generated is of the form (C1, C2).
- **At Receiver End**
  a. The first receiver multiplies its own private key with C1 part of ciphertext as: $(C1.\beta)$.
  b. Then subtract this result from C2 to get $C2 - C1.\beta$.
- **At Intruder End**
  a. If any malicious node tries to access the encrypted data, it needs to compute the key α given G and αG, which is considered as a very hard discrete logarithmic problem to solve.

Mathematically, we can see that how the transmitted data M is encrypted at sender side and how the ciphertext is decrypted at the receiver side:

- **Source End:** Plain Text M
  $= \alpha * G, M + \alpha * Q_D$ >> Encryption (Cipher Text)

Figure 2. The encryption and decryption scheme based on elliptic curve cryptography

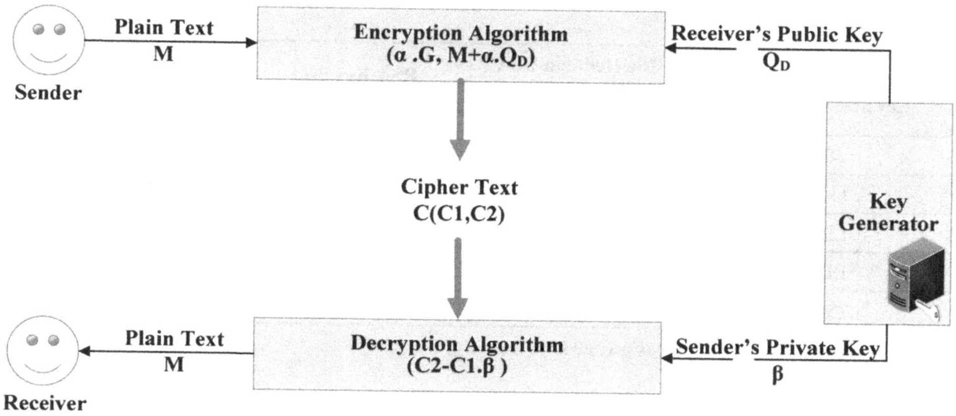

$= M + \alpha * Q_D - \beta * \alpha * G$ >> Decryption
$= M + \alpha * \beta * G - \beta * \alpha * G$
= M Plain Text: (**Receiver end**)

Security Level of Elliptic Curve Cryptography

Level of Security in ECC mainly depends on the difficulty level of computation of key α, given G and αG, that is already defined as a logarithm problem. ECC uses smaller key size and thus, provides computational advantages, shorter storage space, and lesser bandwidth requirements when compared to others algorithms like RSA and Diffie Hellman DSA. The key size of all the schemes is compared based on the computational effort in Table 2.

LITERATURE REVIEW

Gupta et al. (Gupta et al., 2014) introduced a mechanism based on the trust value and cryptographic algorithm. The study considered three parameters for the selection of a trustworthy node, however, the data transmitted through the found trusty node was not found to be sufficiently safe. Therefore, digital signature algorithms were used for providing security. Selection of the gateway has been made by data categories (normal, sensitive). For this, a trust-based gateway selection scheme, where some authentication procedure is employed for transmission of sensitive data, was introduced.

Table 2. Comparable key size with respect to the computational effort (NIST SP-800- 57)

Security Level Symmetric Key Size (in Bits)	Diffie Hellman DSA Key Size (in Bits)	RSA Key Size (in Bits)	ECC Modulus Size (in Bits)
80	L: 1024 N: 160	1024	160-223
112	L: 2048 N: 224	2048	224-255
128	L: 3072 N: 256	3072	256-383
192	L: 7680 N: 384	7680	384-511
256	L: 15360 N: 512	15360	512+

Where L is public key size and N is private key size.

Manoharan et al. (Manoharan et al., 2011) proposed a selection mechanism for gateways during the process of integration of MANET with the Internet. The study categorized the integration challenges of MANET into four categories namely: addressing, gateway, agility, and routing. Normalized security parameters like node trust, route trust, and residual route load capacity were chosen for trust-based selection. The study introduced a hybrid approach in which gateway advertisement message is sent via the gateway node in the proactive zone, and solicitation messages are forwarded from the reactive zone via a mobile node to discover an optimal gateway node. However, when the malicious entities present in the network increased exponentially, the performance of the network throughout decreased considerably.

Ahmad and Khan (Ahmed & Khan, 2013), proposed a light weight mechanism based on trust and security to discover an optimal gateway node for forwarding packets. Two security matrices namely route trust and residual load capacity were employed to build a reliable mechanism for gateway selection. This concept is based on mutual trust and authentication between nodes. The study also discovered that reasons such as congestion over the path, and overflow problem in interface queries of an intermediate node are for packets drop at a normal node and as such it introduced efficient adaptive load balancing scheme for its solution.

Chauhan et al. (Chauhan et al., 2011) introduced an approach to improve the trustworthiness of neighbor nodes. The proposed mechanism calculates the trust value of all neighbor nodes before computing the most secure path, thus, providing a mechanism for secure routing. The proposed mechanism first calculates the trust value of all the neighbor nodes and then computes the most secure path. The computed trust value of each node is refreshed after a predefined interval helping addition and removal of trust nodes periodically. The trust value is broadcast to all other nodes making them aware of malicious behavior of some node thereby, preventing DoS attacks.

The mechanism proposed by (Ferdous & Muthukkumarasamy, 2010) is based on cluster learning, using local mobile agents. In this scheme, the computed trust value of each node is included in the local managing scheme of each node and is saved as history by these agents.

Azer and El-Kassas (Azer & El-Kassas, 2010) proposed a mechanism for the detection and prevention of wormhole attack. In this scheme, each node assigns a weight to another by social science theory.

Matsuda et al. (Matsuda et al., 2010) proposed a trust-based dynamic routing scheme for gateway selection. However, they did not propose any authentication mechanism.

A comparison of various schemes proposed on various factors such as routing protocol used, adapted gateway discovery approach, trust factors of MNS, and the security level is presented in Table 3.

MOTIVATION FOR RESEARCH

The motivation of this research comes from addressing and analyzing several security challenges which arise during the stabling of the path towards the intended gateway from MNs. Monitoring and controlling procedures are required for addressing security challenges due to malicious nodes in a hybrid network. The gateway connecting

Table 3. Comparisons based on security level among proposed scheme

Integration Strategy	Routing Protocol	GWD Approach	Trust Factor of MNS	Security Level in MANET	Handoff Decision
Mewlana (2002)	DSDV	Proactive	No	No	Hop count
Haic (2003)	AODV	Hybrid	No	No	MMCS switching
Icfian (2004)	EDSDV	Reactive	No	No	Infinite Hop count
Fiians (2004)	Any ODP	Reactive	Yes	Low	Hop count
Haimfgmg 2008)	AODV	Reactive	No	No	Hop count
Ttaiim (2008)	CGSR	Hybrid	No	No	Cluster head proximity
Sedymo (2009)	AODV	Hybrid	Yes	Medium	Hop count
Egdiim (2010)	AODV	Proactive	No	No	Pathload Queue length
Isagdhm (2010)	AODV	Reactive	No	No	Hop Count
Tbgdiim (2011)	AODV	Hybrid	Yes	Low	Route Selection value
Tbsgdiim (2013)	AODV	Hybrid	Yes	Medium	Route selection value
Tbsgwsaas (2014)	AODV	Hybrid	Yes	Medium	Trust Route selection value

MANET with the Internet has a dual interface - one based on IP routing mechanism and the other based on routing for ad-hoc networks. Anyone of the gateway discovery methods from proactive, reactive and hybrid is selected while integrating MANET with the Internet. Gateway periodically broadcasts advertisement messages, and an optimum one is chosen for the establishment of a path between a node and the Internet. Thus, the gateway discovery process followed by its registration is performed while integration, which becomes a susceptible point for attacks (Wu et al., 2007). MANET is susceptible to several attacks during the Internet integration process because of its multi-hop nature, where a node may drop packets. Many proposals have discussed the efficient and effective discovery of gateways. However, few have discussed strategies for security during the discovery process, leaving huge scope for further research.

PROPOSED SECURITY PROTOCOL

Monoharan et al. (Manoharan et al., 2011) introduced a novel concept for the discovery and selection of the least congested gateway node using metrics hop count, route trust, node trust, and residual route load capacity. This work is an extension of the approach used by Monoharan et al. and makes use of a modified computation for calculating route trust level to find a highly-trusted path and a different method for calculating the node trust level (Gupta et al., 2014). To imitate a comprehensive estimation of the trust level of the path, this computation is modified to TRSV in the proposed mechanism (Manoharan et al., 2011). The work uses the concept for other available paths to ensure that the robustness of both the network and route is same as introduced in (Ahmed & Khan, 2013). Unlike, (Ahmed & Khan 2013), the work uses elliptic curve cryptography which provides high security with less key size compared to other approaches like Diffie Hellman, RSA, etc.

Gateway Selection Attributes

The current work mainly uses, metrics namely 'Residual Path Load Capacity,' 'Route_Trust Level,' 'Node_Trust Level,' and 'Hop Count' to select an optimal gateway. These parameters are defined below:

Node_Trust Level

For maintaining the dynamic changes that occur in Node_Trust, a new type of data structure known as Neighbor_Table as shown in Figure 3 has been used (Manoharan, 2011). It maintains the field Neighbor_ID and Trust value of the corresponding

Figure 3. Neighbor_Table format maintained by each node

Neighbor's ID	OTV

node. This table is maintained by the node along with the routing table at the corresponding node.

Trust factor of a node n towards another node m has been evaluated as $T^m(n)$. This value is a weighted sum of two factors: first its own trust and second the neighbor node's recommended value as in (Gupta et al., 2014)which is as follows:

$$T_n^m := (1-\mu) X_n^m + \mu R_n^m \quad (1)$$

X_n^m, Trust value hold by node m for node n has been computed as follows:

$$X_n^m := \lambda J_n^m + (1-\lambda) T_n^m \quad (2)$$

- **Neighbor's Recommendation Value Computation: R_n^m**, Aggregate Recommendation value for node n which is computed by using the set K(n) for node n is the aggregation of all the trust values held by its neighbor nodes. This set contains a subset of all the neighboring nodes. To enhance the confidence of recommendation, the subsets of neighbors hold a node which has trust value greater than a defined threshold. Here, the R_n^m represents the aggregation of the recommended value from every node j belonging to K (n).

$$R_n^m = \frac{\sum_{j \in K(n)} T_j^m * S_n^j * A_n^j}{\sum_{j \in K(n)} T_j^m * S_n^j} \quad (3)$$

Here the recommendation action is mainly based on two critical parameters. First one is the accuracy of the trust level of node and second is the stability of trust level of a link among nodes m and n. Standard Deviation methodology is used for computation of Accuracy (Theodorakopoulos & Baras, 2006). This can be written as:

$$A_n^j = N\left(T_n^j, \sigma_n^j\right) \tag{4}$$

S_n^j represents the stability of link among nodes m and n measured by j. This is the time measurement which must be known by these two nodes.

- ***Initial* Trust *Assignment:*** When a new node *p* comes in the range of some node say, *k*, node *p* is considered as a neighboring node of k, and the initial trust value of 0.5 is assigned by node k to node *p*. There are three types of trust value assignment strategies, i.e., 'sensible,' 'optimistic' and 'moderate'. In the 'sensible' strategy, node *p* never assigns trust value because it considers all the newly added neighbors as malicious. A highly-trusted value is assigned by a node to newly added neighbor nodes in case of 'optimistic' strategy. Moreover, if 'moderate' strategy is adopted, it has both possibilities of assigning trust values either 'sensible' or 'optimistic' for a new node. Therefore, a midway trust value is assigned to newly added neighbors. In our proposed proposition, we select a moderate strategy for initial trust value assignment for newly added neighbor nodes, which is denoted by I_k. Table 4, demonstrates notations used in the above equation:

Route_Trust Level

When a path exists between the nodes, then the trust level is considered to find the reliability of the existing route. Computation of Route_Trust level is made with the help of an extended routing table. Figure 4 shows the format of the new extended routing table with the additional field as in (Manoharan, 2011). Here the additional field $(TV)^A$ demonstrates the Advertised Trust value of downstream neighbor node over the path. R_P holds the capacity value of a path to compute the residual load.

In (Manoharan, 2011), the computation of route trust has been made by RREP and RREQ packets format, by which the advertised and observed trust value is being measured. Its advertised value is claiming trustworthiness of node. After receiving the advertised value of a node, receiving node compares it to its own calculated/observed trust factor which is based on the behavior of neighbor nodes like total number of packets forwarded and dropped through that node.

In (Ahmed & Khan, 2013), a modified version for estimation regarding the trustworthiness of route between nodes is proposed. The minimum value of two

Table 4. Notations used in the above equations

Notations	Description
T_n^m	Trust level of node n at node m
X_n^m	Trust value computed by node m for node n. This value ranges from 0 to 1.
R_n^m	Aggregate recommendation value by all neighbors' node, lies in a range from 0 to 1.
A_n^j	The accuracy of trust value of node n computed by node m.
S_n^j	Stability of relation among node n and m.
J_n^m	Based on judgment action of all neighbors, calculates trust value of the node.
σ	Standard deviation used for accuracy.
μ, λ	The parameter used by the equation for most relevant factor computation. Ranges from 0 to 1.
I_k^p	Initial trust value assignment by node p to all newly added neighbor nodes.

Figure 4. Extended routing table

Dest_ID	Seq_No	Rp	—	—	(TV)A	(TV)O	STRSV

factors such as observed trust and advertised trust value are selected and as such the requesting node selects a route with minimum route trust value. As the minimum function finally estimates the Route trust level, it becomes a highly vulnerable point for an attacker.

In this work, to find a better estimation of a trusted route, modification over Route trust level computation is being done. We can prevent the attacks along the route by calculating Route_Trust level based on the average function of observed and advertised value. A route_trust level calculation is being done as follows:

When a Gateway advertises its messages, then initially Route_Trust level is assigned by using a selected approach as:

- Initially $TL^R := 0.5$
- Gateway evaluates the TL^R such as $TL^R := TV_G^A$, which is unicasted along the reverse path towards intermediate node $M_{i.}$
- For all intermediate nodes, Route_Trust level is calculated as follows:
  a. if i=1, then $TL^R := AVG\left(\left(TV\right)_G^O, \left(TV\right)_i^A\right)$
  b. else for $2 \leq i \leq n$ and j = i-1, where n = Hop_count

$$TL^R := AVG\{\left(TV\right)_j^O, \left(TV\right)_i^A$$

Residual Path Load Ability

The current proposal to select a gateway path with maximum accessible load ability and the residual path load capacity, at any node is defined as the smallest accessible load ability while counting all the midway nodes and a gateway node. Let, L_n represents the maximum load ability of a node, C_n the current load ability handled by a node n, then the residual load ability R_n at node n is calculated as:

$$R_n = L_n - C_n \tag{5}$$

Where

$$C_n = \sum_{i=1}^{s} r_i s_i \tag{6}$$

where, C_n is the current load at node *n* which relay traffic from traffic source s. r_i and $s_{i,}$ respectively represent the average arrival rate and average packet size of traffic from source i. Then, we can compute the residual load ability R_p of path p as follows:

$$R_p = \min\left\{R_n, \mu_{current}\right\} \tag{7}$$

where, the residual ability of an Internet gateway $\mu_{current}$ is obtained by subtraction of current traffic load on Internet gateway from the total load C as follows:

$$\mu_{current} = C - \sum_{i=1}^{s} r_i s_i \tag{8}$$

where, s is the number of nodes connected to the Internet gateway.

Trust level and residual load ability of the path is circulated through advertisement message of gateway node which is RREP_I (Manoharan, 2011). This is an extended format of RREP as shown in Figure 5, with extra fields such as Advertised Route_Trust value and identification of recommender nodes. A hop_count value should be incremented by one when the node receives a GWADV message via an intermediate node. Moreover, the node should store the Route_Trust value in its extended routing table with the help of the forwarded message. The node next estimates the value TV^A and R_n with the help of R_ACK, such that GWADV is updated and directed towards the upstream points with an entry of the recommended node's ID.

- **Malicious Node Detection Procedure:** In our proposed work, the malicious node is detected by using the acceptance range of observed trust factor of the node. If any node M publishes an erroneous Route_Trust factor over and again, a continuous decrement in observed trust will be performed. Node M is marked as malicious if its observed Trust factor is less than a predefined threshold value. Another node N which observes its trust factor separates node M from the network by removing its entry from Neighbor_Table till time Tmal. Node N demands an alternative path towards GW by Local Repair Scheme. After the time Tmal, node M is considered as a normal node in the network. Figure 5 illustrates all the additional parameters required for the routing purpose.

Figure 6 depicts the format of R_ACK packet (Manoharan, 2011), which is directed via GW towards the requested node including each intermediate point along the path. By sending this, it notifies the node about the number of receiving packets since the previous receipt of R_ACK.

Calculation of Secure Trusted Route Selection Value

Requestor node (Originator) may receive several RRep_I via all of its neighbor nodes. To find an optimal and most Trustworthy path, source node computes a metric known as Secure Trusted Route Selection Value (STRSV). In our proposed work, this calculation is being modified by including the Route_Trust level factor. Table 5 illustrates all the notations used in equation 9 as below:

$$STRSV := \alpha 1\left({TL_i^R}/{TL_{Avg}^R}\right) + \alpha 2\left({NT_i}/{NT_{avg}}\right) + \alpha 3\left({R_P}/{R_{max}}\right) + \alpha 4\left({H^{avg}}/{H^i}\right) \quad (9)$$

Figure 5. Extended routing table format

TYPE	A	R	I	Reserved	Profix_Size	Hop_Count
RReq_ID						
Destination IP_Address						
Destination Sequence Number						
Originator IP_Address						
Originator Sequence Number						
Recommender_ID	Advertised Route_Trust Value	Rn				

Figure 6. R_ACK packet format

TYPE
Originator ID/Destination ID
Destination ID/Originator ID
Received Packet_Count
Timestamp

Algorithm for Secure Gateway Discovery

```
Initial Setup:
Input: Set of GW.
Output: Secure Trusted Route, Secure Data Transmission.
Presume: Shared a secret key among Source and GW node using Key
exchange protocol.
Step 1:
Source MN should be broadcasted as a message GWSOL to other
nodes in the network such as:
GWSOL [ RREQ, Sid, Did, Pbs, Hi, Tstamp]
Step 2:
If (node! = GW) then {
      All intermediate nodes rebroadcast this message.
      Hi: = Hi +1;
      }
```

Table 5. Notations used in equation 9

Notation	Description
TL_i^R	Neighbor node i, whose RRep_I is being considered has trust level on a route.
TL_{Avg}^R	Average value of trust level of a route by which the RRep_I packet is directed.
NT_i	Node_Trust level for neighbor node i for which RRep_I is considered.
NT_{avg}	Average Trust value being computed for a neighbor node by which RRep_I is directed.
R_p	Residual path load capacity of the path.
R_{max}	Maximum residual path load ability.
H^{avg}	Average hop being computed via every received path.
H^i	The number of Hops in RRep_I along the path.
$\alpha1, \alpha2, \alpha3, \alpha4$	• A parameter whose values lie in the range of 0 to 1. • Must satisfy the given condition as follows: $\alpha1 + \alpha2 + \alpha3 + \alpha4 = 1$

```
else {
      FA record Sid and Pbs and check in its own table for
route existence.
      If a route exists, then go to Step 4 otherwise step 3.
      }
Endif
Step 3:
Gateway informs by unicast RRep message to its first neighbor
only.
Step 4:
Reply with metric information.
Encrypt GWADV embedded with Tstamp, Hi and Seq_no. using the
shared secret key as follows:
Unicast RRep message [RRep, E{GW_ADV, K}, ATVg, RTi, Hi,
Tstamp] to an intermediate node.
Step 5:
While (every intermediate node MNi visited from GW node)
```

(i) Compute TL^R

a). if i=1 then $TL^R := AVG\left((TV)^O_G, (TV)^A_i\right)$

b). else for 2 ≤ i ≤ n and j = i-1
where n = Hop_count.

$$TL^R := AVG\left\{(TV)^O_j, (TV)^A_i\right\}$$

(ii) Rp: = min {Rn}
(iii) Hi: = Hi+1

Node MNi unicast RRep [RRep, ATVi, Rp, Hi, E {GW_ADV, K}, Tstamp] to neighbour node MNj.

(i) Check the observed route trust value is in advertising range of node.

```
If (ATVi ~~ OTVi)
        Increment the OTV of that node i.
Else
Decrement OTV of that node i.
Endif
```

(ii) Decide regarding node, if it is malicious or not.

```
If (OTVi ≥ RThreshold)
        GOTO step 5;
Else
```

Monitor this neighbor node as Malicious and Isolate this node network till time Tmal.

Step 6:

Source Node receive RRep message from its next-hop, source node computes some value in the following way:

- First Decrypt the GW_ADV message using the Shared secret key and own private key.

Also check the Tstamp, Seq_no, Hi with its sending respective value.

- If value Matched

Compute the Secure Trust Route Selection value STRSV as:

$$STRSV := \alpha 1\left(TL^R_i \big/ TL^R_{Avg}\right) + \alpha 2\left(NT_i \big/ NT_{avg}\right) + \alpha 3\left(R_P \big/ R_{\max}\right) + \alpha 4\left(H^{avg} \big/ H^i\right)$$

- Select the Route based on High RSV of the available path through the gateway for data transmission. Moreover, Keep all left (p-1) path in Queue.

```
Authenticate the Source and GW node using a secret key and Data
transfer securely.
```

SECURITY ANALYSIS OF PROPOSED PROTOCOL

Security Analysis Using AVISPA

The study has used "Automated Validation of Internet Security Protocol and Application" (AVISPA) (Ocenasek & Sveda, 2009) simulation and validation tools for the security analysis of the designed protocol. The tool has been chosen because of the following reasons:

- **Animated Feature:** It helps to model the number of objectives like sharing key secretly, authorization, and robust security protocol in contrast to attacks.
- **HLPSL:** High-Level Protocol Specification Language (HLPSL) is more user-friendly for implementing new protocols and validating them.
- **Exploration of Attack:** Various developers and researchers extensively use this tool because it explores the presence of any possible attacks in the network.

Steps involved for experimentation with AVISPA to explore the security protocol based on cryptography are as follows:

- **Step 1:** The new protocol needs to be written in the form of HLPSL specification which comprises of the role of each participant followed by a composition of role to represent the scenario of roles.
- **Step 2:** Translation of HLPSL into IF by using translator HLPSL2IF where IF consists of syntax information regarding backends and operates mathematically, including attacker behaviors.
- **Step 3:** Explore the presence of any attacks, either active or passive by using model checker of AVISPA.

Figure 7, illustrates the architecture of the AVISPA tool (http://www.avispa-project.org/package/user-manual.pdf) and shows how the HLPSL is converted into IF and passed over to model checker.

AVISPA tool comprises of four model checkers as shown in Figure 7, which illustrate the overall activity involved in this tool (Ocenasek & Sveda, 2009). These are:

Figure 7. Architecture of AVISPA tool

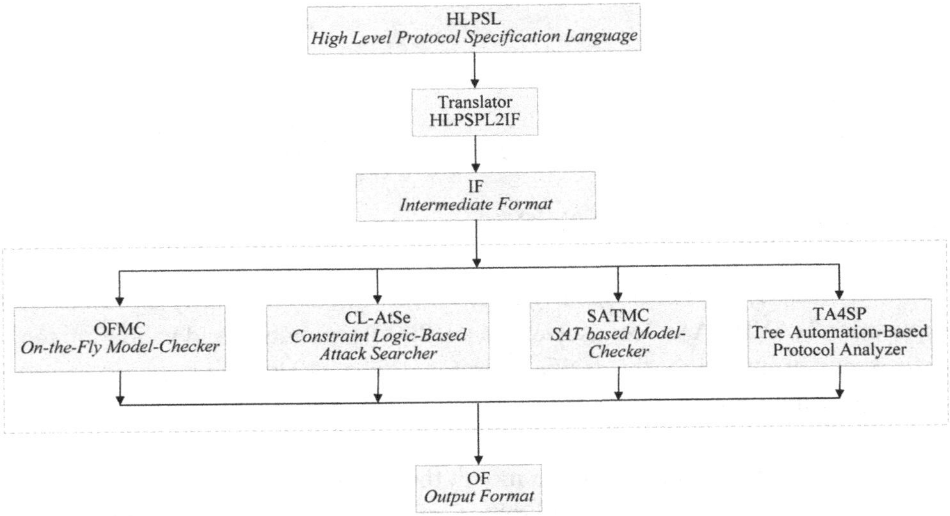

- **On-the-Fly Model Checker:** It creates an infinite tree and is based on Demand-driven nature and performs various activities for search space for the state. It detects the attack and verifies the correctness of the rules till the number of bounded sessions is checked by OFMC backend.
- **Constraint-Logic-Based Attach Searcher:** Constraints are obtained during the translation of security protocol into IF (Intermediate Format). Detection of attack is being performed by using such a set of constraints. Action translation and detection is being performed internally by CL-AtSe because of fully automated adversaries' data.
- **SAT Model Checker:** At this backend, the exploration of state space is performed by using symbolic mechanism. Like OFMC, based on bounded session, the detection of attacks and validation of required security is done.
- **Tree Automated Based Analyzer:** At this backend, valuation of attacker knowledge is computed as the number of unbounded sessions, which can be estimated by using formulae with regular tree language.

Examination and validation of security primitives of proposed SGWDP have been implemented with the help of AVISPA tool using HLSPL specifications. Role of mobile node and gateway including intruder is illustrated in Table 6, in which steps involved in GWSOL and GWADV message specification is presented.

Table 6. HLPSL specification of role played by MN and GW

```
Role SGWDP_GWSOL (M, G: agent, Kmg: Smmetric_Key, Snd, Rcv: Channel (dy))
Played_by M
def =
Local State: Nat,
Nm, Tm: Text,
Tg, Ng: Text,
RReq, RReg, RRep, RACK: Message,
ConstSec_s_Tm, Sec_s_Tg, Sec_s_Nm, Sec_s_Ng: Protocol_id
init State: = 0
Transition
0. State = 0 /\ Rcv (Start) =|>
State': = 1 /\ Snd (RReq)
1. State = 1 /\ Rcv ({Ng', Tg'} _Kmg) =|>
State': = 2 /\ Nm': = new ()
/\ Tm': = new ()
/\ Snd ({Nm', Tm', Ng', Tg'} _Kmg)
/\ Snd (RReg)
/\ Secret (Nm', Sec_s_Nm, {M, G})
/\ Secret (Ng', Sec_s_Ng, {M, G})
/\ Secret (Tm', Sec_s_Tm, {M, G})
/\ Secret (Tg', Sec_s_Tg, {M, G})
/\ witness (M, G, nm, tm, Nm', Tm')
/\ request (M, G, tg, ng, Ng, Tg')
2. State = 2 /\ Rcv ({Nm', Tm'} _Kmg)
State': = 3 /\ Rcv (RACK)
end role
```

```
Role SGWDP_GWADV (M, G: agent, Kmg: Smmetric_Key, Snd, Rcv: Channel (dy))
Played_by G
def =
Local State: Nat,
Ng, Tg: Text,
Tm, Nm: Text,
RReq, RReg, RRep, RACK: Message,
Const Sec_a_Tm, Sec_a_Tg, Sec_a_Nm, Sec_a_Ng: Protocol_id
init State: = 0
Transition
1. State = 0 /\ Rcv (RReq) =|>
State': = 1 /\ Tg': = new ()
/\ Ng': = new ()
/\ Snd ({Tg', Ng'} _Kmg)
/\ Secret (Ng', Sec_a_Ng, {M, G})
/\ Secret (Tg', Sec_a_Tg, {M, G})
/\ witness (G, M, rreq, RReq)
2. State = 1 /\ Rcv ({Nm', Ng', Tg' Tm'} _Kmg) =|>
State': = 2 /\ Snd ({Nm', Tm'} _Kmg)
/\ Snd (RACK)
/\ Secret (Nm', Sec_a_Nm, {M, G})
/\ Secret (Tm', Sec_a_Tm, {M, G})
/\ witness (G, M, nm, tm, Nm', Tm')
/\ request (G, M, tm, nm, Nm', Tm')
end role
```

In addition to this transition state defined for M and G, the role, goal, and session need to be defined for the proposed protocol. The role_environment, Goal, and session have been presented in Tables 7, 8 and 9 respectively.

- **SPAN- Security Protocol Animator:** It is used for simulation of the proposed work. Analysis of the proposed protocol has been done over OFMC, and CL-AtSe model checker and corresponding simulation result are shown in Figures 8 and 9. The results show that the proposed protocol is safe against both active and passive attacks.

Table 7. HLPSL specification for role environment

```
role_environment ()
def=
Const m g: agent,
Kmg, Kmi, Kig: Symmetric_Key,
Tm, Tg, Nm, Ng: Protocol_id,
Intruder Knowledge= {m, g, Kmi, Kig}
Composition session (m, g, Kmg)
/\ session (m, i, Kmi)
/\ session (i, g, Kig)
end role
```

Table 8. HLPSL specification for role goal

```
Goal
% Secrecy_of TM, Tg, Nm, Ng
Secrecy_of Sec_s_Tm, Sec_a_Tg, Sec_s_Nm, Sec_a_Ng.
% SWGDP_GWSOL authenticate SGWDP_GWADV on tg, ng authenticates_on Tg, Ng.
% SGWDP_ADV authenticate SGWDP_GWSOL on tm, nm authenticates_on Tm, Nm.
end Goal
```

Table 9. HLPSL specification for role session

```
role Session (M, G: agent, Kmg, Symmetric_Key)
def=
local SM, RM, SG, RG: channel(dy)
Composition
sgwdp_GWSOL (M, G, Kmg, SM, RM)
/\ sgwdp_GWADV (M, G, Kmg, SG, RG)
end role
```

Figure 8. Detection and verification over OFMC backend

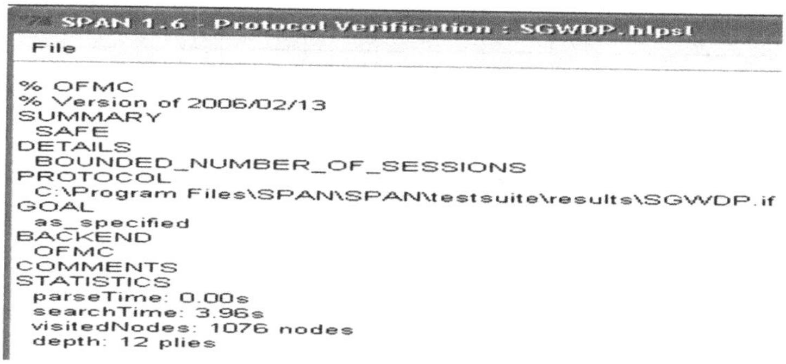

Figure 9. Detection and verification over Cl-AtSe Backend

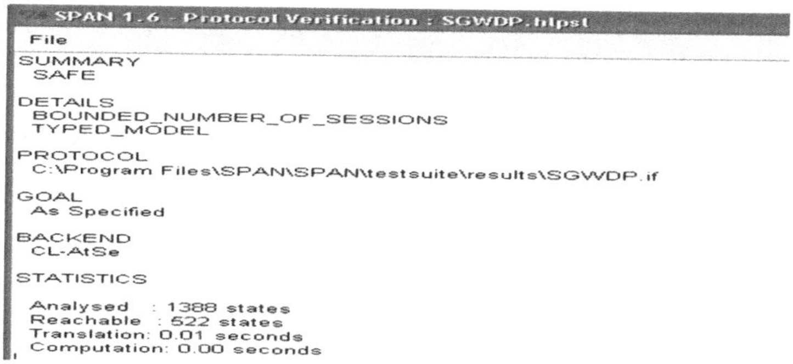

The simulation results obtained through model checker over On-the-Fly model and Constraint Logic Based Attack Searcher model for SGWDP protocol is safe against attacks.

PERFORMANCE EVALUATION BASED ON COMPUTATIONAL TIME

Performance metric computation time is the time required to compute the overall steps involved in a particular protocol. This time has been calculated and used to evaluate the performance of the proposed protocol which has been compared to TBSGDM (Ahmed & Khan, 2013) and TBSGSAAS (Gupta et al., 2014) protocols. Notations used for expressing various times, used in expressing computation time are defined in Table 10.

Table 10. Notations used for various times

Notation	Description
T_A	The time required to compute addition operation
T_S	The time required to compute subtraction operation
T_M	The time required to compute multiplication operation
T_E	The time required to compute exponential operation

Cao et al. (Cao et al., 2010) with the help of MIRCAL have estimated the required execution time for each operation in the compared cryptographic algorithm. They observed that computation time for T_M, T_S, and T_E were .83ms, 1.4ms and 11.20ms, respectively while as the total computation time required by comparison schemes are 46.46ms and 68.86ms, respectively. The total time required by the current approach is 5.6ms which is much less than the total time required in approaches proposed by Ahmed (Ahmed & Khan, 2013) and Gupta (Gupta et al., 2014) as shown in Table 11.

- **Based on Key Size:** Key length besides being a significant factor for enhancing the security level of a protocol also determines the storage requirement of a protocol. Security level increases with the increase in the key length as shown in Table 12. The table also shows a comparison of Diffie Hellman DSA and ECC cryptographic algorithm based on key length of generated keys. The column ratio shows that ECC is best and uses small key length for providing same security level in comparison to DH-DSA with a large key.
- **Based on Storage:** Due to the limitation of memory space in mobile nodes, adequate security using small storage space is highly desired. As observed from Table 12, the key for ECC requires less storage space than that of DH-DSA for providing a particular security level.

Table 11. Comparison on computation times

Scheme	Phase I	Phase II	Total Computation Time	Total Computation Time (ms)
(Ahmed & Khan, 2013)	$2T_E + 1T_M$	$2T_E + 1T_M$	$4T_E + 2T_M$	46.46
(Gupta et al., 2014)	$3T_E + 1T_M$	$3T_E + 1T_M$	$6T_E + 2T_M$	68.86
Proposed Protocol SGWDP	$1T_A + 2T_M$	$1T_S + 2T_M$	$1T_A + 4T_M + 1T_S$	5.60

Table 12. Comparison based on the key length

Security Level (in Bits)	ECC (in Bits)	Ratio	DH-DSA (in Bits)
80	160-223	1:6	L: 1024 N: 160
112	224-255	1:9	L: 2048 N: 224
128	256-383	1:12	L: 3072 N: 256
192	384-511	1:20	L: 7680 N: 384
256	512+	1:30	L: 15360 N: 512

- **Based on Robustness:** The degree of robustness of a network is determined by the type of security protocol used in it. For a particular protocol, robustness can be increased by increasing its key size; however, due to restrictions such as limited storage space, lesser bandwidth, and lesser computational power, it is preferred to use an algorithm that provides maximum security with minimum key size. In comparison with DH-DSA algorithm, ECC provides a better degree of robustness for smaller key length and hence, are preferred in the constrained nodes.

A comparison of the proposed protocol with two prominent protocols namely TBSGDM and TBSGSAAS on various factors including computational time, storage space requirement, bandwidth, type of information security attained, etc. is given in Table 13.

The comparison reports that the proposed protocol requires less key storage space with less computation time and less bandwidth requirement along with the high trust level of the route between the source and the destination node.

CONCLUSION AND FUTURE SCOPE

MANET is an autonomous and stand-alone infrastructure of fewer networks and does not require any centralized authority. MANET can be connected to the Internet through an interface, called gateway. However, there are several security issues concerning this integration of MANET with the Internet. Secure gateway discovery and selection approach defined with the help of security parameters such as route trust, node trust level, and residual path load ability is mainly used to address these security concerns. This work proposed a secure gateway discovery protocol using ECC for MANET which unlike other similar techniques does not use exponential operations. The devised protocol used hardness of ECC discrete logarithmic problem

Table 13. Comparison of the proposed protocol with an existing protocol

Parameter	Existing Strategy 1: TBSGDM	Existing Strategy 2: TBSGSAAS	Proposed Protocol: SGWDP
Computation Time	Medium	High	Very Low
Storage Space	High	High	Low
Bandwidth	Medium	Medium	Very Low
Key Size	Large	Large	Small
Confidentiality	Yes	Yes	Yes
Authentication	Yes	Yes	Yes
Non-Repudiation	Yes	Yes	Yes
Trust Level	Medium	Low	High
Attack	Found	Found	None
Local Repair Scheme	Yes	No	Yes

with smaller key size to provide adequate security, at the lesser requirement of storage space, and computational power which is highly desired in low resource nodes. Performance evaluation through computation metric and security analysis against different types of active and passive attacks carried out using SPAN for AVISPA have demonstrated the efficiency in terms of both execution time and level of security of the proposed scheme.

REFERENCES

Ahmed, M., & Khan, K. (2013). Trust-Based Secure Gateway Discovery Mechanism for Integrated Internet and MANET. *International Conference on Distributed*. Retrieved from http://link.springer.com/chapter/10.1007/978-3-642-36071-8_7

Azer, M., & El-Kassas, S. (2010). An innovative approach for the wormhole attack detection and prevention in wireless ad hoc networks. *Networking, Sensing and*. Retrieved from http://ieeexplore.ieee.org/abstract/document/5461523/

Cao, X., Kou, W., & Du, X. (2010). A pairing-free identity-based authenticated key agreement protocol with minimal message exchanges. *Information Sciences*. Retrieved from http://www.sciencedirect.com/science/article/pii/S0020025510001519

Chauhan, A., Patle, A., & Mahajan, A. (2011). A Better Approach towards Securing Mobile Adhoc Network. *International Journal of Computer*. Retrieved from http://citeseerx.ist.psu.edu/viewdoc/download?doi=10.1.1.206.2993&rep=rep1&type=pdf

Dorri, A., Kamel, S. R., & Kheirkhah, E. (2015). *Security challenges in mobile ad hoc networks: a survey*. doi:10.5121/ijcses.2015.6102

Ferdous, R., & Muthukkumarasamy, V. (2010). A node-based trust management scheme for mobile ad-hoc networks. *Network and System*. Retrieved from http://ieeexplore.ieee.org/abstract/document/5635570/

Gupta, A., Kumar, R., & Gupta, N. (2014). A trust based secure gateway selection and authentication scheme in MANET. *Contemporary Computing and*. Retrieved from http://ieeexplore.ieee.org/abstract/document/7019816/

Koblitz, N. (1987). Elliptic curve cryptosystems. *Mathematics of Computation*. Retrieved from http://www.ams.org/mcom/1987-48-177/S0025-5718-1987-0866109-5/

Manoharan, R. (2011). A trust based gateway selection scheme for integration of MANET with Internet. *Recent Trends in*. Retrieved from http://ieeexplore.ieee.org/abstract/document/5972415/

Matsuda, T., Nakayama, H., Shen, X., & Nemoto, Y. (2010). Gateway selection protocol in hybrid manet using dymo routing. *Mobile Networks and*. Retrieved from http://link.springer.com/article/10.1007/s11036-009-0173-6

Miller, V. (1998). Use of elliptic curves in cryptography. *Exploratory Computer Science*. Retrieved from https://www.researchgate.net/profile/Victor_Miller/publication/227128293_Use_of_Elliptic_Curves_in_Cryptography/links/0c96052e065c94b47c000000.pdf

Ocenasek, P., & Sveda, M. (2009). AVISPA: Towards Practical Verification of Communication Properties. *IFAC Proceedings Volumes*. Retrieved from http://www.sciencedirect.com/science/article/pii/S1474667016324624

Sarika, S., Pravin, A., & Vijayakumar, A. (2016). Security Issues in Mobile Ad Hoc Networks. *Procedia Computer*. Retrieved from http://www.sciencedirect.com/science/article/pii/S1877050916316106

Theodorakopoulos, G., & Baras, J. (2006). On trust models and trust evaluation metrics for ad hoc networks. *IEEE Journal on Selected*. Retrieved from http://ieeexplore.ieee.org/abstract/document/1589111/

Wu, B., Chen, J., Wu, J., & Cardei, M. (2007). A survey of attacks and countermeasures in mobile ad hoc networks. *Wireless Network Security*. Retrieved from http://link.springer.com/chapter/10.1007/978-0-387-33112-6_5

Chapter 8
Preserving Security of Mobile Anchors Against Physical Layer Attacks:
A Resilient Scheme for Wireless Node Localization

Rathindra Nath Biswas
A. J. C. Bose Polytechnic, India

Swarup Kumar Mitra
MCKV Institute of Engineering, India

Mrinal Kanti Naskar
Jadavpur University, India

ABSTRACT

This chapter introduces a new security scheme for mobile anchors avoiding the physical layer attacks towards localization in wireless sensor networks (WSNs). In a network, anchors are made location-aware equipping them with GPS (global positioning system) receivers. Direction finding capabilities are also incorporated with smart antennas. The proposed algorithm is based on adaptive beamforming of smart array that always minimizes the probabilities of successful attacks, keeping the adversaries beyond its beam coverage. Particle swarm optimization (PSO) technique is used to compute array excitation coefficients, generating the desired pattern. Thus, anchors remain secured through pattern irregularities, deteriorating the information retrieval process even though chances of occurring adequate RSS (received signal strength)/AoA (angle of arrival) measurements may exist. Moreover, anchors are assumed to send pseudo references towards stationary nodes over private links, preserving data integrity for localization. Simulation results validate its effectiveness over the existing methods.

DOI: 10.4018/978-1-5225-5742-5.ch008

INTRODUCTION

During the last decades, continuous efforts were made to bring the diverse technologies in a common platform. The outcome can be viewed as an Internet of Things (IoT), an amalgamation of the Internet and smart sensors to ensure connectivity, computation and communications among the heterogeneous entities (Al-Gburi et al., 2018; Misra et al., 2017). Wireless sensor networks might be regarded as an example of such infrastructures. It inherently possesses numerous attractive features such as scalability, fault-tolerance capability, low power requirements, and less establishment cost, etc. Hence, such network architectures, comprising a considerable number of battery-driven tiny sensors, have now become much famous for data gathering applications under the hostile environments (Akyildiz et al., 2002; Biswas et al., 2014). For example, several essential services, both in civil and military sectors, often deploy such kind of network structures for various purposes like continuous monitoring of the environments, security surveillance, target detection, and tracking, etc. in the areas of interest. However, such applications frequently need location-based data to be relayed at the sink or base station (BS) for the realization of any event occurring within the networks. Usually, sensor devices are randomly deployed over the harsh fields from aircraft/ space vehicles to collect raw data from their surroundings. Accordingly, they remain scattered, unattended and unaware of their locations unless they are made location-aware by some system supports or being localized with the help of a localization system (Ou, 2011; Akter et al., 2018). In practice, a variety of network architectures are commonly existing. They are classified as (i) static networks consisting of stationary nodes only (ii) mobile networks comprised of mobile nodes only and (iii) quasi-static networks involving few mobile nodes along with the plentiful stationary nodes. However, random deployment causes some coverage problem in the first configurations because there is no provision of node relocations. Instead, the second arrangements could provide adequate coverage, but they seem to be much more energy inefficient. In this context, a more feasible solution might be obtained with the third configurations, and hence, it has now become the basis for the development of the state-of-the-art WSN architectures (Halder and Ghosal, 2016; Lin et al., 2017). Throughout the entire networks, mobile nodes can move freely, and they act as mobile data collectors (MDC) (Pazzi and Boukerche, 2008). For several location-based services (LBS), they also need to be location aware along their trajectories. Hence, they usually are made as embedded systems with GPS (Global Positioning System) receivers. Such nodes are referred to as the mobile anchors or beacons in WSNs literature. By employing suitable localization systems, on the other hand, stationary nodes are made capable of relaying location-based data to the base station in a cooperative manner. In most of the cases, anchors are also used as reference nodes for the localization process (Ssu et al., 2005; Naraghi-Pour and Rojas, 2014). Thus, mobile anchor based WSN architectures frequently possess several useful attributes like portability, self-configuration capability, self-localization capability, ease of installation and maintenance, etc. Therefore, they are frequently found to have their extensive use in various application domains.

Currently, the versatile applications of such wireless networks also make them tempting targets of several malicious attacks (Zou et al., 2016; Shiu et al., 2011). There are two types of attacks: internal and external, usually present in WSN environments. In case of internal attacks, the adversaries capture few static and/or mobile benevolent nodes and make them compromised either by directly accessing their control systems or tampering the radio environments of those particular areas over the networks. They usually aim to mislead the decision to be made upon analyzing all the collected data at the base station and hence, provide erroneous information. Sybil, replay and wormhole (Boukerche et al., 2008), etc. are typical examples of such attacks. On the contrary, adversaries enter into the networks from outside as different entities in external type attacks. They also make efforts to route spoofed information over the networks, suppressing their actual identities to the others. Although cryptographic solutions are found to be very effective against the external attacks, they often show vulnerability against the internal attacks (Chen et al., 2010). Moreover, such attacks would be more severe in the physical layer because the entire node set must share a shared wireless medium for relaying their information over the networks (Zhou et al., 2014). Hence, adversaries eavesdropping at some specific region or few compromised nodes might be able to capture the vital information during data transmission among the anchors and the stationary nodes (Kang, 2009). Anchors may also have the possibility of being detected and tracked while attackers can make sufficient measurements of the received signal strength (RSS) or the angle of arrival (AoA) information from their broadcast messages. Thus, they could corrupt the reference data easily by estimating the corresponding locations using trilateration or triangulation (Gezici, 2008; Wong et al., 2007) principles. They would also be able to disrupt the localization process by relaying these data throughout the entire networks. Moreover, the attackers can produce jamming signals or noise, introducing errors in the GPS receiver outputs. Consequently, preserving the security of mobile anchors over the sensor fields has now become a challenging task for many critical applications.

Several approaches have been adopted so far towards protecting the privacy of mobile users/ anchors at the upper layers (Sweeney, 2002; Meyerowitz and Roy Choudhury, 2009). These schemes are usually based on the principles of obscuring their actual location information or changing pseudonyms at appropriate intervals. Such techniques may not be suitable for preventing the attacks occurred in the physical layer. Because the anchors remain insecure and may be captured by the illegal hunters whenever they emit signals into air/freespace. Hence, the attackers need to be kept beyond their radio coverage. This important criterion was overlooked in most of the existing methods making them fragile in the presence of attackers.

Design of a security model for the mobile anchors defending the adversarial attacks at the physical layer and keeping the reference data intact towards the localization process is the primary concern of this chapter. The proposed algorithm is based on the adaptive beamforming principles of smart antennas. Particle Swarm Optimization (PSO) technique is used here to calculate the array element excitation coefficients producing the optimal pattern. Mobile anchors are considered to be equipped with smart antenna arrays. The desired pattern must consist of the main lobe focused at the desired node, and also several deep nulls steered towards the neighboring nodes during each time of data collection. It always ensures security in the networks reducing the probability of successful attacks and keeping the adversaries beyond the exposure of such patterns. Since the precise measurement of RSS/AoA data is dependent on the radio characteristics and the physical environments of the networks, the pattern irregularities each time enforce erroneous data estimation. Moreover, the algorithm provides an extra layer of protection for data integrity allowing pseudo anchor references along the trajectories. Thus, this scheme leads to a robust localization in wireless sensor networks.

RELATED WORKS

The research area of preserving security in WSNs has been much enriched with various pioneering works during past decades. Most of these methods are usually based on the k-anonymity, dummy/ fake ID transfer, and obfuscation principles, etc. Such schemes could guarantee the protection of nodes against the adversarial attacks acquiring accumulated data in the upper/application layer (Huang et al., 2005; Myles et al., 2003). However, they fail to perform well in the physical layer because the nodes might be exposed to the adversaries each time during signal transmission over the radio (Rios & Lopez, 2011). The design of security model for this layer is slightly more complicated than that of earlier cases, and thus, very little research work was found satisfying all the necessary conditions (Bloch & Barros, 2011). In WSN scenarios, the attackers could make a threat to the privacy of sensor nodes by getting access to their RSS, AoA, ToA (time of arrival) and TDoA (time difference of arrival) information. Accordingly, they could break down the localization process corrupting this data and conveying such distorted information throughout the networks. Several innovative works to mitigate malicious attacks on the localization systems are discussed over here. Research work (Oh et al., 2011) proposed a novel jamming technique that mixes jamming signal from the neighboring nodes keeping similar link throughputs. Moreover, it introduced a multi cooperator power control

(MCPC) algorithm to control the jamming noise power. Thus, it claims to ensure an additional increase of privacy through an active control on the strength of jamming noise. Another work (Wong et al., 2007) also described a privacy protection scheme under AoA based localization systems. It usually aims at decreasing the number of possible AoA measurements by using adaptive beamforming of smart antennas. Performance of this method is also dependent on the security margin defined with a pre-specified signal to noise ratio (SNR). Again, it has been shown that an acceptable performance could be obtained against the adversarial attacks on RSS based localization systems with a directional antenna made of tin cans (Bauer et al., 2009). However, this is an unrealistic approach because integrating directional antennas to each sensor makes the system bulky and expensive. A new method has also been introduced by altering anchor transmit power dynamically and adding a significant amount of noise with its transmitted signal (El-badry et al., 2010). Thus, it guarantees to avoid the precise RSS measurement of the radiated signal from an adversary in its vicinity. However, this approach makes a significant reduction in link throughput. Similarly, a security scheme has been described for mobile users against RSS based attacks on localization systems in wireless local area networks (WLAN) (Wang & Yang, 2011). An intelligent antenna pattern synthesis method was used to protect the location information of mobile users in the physical layer. However, this is also a simple scheme to perform well within network regions with a lower density of nodes and in lower communication ranges. Some researchers (Jiang et al., 2007) have also proposed a simple technique using intelligent transmit power control (TPC) in wireless nodes. It decreases the number of adversaries in range, thus, reducing the possibility of being captured. A physical layer spoofing detection scheme has also been proposed (Wang et al., 2017). Utilizing signal processing and feature recognition, improves the detection performance to some extent. Further, few (Soosahabi & Naraghi-Pour, 2012) described a scalable security method randomizing the key distributions to defeat any keyspace exploration attack. An analysis of outage probability for secrecy rate in multiple input multiple output (MIMO) wireless systems in the presence of eavesdroppers and jammers, has also been presented (Rawat et al., 2017). Further, research works (Mehta et al., 2012) proposed two techniques in each of the cases providing privacy both at the source and sink locations, making trade-offs between privacy, communication cost, and latency. However, the effectiveness of this method is also restricted to lower node density areas in the WSNs.

Therefore, new security model should be developed that must not only preserve the robustness of localization process but also ensures an uninterrupted data communication in location-based services, even over the higher node density regions of the WSNs. The proposed security scheme considers both of these aspects and becomes more resilient compared to other existing methods.

SECURITY ISSUES IN WIRELESS SENSOR NETWORKS

As mentioned in the earlier sections, wireless sensor networks constitute plentiful smart battery-driven tiny sensor devices. In most of the cases, after a random deployment in remote and hostile environments, they remain scattered, unattended and unaware of their locations. So, several issues regarding energy efficiency, coverage and security, etc. are pervasive to exist there. Towards fulfilling these conditions, network architectures and protocols should be appropriately framed. For example, energy efficiency can be enhanced by selecting appropriate operating modes (e.g., active, route, sleep, etc.) as per the requirements, to reduce the power consumption on each node in the networks. Likewise, an improvement in coverage can be made by introducing some mobility to facilitate the node relocation process. Preserving security in WSNs, on the other hand, appears to be a rather great challenging task and now attracts more research attention. Both in civil and military sectors, there is an increased demand for location-based services today. So, all sensor nodes need to be incorporated with GPS receivers, or there must have a suitable localization system enabling them to determine their locations autonomously. In this regard, the installation of a GPS to each node might be an unrealistic approach because it makes sensors bulky and expensive. In contrast, localization systems could play a crucial role through observation and detection of an event conveniently occurring within the networks. As a result, they are now becoming the tempting targets to the attackers. Attacks may occur in different ways such as direct (or external) and indirect (or internal) to the localization systems. However, localization systems are generally classified into two categories namely range-free and range-based methods depending on the requirement of range information (e.g., distance/angle) in position computation (Yao et al., 2016; Patwari et al., 2005). Although range-free schemes are simple enough, range-based systems are often used due to their higher accuracy. All range-based localization systems normally function with three successive parts which are range estimation, position computation, and localization algorithm. Thus, attacks may occurr on one or more segments to hamper their normal operations causing the overall breakdown of the localization systems (Boukerche et al., 2008; Chen et al., 2006). Moreover, GPS data could be corrupted with jamming signals or noise in WSNs.

Wireless Sensor Networks Preliminaries

The topic of preserving security in WSNs has become an emerging issue at present. From these perspectives, development of a useful security model to ensure continuous data gathering and routing through the nodes is urgently required. As the adversaries are supposed to attack the localization systems, the key feature of such schemes is to preserve the necessary data intact at each part keeping the attackers outside (Srinivasan and Wu, 2008). For this purpose, the reference data of all anchors along their trajectories also need to be protected from the adversarial attacks. All necessary assumptions on the network configurations, radio characteristics, and attack scenarios are introduced here to expedite the description and analysis of the proposed scheme in the following sections.

Network Topologies and Protocols

To implement the proposed security model, several assumptions are made at network architectures and protocols (as shown in Figure 1). These are furnished as follows:

1. The wireless networks are constructed with a random deployment of few mobile anchors and adequate stationary sensors over the areas of interest. The sensor fields must have many RF (radio frequency) reflectors making the adversaries challenging to find the direct/ dominant signal path.
2. Anchors are equipped with both the GPS receivers and smart antennas. The mobility features are also incorporated by mounting them on wheels/vehicles. They have an extra capacity for memory and refilling options to a power source.
3. Each sensor is configured with a unique ID and activated to broadcast message over the networks in a synchronous manner and with a periodic interval of time (τ). Also, they must have a localization system and some specific operating modes.
4. Anchors are capable of estimating the range information while the RSS exceeds the prescribed threshold limit on signal to noise ratio (SNR_{th}) using path loss model and ESPRIT (estimation of signal parameters via rotational invariance technique) algorithm.
5. Anchors must have the ability to establish secure communication links with the desired nodes, suppressing the effect of interferences from their surroundings by using an adaptive beamforming mechanism.
6. Anchors move in random trajectories within the networks and run with a scheduling technique.
7. The base station (BS) is fixed and located at a highly protected area in WSNs.

Radio Propagation Characteristics

The physical environments always cause various propagation features on the transmitted signal such as reflection, refraction, diffraction, and dispersion, etc. over the networks. Accordingly, the mean power of the received signal could be estimated

Figure 1. Wireless sensor network architectures

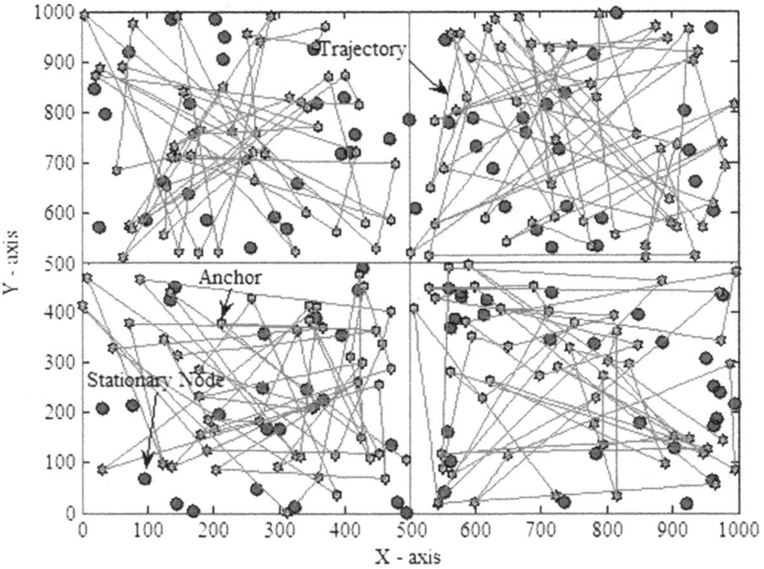

with an exponentially decaying function of distance traveled. This phenomenon is known as path loss and is mostly used for the measurement of distance information in many RSS based localization systems (Wang and Yang, 2011; Patwari et al., 2005). However, selection of a proper signal propagation model, defining the path loss more realistically, is another important aspect for developing the security model in WSNs. The assumptions made in this regard are described as below:

1. Signals flowing through the radio environments are usually a composite form of large-scale path loss component, medium scale slow varying component, and small-scale fast varying component. The medium scale slow varying component uses log-normal distributions, and small-scale fast varying component uses Rician/ Rayleigh distributions in LoS (line of sight)/ NLoS (non-line of sight) data communications respectively (Liberti & Rappaport, 1999).
2. Path loss is determined using small-scale propagation characteristics with fast signal variations due to multipath fading over short distances (order of few wavelengths)/ short duration of time (order of few seconds).
3. The link budget equations are formulated assuming equal energy dissipation per bit in the electronic circuits of wireless sensor transceivers (transmitters/ receivers). However, extra energy consumption of the power amplifier circuit is considered in the transmission of each data bit at a unit distance over the free space (Biswas et al., 2014).

Attack Scenarios in Physical Layer

In general, the objective of attacks could be viewed as to mislead important plans/decisions taken over the accumulated data in WSNs. As mentioned earlier, localization systems take a significant role of detecting/tracking the events occurred in various location-based services. Hence, this chapter is focused on the description of possible attack scenarios for localization systems in the physical layer and effective countermeasures against them. Attacks may occur in direct/indirect ways to malfunction any segment of the localization systems, leading to overall systems break down (Bettini et al., 2005).

Indirect Attacks

Adversaries could establish passive links to control few benevolent nodes getting access to their stored data. Otherwise, they could compromise the radio environments of specific areas in WSNs deteriorating the propagation characteristics of some benevolent nodes over there. Such types of attacks are also termed as internal attacks, and it causes the localization process very tricky.

1. **Through Compromised Nodes:** Distance estimations could be made erroneous by varying the transmission power or delaying the data packets transmission time of compromised nodes towards RSS based or ToA/TDoA based measurement techniques respectively (Li and Ren, 2010). To make tampering of angle estimations through AoA based measurement methods, compromised nodes could send signals with reduced SNR. Besides, position computations could be made incorrect, corrupting the anchor references.
2. **Through Compromised Environments:** By introducing obstacles, smoke or noise, etc. to change the physical medium over the WSNs, both RSS based or ToA/TDoA based measurement methods could be made inaccurate. However, AoA based measurement schemes could be compromised deploying magnets over the sensor fields. Also, position computations could be hampered, jamming the GPS signals to make erroneous anchor references (Myles et al., 2003).

Direct Attacks

Adversaries could install large advanced electronic devices and circuits to eavesdrop at few nodes and capture MAC IDs from broadcast messages over the networks. Then they might appear with such IDs and communicate with the benevolent nodes. During communications, they could inject garbage/deceived information to these nodes, causing erroneous data routing throughout the entire networks in a convenient manner. Such attacks are most often termed as external attacks (Yilmaz and Arslan 2015).

PROPOSED SECURITY MODEL PERSPECTIVES

The IoT systems include all significant types of wireless network architectures. The entities of such systems usually interconnect themselves and operate through the exploitation of capabilities like data sensing, communication, and actuation, etc. So, they are also prone to be under security threats and vulnerabilities at various functional segments (Jeyanthi, 2016). Cryptographic approaches, checking authentication and data integrity of broadcast messages, well suited to provide security against external attacks. However, they become fragile to internal attacks because compromising few nodes; adversaries may get access to their stored keys and passwords. So, some methods based on the principles of encountering the compromised nodes and blocking them from data communications exist in the literature. Moreover, the performance of some schemes is validated with their reliability on position computation in the presence of compromised nodes. The proposed security model tries to trade off these two objectives as blocking the adversaries using optimal patterns and computing positions generating pseudo anchor references (as shown in Figure 2).

Adaptive Beamforming of Smart Antennas

In WSNs, most of the power is wasted while sensor nodes set up communication links producing an omnidirectional pattern with their conventional dipole antennas. The unused power may create interferences to the neighboring nodes deteriorating their quality of service (QoS) in the networks. Conversely, smart antennas can enhance the signal-to-interference-plus-noise ratio (SINR) in the data links mitigating multipath fading through spatial isolation (Winters, 2006). Therefore, adaptive beamforming means shaping of an optimal pattern by steering main-lobe and nulls at appropriate angles as per the direction-of-arrival (DoA) information (Godara, 1997). This improves channel capacity in the wireless links making them stable and secure to guarantee higher throughputs in data transmission. Towards localization, the precision of information regarding distance/angle and anchor references, etc. is vital. Hence, such a method may be advantageous to protect them against the adversarial attacks, establishing private and point-to-point links. In this chapter, the beamforming mechanism is realized using particle swarm optimization (PSO) to determine the element excitation coefficients of a linear array with uniform spacing. A brief overview of smart antennas and PSO algorithm is presented here to expedite the description and analysis of adaptive beamforming in smart antennas.

Figure 2. Block diagram representation of the proposed security model

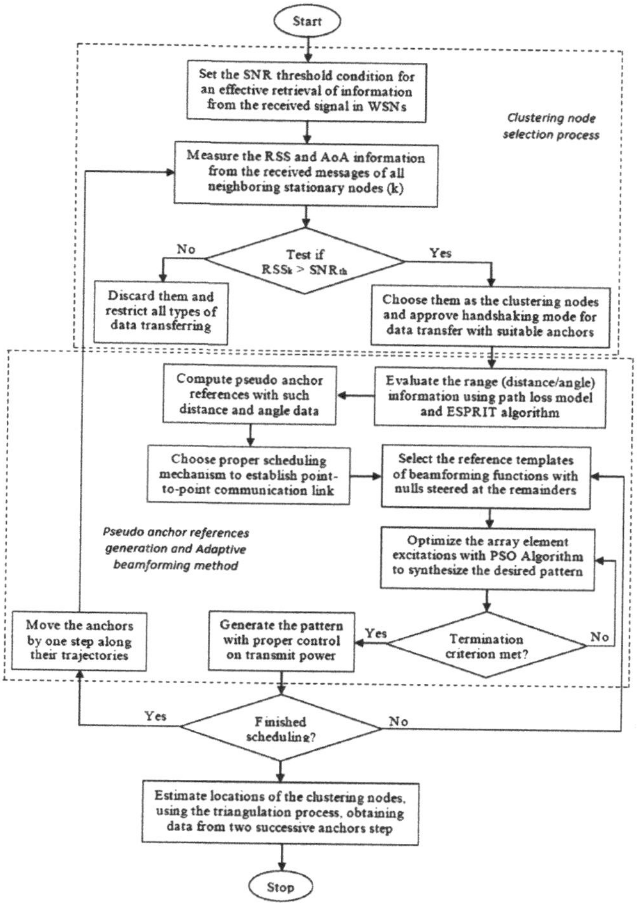

Basics of Smart Antennas

A smart antenna system (as shown in Figure 3) is comprised of three major components as (i) an antenna unit (ii) a signal processing unit and (iii) a beamforming network (Godara, 2004). Here, the antenna unit involves an array of 2N spatially separate antenna elements, providing space division multiple access (SDMA). Signal processing unit usually estimates DoA from the intercepted signals, x(t). Also, beamforming network updates the weight vectors, W, in an iterative process producing the output signal, y(t) by a reference template, r(t). Therefore, the output is obtained while the error function, e(t) = r(t)-y(t) reaches within an allowable limit. This can be expressed as follows:

$$y(t) = W^T x(t) \tag{1}$$

where, $x(t) = a(\theta_d)s(t) + \begin{bmatrix} a(\theta_1) & a(\theta_2) & \cdot & \cdot & a(\theta_{D-1}) \end{bmatrix} . \begin{bmatrix} i_1(t) \\ i_2(t) \\ \cdot \\ \cdot \\ i_{D-1}(t) \end{bmatrix} + n(t)$

(2)

or, $x(t) = x_s(t) + x_i(t) + n(t)$

Thus, it signifies a composite vector form of the desired signal, $x_s(t)$ arriving at an angle, θ_d plus (D-1) number of interfering signals, $x_i(t)$ arriving at different angles from θ_1 to θ_{D-1} and zero mean AWGN (additive white Gaussian noise), n(t) for each channel. Again, W^T means weight vector of excitation coefficients. For an array with 2N-elements, it can be expressed as follows:

$$W^T = \begin{bmatrix} W_1 & W_2 & \cdot & \cdot & W_{2N} \end{bmatrix} \tag{3}$$

For a particular scanning angle (θ_i), $a(\theta_i)$ represents an array steering vector that takes the form as follows:

$$a(\theta_i) = \begin{bmatrix} 1 & e^{j\beta\Delta\sin\theta_i} & e^{j2\beta\Delta\sin\theta_i} & \cdot & \cdot & e^{j(2N-1)\beta\Delta\sin\theta_i} \end{bmatrix}^T \tag{4}$$

Where $\beta = 2\pi/\lambda$ is the wave number, and λ is the wavelength of the transmitted/received signal. Again, Δ indicates inter-element spacing of the array.

Although two types of smart antennas such as (i) switched-beam and (ii) adaptive arrays often exist in practice (Gross, 2005), the latter can estimate signals more intelligently incorporating channel propagation characteristics under fluctuating radio environments. The state-of-the-art DoA estimation methods are based on time series analysis, spectrum analysis, Eigenstructure methods, parametric methods, and linear prediction methods, etc. Among some popular DoA estimation methods, Bartlett, Capon, ESPRIT (estimation of signal parameters via rotational invariance techniques), MUSIC (multiple signal classification) and Root-MUSIC, etc. are ubiquitous. On the other hand, beamforming algorithms usually work on the principles of maximizing the signal to interference ratio (SIR), minimizing the variance and minimizing the mean square error (MSE), etc. For example, least mean squares (LMS), sample matrix inversion (SMI), recursive least squares (RLS), constant modulus (CM) and conjugate gradient (CG) methods, etc. are usually used in various beamforming applications.

Overview of PSO Algorithm

Particle swarm optimization (PSO) is a population-based, stochastic evolutionary technique (Clerc and Kennedy, 2002). It inherently possesses useful features as a simple structure and higher convergence speed. Hence, it is now widely used to solve many multi-objective and complex optimization problems in various fields of applications. It's performance is further improved, avoiding local optima trapping, by introducing an inertia weight (w) or constriction factor to the velocity update equation. In this algorithm, each potential solution is termed as a 'particle' in the search space and must have a fitness value obtained by evaluating the objective function (also termed as cost/ fitness/ error function). Each particle begins the movement, in fact, with random position (X) and random velocity (V) over the search space. It is an iterative process, and each particle tries to find out the position with possibly higher fitness value at its every movement. Using previous knowledge of personal best position (P_{best}) and the global best position (G_{best}) attained ever in

Figure 3. Smart antennas configurations

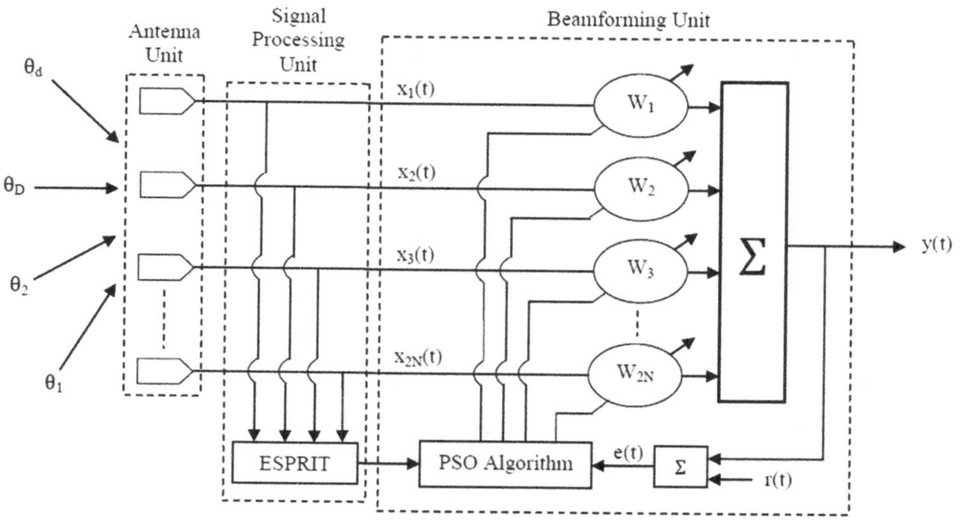

the solution space, each particle must update its velocity and position as per the following relations:

$$V = w.V + 2.rand().\left(P_{best} - X\right) + 2.rand().\left(G_{best} - X\right) \quad (5)$$

$$X = X + V \quad (6)$$

Here, t is taken as a unit time step. Also, P_{best} and G_{best} are chosen by particles fitness values during the search process.

The second and third terms of equation (5) are known as a 'cognitive' and a 'social' component respectively. Cognitive component encourages each particle to move toward its own best position, and the social component explores the optimal global solution, exploiting swarm behaviors. The constants represent the relative weights on stochastic acceleration, pulling each particle towards P_{best} and G_{best} positions. The 'Rand ()' is a function of uniformly distributed random numbers in the range [0, 1] that incorporate some randomness to mimic the analogy of a real scenario. The inertia weight is usually introduced to keep a balance between global exploration and local exploitation abilities in the search. It is found empirically that the process converges faster while inertia weight is linearly decreased from 0.9 to 0.4. The termination criterion for such methods is usually set by choosing a maximum number of iterations or allowing the fitness value within a predefined limit. Also, boundary conditions are applied to reinforce the particles movements inside the desired domain of interest. The dynamic range of the search space is defined with the maximum and minimum value in velocity and position respectively. Whenever any particle exceeds this limit, i.e. (V_{max},V_{min}) and (X_{max},X_{min}), its velocity and position are to be reset forcefully between the upper and lower boundaries towards an effective controlling on the convergence speed (Robinson and Rahmat-Samii, 2004).

PSO-Based Adaptive Beamforming Method

Patterns with higher directivity, narrower beam width, and lower side-lobes level are highly desirable for secured data transfer through long-haul point-to-point wireless communication links. As the single antenna is unable to generate such patterns, an array configuration is frequently used (Balanis, 2005). The optimum tradeoff among these beamforming attributes can be achieved by optimizing the electrical/physical parameters of the antenna array (Zurita, 2014). Although such an optimum pattern alone cannot always offer security against several malicious attacks in WSNs, hence, the flexibility of placing deep nulls in the direction of interferences is crucial for providing a second layer of protection (Zhu, 2016). This makes the design problem very complicated, and there is always a probability of deteriorating the trade-off issues. However, the desired beam pattern with steered deep nulls towards the interferers can be synthesized by the PSO algorithm, evaluating the element excitation coefficients (W) conveniently. Assuming symmetry in amplitudes of the array element excitation coefficients about the origin, the normalized form of array factor (AF) for a linear array (as shown in Figure 3) with uniform inter-element spacing (Δ) can be written as follows:

$$AF_p(\theta) = \sum_{n=1}^{N} W_n \cos\left[\left(n - \frac{1}{2}\right)\beta.\Delta(\sin\theta - \sin\theta_d)\right] \tag{7}$$

Therefore, the optimization problem reduces to only half (N) dimensions for symmetrical array structures. Again, minimum and maximum boundary value in each dimension is set as [0, 1] giving a dynamic range of unity in the optimization process. Now, all the necessary beamforming attributes of desired patterns are stipulated on the reference templates of a simple time-scaled cosine function as follows:

$$AF_d(\theta) = \begin{cases} \cos\left[(\theta - \theta_d)\dfrac{\pi}{FNBW_d}\right] & if \quad |\theta - \theta_d| \le \dfrac{FNBW_d}{2} \\ \eta & if \quad \theta = \theta_n \\ SLL_d & elsewhere \end{cases} \tag{8}$$

Here, desired beam width ($FNBW_d$) is adjusted by choosing the appropriate value of phase angle for the cosine function. Also, desired side-lobes level (SLL_d) and depth of nulls (η) at interfering directions (θ_n) can be set as per the needs of the design.

Again, considering the perspectives of lower computational complexity in the optimization process, a simple formula is adopted here for calculation of the objective function (F) as:

$$F = \min\left\{\sum_{\theta=-90^0}^{90^0} \delta(\theta)\right\} \tag{9}$$

$$\text{where, } \delta(\theta) = \begin{cases} 1 & \text{if} \quad AF_d(\theta) - AF_p(\theta) \le 0 \\ 0 & \quad otherwise \end{cases} \tag{10}$$

Here, $AF_d(\theta)$ and $AF_p(\theta)$ are taken as the desired and produced pattern components respectively. Also, $\delta(\theta)$ represents a weight assigned for each deviation obtained at any sample angle (θ) over the range [-90^0, 90^0].

Since each particle has (N) dimensions within the solution space, and now considering (M) particles, the algorithm would yield both position (X) vector and velocity (V) vector as (M × N) dimensional matrices. They are also randomly initialized towards faster convergence. The objective function is evaluated for each particle to find its P_{best} value as $P_{best} = [P_{best1}, P_{best2} \ldots P_{bestM}]^T$ and G_{best} value as $G_{best} = \min\{P_{best}\}$ in an iterative way. The P_{best} and G_{best} value along with their respective positions are recorded and used to update velocity and position according to equation (5) and (6) respectively. This algorithm is set to be terminated on attaining a maximum iteration of 1000.

Generation of Pseudo Anchor References

As mentioned in the earlier sections, localization systems involve anchor references in position computation of sensor nodes. However, attacks may occur to distort anchor references causing erroneous position estimation. Hence, such reference data needs to be kept secure and intact for the localization process. This is ensured in the proposed scheme considering anchors to send pseudo references along with their trajectories rather than the actual one. Thus, sensor nodes can autonomously estimate their locations having two such pseudo anchor references, spoofing the attackers in WSNs. The steps for generating pseudo anchor references are discussed as follows:

Calculation of Distance Information

Formulating an appropriate radio propagation model, distance information can be estimated with path loss component. In long-distance distributions (Liberti and Rappaport, 1999), large-scale path loss component (L_p) can be defined by a function of distance (d) and usually expressed (in dB) as:

$$L_p(d) = L_p(d_0) + 10\alpha \log\left(\frac{d}{d_0}\right) \tag{11}$$

Where α is known as path loss exponent. It indicates the rate of increase in path loss with distance. Also, d_0 denotes a small reference distance from the transmitter.

Now, considering variable cluttering effects of environments, the expression of path loss component is modified and defined with log-normal shadowing model (in dB) as:

$$L_{ps}(d) = L_p(d) + X_\sigma \tag{12}$$

where X_σ is a random variable of zero mean Gaussian distributions with standard deviation σ.

The link budget of LoS propagation can be described with Frii's free space equation as:

$$P_r = \frac{P_t G_t G_r \lambda^2}{(4\pi d)^2} \tag{13}$$

Where P_t and G_t signify power output and gain of the transmitting antenna. P_r and G_r imply power intercepted and gain of the receiving antenna.

Again, the equation (13) can also be expressed (in dB) as:

$$P_r = P_t + G_t + G_r - 32.45 - 20\log_{10}(d / KM) - 20\log_{10}(f / MHz) \tag{14}$$

where $L_p = 32.45 + 20\log_{10}(d / KM) + 20\log_{10}(f / MHz)$ is the path loss component.

To estimate distance (d_k) for the k-th node using received signal power (P_k), log-normal shadowing condition is to be applied in equation (14) and can be written as:

$$P_k = P_t + G_t + G_r - L_p(d_0) - 10\alpha \log(\frac{d_k}{d_0}) - X_\sigma \tag{15}$$

P_t and P_r are normally represented in dB/dBm. Also, G_t and G_r are represented in dBi. Parametric settings are made as per the Crossbow MICAz motes keeping compatibility with FCC limits (MICAz 2018). For low power tiny sensors, they are chosen as P_t = 30 dBm, G_t = 10 dBi, G_r = 0 dBi, d_0 = 1 m, SNR_{th} = -40 dBm, X_σ = 0 dB and α = 2.

Estimation of Angle Information

The angle information of all received signals can also be determined using one common high precision direction of arrival (DoA) technique known as ESPRIT in smart antennas literature (Roy and Kailath, 1989). ESPRIT algorithm exploits the rotational invariance property in the signal subspace. It usually utilizes a translational invariance structure that consists of two identical sub-arrays with a finite separation Δ (also known as doublets). Hence, assuming the number of signal sources (D) is less than that of array elements (2N), the signals induced on each of the sub-arrays can be written as:

$$x_1(t) = A_1.s(t) + n_1(t) \tag{16}$$

and $x_2(t) = A_2.s(t) + n_2(t) = A_1.\Phi.s(t) + n_2(t)$ (17)

Where, $\Phi = diag\{e^{j\beta.\Delta \sin\theta_1}, e^{j\beta.\Delta \sin\theta_2}, ..., e^{j\beta.\Delta \sin\theta_D}\}$ is a diagonal unitary matrix with progressive phase shifts. Also, A_1 and A_2 are called Vandermonde matrix of steering vectors for two sub-arrays.

Now, considering the contributions of both sub-arrays, the total received signal and correlation matrix for the complete array can be expressed as:

$$x(t) = \begin{bmatrix} A_1 \\ A_1.\Phi \end{bmatrix}.s(t) + \begin{bmatrix} n_1(t) \\ n_2(t) \end{bmatrix} \tag{18}$$

$$R_{xx} = E[x.x^H] = A_1 R_{ss} A_1^H + \sigma_n^2 I \tag{19}$$

Again, correlation matrices for two sub-arrays are usually represented as:

$$R_{11} = E[x_1.x_1^H] = A_1 R_{ss} A_1^H + \sigma_n^2 I \tag{20}$$

and $R_{22} = E[x_2.x_2^H] = A_1 R_{ss} A_1^H + \sigma_n^2 I$ (21)

Due to the invariance array structure, signal subspace (E_x) can be decomposed into two subspaces: E_1 and E_2 whose columns include the D eigenvectors corresponding to the largest eigenvalues of R_{11} and R_{22}. Since these arrays are related with translational invariance features, E_1 and E_2 would be related by a unique non-singular transformation matrix Ψ such that $E_1\Psi = E_2$.

Similarly, there must also be a unique non-singular transformation matrix Γ such that $E_1 = A_1\Gamma$ and $E_2 = A_1\Phi\Gamma$.

From the above relationships, it can be derived that $\Gamma\Psi\Gamma^{-1} = \Phi$.

Thus, the eigenvalues of Ψ must be equal to the diagonal elements of Φ such that

$$\lambda_1 = e^{j\beta.\Delta\sin\theta_1}, \lambda_2 = e^{j\beta.\Delta\sin\theta_2}, \ldots\ldots, \lambda_D = e^{j\beta.\Delta\sin\theta_D}$$

Also, the columns of Γ must be the eigenvectors of Ψ.

Now, the angle information of signals arriving at k-th node (θ_k) can be estimated as:

$$\theta_k = \sin^{-1}\left(\frac{\arg(\lambda_k)}{\beta.\Delta}\right) \tag{22}$$

where, k = 1,2,….,D

Formation of Anchor References

In WSNs, anchors are aware of their own locations through GPS receivers. As discussed earlier, they estimate distance and angle information from broadcast messages having SNR greater than a prescribed value. Such neighboring nodes (also termed as clustering nodes) are selected for serial data transfer from present anchor position. This anchor reference is essential for estimating the position of each clustering node. Hence, it needs to be kept confidential so that data integrity is retained in relayed data packets. Accordingly, pseudo forms of such references are prepared along the corresponding directions of each clustering node. For k-th clustering node, pseudo anchor reference (x_{pk},y_{pk}) is generated as follows:

$$\left.\begin{aligned} x_{pk} &= x_a + rand().d_k\cos\theta_k \\ y_{pk} &= y_a + rand().d_k\sin\theta_k \end{aligned}\right\} \tag{23}$$

Where, (x_a,y_a) denotes actual position in present anchor step.

PERFORMANCE EVALUATION FRAMEWORK

As discussed earlier, security of anchors is preserved through adaptive beamforming and pseudo references. Beamforming aims to provide a stable link with the desired node keeping all neighboring nodes away from its radio coverage. In contrast, the objective of generating pseudo references is to keep anchors' trajectories secured, reducing the chances of being detected/ tracked directly. This section deals with the formulation of security conditions, selection of benchmarks for evaluating performance and simulation results.

Security Criterions

All neighboring nodes are assumed to be suspicious because some of them might be compromised or externally implanted. So, anchors must control their transmission power in beamforming as per the least requirement of signal to noise ratio (SNR_{th}), maintaining reliable data transfer with the desired node. This would also cause deterioration of SNR at all adjacent nodes keeping them always below the threshold limit. Moreover, the second layer of protection is provided by steering deep nulls towards them. As the retrieval of contents is quite impossible at such a lower SNR level, the integrity of the relayed data packets is ensured. Hence, the conditions for preserving anchors security can be expressed (in dBm) as below:

For the desired node

$$P_0 \left| AF_d(\theta_d) \right|^2 \geq SNR_{th} \tag{24}$$

And in the case of all other neighboring nodes,

$$P_0 \left| AF_d(\theta_k) \right|^2 < SNR_{th} \tag{25}$$

where P_0 is the effective isotropic radiated power (EIRP) at a reference distance from anchors.

However, SNR gives a quantitative measure of signal power to noise power. In the case of AWGN (additive white Gaussian noise) distribution, it usually varies with distance from the transmitter in free space ($X_\sigma = 0$ dB). Thus, SNR level for a k-th node with distance d_k can also be defined as:

$$SNR_k = P_k(d_k) \tag{26}$$

On the other hand, transmitting data packets along with pseudo anchor references may be helpful in camouflaging their actual positions to the attackers. However, the desired node can estimate its position, as an intersection point of lines originating from two distinct anchor positions with such reference data. In contrast, security conditions for anchors may also be violated if two or more neighboring nodes remain on and above SNR_{th} within patterns.

Performance Metrics

Performance of the proposed security algorithm depends typically on the accuracy of the beamforming process, and hence, it is verified under two metrics as follows:

- **Beamforming efficiency (γ):** It is the capability of reproducing the patterns as per the attributes defined on the desired beamforming functions. It measures all the deviations of the optimal pattern from the desired specifications and expressed (in percentage) as:

$$\gamma = (1-\varepsilon)\times 100\% \tag{27}$$

Where ε denotes the error associated with the beamforming process. It is here defined as a ratio of the aggregated value of deviation weights to the total number of sample points (Ω) and expressed as:

$$\varepsilon = \frac{\sum_{i=1}^{\Omega} \delta(\theta_i)}{\Omega} \tag{28}$$

Typically, θ_i is the i-th sample angle over the range $[-90^0, 90^0]$.

- **Success rate (μ):** It measures the degree of effective attempts preserving security on particular anchor movements in WSNs. Therefore, it can also be defined as the ratio of the number of successful attempts (Λ_s) to total attempts (Λ) made by anchors over a specific time duration. It is expressed (in percentage) as:

$$\mu = \frac{\Lambda_s}{\Lambda}\times 100\% \tag{29}$$

where successful attempt means permitting not more than one neighboring node (in the worst case) within patterns at a time.

Simulation Environments

Simulation environments are implemented on MATLAB software (version 7) platform. Several off-line PC (personal computer) generated data, making an analogy with the real-time WSNs scenarios are assumed here. A random deployment of 100, 200 and 300 stationary sensor nodes (making different node density) over a two-dimensional (2-D) field of 1000m×1000m area are considered as network architectures. Sensors are supposed to be with a reasonable far space for increasing network coverage avoiding interferences among them. Anchors are also considered to move along random trajectories over the sensor field and relay necessary data packets via private links for localization of the nodes. For connecting nodes, scheduling mechanism is adopted by their corresponding distances. Adversaries are assumed to either capture few nodes making them compromised or participate directly in data communications over the networks. As radio propagation over free space, log-normal shadowing model is assumed.

Simulation Parameters

Simulation parameters are set in keeping similarity with common wireless narrowband transmission systems such as WLAN IEEE 802.11 (IEEE 2010) and are given in Table 1. Antenna array design parameters and specifications of the desired patterns for producing optimal patterns are chosen as per Table 2. In the PSO algorithm, a maximum of 1000 iterations are set as termination condition, and boundary limits for optimization variables are kept in the range of {0,1}.

Simulation Results

The proposed security model is tested under extensive simulations on its performance parameters as mentioned above. Such parameters are usually varied with array length and node density in WSNs. However, empirical cumulative distribution functions (ECDF) of the results are made, by taking 30 runs of the program, towards proper explanations in all the cases. Also, convergence curves and corresponding optimal patterns are shown in Figure 4 and Figure 5 respectively. The optimized values of array element excitation coefficients are given in Table 3. Beamforming efficiency is illustrated in Figure 6. Success rate (considering only 25 anchor steps in each run) under variable array lengths and node density is also shown in Figure 7 and Figure 8 respectively.

Table 1. Simulation parameters

Parameters	Values
Network size	1000m x 1000 m
Number of nodes	100, 200, 300
Number of anchors	2,4,6
Number of compromised nodes	10,20,30
Maximum transmission range (d_{max})	100 m
Transmit power of an anchor (P_t)	30 dBm
Threshold level in SNR (SNR_{th})	–40 dBm
Path loss exponent (α)	2
Shadowing noise variance (σ^2)	1

Table 2. Antenna design parameters and pattern attributes

Parameters	Values
Array size (2N)	20,30,40
Frequency (f)	2.4 GHz
Inter-element spacing (Δ)	0.5λ
Phase shift (ζ)	0
SLL_d	0.01 (-40 dB)
$FNBW_d$	20^0
η	0.00001 (-100 dB)
θ_d	30^0
θ_n	-20^0, -5^0, 10^0, 45^0, 60^0

Performance Analysis

Performance of any security scheme can be explained under two key factors as (i) node deployment scenario and (ii) attack model in WSNs. Thus, attacks might be more severe in case of the networks with higher node density rather than its counterpart. Also, the complexity of the attack model might have a significant impact on the performance of a security algorithm. The ordinary security models often ignore to take up necessary preventive measures against such conditions and hence, fail to perform well in most of the cases. The proposed security model becomes fragile against replay type attacks to some extent at higher node/ compromised node density regions. Although combining cryptographic approaches, using pairwise key distribution at

Figure 4. Convergence curve for optimization process (Node = 100)

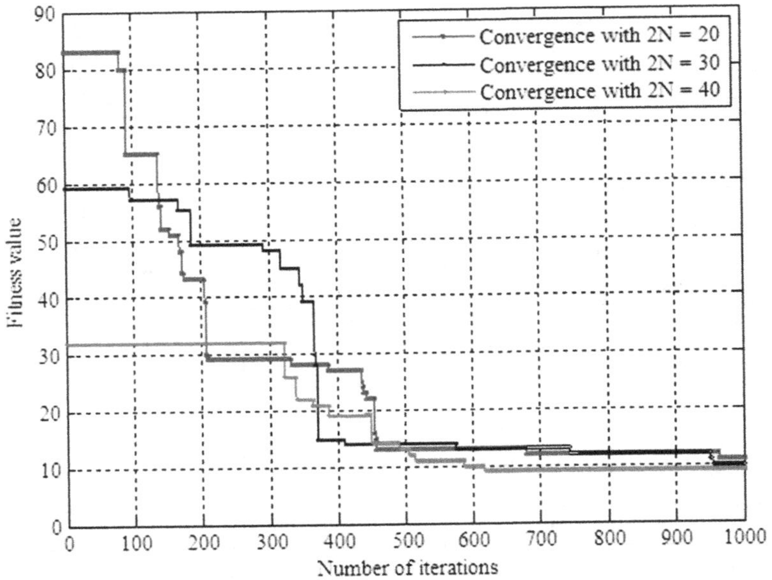

Figure 5. Optimal patterns with various array lengths (Node = 100)

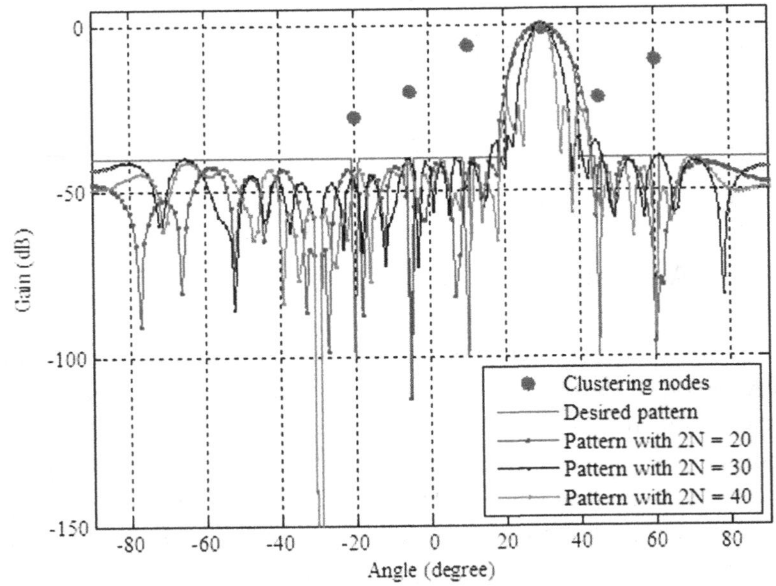

Figure 6. Beamforming efficiency with various array lengths (Node = 100)

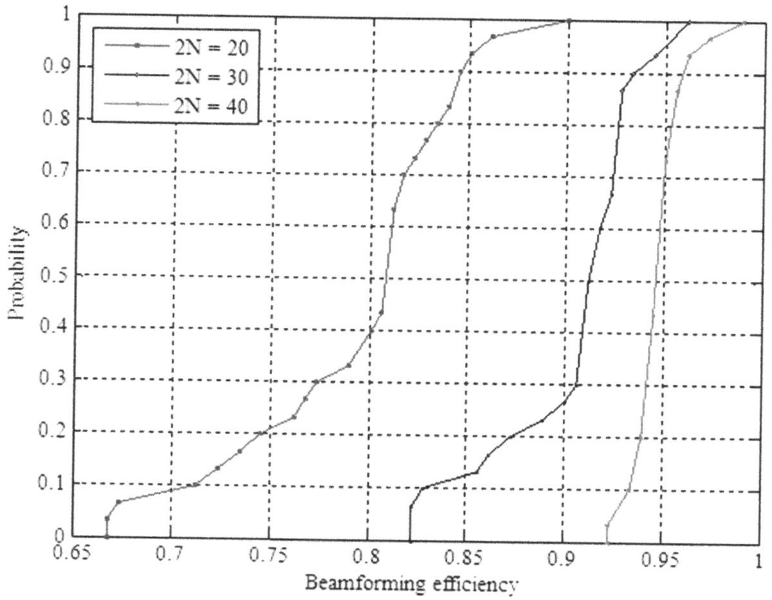

Figure 7. Success rate attained with various array lengths (Node = 100)

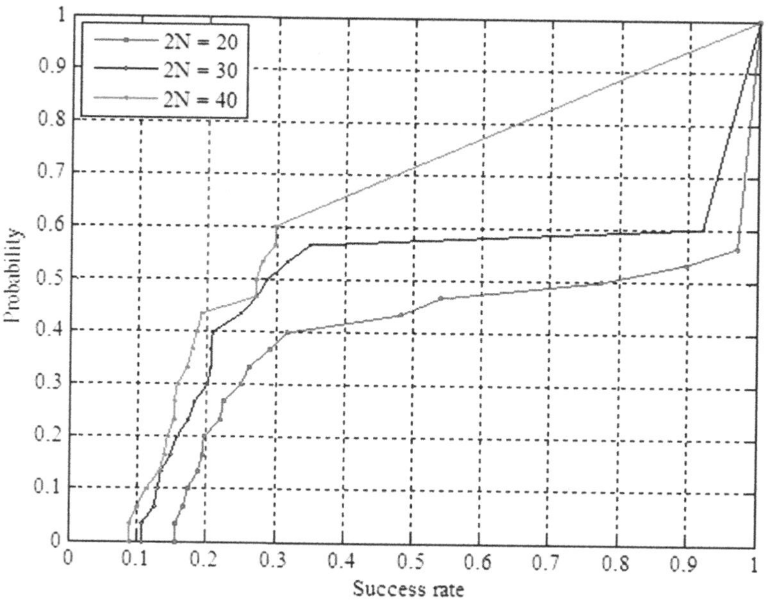

Figure 8. Success rate attained with various node density (2N = 20)

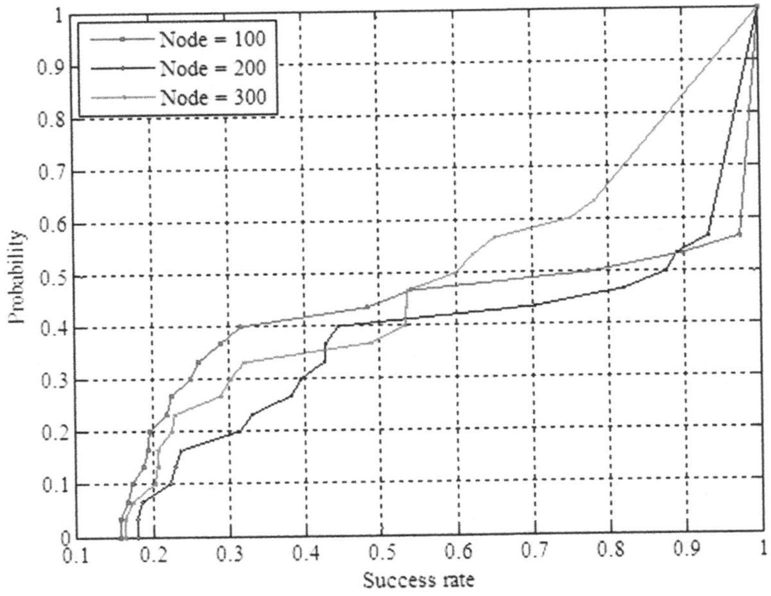

the time of data transfer with anchors might be a viable solution, it also becomes vulnerable. Because having no previous knowledge of compromised nodes' behaviors over the networks, anchors could share their secret keys with compromised nodes via direct links. Otherwise, a compromised node prevailing on the patterns of another link could capture anchor generated data packets. In both cases, they might be able to replay the data packets, tampering its contents towards adjacent nodes. Obviously, it would mislead the localization process on those particular benevolent nodes. Hence, some alternative measures should also be taken to identify the compromised nodes and eliminate their effects on the localization process.

CONCLUSION

A new security model using adaptive beamforming of smart antennas is presented in this chapter. It can ensure privacy protection of mobile anchors against the attacks at the physical layer. As anchors are used as reference nodes in the localization process, preserving their location privacy over networks is always essential. In the proposed method, data transmission is secured via establishing more stable links with the optimal patterns. In most cases, such patterns reduce the chances of attacks keeping the adversaries beyond the radio coverage of anchors. Moreover, pattern

Table 3. Optimized element excitation coefficients

Parameters	Values		
Index (n)	Number of Array Elements (2N)		
	N = 10	N = 15	N = 20
1	1.0000	1.0000	1.0000
2	0.9340	0.9693	0.9873
3	0.8505	0.9307	0.9297
4	0.7358	0.8813	0.8912
5	0.6098	0.7999	0.8971
6	0.4618	0.7324	0.8106
7	0.3389	0.6745	0.7440
8	0.2083	0.5832	0.7555
9	0.1252	0.4907	0.7060
10	0.0636	0.4307	0.6783
11	--	0.3050	0.6354
12	--	0.2282	0.6038
13	--	0.1689	0.5556
14	--	0.1298	0.4760
15	--	0.0615	0.4152
16	--	--	0.3317
17	--	--	0.2565
18	--	--	0.1964
19	--	--	0.1335
20	--	--	0.0661

irregularities cause data retrieval process trickier even if some attackers remain within the links. The relaying of pseudo anchor references also helps to keep data confidentiality against direct attacks. Simulation results validate its competency with higher success rates and accuracy in the localization process. However, this scheme is developed with several assumptions on attack models. Adversaries could also install large, sophisticated equipment/code to crack the relayed data packets accessing its contents. So, the feasibility of this scheme should be verified under several complex attack scenarios in the future works.

REFERENCES

Akter, M., Rahman, M. O., Islam, M. N., Hassan, M. M., Alsanad, A., & Sangaiah, A. K. (2018). Energy-efficient tracking and localization of objects in wireless sensor networks. *IEEE Access: Practical Innovations, Open Solutions*, *6*, 17165–17177. doi:10.1109/ACCESS.2018.2809692

Akyildiz, I. F., Su, W., Sankarasubramaniam, Y., & Cayirci, E. (2002). A survey on sensor networks. *IEEE Communications Magazine*, *40*(8), 102–114. doi:10.1109/MCOM.2002.1024422

Al-Gburi, A., Al-Hasnawi, A., & Lilien, L. (2018). Differentiating security from privacy in internet of things: A survey of selected threats and controls. In K. Daimi (Ed.), *Computer and network security essentials* (pp. 153–172). Springer International Publishing. doi:10.1007/978-3-319-58424-9_9

Balanis, C. A. (2005). *Antenna theory: Analysis and design*. New York: John Wiley and Sons Inc.

Bauer, K., McCoy, D., Anderson, E., Breitenbach, M., Grudic, G., Grunwald, D., & Sicker, D. (2009). The directional attack on wireless localization-or-How to spoof your location with a tin can. In *Proceedings of Global Telecommunications Conference* (pp. 1-6). Honolulu, HI: IEEE. 10.1109/GLOCOM.2009.5425737

Bettini, C., Wang, X. S., & Jojodia, S. (2005). Protecting privacy against location-based personal identification. In *Proceedings of the Second VDLB International Conference on Secure Data Management* (vol. 1, pp. 185-199). Trondheim, Norway: Springer. 10.1007/11552338_13

Biswas, R. N., Mitra, S. K. & Naskar, M. K. (2014). A robust mobile anchor based localization technique for wireless sensor networks using smart antenna. *International Journal of Ad-Hoc and Ubiquitous Computing*, *15*(1/2/3), 23-37.

Bloch, M., & Barros, J. (2011). *Physical-layer security: From information theory to security engineering*. New York: Cambridge University Press. doi:10.1017/CBO9780511977985

Boukerche, A., Oliveira, H. A. B. F., Nakamura, E. F., & Loureiro, A. A. F. (2008). Secure localization algorithms for wireless sensor networks. *IEEE Communications Magazine*, *46*(4), 96–101. doi:10.1109/MCOM.2008.4481347

Chen, Y., Kleisouris, K., Li, X., Trappe, W., & Martin, R. P. (2006). The robustness of localization algorithms to signal strength attacks: A comparative study. In *Proceedings of International Conference on Distributed Computing in Sensor Systems* (vol. 1, pp. 546-563). San Francisco, CA: Springer. 10.1007/11776178_33

Chen, Y., Yang, J., Trappe, W., & Martin, R. P. (2010). Detecting and localizing identity-based attacks in wireless and sensor networks. *IEEE Transactions on Vehicular Technology*, *59*(5), 2418–2434. doi:10.1109/TVT.2010.2044904

Clerc, M., & Kennedy, J. (2002). The particle swarm: Explosion, stability, and convergence in a multidimensional complex space. *IEEE Transactions on Evolutionary Computation*, *6*(1), 58–73. doi:10.1109/4235.985692

Data sheet for Crossbow MICAz mote. (n.d.). Retrieved on August 14, 2018, from http://edge.rit.edu/edge/P08208/public/Controls_Files/MICaZ-DataSheet.pdf

El-badry, R., Sultan, A., & Youssef, M. (2010). HyberLoc: Providing physical layer location privacy in hybrid sensor networks. In *Proceedings of International Conference on Communications* (pp. 1-5). Cape Town, South Africa: IEEE. 10.1109/ICC.2010.5502104

Gezici, S. (2008). A survey on wireless position estimation. *Wireless Personal Communications*, *44*(3), 263–282. doi:10.100711277-007-9375-z

Godara, L. C. (1997). Application of antenna arrays to mobile communications, part II: Beam-forming and direction-of-arrival considerations. *Proceedings of the IEEE*, *85*(8), 1195–1245. doi:10.1109/5.622504

Godara, L. C. (2004). *Smart antennas*. Boca Raton, FL: CRC Press LLC. doi:10.1201/9780203496770

Gross, F. B. (2005). *Smart antennas for wireless communications*. New York: McGraw-Hill Companies, Inc.

Halder, S., & Ghosal, A. (2016). A survey on mobile anchor assisted localization techniques in wireless sensor networks. *Wireless Networks*, *22*(7), 2317–2336. doi:10.100711276-015-1101-2

Huang, L., Matsuura, K., Yamane, H., & Sezaki, K. (2005). Enhancing wireless location privacy using silent period. In *Proceedings of Wireless Communications and Networking Conference* (vol. 2, pp. 1187–1192). New Orleans, LA: IEEE.

Jeyanthi, N. (2016). Internet of things (IoT) as interconnection of threats (IoT). In F. Hu (Ed.), *Security and privacy in internet of things (IoTs): Models, algorithms, and implementations* (pp. 1–19). Boca Raton, FL: Taylor & Francis Group, LLC. doi:10.1201/b19516-3

Jiang, T., Wang, H. J., & Hu, Y.-C. (2007). Preserving location privacy in wireless LANs. In *Proceedings of the 5th International Conference on Mobile Systems, Applications and Services* (pp. 246-257). San Juan, Puerto Rico: ACM.

Kang, L. (2009). Protecting location privacy in large-scale wireless sensor networks. In *Proceedings of the International Conference on Communications* (pp. 603-608). Dresden, Germany: IEEE. 10.1109/ICC.2009.5199372

Li, Y., & Ren, J. (2010). Source-location privacy through dynamic routing in wireless sensor networks. In *Proceedings of 29th IEEE Conference on Computer Communications* (pp. 1-9). San Diego, CA: IEEE. 10.1109/INFCOM.2010.5462096

Liberti, J. C., & Rappaport, T. S. (1999). *Smart antennas for wireless communications: IS-95 and third generation CDMA applications*. Englewood Cliffs, NJ: Prentice-Hall.

Lin, C.-F., Chi, K.-H., Hsu, Y.-Y., & Liu, C.-Y. (2017). Mobile anchor-assisted localization over android. *Wireless Networks*, *23*(8), 2379–2394. doi:10.100711276-016-1295-y

Mehta, K., Liu, D., & Wright, M. (2012). Protecting location privacy in sensor networks against a global eavesdropper. *IEEE Transactions on Mobile Computing*, *11*(2), 320–336. doi:10.1109/TMC.2011.32

Meyerowitz, J., & Roy Choudhury, R. (2009). Hiding stars with fireworks: location privacy through camouflage. In *Proceedings of the 15th Annual International Conference on Mobile Computing and Networking* (pp. 345–356). Beijing, China: ACM. 10.1145/1614320.1614358

Misra, S., Maheswaran, M., & Hashmi, S. (2017). *Security challenges and approaches in internet of things*. Springer International Publishing. doi:10.1007/978-3-319-44230-3

Myles, G., Friday, A., & Davies, N. (2003). Preserving privacy in environments with location-based applications. *IEEE Pervasive Computing*, *2*(1), 56–64. doi:10.1109/MPRV.2003.1186726

Naraghi-Pour, M., & Rojas, G. C. (2014). A novel algorithm for distributed localization in wireless sensor networks. *ACM Transactions on Sensor Networks*, *11*(1), 1–25. doi:10.1145/2632150

Oh, S., & Gruteser, M. (2011). Multi-node coordinated jamming for location privacy protection. In *Proceedings of the Military Communications Conference* (pp.1243-1249). Baltimore, MD: IEEE.

Ou, C.-H. (2011). A localization scheme for wireless sensor networks using mobile anchors with directional antennas. *IEEE Sensors Journal, 11*(7), 1607–1616. doi:10.1109/JSEN.2010.2102748

Part 11: Wireless LAN medium access control (MAC) and physical layer (PHY) specifications. (n.d.). Retrieved on August 14, 2018, from http://www.di-srv.unisa.it/~vitsca/RC-0809I/IEEE-802-11.pdf

Patwari, N., Ash, J. N., Kyperountas, S., Hero, A. O., Moses, R. L., & Correal, N. S. (2005). Locating the nodes: Cooperative localization in wireless sensor networks. *IEEE Signal Processing Magazine, 22*(4), 54–69. doi:10.1109/MSP.2005.1458287

Pazzi, R. W. N., & Boukerche, A. (2008). Mobile data collector strategy for delay-sensitive applications over wireless sensor network. *Computer Communications, 31*(5), 1028–1039. doi:10.1016/j.comcom.2007.12.024

Rawat, D. B., White, T., Parwez, M. S., Bajracharya, C., & Song, M. (2017). Evaluating secrecy outage of physical layer security in large-scale MIMO wireless communications for cyber-physical systems. *IEEE Internet of Things Journal, 4*(6), 1987–1993. doi:10.1109/JIOT.2017.2691352

Rios, R., & Lopez, J. (2011). Analysis of location privacy solutions in wireless sensor networks. *IET Communications, 5*(17), 2518–2532. doi:10.1049/iet-com.2010.0825

Robinson, J., & Rahmat-Samii, Y. (2004). Particle swarm optimization in electromagnetics. *IEEE Transactions on Antennas and Propagation, 52*(2), 397–402. doi:10.1109/TAP.2004.823969

Roy, R., & Kailath, T. (1989). Esprit - estimation of signal parameters via rotational invariance techniques. *IEEE Transactions on Acoustics, Speech, and Signal Processing, 37*(7), 984–995. doi:10.1109/29.32276

Shiu, Y.-S., Chang, S. Y., Wu, H.-C., Huang, S. C.-H., & Chen, H.-H. (2011). Physical layer security in wireless networks: A tutorial. *IEEE Wireless Communications, 18*(2), 66–74. doi:10.1109/MWC.2011.5751298

Soosahabi, R., & Naraghi-Pour, M. (2012). Scalable PHY-Layer security for distributed detection in wireless sensor networks. *IEEE Transactions on Information Forensics and Security, 7*(4), 1118–1126. doi:10.1109/TIFS.2012.2194704

Srinivasan, A., & Wu, J. (2008). *A survey on secure localization in wireless sensor networks. In Encyclopedia of Wireless and Mobile Communications*. Taylor and Francis Group.

Ssu, K.-F., Ou, C.-H., & Jiau, H. C. (2005). Localization with mobile anchor points in wireless sensor networks. *IEEE Transactions on Vehicular Technology*, *54*(3), 1187–1197. doi:10.1109/TVT.2005.844642

Sweeney, L. (2002). k- Anonymity: A model for protecting privacy. *International Journal of Uncertainty, Fuzziness and Knowledge-based Systems*, *10*(5), 557–570. doi:10.1142/S0218488502001648

Wang, N., Li, W., Jiang, T., & Lv, S. (2017). Physical layer spoofing detection based on sparse signal processing and fuzzy recognition. *IET Signal Processing*, *11*(5), 640–646. doi:10.1049/iet-spr.2016.0378

Wang, T., & Yang, Y. (2011). Location privacy protection from RSS localization system using antenna pattern synthesis. In *Proceedings of International Conference on Computer Communications* (pp. 2408-2416). Shanghai, China: IEEE. 10.1109/INFCOM.2011.5935061

Winters, J. H. (2006). Smart antenna techniques and their application to wireless ad hoc networks. *IEEE Wireless Communications*, *13*(4), 77–83. doi:10.1109/MWC.2006.1678168

Wong, F. L., Lin, M., Nagaraja, S., Wassell, I., & Stajano, F. (2007). Evaluation framework of location privacy of wireless mobile systems with arbitrary beam pattern. In *Proceedings of Fifth Annual Conference on Communication Networks and Services Research* (vol. 2, pp. 157-165). Fredericton, Canada: IEEE. 10.1109/CNSR.2007.30

Yao, Y., Zou, K., Chen, X., & Xu, X. (2016). A distributed range-free correction vector based localization refinement algorithm. *Wireless Networks*, *22*(8), 2667–2680. doi:10.100711276-015-1129-3

Yilmaz, M. H., & Arslan, H. (2015). A survey: Spoofing attacks in physical layer security. In *Proceedings of 40th Annual IEEE Conference on Local Computer Networks* (pp. 812-817). Clearwater Beach, FL: IEEE. 10.1109/LCNW.2015.7365932

Zhou, X., Song, L., & Zhang, Y. (Eds.). (2014). *Physical layer security in wireless communications*. Boca Raton, FL: Taylor & Francis Group, LLC.

Zhu, J. (2016). *Physical layer security in massive MIMO systems* (Unpublished doctoral dissertation). The University of British Columbia, Vancouver, Canada.

Zou, Y., Zhu, J., Wang, X., & Hanzo, L. (2016). A survey on wireless security: Technical challenges, recent advances, and future trends. *Proceedings of the IEEE, 104*(9), 1727–1765. doi:10.1109/JPROC.2016.2558521

Zurita, L. N. R. (2014). *Optimising multiple antenna techniques for physical layer security* (Unpublished doctoral dissertation). The University of Leeds, Leeds, UK.

Chapter 9
An Adaptive Security Framework for the Internet of Things Applications Based on the Contextual Information

Harsuminder Kaur Gill
Jaypee University of Information Technology, India

Anil Kumar Verma
Thapar University, India

Rajinder Sandhu
Jaypee University of Information Technology, India

ABSTRACT

With the growth of Internet of Things and user demand for personalized applications, context-aware applications are gaining popularity in current IT cyberspace. Personalized content, which can be a notification, recommendation, etc., are generated based on the contextual information such as location, temperature, and nearby objects. Furthermore, contextual information can also play an important role in security management of user or device in real time. When the context of a user or device changes, the security mechanisms should also be updated in real time for better performance and quality of service. Access to a specific resource may also be dependent upon user's/device's current context. In this chapter, the role of contextual information for IoT application security is discussed and a framework is provided which auto-updates security policy of the device based on its current context. Proposed framework makes use of machine learning algorithm to update the security policies based on the current context of the IoT device(s).

DOI: 10.4018/978-1-5225-5742-5.ch009

INTRODUCTION

With the advancements and successful adoption of network connecting technologies such as LTE, 3G, WiMax, etc., the Internet has become a necessity in a current era of living. Around 3.5 billion Internet users are available in the world which is around 40% of the total population ("Internet Live Stats," 2014). Due to such colossal connectivity, a new paradigm has evolved in which not only humans but other things such as fan, machine, car, etc., also connect to the Internet, share data and execute certain tasks with or without any human intervention. This novel paradigm is known as the Internet of Things (IoT). As the name suggests, it is the interconnection of things (sensors, RFID tags, smart devices, etc.) with each other using the Internet so that these things can share information and make some useful decisions (Sandhu and Sood, 2016). In 1998, IoT was first coined by Kevin Auston in his presentation on future of networks. Later, it has been introduced in the Oxford dictionary with the following definition: *"The interconnection via the Internet of computing devices embedded in everyday objects, enabling them to send and receive data."* IoT has multiple application areas such as smart healthcare, smart home, smart school, smart transport and many more. Out of the many challenges of IoT, effective decision making with relevance to the current context of the user or the thing is very important. Any decision made by IoT based application which is out of the current context of the user/thing affects the overall performance and accuracy of the system. However, with real-time data available through the IoT devices, smart context-aware applications can be developed. On the other hand, the IoT framework consists of billions of sensors deployed around the world where the analysis of the data generated by all connected sensors is not feasible. Integration of context awareness in the deployment and usage of IoT devices will provide a method in which only suitable sensors can be prompted to make any decision. This will yield the better performance and scalability of IoT based applications.

Context-aware IoT paradigm proves to be novel for application users. However, security remains the essential requirement in any application. Security mechanism in IoT applications is usually handled in a traditional way such as assigning a role to the application user, grant for resources, etc. These traditional methods are independent and proved to provide the desired security, but the consideration of context also plays an important role and can be very helpful. The security in IoT applications should be highly dependent upon the context of the device and security policies should be updated if the context of the IoT device changes. Consider a scenario when the context (location) of a user/device changes from a public Internet access area to private network. Based on the context, security policies can be updated so that overall QoS of application is optimized. This will make IoT based applications more secure and reliable.

Securing data during transmission and at the interfaces is one of the significant challenges of IoT based smart applications. Any unauthorized change in data can lead to unintended results which further decreases the reliability of IoT based applications. Proper cryptographic techniques should be employed so that IoT based applications are not hacked. However, memory and energy constraints on IoT devices do not allow the use of heavy cryptographic algorithms. Lightweight cryptography is used for most of the IoT based applications which can be prone to attacks. Adding context to the cryptographic techniques can further enhance the security. Contextual information can be used to dynamically allocate the light cryptographic solutions to any IoT based smart applications.

In this chapter, a security framework has been proposed which considers context for managing the security policies of IoT based applications and IoT devices. Three context values associated with IoT devices are used which are when (time of record), where (location of the sensor), whom (surrounding sensor devices) for the security policies upgradations. Medical sensor recording heart rate, GSR values, and respiratory rate are used in the use case to test the proposed framework. Naïve Bayes algorithm which provides the probability-based selection of the security policy to be updated is used in the proposed framework.

BACKGROUND

Internet of Things (IoT)

Over the last decade, Internet of Things (IoT) has attained considerable attention in industrial and academic fields. Major companies like Google, Amazon, IBM, Microsoft, CISCO, etc. are putting efforts in the field of IoT. Concerning academic research, renowned universities such as Stanford University, Harvard University have started dedicated research and courses related to IoT (Xing Liu and Baiocchi, 2016). Apart from these important organizations, many small and medium international organizations are also contributing to the evolution of IoT in our day to day life. Some of the organizations working on the standardization of IoT are International Telecommunication Union (ITU), National Institute of Standards and Technology (NIST), Internet Engineering Task Force (IETF), etc.

IoT is being promoted in all the fields because of its capabilities (Atzori, Lera, & Morabito, 2010; Miorandi, Sicari, De Pellegrini, & Chlamtac, 2012). The eventual objective of IoT is to make the world a convenient place where objects, referred to as "smart objects" (Kortuem, et al., 2010) work seamlessly with the humans. Smart objects predict likes and dislikes, needs and desires of human beings by communicating with each other over the Internet with minimum or least human intervention. In summary, IoT is the interconnection between three types of things a) human-to-human b) machine-to-human c) machine-to-machine, over the Internet.

According to the study by (Sundmaeker, Guillemin & Friess, 2010), IoT is at its initial stage and possesses some fuzziness. Different researchers have defined IoT differently. Figure 1 shows some of the features of IoT. Some of the definitions are stated below:

1. **Cluster of European research projects** (Sundmaeker et al., 2010): *"Things" are active participants in business, information and social processes where they are enabled to interact and communicate among themselves and with the environment by exchanging data* and *information sensed about the environment, while reacting autonomously to the real/physical world events and influencing it by running processes that trigger actions and create services with or without direct human intervention."*
2. **RFID Group** (Gubbi, Buyya, Marusic and Palaniswami, 2013): *"The worldwide network of interconnected objects uniquely addressable based on standard communication protocols."*
3. **Definition as in** (Vermesan et al., 2009): *"The Internet of Things allows people and things to be connected anytime, anyplace, with anything and anyone, ideally using any path/network and any service."*

The definition of IoT as stated by (Vermesan et al., 2009) expresses the essential features of IoT and covers the broader vision. Therefore, in this work, the definition stated by (Vermesan et al., 2009) is widely accepted. Many researchers have identified the necessary characteristics of IoT. Quoting to (Atzori et al., 2010; Gubbi et al., 2013; Miorandi et al., 2012; Perera, et al., 2014) following characteristics have been listed:

- **Intelligence:** Intelligence refers to the meaningful information extracted from the raw data by the sensors. Once context-aware data has been generated, it can be utilized to form intelligent systems and communication.
- **Complex System:** Over a period in IoT based applications, many devices are added to the network while others may vanish from the network, and this makes the IoT system very complicated.
- **Architecture:** There are generally two types of architectures in IoT: system-event driven and time driven. Event-driven architecture collects data when a specified event occurs whereas time driven architectures collect data periodically.
- **Scalability:** IoT devices need to be scalable because ultimately, they must communicate to information infrastructure globally.

- **Space Considerations:** In IoT, communications between devices are highly dependent upon location, the presence of other objects or people and surroundings of a device. Hence, the IoT device needs to possess location and tracking capabilities.
- **Energy Considerations:** IoT infrastructure should employ energy efficient algorithms and conserve energy to prolong the battery life of a device over a more extended period.
- **Time Considerations:** Although there are billions of devices that IoT can handle through simultaneous and parallel executions, real-time executions and data processing are essential. Therefore, time consideration is an essential characteristic of IoT.
- **Size Considerations:** According to (Sundmaeker et al., 2010), by the year 2020, there will be approximately hundred billion devices connected over the Internet. By increase in some devices, there would be a significant increase in some interactions too.
- **Everything-as-a-Service:** IoT would instead require a large number of services to build up a massive infrastructure and to process in real time. Hence, sharing and everything-as-a-service model is best suited for IoT.
- **Privacy-Preserving and Security Mechanism:** For the technology to be widely adopted, it should be secure and possess privacy mechanisms. Hence, security is the critical characteristic of IoT design and infrastructure.

Context Awareness

Humans can exchange ideas with each other very efficiently. They can understand each other because they know the context in which the person is talking about. However, this is not true in case of human to computer communication. Users can take full advantage of computational services by providing contextual information to computers. One way to provide contextual information to computers is by the user explicitly. However, this approach can sometimes make awkward situations because many users may know which information is potentially relevant according to various situations. The better approach is to develop context-aware applications. These applications automatically collect contextual information and make them available to computers during run-time.

Many authors agreed that context plays a vital role in IoT based applications. However, the cardinality of literature studying context for IoT based applications is feeble. So, while conducting the literature review, the focus was on exploring the background, classification, characteristics, and evolvement of context. This is required for the better understanding of context and its relationship with IoT based applications. In this section, context-aware literature has been discussed, and its relevance has been studied with IoT based applications. So, a literature review has been divided into following subsections for better understanding:

Context Classification

Many authors have studied the classification of context in which Abowd et al. (Dey & Abowd, 1999), Schilit et al. (Schilit, Adams and Want, 1994), Henricksen (Henricksen, 2003), Bunningen et al. (Bunningen, Feng & Apers, 2005) and Perera et al. (Perera et al., 2014) are some of the notable contributors. Abowd et al. (Dey and Abowd, 1999) classified the context into two basic categories as the primary context and secondary context. Primary contexts are collected directly from the sensors or any other devices whereas secondary context is calculated using data collected for the primary context. However, the proposed classification is not possible in IoT based applications because it is challenging to predict the classification of any context. For example, the location of the home can be first context collected from a GPS device, and it can be secondary context found from the social security number of the user. Schilit et al. (Schilit et al., 1994) classified context into three major classifications: a) where you are b) who you are with c) what resources are nearby. They argued that based on these three context parameters, applications could make effective decisions. However, this classification fails to address the configuration, deployment and selection issues of devices in any IoT based application. Henricksen (Henricksen, 2003) stated the classification of context based on how the environment of sensors is modeled and setup.

Four classifications provided in this research are: a) Real-time data generated by sensors, b) Static information which does not change, c) Information that changes with low-frequency, and, d) Derived information which can be computed using information of other three categories. He lists detailed information from the perspective of sensor data frequency, but the relationship between contexts is not studied in this classification. Bunningen et al. (Bunningen et al., 2005) classified the schemes of context classification into two main categories which are conceptual schemes and operational schemes. All the classification schemes discussed above can be efficiently allocated to one of these categories. Perera et al. (Perera et al., 2014) studied all the classifications and provided a high and low-level hierarchy of context classifications for IoT based applications. All this context information is valuable in any smart environment. However, the smart application should be aware of what type of information needs to be processed at any given instant of time.

Application Features Using Context

Any application developed using IoT can provide multiple features, such as it can present any data value, perform any action, alert any specific user, etc. Based on the studies conducted in (Barkhuus and Dey, 2003; Dey and Abowd, 1999; Pascoe, n.d.; Schilit et al., 1994), application features categorization is shown in Figure 1.

Applications using IoT device may collect a diverse and large amount of information which can be extremely confusing for the end user. Context can be used to decide which information should be presented to the user. For example, when any user is in the shopping mall, using the current context, a shopping list should be provided to the user automatically on his/her mobile device. Rest of the non-relevant information can be delayed. Presentation of the information can be further divided into two sub-parts. First is the primary information such as current temperature or rainfall estimation. Secondary information is derived from the primary information. For example, based on temperature and rainfall data, the application can suggest the type of clothes to wear or whether to carry an umbrella or not.

Execution of any action automatically by devices is also an essential aspect in any application using IoT devices. In (Barkhuus and Dey, 2003; Perera et al., 2014), the importance of effective executive action and its characteristics are studied. For example, the smart home cooling system should automatically turn on or off based on the movement in the home. Execution can further be divided into three parts which are explained in detail below.

- **Manual:** In this type of execution, user sets the preference or changes the environment manually. For example, setting the temperature in the home.
- **Passive Execution:** In this type of execution, application continuously monitors the system and asks the user to choose some actions from the

Figure 1. Features of IoT based applications

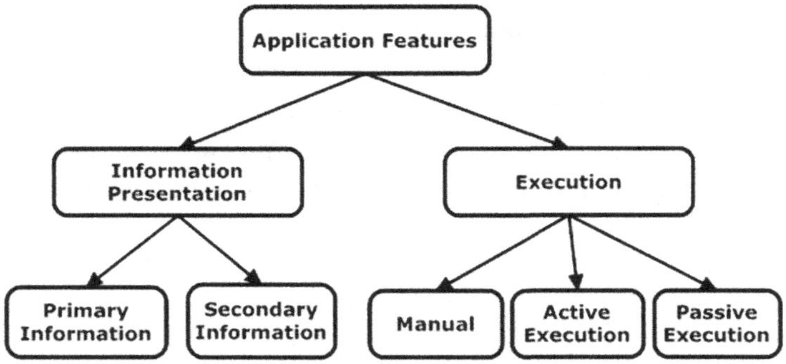

available actions. For example, when the user enters a shopping mall, the application should present him/her a list of items available on discount.

- **Active Execution:** In this type of execution, the smart application automatically adjusts the settings and takes appropriate actions. For example, calling fire services in case of fire detection in the house.

The Lifecycle of Context-Aware Applications

Hynes et al. (Hynes, Reynolds and Hauswirth, 2009) stated that lifecycle of any smart application could be classified into enterprise lifecycle and context lifecycle. Perera et al. (Perera et al., 2014) argued that enterprise lifecycle is well studied and standardized whereas context lifecycle is still is in its initial stages. Some of the notable context lifecycles are listed in Table 1. After studying the relevant literature, lifecycle of the context-aware application using IoT can be divided into four distinct steps which are shown in Figure 2.

- **Data Acquisition:** Data acquisition is one of the most critical steps in any IoT based application development. If the data is not collected correctly and promptly, other steps fail automatically (Perera et al., 2014; Pietschmann et al., 2008).

Table 1. Context lifecycles

S. No.	Author	Context Lifecycle
1.	Chantzara and Anagnostou(Chantzara & Anagnostou, 2005)	Sense → process → disseminate → use.
2.	Ferscha et al. (Ferscha, Vogl, & Beer, 2005)	Sensing → transformation → representation → rule base → actuation
3.	Wrona and Gomez(Wrona & Gomez, 2005)	Context information discovery → context information acquisition → context information reasoning
4.	Hynes et al. (Hynes et al., 2009)	(Context sensing →context transmission →context acquisition) →context classification →context handling → (context dissemination →context usage →context deletion →context request) →context maintenance →context disposition.
5.	Baldauf et al. (Baldauf, Dustdar, & Rosenberg, 2007)	Sensors → raw data retrieval →reprocessing → storage → application.
6.	Perera et al. (Perera et al., 2014)	Context acquisition → Context modelling → Context reasoning → Context dissemination.

Figure 2. The lifecycle of context-aware application

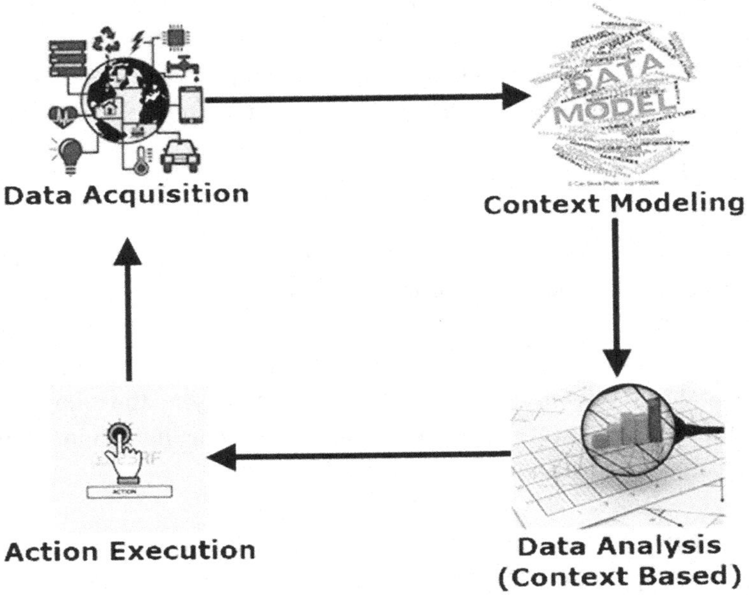

- **Modeling the Context:** Appropriate modeling techniques for creation and derivation of context are very important. Modeling provides an overview of the application and its usage for the context information. Based on context modeling techniques described in (Bettini et al., 2010; Henricksen and Indulska, 2004) the types of context modeling can be classified as: Key-Value Modeling, Markup Modeling (Knappmeyer at al., 2010; Yanwei et al., 2011), Graph-Based Modeling (Henricksen, 2003; Myeong, Chang and Lee, 2012; Van et al., 2008), Object-Based Modeling, Ontology-Based modeling (Allemang and Hendler, 2011; Sheth, Henson and Sahoo, 2008; Yu, 2011). Ontology is the most suitable context modeling technique for IoT based smart application among the mentioned techniques.
- **Data Analysis:** After modeling the context, data analysis step should be used to extract useful information from the collected and modeled data points (Bettini et al., 2010; Ejigu, Scuturici and Brunie, 2007; Guan et al., 2007; Jie and ZhaoHui, 2006; Perttunen et al., 2009). Based on these data analysis tools, specific actions to be carried out will be formulated by the smart application. Literature of data analysis is very vast and itself a subject to study. To keep the brevity of this report, some of the related literature analysis has been presented (Perera et al., 2014). Table 2 below presents different

Table 2. Different data analysis algorithms in projects studied (Perera et al., 2014)

S. No.	Name	Count out of 109	Percentage
1.	Rule-Based Approach	58	54
2.	Decision Tree	16	15
3.	Naïve Bayes	14	13
4.	Hidden Markov Models	14	13
5.	Support Vector Machines	5	4
6.	K-Nearest Neighbor	2	2

types of decision-making algorithms used in 109 projects studied by (Perera et al., 2014).

- **Action Execution:** After all the steps in the context-aware application lifecycle, the final step is to distribute the information so that appropriate action can be taken. Information can be shared with some users, devices or other applications. The first step in action execution is the distribution of the information which can be done in two ways (Perera et al., 2014):
  - **Query Based:** In this case, an application, a device or a user that requires the information sent a query to the application and based on that query, the application returns the results.
  - **Subscribe:** In this case, the application automatically sends the information to other application, device or user after some pre-specified interval of time. Subscription can be of two types:
    - **Trigger-based:** When new information is generated, or interaction is required, it sends the information.
    - **Periodic based:** Information is sent after each pre-specified interval of time.

After the information is communicated to the end device, it performs the required action.

IoT and Context-Aware Applications

Forecasting its benefits and need, researchers started to work more progressively on context-aware, intelligent services using IoT in 2016. Some of the notable contributions are discussed in this section and compared in Table 3.

In 2012, Yanwei et al. (Yanwei et al., 2011) stated the importance of studying the context in case of an IoT environment. They argued that thing-to-thing context for any IoT based smart application is essential and can result in better result formation.

They also proposed a framework which uses different contexts to pass critical information. In 2016, Gil et al. (Gil, Ferrndez, Mora-Mora & Peral, 2016) surveyed different context-aware intelligent services from IoT perspectives. They provided the taxonomy of IoT research based on technologies (cloud computing, big data, etc.), applications (smart grid, health, cities, etc.), data and context. They identified some open issues and role of contextual information in providing intelligent services using IoT. In 2016, Sachdeva et al. (Sachdeva, Dhir & Kumar, 2016) studied different machine learning techniques for context-aware recommendation systems that use the IoT data. They compared multiple machine learning algorithms and concluded that genetic algorithm based artificial neural network produced best results. In 2016, Du et al. (Du, Putra, Yamamoto, & Nakao, 2016) proposed a prototype which uses software-defined networks data plane to use the context information and provide better results. Their proposed prototype processes the IoT traffic in the software-defined network's data plane based on the contextual header information. If the sensor's contextual information matches the high-end application, it performs some processing in the data plane for providing better results. In 2016, Gill et al. (Gill, et al., 2016) developed an application for older adults using IoT and supply chain methodology. The proposed application reads the alert or warning message delivered to the older adults based on their current context. In 2016, Amin et al. (Amin, Ali-Eldin & Ali, 2016) studied the relevance of context awareness in IoT systems by building a layer of context features on the top of the IoT layer. They used fault management in electric power distribution using IoT and context awareness. They selected fault management areas based on the context information of that area. In 2016, Khan et al. (Khan et al., 2016) developed a context-aware low power intelligent, smart home using a unified communication channel and methods. All devices deployed in the smart home use the same communication methods for sharing information among each other. This increases the overall performance of the system. In 2016, Chen et al. (Y. Chen, Zhou and Guo, 2016) worked on the searching technique for appropriate IoT device for acquisition of respective information. They argued that traditional search techniques would not be able to handle the context relationship in IoT based environments. They used the ontology-based hierarchical search system for selection of appropriate smart objects to be deployed in any smart application. In 2016, Kamienski et al. (Kamienski et al., 2016) proposed a context-aware application development platform for smart applications using different smart objects. They took energy management in smart buildings as a use case and found the effectiveness of the proposed framework. In 2016, Rokni and Ghasemzadeh (Rokni and Ghasemzadeh, 2016) argued that currently available sensors behave only the way their algorithm is developed. However, a smart object should be able to behave differently based on the current context of the user or application. They proposed to develop a platform in which smart sensors can use the algorithms of other smart sensors to carry out the work based on different context. In 2016, Sandhu and Sood (Sandhu and Sood, 2016) devised a game theory based framework which selects the appropriate sensors in real-time to make any decision. A decision on the selection of sensor is made based on the calculated Nash equilibrium of triggered sensors. They evaluated their proposed framework based on the use case of the smart home.

ADAPTIVE SECURITY FRAMEWORK USING CONTEXT

In this chapter, an adaptive security framework has been proposed for the security of IoT devices based on the contextual information. Figure 3 provides the proposed framework for change in security policies of IoT devices based on the contextual information received by the machine learning component. IoT devices are sending their data to Cloud infrastructure for processing which is being sent using some

Table 3. Comparison of different IoT based context-aware systems

S. No.	Article	Context Lifecycle	Type of Application	IoT Devices	Technique Used
1	(Yanwei et al., 2011)	Data Acquisition	Smart grid application is used to test the thing-to-thing context.	Yes	Six tuple-based descriptions of context.
2	(Sachdeva et al., 2016)	Data Analysis	Chicago Restaurant Dataset	No	Compared using MATLAB
3	(Du et al., 2016)	Context Modeling	Smart GPS Monitoring	Yes	Implemented with Intel Edison Board
4	(Gill et al., 2016)	Execution	Smart Home for Elder Users	Yes	Raspberry Pi and Other Devices
5	(Amin et al., 2016)	Context Modeling	Fault Management in Power Grid	Yes	Message Passing, Layered Architecture
7	(Khan et al., 2016)	Execution	Smart Home	Yes	Hadoop, Medical and Fire Dataset
8	(Y. Chen et al., 2016)	Context Modeling	Smart Search System	Yes	Ontology, Hidden Markov Models
9	(Kamienski et al., 2016)	Execution	Smart Building	Yes	Data Mining and Message Passing
10	(Rokni & Ghasemzadeh, 2016)	Context Modeling	Smart Fitness	Yes	Software reuse and Machine Learning
11	(Sandhu & Sood, 2016)	Context Modeling	Smart Home	Yes	Game Theory

security policy. If there is any change in the contextual information of IoT device, it will send that information to a machine learning component that predicts which security policy is to be used in real-time. Security policy will be updated, and IoT device will start sending data based on new security policy.

Machine Learning Component

In this chapter, the Naïve Bayes algorithm has been proposed to select the security policy based on the contextual information received from the IoT device. Naïve Bayes will take a change in contextual information and predicts the conditional probability of each security policy to be used at that instance of time. Naïve Bayes predicts the probabilities using Bayes theorem which provides conditional probability formula as:

$$P(C_i|Y) = \frac{P(Y|C_i)P(C_i)}{P(Y)}$$

Where Ci is the ith security policy, and Y is the contextual information.

Figure 3. Proposed security framework for IoT devices

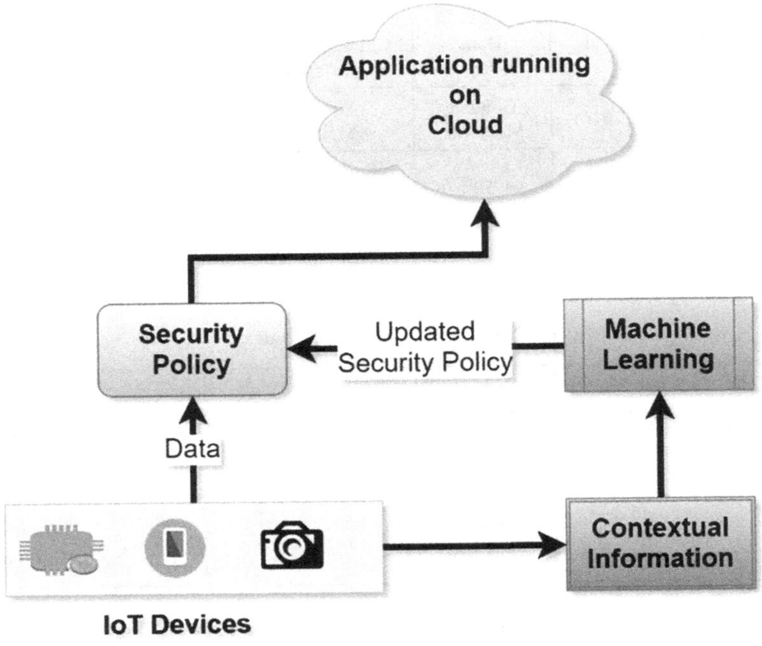

Figure 4. Naïve Bayes algorithm to predict security policy

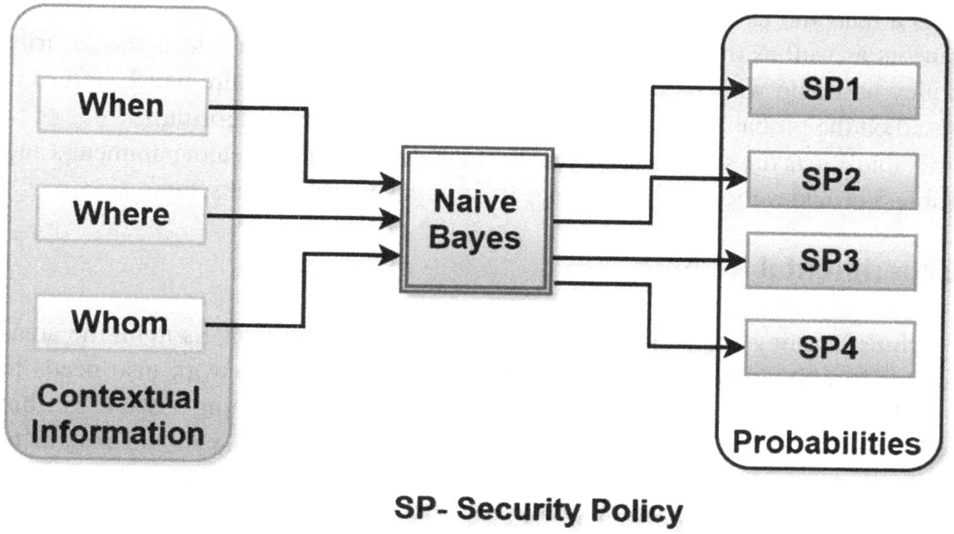

Category of security policy to be used cannot be fixed to a particular policy strictly. The new security policy may require a combination of different contextual information such as when, where, whom, etc. So, a probabilistic association of security policy to contextual information of IoT device is required in the proposed framework. Naïve Bayes classifier predicts the probability of each IoT device to fall in any of the pre-specified security policies. By default, the IoT is assumed to fall in general security policy. Figure 4 shows are linking of contextual information with the selection of security policy derived by the Naïve Bayes algorithm.

EXPERIMENTAL EVALUATION

The proposed framework has been experimentally evaluated using a real-time scenario which involves real sensors sending data to the cloud. For better understanding, this section has been divided into three sections which are explained in detail ahead.

Testbed for Evaluation

Figure 5 shows experimental testbed designed to evaluate the proposed framework experimentally. It contains three sensors which are a heart rate sensor, a respiratory sensor, and Galvanic Skin Response (GSR) sensor. All these sensors collect data of a subject and send that data to an android mobile device. Android mobile device runs a machine learning component which receives contextual information from sensors as well as the mobile device. The mobile device then selects the security policy based on what data should be sent to cloud infrastructure which in turn is based on the probabilities calculated using the Naïve Bayes algorithm.

Table 4 lists the sensors used to collect the data related to health parameters and Table 5 provides the security policies used in the experimental setup.

Experimental Results

Machine learning algorithms have been introduced by researchers in all the areas related to effective decision making. As the proposed framework also needs to decide which security policy to use in real-time, machine learning based algorithm is required. Many machine learning algorithms are available in the market to perform such an operation. However, as a total number of policies among which system has to select a policy is fixed, supervised machine learning algorithm is best suited for the proposed framework. Classification (supervised learning) contains many algorithms, but the relationship between attribute and context can be correctly represented using conditional probabilities which contributed to the decision to use naïve Bayes algorithm. Naïve Bayes algorithm has been used to train the machine learning component so that it can predict the probability of choosing security policy at any instant of time. Raw data collected by sensors and manual setting of security policy is fed into Naïve Bayes classifier of Weka 3.7 (Hall et al., 2009). Data were collected for two weeks for the movement of two subjects within the area of Melbourne region of Australia. Total instances collected for change in

Figure 5. Testbed for the experiment of the proposed framework

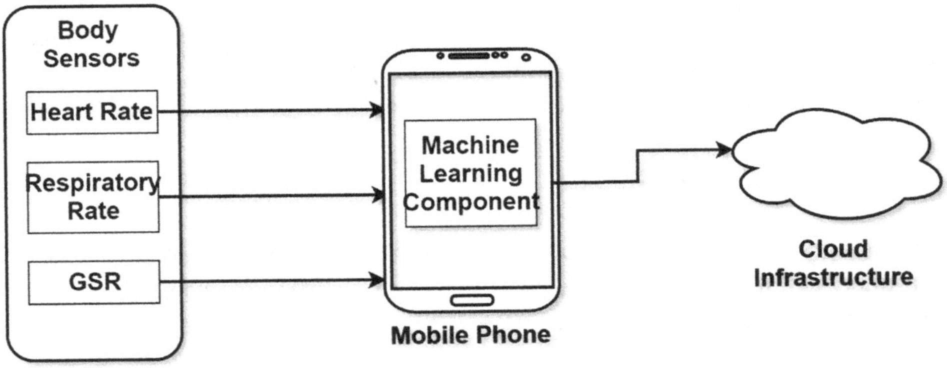

Table 4. Different sensors used in the experimental evaluation

S. No.	Name of Sensor	Data Send per Reading	Connected Via
1	Heartrate Monitor	92kb	Wi-Fi
2	Respiratory Rate Monitor	71kb	Wi-Fi
3	GSR	149kb	Bluetooth

Table 5. Different security profiles created in the mobile device

S. No.	Name	Security Level	Encryption	Verification Using MD5
1	SP1	Lowest	None	No
2	SP2	Low	Low	No
3	SP3	Medium	Single Side	Yes
4	SP4	Highest	Both Sides	Yes

contextual information were recorded equal to 604. Same data has been fed to Weka with 10-fold cross-validation, and Table 6 shows different metrics of the training.

The proposed system was also testing with some minor attacks generated by Pytbull ("Pytbull," 2017) and the results obtained are shown in Figure 6, Figure 7 and Figure 8. Different levels of attacks were generated and send to both the machine learning components.

Results obtained from the experimental evaluation are shown in Figure 6, Figure 7 and Figure 8. Figure 6 shows the number and level of attacks generated by Pytbull to the mobile device which sends data to cloud computing infrastructure. Figure 7 shows the average utilization of resources of the mobile device by sensor data analysis component which is continuously sending data to cloud from sensors. As proposed framework follows security policies based on the context of the user, it does not use encryption when in the private network reducing the resource utilization of sensor analysis component. For the same reason, the battery was consumed less in case of the proposed framework as shown in Figure 8. Experimental evaluation proved the concept about the proposed framework which changes the security policies based on the contextual information of sensors.

Table 6. Summary of 10-fold cross-validation training of Naïve Bayes in Weka 3.7

Stratified Cross-Validation		
Summary		
Correctly Classified Instances	544	90%
Incorrectly Classified Instances	60	10%
Kappa Statistic	0.92	
K&B Relative Info Score	11812.098	
K&B Information Score	225.5791 bits	1.4727 bits/instance
Class Complexity I Order 0	247.7121 bits	1.3152 bits/instance
Class Complexity I Scheme	25.5260 bits	0.1714 bits/instance
Complexity Improvement (Sf)	210.2571 bits	1.2712 bits/instance
Mean Absolute Error	0.0232	
Root Mean Squared Error	0.135	
Relative Absolute Error	8.3481%	
Root Relative Squared Error	38.1497%	
Total Number of Instances	604	

Figure 6. Different levels of attacks generated by Pytbull to the mobile device

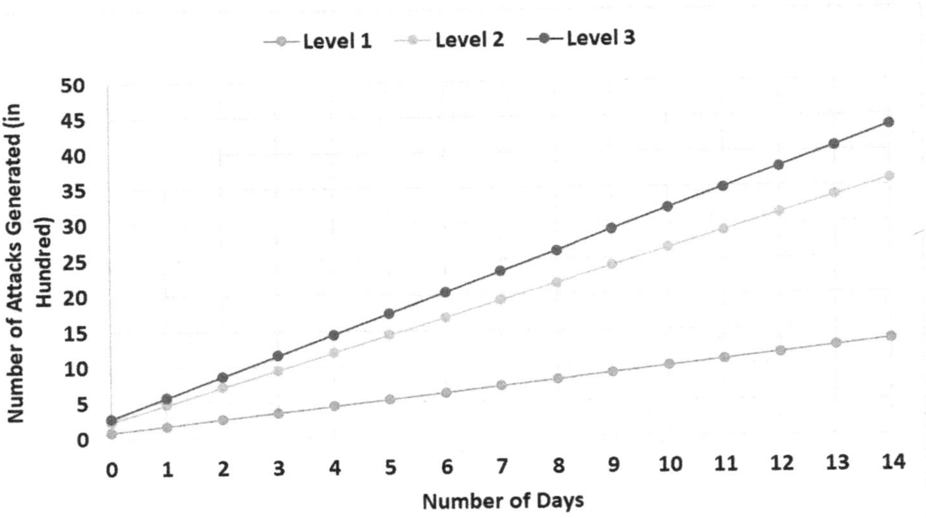

Figure 7. Average resource utilization of mobile device for sensor data analysis

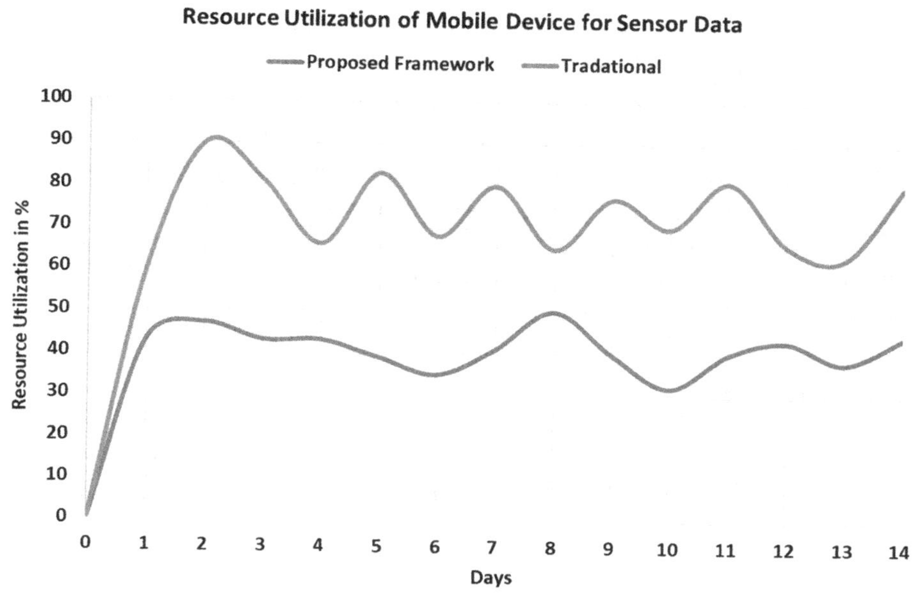

Figure 8. Average battery consumption of mobile device

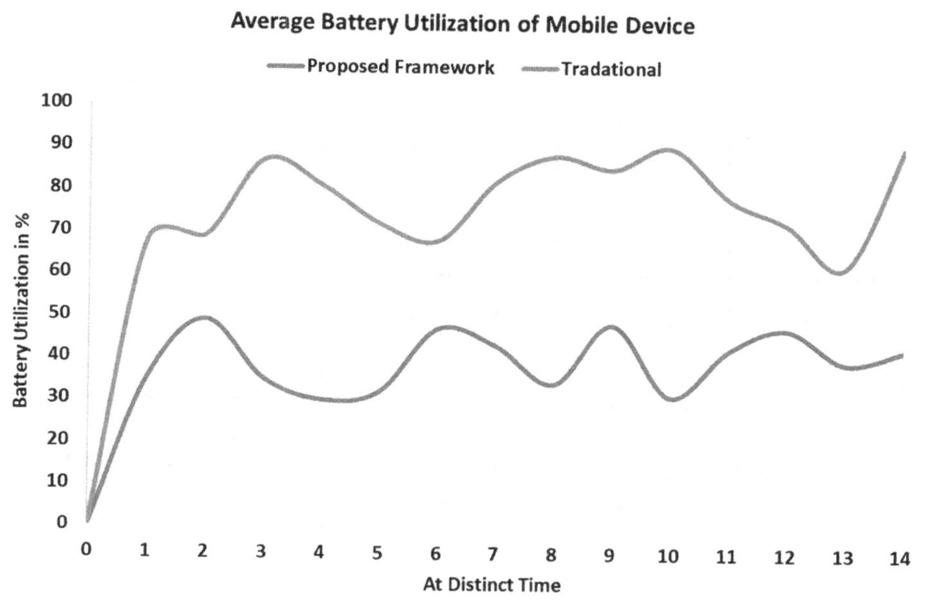

CONCLUSION

Contextual information is key to the development of many smart applications where real-time decisions are required to be taken. Contextual information will provide a better experience and increase the usability of any smart application. Many non-functional attributes of any smart application can be easily enhanced using contextual information. In this chapter, the security of any smart device is updated based on the contextual information of the device. Results from experimental evaluation proved the hypothesis and contextual information was able to enhance the performance as well as the battery utilization of the mobile device.

REFERENCES

Allemang, D., & Hendler, J. (2011). *Semantic Web for the Working Ontologist: Effective modeling in RDFS and OWL*. Semantic Web for the Working Ontologist. doi:10.1016/B978-0-12-385965-5.10016-0

Amin, S. A. A., Ali-Eldin, A., & Ali, H. A. (2016). A context-aware dispatcher for the Internet of Things: The case of electric power distribution systems. *Computers & Electrical Engineering*, *52*, 183–198. doi:10.1016/j.compeleceng.2015.05.012

Atzori, L., Lera, A., & Morabito, G. (2010). Internet of Things: A Survey. *Computer Networks*, *54*(15), 2787–2805. doi:10.1016/j.comnet.2010.05.010

Baldauf, M., Dustdar, S., & Rosenberg, F. (2007). A survey on context-aware systems. *International Journal of Ad Hoc and Ubiquitous Computing*, *2*(4), 263. doi:10.1504/IJAHUC.2007.014070

Barkhuus, L., & Dey, A. K. (2003). Is Context-Aware Computing Taking Control away from the User? Three Levels of Interactivity Examined. In Ubicomp 2003: Ubiquitous Computing (Vol. 2864, pp. 149–156). Springer Berlin Heidelberg. Retrieved from doi:10.1007/978-3-540-39653-6_12

Bettini, C., Brdiczka, O., Henricksen, K., Indulska, J., Nicklas, D., Ranganathan, A., & Riboni, D. (2010). A survey of context modelling and reasoning techniques. *Pervasive and Mobile Computing*, *6*(2), 161–180. doi:10.1016/j.pmcj.2009.06.002

Chantzara, M., & Anagnostou, M. (2005). Evaluation and Selection of Context Information. *Second International Workshop on Modeling and Retrieval of Context*. Retrieved from http://ceur-ws.org/Vol-146/paper7.pdf

Chen, H., Finin, T., Joshi, A., Kagal, L., Perich, F., & Chakraborty, D. (2004). Intelligent agents meet the semantic Web in smart spaces. *IEEE Internet Computing*, *8*(6), 69–79. doi:10.1109/MIC.2004.66

Chen, Y., Zhou, J., & Guo, M. (2016). A context-aware search system for Internet of Things based on hierarchical context model. *Telecommunication Systems*, *62*(1), 77–91. doi:10.100711235-015-9984-x

Dey, A. K., & Abowd, G. (1999). Towards a Better Understanding of Context and Context-Awareness. In *Handheld and Ubiquitous Computing* (pp. 304–307). Springer Berlin Heidelberg. doi:10.1007/3-540-48157-5_29

Du, P., Putra, P., Yamamoto, S., & Nakao, A. (2016). A context-aware IoT architecture through software-defined data plane. In *Proceedings - 2016 IEEE Region 10 Symposium, TENSYMP 2016* (pp. 315–320). IEEE. 10.1109/TENCONSpring.2016.7519425

Ejigu, D., Scuturici, M., & Brunie, L. (2007). An ontology-based approach to context modeling and reasoning in pervasive computing. In *Proceedings - Fifth Annual IEEE International Conference on Pervasive Computing and Communications Workshops, PerCom Workshops 2007* (pp. 14–19). IEEE. 10.1109/PERCOMW.2007.22

Ferscha, A., Vogl, S., & Beer, W. (2005). Context Sensing, Aggregation, Representation and Exploitation in Wireless Networks. *Scalable Computing: Practice and Experience*, *6*(2), 71–81. Retrieved from http://scpe.org/index.php/scpe/article/view/327

Gil, D., Ferrández, A., Mora-Mora, H., & Peral, J. (2016). Internet of things: A review of surveys based on context aware intelligent services. *Sensors (Switzerland)*, *16*(7), 1069. doi:10.339016071069 PMID:27409623

Gill, A. Q., Phennel, N., Lane, D., & Phung, V. L. (2016). IoT-enabled emergency information supply chain architecture for elderly people: The Australian context. *Information Systems*, *58*, 75–86. doi:10.1016/j.is.2016.02.004

Guan, D., Yuan, W., Lee, S., & Lee, Y. K. (2007). Context selection and reasoning in ubiquitous computing. In *Proceedings The 2007 International Conference on Intelligent Pervasive Computing, IPC 2007* (pp. 184–187). Academic Press. 10.1109/IPC.2007.102

Gubbi, J., Buyya, R., Marusic, S., & Palaniswami, M. (2013). Internet of Things (IoT): A vision, architectural elements, and future directions. *Future Generation Computer Systems*, *29*(7), 1645–1660. doi:10.1016/j.future.2013.01.010

Hall, M., Frank, E., Holmes, G., Pfahringer, B., Reutemann, P., & Witten, I. H. (2009). The WEKA data mining software. *SIGKDD Explorations Newsletter, 11*(1), 10. doi:10.1145/1656274.1656278

Henricksen, K. (2003). *A framework for context-aware pervasive computing applications.* The School of Information Technology and Electrical Engineering, The University of Queensland. Retrieved from http://henricksen.id.au/publications/phd-thesis.pdf

Henricksen, K., & Indulska, J. (2004). Modelling and using imperfect context information. In *Proceedings - Second IEEE Annual Conference on Pervasive Computing and Communications, Workshops, PerCom* (pp. 33–37). IEEE. 10.1109/PERCOMW.2004.1276901

Hynes, G., Reynolds, V., & Hauswirth, M. (2009). A context lifecycle for web-based context management services. In Lecture Notes in Computer Science (including subseries Lecture Notes in Artificial Intelligence and Lecture Notes in Bioinformatics) (Vol. 5741, pp. 51–65). Springer Berlin Heidelberg. doi:10.1007/978-3-642-04471-7_5

Indulska, J., & Sutton, P. (2003). Location management in pervasive systems. In *Proceedings of the Australasian information security workshop conference on ACSW frontiers* (Vol. 34, pp. 143–151). Retrieved from http://dl.acm.org/citation.cfm?id=828003

Internet Live Stats. (2014). *Number of Internet Users (2014) - Internet Live Stats.* Retrieved February 9, 2017, from http://www.Internetlivestats.com/Internet-users/

Jie, S., & ZhaoHui, W. (2006). Context Reasoning Technologies in Ubiquitous Computing Environment. *Embedded and Ubiquitous Computing. Proceedings, 4096*, 1027–1036. doi:10.1007/11802167_103

Kamienski, C., Jentsch, M., Eisenhauer, M., Kiljander, J., Ferrera, E., & Rosengren, P. … Sadok, D. (2016). Application development for the Internet of Things: A context-aware mixed criticality systems development platform. *Computer Communications.* doi:10.1016/j.comcom.2016.09.014

Khan, M., Din, S., Jabbar, S., Gohar, M., Ghayvat, H., & Mukhopadhyay, S. C. (2016). Context-aware low power intelligent SmartHome based on the Internet of things. *Computers & Electrical Engineering, 52*, 208–222. doi:10.1016/j.compeleceng.2016.04.014

Knappmeyer, M., Kiani, S. L., Frà, C., Moltchanov, B., & Baker, N. (2010). ContextML: A light-weight context representation and context management schema. In *ISWPC 2010 - IEEE 5th International Symposium on Wireless Pervasive Computing 2010* (pp. 367–372). IEEE. 10.1109/ISWPC.2010.5483753

Kortuem, G., Kawsar, F., Fitton, D., & Sundramoorthy, V. (2010). Smart Objects as Building Blocks for the Internet of Things. *IEEE Computer Society, 10*, 1089–7801. doi:10.1109/MIC.2009.143

Liu, X., & Baiocchi, O. (2016). A comparison of the definitions for smart sensors, smart objects and Things in IoT. In *2016 IEEE 7th Annual Information Technology, Electronics and Mobile Communication Conference (IEMCON)* (pp. 1–4). IEEE. 10.1109/IEMCON.2016.7746311

Miorandi, D., Sicari, S., De Pellegrini, F., & Chlamtac, I. (2012). Internet of things: Vision, applications and research challenges. *Ad Hoc Networks, 10*(7), 1497–1516. doi:10.1016/j.adhoc.2012.02.016

Myeong, H., Chang, J. Y., & Lee, K. M. (2012). Learning object relationships via graph-based context model. In *Proceedings of the IEEE Computer Society Conference on Computer Vision and Pattern Recognition* (pp. 2727–2734). IEEE. 10.1109/CVPR.2012.6247995

Pascoe, J. (n.d.). Adding generic contextual capabilities to wearable computers. In *Digest of Papers. Second International Symposium on Wearable Computers (Cat. No.98EX215)* (pp. 92–99). IEEE Comput. Soc. 10.1109/ISWC.1998.729534

Perera, C., Zaslavsky, A., Christen, P., & Georgakopoulos, D. (2014). Context aware computing for the Internet of things: A survey. *IEEE Communications Surveys and Tutorials, 16*(1), 414–454. doi:10.1109/SURV.2013.042313.00197

Perttunen, M., Riekki, J., & Lassila, O. (2009). Context Representation and Reasoning in Pervasive Computing.pdf. *International Journal of Multimedia and Ubiquitous Engineering, 4*(4), 1–28.

Pietschmann, S., Mitschick, A., Winkler, R., & Meißner, K. (2008). CROCO: Ontology-based, cross-application context management. In *Proceedings - 3rd International Workshop on Semantic Media Adaptation and Personalization, SMAP 2008* (pp. 88–93). Academic Press. 10.1109/SMAP.2008.10

Pytbull. (2017). Retrieved August 20, 2017, from http://pytbull.sourceforge.net

Rokni, S. A., & Ghasemzadeh, H. (2016). Autonomous sensor-context learning in dynamic human-centered Internet-of-things environments. In *Proceedings of the 35th International Conference on Computer-Aided Design - ICCAD '16* (pp. 1–6). New York: ACM Press. 10.1145/2966986.2967008

Sachdeva, N., Dhir, R., & Kumar, A. (2016). Empirical analysis of Machine Learning Techniques for context aware Recommender Systems in the environment of IoT. In *Proceedings of the International Conference on Advances in Information Communication Technology & Computing - AICTC '16* (pp. 1–7). New York: ACM Press. 10.1145/2979779.2979818

Sandhu, R., & Sood, S. K. (2016). A stochastic game net-based model for effective decision-making in smart environments. *Concurrency and Computation*. doi:10.1002/cpe.3843

Schilit, B., Adams, N., & Want, R. (1994). Context-aware computing applications. In Wmcsa (pp. 85–90). IEEE Comput. Soc. Press. doi:10.1109/WMCSA.1994.16

Schmidt, A., & Van Laerhoven, K. (2001). How to build smart appliances? *IEEE Personal Communications*, *8*(4), 66–71. doi:10.1109/98.944006

Sheth, A., Henson, C., & Sahoo, S. S. (2008). Semantic sensor web. *IEEE Internet Computing*, *12*(4), 78–83. doi:10.1109/MIC.2008.87

Sundmaeker, H., Guillemin, P., & Friess, P. (2010). *Vision and challenges for realising the Internet of Things. ... the Internet of Things*. doi:10.2759/26127

Van Bunningen, A. H., Feng, L., & Apers, F. M. G. (2005). Context for ubiquitous data management. In *Proceedings of the International Workshop on Ubiquitous Data Management, UDM 2005* (pp. 17–24). IEEE. 10.1109/UDM.2005.7

Van Nguyen, T., Lim, W., Nguyen, H. A., & Choi, D. (2008). Context awareness framework based on contextual graph. *5th IEEE and IFIP International Conference on Wireless and Optical Communications Networks, WOCN 2008*. 10.1109/WOCN.2008.4542542

Vermesan, O., Friess, P., Guillemin, P., Gusmeroli, S., Sundmaeker, H., Bassi, A., ... Pat, D. (2009). Internet of Things Strategic Research Roadmap. *Internet of Things Strategic Research Roadmap*, 9–52.

Wrona, K., & Gomez, L. (2005). Context-aware security and secure context-awareness in ubiquitous computing environments. In *Proceedings of the XXI Autumn Meeting of Polish Information Processing Society* (pp. 255–265). Academic Press.

Yanwei, S., Guangzhou, Z., & Haitao, P. (2011). Research on the context model of intelligent interaction system in the Internet of Things. In *IT in Medicine and Education (ITME), 2011 International Symposium on* (Vol. 2, pp. 379–382). IEEE. 10.1109/ITiME.2011.6132129

Yu, L. (2011). *A Developer's Guide to the Semantic Web. Language*. Berlin: Springer Berlin Heidelberg. doi:10.1007/978-3-642-15970-1

Section 4

Social/Legal Issues and Forensics

This section illustrates various concerns regarding the social and legal aspects of the internet of things through a case study. It also discusses the importance of digital forensics for the Internet of Things and its underlying challenges.

Chapter 10
Emerging Social and Legal Issues of the Internet of Things:
A Case Study

Valentina Amenta
National Research Council, Italy

Adriana Lazzaroni
National Research Council, Italy

Laura Abba
National Research Council, Italy

ABSTRACT

The advent of internet represents a revolution for the contemporary era, having brought about a striking series of changes in social, institutional, political, and economic life. This ongoing revolution has spread and absorbed within itself all the problems related to its own development. Objects become recognizable and acquire intelligence in that they are able to communicate data regarding themselves and also access other information aggregated by other devices. They are able to participate in a dialogue and interact among themselves within electronic communication networks without human intervention. All objects can acquire an active role thanks to connection with the web. The associated problems, which can no longer be ignored, draw attention above all to the lack of data control, which is to the vast extent of the data collected and more generally to the security of these data. This chapter has the aim of analyzing the ways in which European legislators, and consequently also Italian representatives, have intervened in order to stem the tide of emerging issues.

DOI: 10.4018/978-1-5225-5742-5.ch010

THE 'INTERNET OF THINGS' MODEL

We begin to speak of the "Internet of Things (known as IoT)" in 1999, during a presentation at Procter & Gamble by Kevin Ashton, the British technological pioneer. In its first accepted meaning, IoT referred to those objects which, using banal tags, were identified unequivocally and then represented within the Web.

The first clear definition of IoT dated to 2009 when Ashton wrote: "*We need to empower computers with their means of gathering information so that they can see, hear and smell the world for themselves, in all its random glory. RFID and sensor technology enables computers to observe, identify and understand the world—without the limitations of human-entered data* (Ashton, 2009)".

A further definition is found in 2012, when a non-profit making research institute, Rand Europe, attempted to define IoT in research work for the European Commission. It is defined as: *"The Internet of Things (IoT) builds out from today's Internet by creating a pervasive and self-organizing network of connected, identifiable and addressable physical objects, enabling application development in key vertical sectors through the use of embedded chips, sensors, actuators, and low-cost miniaturization. The IoT is developing rapidly, challenging assumptions underlying the future Internet business, market, policy, and societal models. Connecting billions of objects to facilitate smarter living, the IoT may help us address global and societal challenges, making Europe a sustainable and inclusive economy. However, IoT-driven "smart meters", grids, homes, cities and transportation systems also raise some important issues that will need to be addressed* (Rand Europe, 2012)".

From these definitions it is possible to extrapolate the first vital data, that is, we can use the term IoT to refer to "intelligent objects". These include devices or sensors, computers, tablets, and smartphones, which have the privilege of connecting, communicating and transmitting information with or using each other through the Internet.

The paradigm which includes the intelligence of objects can be broken down into three directions (naturally the intelligent object must possess a capacity for connection in order to move the information collected at a local level towards remote applications, creating in this way a network of things):

1. Functionality of self-awareness identification, that is the possession of an unequivocal digital identification number (this is a basic functionality, present in all Internet of Things applications); localization, that is the capacity of objects to be aware of their position (this may occur in real time, or through elaboration of tracing information collected during the productive or logistic process); diagnosis of state, that is the capacity to monitor the object's internal

parameters so as to control its correct working state and possible need for assistance.

2. Functionality of interaction with the surrounding environment, that is data acquisition, conventionally divided into 'Sensing' (the measurement of variables of state that describe the physical system and/or surrounding environment) and 'Metering' (measurement of flow variables, such as consumption of electric energy, gas, water, heat, etc.) and implementation, that is the capacity to carry out commands remotely, by means of the distance control of actuators, or deriving from data elaboration in loco.
3. The functionality of data elaboration that is, precisely, basic elaboration. This means the treatment of the fundamental data collected, for example through filtering, correction, algebraic aggregation, conversion, cryptography, etc., and advanced elaboration, that is the extraction of information from the primitive data, for example., using statistical analysis, inferences and forecasts.

IoT is not yet an accomplished and mature model. It is instead a pathway of development which, starting from discrete-time identification based on RFID tags, has developed to the point of including sensor networks which connect the physical world to the digital world in real time.

IoT FRAMEWORK WITHIN REGULATION (EU) 2016/679

The enormous amount of data which connected devices generate, often in an autonomous way, arouse concerns regarding privacy and security. The Global Privacy Enforcement Network (GPEN), the international network founded in order to reinforce cooperation between the privacy authorities of various countries, launched an investigation (Privacy Sweep, 2016) in 2016 at an international level dedicated to the verification of the respect of privacy within IoT. In addition to Italy, another 28 national privacy authorities participated in the investigation. From the data, it emerges that out of more than three hundred electronic devices connected to the Internet – such as watches and intelligent bracelets, electronic counters and new generation thermostats – more than 60% did not pass the exam of the privacy authorities.

The confirmations obtained by the experts of the Authorities (Soro, 2016): out of more than three hundred devices of the leading companies of the sector brought to light at a global level, severe deficiencies in the protection of the privacy of users include:

- 59% of devices offer no adequate information regarding how users' personal data are collected, utilized and communicated to third parties;
- 68% do not supply appropriate information regarding the way in which data are stored;
- 72% do not explain to users how to delete the data from the device;
- 38% do not guarantee simple ways of contacting those clients who require clarification regarding respect of their privacy.

Some analyzed devices also presented problems regarding data security, for example., sending "unencoded" (that is unencrypted) transmissions to the local medical practitioner containing information relative to users' health and therefore, involving the sensitive data of users.

Despite the topical nature of the subject, above all in juridical terms, a clear and unequivocal picture regarding IoT does not exist. The directions to follow are those offered by already existing directives and regulations. Also, further complicating the legislative panorama, there is the moment of transition due to the issue of the new EU regulation regarding the protection of personal data which repealed the previous directive. In fact, on 4 May 2016, there was a publication in the Official Journal of the European Union of "Regulation (EU) 2016/679 of the European Parliament and Council, of 27 April 2016, on the protection of natural people with regard to the processing of personal data and on the free movement of such data, and repealing Directive 95/46/EC".

The regulation came into effect on 25 May 2016 but became operational in EU countries from 25 May 2018. This left a two- year period for all interested parties to carry out the necessary adjustments to their data treatment policies.

In order to apply the new EU Regulation 2016/679, the treatment of personal data must be carried out within the context of activities in the location of the data controller in the EU (Art. 3, para .1, Regulation (EU) 2016/679). Furthermore, it is clear that this regulation applies to entirely or partially automated treatment of personal data and to the non-automated treatment of personal data contained in an archive or due to be inserted in one (Art. 2, para. 1, Regulation (EU) 2016/679).

For our research, it follows that all the objects used to collect and process individual data within the supply of IoT services (pace counter, thermostats, refrigerators, smartphones, and tablets) qualify as tools.

A first problem is raised about the identification of the Data Controller (Art. 4, subs. 1, p. 7, Regulation (EU) 2016/679). Such a heterogeneous area as IoT involves a combination of actions by various stakeholders such as device producers and social platforms, the providers or leasers of data brokers or data platforms.

The complex network of stakeholders involved implies the need for a precise attribution of responsibility as regards the treatment of personal data, based on the specific nature of their related tasks. The producers of devices, besides selling objects to their clients or products to other organizations, also develop or modify the operating systems of intelligent objects or install software which determines their operation, including the gathering of data and their successive transmission. We confirm: Whom are these data transmitted to? The sharing of the gathered and aggregated data belongs to the standard settings predefined by the producers, and therefore, the legislation would seem to identify the Data Controller as the figure or entity that has had an active role in the management of data collection, such as, an application developer or software programmer.

Shifting attention to the figure of the user, that is, the natural people who use the technologically sensitive devices and to whom the personal data refer, we immediately face the problem of exclusion from the application of Regulation 679/2016. The new regulation retraces the old directive in the section in which in Art. 2 it is explicitly sanctioned that it cannot be applied to the treatment of personal data carried out by natural people for activities that are exclusive of a personal or domestic nature. What occurs in practice is a transfer of one's own personal data to the producers of devices, application developers and other third parties at the moment various devices are utilized. This generalized lack of awareness on the part of the user is at the center of the debate concerning IoT, bringing to light critical situations and risks for the total effective loss of control over one's own data. The user, indeed, for the most part, is unaware that the technological interaction involving IoT is founded on a massive and ongoing process of collection and manipulation of their personal data. This situation is particularly suited for allowing an intrusion, more or less penetrating, into the individual's sphere of privacy (Justice Option, 2014).

If it is true, in fact, that the emergence of new technologies based on dialogue between devices involves risk profiles as yet unknown to users, it is absolutely essential to provide users with suitable information in order to make them effectively aware of the single activities of elaboration and transmission of data involved in the services being used, with particular attention paid to the purposes of this treatment.

The need for appropriate information was advanced by WP29 which expressly specifies that for the treatment to be lawful, the users must remain in complete control of their personal data throughout the product lifecycle.

IoT and Anonymous Personal Data

Within the context of IoT, it often occurs that the data originating from devices can identify an individual. It may be that the subjects interested by the personal data treatment are not themselves IoT users. For example, a wearable device, such as intelligent glasses, can gather data regarding other exciting subjects, to third parties about the possessor of the device. It follows, therefore, that the possession of a device is not the essential prerequisite for being the interested party to the treatment of data.

Despite various efforts to create techniques of anonymization and pseudonymization, this data remains very much within the category of personal data (Art. 4, Parag. 1, EU Regulation 2016/679).

As regards the legitimacy of the process of anonymization, first of all, this is a technique applied to personal data with the aim of obtaining an irreversible de-identification. Therefore, the initial assumption is that the personal data must be gathered and treated in conformity with the applicable legislation regarding the storage of data in an identifiable format. Within this context, the process of anonymization, understood as treatment of personal data to obtain anonymous data, represents "successive treatment."

In light of what has been specified above, we can arrive at the conviction that the techniques of re-identification have prevailed and that we have already surpassed the legislative apparatus based so far on the belief that to protect a consumer from aggression to their private sphere, it was enough to share information anonymously.

As an example, Fitbit, a producer of bracelets and connected scales which monitor respectively physical fitness and weight loss, could introduce a de-identification of the data. This may be done by removing the name, address and other information which can identify the user before sharing this information with others. All this will, however, not be sufficient due to the ease of re-identifying this data set. The reason is very intuitive: each of us has a unique gait. This means that if we know the gait and walking style of a user, it could be possible to identify that individual among the millions of anonymized data belonging to the Fitbit users.

In Italy, legislation has dealt with anonymous data, identifying it as that data which in its original form, or following treatment, cannot be associated with an identified or identifiable interested party (Art.4, Data Protection Code).

Furthermore, Italian legislation puts anonymization within one of the fundamental principles of the Italian Privacy Code, which is the "principle of necessity (Art.3 Data Protection Code)". According to the regulation, information systems and the software used within them must be configured in such a way as to minimize the recourse to personal and identifying data, substituting the treatment with the use of anonymous data or pseudonyms when there is no significant impact on the purpose for which the data is required. This foresees identification of the interested party only in case of absolute necessity. This represents a veritable revolution in the approach to the protection of data processed with automated systems, above all as regards electronic commerce and telecommunications services. It is worth noting that this principle appears neither in Directive n. 95/46 nor in Law n. 675/96 and imposes a rather onerous obligation. How is it possible to establish if the purposes of a program can be satisfied using anonymous data? Each time data treatment is carried out relative to a subject, even if the processing occurs regarding data that are anonymous, these must inevitably be defined as personal given that, directly or indirectly, they are relative to a specific subject.

To be precise, the anonymization techniques of particular importance are those which can be termed “issue and forget”. After having released a piece of information, publicly or privately, to third parties or internally with the same organization, this is forgotten, in the sense that there is no attempt to monitor what occurs to the data after they have been issued. Rather than putting at risk the interested party, the information regarding the data subject is modified before being issued.

These techniques are prevalent because they enable diffusion of the data while at the same time safeguarding privacy. In practice, therefore, before issuing the data, the following steps should be taken:

- Locate identifying information: Any field which may be used to identify individuals should be ascertained. Often there can be the identification of combinations of fields which when analyzed together could create a link between the record in a table and the identity of a patient.
- Repression: Following this the identifying fields are modified, for example., by removing the fields from the table. In doing this, concerns regarding the protection of personal data are reduced. However, if someone knows the birthday, sex, ZIP code and race of an individual, their identity could be deduced. This method, however, could make these data useless for research within a medical field.
- Generalization: There is an attempt to reach the best balance between usefulness and privacy concerning the repression of the data. This means altering rather than completely canceling the identifying values. Whoever decides to use this method could, for example, choose the name in the field and generalize the date of birth (by entering only the year, and not even the day and the month) and ZIP code (leaving only the first three figures).
- Aggregation: In this case, we are considering, a more statistical synthesis rather than raw data. Therefore, we can put together, for example, sex, illness and a single figure of the ZIP code. If someone knows no further information regarding the individual, it is much more difficult to identify them.

COMPARISON OF THE ANONYMIZATION PROCESS OF USA: EUROPE

In the US, the issue of anonymization was considered to balance out problems of privacy which regarded the field of healthcare. In 1996, the HIPAA (Health Insurance

Portability and Accountability Act) was established. This law, besides having the aim of improving healthcare assistance and insurance, is intended to solve the problems of privacy and security concerning healthcare information. More precisely, as regards the latter, there is the "HIPAA Privacy Rule" which establishes national standards to safeguard information regarding personal health, and is applied to personal healthcare plans, and more in general, to the suppliers of healthcare services that carry out certain operations of personal healthcare assistance through electronic means (these are defined as "covered entities"). The rule specifies adequate guarantees in order to protect the privacy of healthcare information and establish limits and conditions regarding the uses that can be made of this information without the authorization of the patient.

In Europe, the situation is different. The Data Protection Directive claims to cover each "piece of personal data," of which we have already analyzed the definition (Art. 4, Regulation (EU) 2016/679, p. 1.). Reiterating the concept, Europe does not intend to apply the directive to all data, excluding those who do not identify an individual directly or indirectly, such as, anonymized data.

The European legislators, like in the U.S., are convinced of being able to reach a balance using the power of technology. If they are in an anonymous form, the data could be freely shared, implementing innovation and free expression, it is understood that the interested parties are not identified directly or indirectly.

For many years debates have developed, above all with companies such as Google, Microsoft, and Yahoo, on the way in which these should protect the databases which trace the online movements of their users. Many of these discussions have focused on IP addresses. In the same way that a social security number identifies a person, an IP address identifies a computer, which may then link online movements to the position and identity of an individual.

Remembering that an IP address is generally made up of 32 bits, sub-divided into four equal groups of 8 bits, each one referred to as an octet, Google intended to safeguard the privacy of its users by memorizing only the first three octets and canceling the final one. Microsoft and Yahoo wanted to be even more drastic, by canceling the entire IP address. This was also a debate on the search for an equilibrium between the innovations provided by Google which studies individuals' behavior, and possible harm caused to the users, whose IP addresses are revealed and known (Schwartz & Solove, 2011).

Technology poses new challenges in the field of so-called "non-PII (Non-Personally identifiable information)." Information scientists are constantly seeking creative methods in order to combine various pieces of non-PII and make them PII, enabling the de-identified information to be re-personalized. As proof of this, in 2006, America Online (AOL), released 20 million search queries for the benefit of researchers. These "queries" were considered to be anonymized. However, journalists of the New York Times showed that at least some of this information was easily re-personalized. They were able to identify people by their search queries. All this was possible thanks to the aggregation of apparently disassociated information such as "landscape painters in Lilburn', 'persons with the surname Arnold' and 'houses sold near the lake in the county of Gwinnett'." AOL apologized for the diffusion of information, recognizing that it had violated the privacy of its users despite attempts to anonymize the data.

In order to demonstrate yet again the ease of re-identifying data, Latanya Sweeney, professor of computer science at Carnegie Mellon University, by means of a study, reached the conclusion that by combining Zip Code, date of birth, and sex, it is possible to identify 87% of the individuals in the United States. This was quite a shocking result given that these pieces of data are generally considered to be non-PII (Sweeney, 2000).

A further problem with "non-PII" is that much of this information that regards persons is readily available, and this increases the possibility of reconstructing PII through non-PII.

This aspect of the problem of re-personalization stems from an aspect of the privacy issue known as "aggregation," which involves the combination of various pieces of data. An individual who thinks that they are anonymous when using certain websites can supply information that can identify the people explicitly, such as, when one is making a purchase. IP addresses can be used to connect de-identified data to names and addresses.

A further example involves a studio of Netflix, a popular online film rental service. After some research, two information scientists (Narayanan & Shmatikov, 2008) demonstrated that some people could be identified using a set of apparently anonymous data, by evaluation regarding the films within a website. Netflix made a de-identified database of film rating available to the public in order to improve the predictive capacity of its software to recommend certain films for rental. This study essentially demonstrates that a single piece of non-PII does not exist in isolation, but there are other data sources which enable the re-identification of a piece of data that has been made anonymous.

Data miners and market operators currently use these techniques. Let us suppose we have data on age (13 years), name (single alphanumerical identifier), favorite toy (Lego), favorite film (Batman), favorite candy (Snickers), favorite restaurant (McDonald's), Zip code (20052). In a world without other sources of data, this information would remain anonymous, but in current society crisscrossed by a plethora of data originating from a wide range of different sources, this is impossible. This anonymous child, could, for example, have a Facebook profile where, with a precise name, they can share their interests and preferences which can coincide with those mentioned above. Besides a social network, there could also be other databases that can specify, name, date of birth and addresses. All these pieces of apparently anonymous data can be gathered and linked together in order to give a particular identity to a precise individual.

The Health Insurance Portability and Accountability Act (hereinafter HIPAA) deals with 18 categories of information as being identifying, excluding from this list such data as those on patients such as hospital name, diagnosis, year of medical exam, patient's age and the first three figures of the ZIP code, which an individual possessing other external information can use to defeat the state of anonymity.

The same approach in following categorization of data is faced by the "Driver's Privacy Protection Act," which requires special treatment for "personal information", which includes among other items: social security number, driver identification number, name, address, and telephone number. On the other hand, less protection is required for a Zip code and any information on accidents, driving violations drivers' conditions.

In the same way, the Federal Education Rights and Privacy Act (FERPA) refers to the safeguarding of "directory information", including among other things: name, address, telephone number, date and place of birth and primary fields of education.

In light of this easy re-identification, such regulations appear to be somewhat arbitrary and not protective. In this case, there is, however, the need to consider recital 26, which beyond what has already been mentioned, adds that, in order to determine whether a natural person is identifiable, account should be taken of all the means reasonably likely to be used by the data controller or other people to identify the individual. Given that, the directive deals with all the information that is directly or indirectly connected with a person, each re-identification of an anonymous database extends the coverage of the directive to that database. As a consequence, the regulation which has the aim of having limits becomes unlimited. The easy re-identification has an opposite impact on the HIPAA, whose safeguards are revealed to be illusory and incomplete, in that it does not consider the treatment of types of data that can be used in order to re-identify and cause harm. In one way or another, both do not reach the balance established at the outset and the vagueness of the regulations inevitably cannot avoid fueling controversy and may very well bring about irrational distinctions between jurisdiction and law.

TOWARDS PII 2.0

There is a need to abandon the idea that the protection of interested parties can be accomplished merely by removing PII. It is not essential how the regulating authorities follow the developments of re-identification because the researchers continually seek out other types of data fields that are still uncovered by the regulations. The list of potential PII will never cease to grow until it includes everything literally. Legislators and regulating authorities should re-evaluate laws and regulations that make distinctions based only on the fact that particular types of data can be associated with identity and should avoid the drawing up of new laws and regulations founded on this distinction. The transformation into an anonymous form, in this way, should no longer be considered when supplying guarantees of privacy.

The best solution would seem to be that of re-orienting privacy according to a concept different from that of PII (in this case there would not be limits to the scope of the law on privacy), and following the proposal whereby regulators should attempt to safeguard interested parties by restricting and reducing the flow of information within the society, although this could obviously sacrifice values such as innovation, freedom of expression and security.

It seems appropriate, therefore, to carry out a cost-benefit analysis for all the data treated and gathered. However, this is very difficult to undertake, above all because costs and benefits are often not known in advance.

The European expansionist approach, as previously mentioned, appears open to criticism given that privacy rules concerning an identified natural people are equivalent to that of the data concerning an identifiable person.

In this way, we come to the definition of the so-called "PII 2.0", as sustained by Solove and Schwartz (2011). The benefit of having two categories of PII, data that regard identified or identifiable persons, paves the way to correct legal protection. This approach enables the safeguarding of both categories of information.

In this model, the information refers to a person:

1. **Identified:** The information identifies a specific person concerning others, and therefore, verifies their identity.
2. **Identifiable:** A specific identification, albeit possible, does not represent a very probable event. In other words, an individual is identifiable when there is some possibility of future identification, albeit not too far into the future. The level of risk for the law is moderate. This information should be treated differently from the category of nominally identifiable information, where a connection to a specific person has not yet been established, but it is much more probable that this can occur.
3. **Non-Identifiable:** This data is not readily associated with people, considering the means that can be reasonably used for the identification. This is the classic case in which we have enormous amounts of data (e.g., the population of a state).

A clear way of demonstrating the working of this new approach is that of considering the applicability of FIPs. This is with the aim of limiting the use of information, limiting data collection, limiting the diffusion of personal information, gathering and using the information only if it is accurate, pertinent and updated (principle of data quality), creating treatment systems that the interested party is familiar with and understands (systems of transparent treatment) and guaranteeing security for personal data.

When the information refers to identified people, all these practices should be applied. It must be specified, however, that the precise content of the ensuing obligations will often be different depending on the context in which the data is treated, on the nature of the information gathered, and on the specific legislative, normative and organizational context in which the rules are formulated. In the opinion of the authors, it is not opportune to treat the category of identifiable information in the same way as the information that enables direct identification.

Within the context of identifiable information, it is necessary that companies pay attention to the treatment of identifiable information by third parties. If a piece of information is not identifiable, a company can publically release it and allow access to third parties.

One of the advantages of this approach is that of adapting practices to the nature of the identified or identifiable information. A further advantage is that it is an incentive for companies to maintain information in the least identifiable form possible. If the concept of PII is abandoned, or if the treatment of identified data is considered as that of identifiable data, firms will be less prepared to use resources to maintain the data in an anonymous form.

Regarding this theme, Federal Trade Commission has expressed the opinion that as long as a specific data set is not reasonably identifiable, the company makes a public commitment not to re-identify it (FTC report, 2012).

In brief, FTC has attempted to distinguish between data that are "reasonably identifiable" and data that are not, and also between those firms that are taking the necessary measures to prevent re-identification.

Although both approaches (PII 2.0 and that of FTC) are attempting to use this new third category of identifiable information to avoid the complete collapse of all the data in the category of PII, this may be inevitable within the context of IoT.

More precisely, within the context of IoT, there is often confusion in judging data originating from sensors or biometric data as personal information. Some privacy policies of companies define "personal information" (or "PII") traditionally, including names, postal addresses, telephone number, e-mail addresses, etc. For these policies, the data originating from sensors should not have the highest protection guaranteed for PII. Other policies are less clear and may mislead to the point of appearing to be contrary to what has been stated above.

The privacy policy of "Breathometer" for example, defines "personal information" as "information that directly identifies you, like your name, address of delivery and invoicing, e-mail address, telephone number, and data regarding your credit card". Although there is no trace of "sensor data", an information scientist or regulator who understands the problem of re-identification could very well include the test results in the category of personal data.

In the same way, the privacy policy of "Nest Thermostat" defines "PII" as data that can reasonably be associated with a specific individual or family.

Given the threat of re-identification of data in IoT, it is difficult to understand whether the policy mentioned above considers the data are originating from the thermostat as personal data or not.

Many other examples could be given, but the point remains the same. Regulators and legislators have not yet faced the reality of this "new" data that can all be identifiable.

The European approach is different where some regulations, before the directive and now in the new regulation, leave a different margin of flexibility. They attempt to reach a correct balance between the rights of the interested person and the legitimate interests of the parties involved which appears somewhat fragile.

Some examples of these regulations, to cite only a few, which appear in the new Regulation n. 679/2016 follow:

- **Art. 5, lett. e):** Kept in a form which permits identification of data subjects for no longer than is necessary for the purposes for which the personal data is processed; personal data may be stored for more extended periods insofar as the personal data will be processed solely for archiving purposes in the public interest, scientific or historical research purposes or statistical purposes in accordance with Article 89(1) subject to implementation of the appropriate technical and organizational measures required by this Regulation in order to safeguard the rights and freedom of the data subject ('storage limitation');
- **Art. 6, letter f):** Processing is necessary for legitimate interests pursued by the controller or by a third party, except where such interests are overridden by the interests or fundamental rights and freedom of the data subject which require protection of personal data, in particular where the data subject is a child;
- **Art. 9, letter c):** Processing is necessary to protect the vital interests of the data subject or other natural people where the data subject is physically or legally incapable of giving consent;
- **Art.10:** Processing of personal data relating to criminal convictions and offenses or related security measures based on Article 6(1) shall be carried out only under the control of official authority or when the processing is

authorized by Union or Member State law providing for appropriate safeguards for the rights and freedoms of data subjects. Any comprehensive register of criminal convictions shall be kept only under the control of official authority.

According to a European approach, therefore, data protection is aimed at protecting the forms of treatment which typically present a higher risk of "easy access to personal data." Furthermore, the new Data Protection, being configured as a Regulation and not as a Directive, deprives the single states of the possibility of approving national laws in this regard which would conflict with each other. The objective to be reached is harmonization of the discipline in the European environment.

This did not occur with Directive 95/46 where, as the Court of Justice of the European Union (C-101/2001) stated, nothing impeded a member state from extending the scope of its national law with regard to the enactment of Directive 95/46 to sectors not included in the area of interest of application of the directive, as long as they did not infringe any other regulation of EU legislation.

THE 'NOTICE AND CONSENT' MODEL IN SAFEGUARDING THE CONSUMER

It is now necessary to go into greater depth regarding the principles relative to the quality of data. It is clear that personal data must be fairly and lawfully (Article 5 (a) Regulation (EU) 679/2016) treated with the effective awareness of the individual. This is an essential requisite about the new technological context, where sensors should be designed so as not to be excessively intrusive. For example, a device that uses a small light to monitor blood flow in the veins is also able to detect information regarding heartbeat. The device can include, moreover, other sensors which measure the oxygen level of the blood, but no information is available on the collection of this data either from the device in general or from the user interface. Even if this sensor is working, it should not be enabled without having first informed the user. It follows that explicit consent is required in order to enable the sensor.

In this context, at least three critical principles deserve attention:

1. **Principle of purpose limitation (Article 5 (b) Regulation (EU) 679/2016):** That of "purpose limitations", according to which the treatment is lawful as long as it is not incompatible with the original purpose for which the processing was carried out (this principle is very close to the idea).

2. **Principle of data minimization:** The data collected on the interested parties must be strictly necessary for the specific purpose pre-emptively determined by the data controller.
3. **Principle of storage limitation:** For which the personal data can be stored for the time required to reach the original aim and only exceptionally can they be stored for long periods on condition that they are processed exclusively for archiving in the public interest, for scientific or historical research or statistical purposes. These public interests balance the personal interest in privacy with the public interest in data collection. This final principle is what can limit the potential opportunities of IoT, becoming a real barrier to innovation.

An example may clarify the final concept expressed in a better way. Let us suppose we have a wearable device, such as a sticking plaster, which can assess the skin conditions of an individual. The device does not need to gather precise geolocational information to work efficiently. However, the device producer could believe that such information can be useful for implementing future features of the product, which may enable the user to choose further treatment options regarding their particular medical condition. As part of the exercise of minimizing the data, the producing company should wait before gathering geolocational data until beginning to offer the new features of the product. There may also be the possibility for the company of gathering less detailed information, such as a ZIP code, rather than more precise information of geolocation. If the company decides that the collection of the latter be necessary, it must supply clear information regarding the gathering and use of the information, and obtain explicit consent from the consumer. Finally, the company must establish the limits of reasonable maintenance of the data gathered. Once this necessity is established in order to satisfy business requirements, this can also be the possibility of conserving the data in a de-identified form. This could be a solution, as already discussed, in order to establish a balance between consumer protection and benefits for the company regarding using the information collected.

Here we arrive at a much-debated area of the Internet of Things that is the so-called "notice and consent" model, which we should contextualize in order to highlight its limits.

Consent (Article 7, Regulation (EU) 679/2016) is whatsoever display of free, specific and informed will with which the interested party accepts, by means of declaration or unequivocal positive action, that the personal data regarding them are an object of treatment (Article 4 (11), Regulation (EU) 679/2016). This offers a way to reconcile, on the one hand, the problem of damage to the consumer about the data deriving from connected devices, and on the other hand, the desire to possess the device which inevitably implies benefits, already previously analyzed. Therefore, if the consumer were aware of and consented to the flow of data generated by the various devices, there would be no cause for concern.

The point is that within the current context, where the "transformative" use of Big Data makes it impossible to describe all the possible uses of information at the moment of initial data collection, this type of approach is inadequate. Furthermore, the digital world is characterized by an asymmetric distribution of control over information, regarding access to quality data and the ability to use them. In this sense, control over information deriving from the predictive analysis is not accessible to everyone, because it is based on the availability of great quantities of data, costly technology and specific human skills able to develop sophisticated systems of analysis and interpretation. A final restraining aspect is that in the current digital economy, consumers often seem to accept that they have no negotiating power regarding their personal information, essentially due to the concentration of the market and relative social and technological lock-in effects, which are a further limitation to "self-determination" and to the user's choices.

For these and other reasons, we need to reconsider the "notice and consent" paradigm within existing regulations that regard data protection and define new rules able to face the various problems of the current and future digital environment (Mantelero, 2014).

At this point, all the legislative apparatus seems to be in difficulty. Analysis of Big Data is designed to remain hidden. Therefore, it appears that the description of purposes, as we have seen, at the center of the regulations on data protection, is becoming increasingly tenuous.

It follows that the difficulty in defining the expected result of data treatment prompts the production of generic and vague declarations for the consumer regarding the purpose of the data collection. Furthermore, in the hypothetical adoption of lengthy and detailed information, the complexity of data processing within the new context does not offer users a real opportunity to understand it, interpret it and therefore, make informed choices.

This all prompts reconsideration of the role of user self-determination, in a situation in which the consumer is no longer able to understand the data processing and its purposes fully, or is not in a position to make decisions. In this regard, initially, the EU Regulation proposed that "consent does not constitute a juridical basis for the treatment when there is a notable imbalance between the position of the interested party and the data controller (Article 7 (4) PGDPR)".

To further complicate the situation, there are various technical issues regarding IoT devices. The devices are often small, without a screen, have meager input-output capacities, such as a keyboard or touchscreen. From here, there arises the need to channel elsewhere the user's privacy information: in the device's box, on the producer's website or within a cell phone application.

Currently, the preferred solution on the part of producers is to supply information on data treatment within a privacy policy published on a website. However, this system does not consider that a consumer's purchasing experience may very well be different from their Internet navigation skills. Also, there is an unjustified belief in the association between devices and a smartphone app or Internet account.

Confusion also reigns when it is decided to apply two privacy policies: one for the website and one regarding the use of the device. This kind of solution doubles the cognitive and attention load of the consumer.

Mainly, as asserted by S. Peppet (Peppet, 2014), the issues regarding privacy policy focus on the ambiguity of the language of the policies – this has already been discussed regarding the "PII" issue – and on the obvious omissions in the policies. It often occurs that the privacy policy does not mention the owner of the data of the device consumer, which type of data the device gathers and which type of sensors are used by the device. These policies are often contradictory when one speaks of the rights of access, modification, and cancellation by the consumer, and the policies frequently confer these rights only for personal data, for which there remains the problem of correct categorization.

To conclude regarding policy omissions, we cannot help but mention the lack of a precise and clear explanation of how these data are processed in the device itself and on the companies' remote servers to which the data are transmitted.

POSSIBLE DEVELOPMENTS: TOWARDS AN OPT-OUT SCHEME

In the light of what has already been said, the user's role must inevitably be restricted, and the importance of the independent authorities must increase. The latter, concerning the consumer, have the technological know-how to assess the risks associated with the various data treatments and can adopt legal remedies to tackle them. Moreover, the authorities are those in the best position to balance all the different interests of the various stakeholders regarding the vast collection of data and their extraction.

This does not mean canceling the old model, but merely reinforcing it, increasing transparency, the responsibility of service providers, and architectures oriented towards the protection of data.

Transparency

Transparency is an instrument which aims to improve the user's understanding and control of personal data. This can occur only if the user's notice is provided and is clear as regards various aspects. These include the purposes of data collection, the memorization and treatment of the data, an overview of the type of data made known, information regarding the data controller, correctly which policy is being used and if there is online access for personal data. Also, it must be made clear the way in which the data are processed, and if a sort of counter of profiling capacity has been put into effect to help users to prepare a group filing using their data (Weber, 2015).

The notice can be provided on the device, using wireless connectivity, or using the location through privacy-preserving proximity testing, done by a central server. This information must be supplied in a clear and understandable way by the principle of correctness in data treatment. For example, the producer of devices could insert in the "things" equipped with sensors, a QR code or an instantaneous code able to describe the types of sensors and the information they capture together with the purpose of data collection.

As also stated in a report of FTC97, the privacy notice should be as clear, brief and standardized as possible to be easily understood and also enable the user to compare privacy practices.

One of the first attempts to develop a standardized privacy notice for the user was the "multilayer privacy notice", which included a standardized page, sub-divided into sections, in which various aspects of privacy were explained.

Others supported the so-called "nutrition label" approach for the standardization of privacy policies (Cranor, 2012). This approach enabled consumers to search for information more rapidly and precisely compared with a traditionally written privacy policy. It is indeed shorter, easier to read and its standardized table enabled the user to understand the search modes (what and where to search) and facilitated comparison with other policies.

Although privacy policies are not exactly a useful tool for communicating with most users, they do play an essential role in promoting transparency, accountability, and competition between companies as regards issues of privacy. This is all made possible only if the policies are clear, concise and easy to read, as in the case of the "nutrition label". There is often the need for small icons that can be integrated into web pages or in a browser to allow users to obtain a rapid understanding of the policy without having to go through the "nutritional label privacy". In the studies carried out by Lorrie F. Cranor on the users of the "Privacy Finder", it was discovered that creating points in terms of privacy, in this case by using green and white boxes, helped users to rapidly search sites with the best privacy policies, thereby influencing consumers' decisions as to where they could make purchases.

To conclude on this theme of maximum transparency regarding privacy policies, one must also consider the "machine-readable privacy policy", which is none other than a declaration regarding the privacy practices of a website, such as the collection and use of data, written in standard programming language, which software tools, like a consumer's browser, can read automatically. For example, when the browser reads a "machine-readable policy", it can compare the policy for the preferences regarding privacy of the consumer's browser, and inform the consumer when these preferences do not correspond to the practices of the website being visited. If, for example, the consumer decides not to visit websites that sell information to third parties, they can set a rule that can recognize this type of policy, to block these sites and set a warning notice.

Accountability

Moving our attention to accountability, this should include two main objectives. It should promote a public understanding of the business system and also a certain level of trust in the system, and ensure an adequate level of protection for the consumer.

Today, it is increasingly necessary and vital that data controllers adopt effective measures for real protection of data and there are many reasons for doing this.

Above all, concerning data, we are witnessing a so-called "flood effect", with a constant increase in the amount of personal data existing, being processed and transferred. This phenomenon is favored both by technological progress, that is ongoing development of information and communication systems, and by the growing capacity of users to exploit technologies and interact with them.

With the growth in the quantity of data being transferred worldwide, the risks of abuse also increase. This further highlights the need for data controllers, in both public and private sectors, to put into effect real and efficient internal mechanisms to safeguard personal information.

Secondly, the increasing amount of personal data is accompanied by an increase in their value in social, political and economic terms. In some sectors, particularly in the online environment, personal data have become the de facto currency of exchange for online contents. At the same time, from a social point of view, there is a growing recognition of data protection as a social value. In brief, as personal data gradually become increasingly precious for data controllers in all sectors, citizens, consumers, and society, in general, are also increasingly being aware of their relevance. This fact, in turn, reinforces the need for applying rigorous measures to safeguard these data.

Finally, it follows from what has been said that violation of privacy may have important negative repercussions for data controllers in the public and private sectors, with further repercussions in both economic terms and, above all, as regards reputation. Therefore, reducing as much as possible risks, building and maintaining a good reputation and guaranteeing the trust of citizens and consumers are becoming fundamental tasks of data controllers across all sectors. From this, it emerges that there is an absolute necessity for data controllers to apply real and effective measures for data protection aimed at the correct management of their protection, but also reducing to a minimum juridical, economic and reputational risks which may stem from inadequate practices in this regard.

In brief, the data controller or processor must carry out an analysis of the risks of the potential impact of the treatment on the rights and freedom of people (Art 32 (a) (1) (2) PGDPR-LIBE) and appoint, when necessary (Art 32 (a) (3b) PGDPR-LIBE), a data protection officer. In cases where there are specific risks (Art. 32 (a) (3c) PGDPR-LIBE), the data controller must perform a "data protection impact assessment (Art. 33 PGDPR-LIBE) ", which must include the entire management of personal data from initial collection to cancellation. The assessment must be documented and a plan drawn up for periodical conformity checks regarding data protection. The assessment must be updated without delay in discovering any lack of conformity. Furthermore, on request, the data controller and processor must make this assessment available for inspection by surveillance authorities.

Therefore, the data controller must consult the data protection officer, or, in the absence of this position, a supervision authority, before beginning data treatment. The purpose is that of ensuring conformity of the data treatment foreseen by this regulation and a reduction in the risks for the interested party. This consultation must take place every time that an impact assessment indicates that, by their nature, content or purposes, the data treatments may represent a high degree of specific risk or whenever data protection officer or surveillance authority considers it necessary.

Finally, it may also occur that in order to reinforce the mechanism of transparency, a data controller may apply to any authority of the European Union, on payment of a limited fee, for a certification of the treatment of personal data, which attests conformity with the regulation on data protection, considering the obligations of who deals with the data and rights of the interested parties (Article 34 (2) PGDPR-LIBE).

Final Considerations: An 'Opt-Out' Scheme

Returning to the notice and consent model, we should add the consideration of the FTC121, which foresees those cases in which companies have no obligation to provide a choice for the consumer before the collection and use of their personal data.

These cases refer to transactions or consumer-company relations. As the uses of the data are generally coherent with the reasonable expectations of the consumer, the cost for consumer and companies in providing notices and choices exceed the benefits. This is a principle that also applies to IoT. Consider an example where a consumer purchases an intelligent oven from company X. The oven is connected with an app to the company which enables the consumer to switch on the oven remotely. If the company decides to use the consumer's usage information to improve the sensitivity of the temperature regulation, there is no need to offer the consumer a choice regarding this use. In this sense, the staff has incorporated some aspects of the so-called "use-based model" in the new approach to the notice and consent. The idea of associating the choices with the context considers how the data will be used. If the use is not coherent with the context of interaction (unforeseen use), the company does not need to offer the consumer a choice and vice versa. It is understood that companies should not gather data without express consent. Furthermore, if a company allows the data collection of consumers and it de-identifies the data immediately and efficiently, a choice does not need to be offered to the consumer.

However, adopting only a used-based model for IoT is not the best solution. This is for a series of reasons. Use-based limitations have not been fully incorporated into legislation or any other code of conduct, and it is not clear who decides whether or not a data use is harmful. The limitations of using themselves do not address the risks regarding privacy and security created by the collection and expensive maintenance of data, since, as mentioned before, maintaining a significant amount of data may increase the attractiveness of the company to the point of being a target for data violation. Finally, this model does not take into consideration the gathering of sensitive data originating from inferences among various pieces of data.

In conclusion, the new pillars on which the new model should be based refer to rigorous multiple assessments of the impacts of data treatment. This must be ongoing throughout the life cycle of the product-services and the adoption of an "opt-out scheme".

In the presence of complex data processing systems or data gathering affected by lock-in effects, the assessment of risks and benefits should not be carried out by consumers or companies, but by third parties, under the supervision of the data protection authorities. Consumers must only decide whether to exercise their right to opt out or not.

Once the data protection authority has approved the assessment, the process is considered to be secure regarding protection of personal information and the potential social consequences. This is the reason for companies involving users in specific treatments, without prior consent, although they must be given notice regarding the results of the assessment and they must be offered the opt-out option (Article 19 - PGDPR.).

Therefore, from the user's point of view, on the one hand, there is a guarantee of assessment of the risks relative to data treatment, thanks to the analysis carried out by the data protection authorities, and on the other hand, the opt-out enables users to receive information regarding treatment and to decide whether or not to consent to data collection.

It follows that this kind of model is more appropriate and gives more guarantees compared with the "notice and consent" model, which within this context is unreliable. It is understood that a solution to cover all fields within the new context as yet does not exist, the themes dealt with here are attempting to find the most reliable solution for facing the issue of privacy.

CONCLUSION

The subject matter has enabled us to reflect on the change in approach with which legislators are facing new technological challenges. This is mainly as regards privacy understood in its new interpretation as opposed to the classic "right to be alone". After briefly examining definitions and advantages originating from this new phenomenon, we moved on to deal with the aspect which technically distinguishes this new technology and consequently the associated problems.

However, the firm belief exists that there remains an inevitable lag between the evolution of the Internet of Things and the development of its legislative regulation.

We have underlined how the issue of privacy includes not only the concealment of personal information but also the capacity to control what is happening to that information. The attribution of tags to objects may not be known to users, and there may very well not be any acoustic or visual signal that draws the user's attention to the device. In this way, individuals can be followed unbeknown to them.

In order to limit this, a certain number of technologies have been developed, the so-called Privacy Enhancing Technologies (PETs). Briefly, these include:

- **Virtual Private Networks (VPNs):** Extranets established by closed groups of commercial partners. This is a private telecommunications network, set up by subjects who use a public transmission system (e.g., Internet) as transport infrastructure. Only partners have access to this network.
- **Transport Layer Security (TLS):** Refers to cryptographic protocols which enable secure communication from source to destination (end-to-end), providing, among other things, the integrity and confidentiality of IoT data.
- **DNS Security Extension (DNSSEC):** Uses cryptographic public keys to sign "resource records", in order to ensure the authentication and integrity of the information provided.
- **Onion Routing:** Encrypts and mixes Internet traffic from many different sources. The data are enveloped in various encrypted layers, using the public keys of the onion routers on the transmission route. This process impedes the correspondence of a particular source with an IP packet. The sender remains anonymous because anyone intermediate subject only knows the position

of the directly preceding nodes. On the other hand, there is an increase in waiting times which affect performance.

- **Private Information Retrieval (PIR) systems:** These enable a user to recover an element from a server possessing a database, without indicating which element is recovered, once EPCIS have been located. However, there are problems of scalability and key management, and also of performance in a globally accessible system such as ONS, which makes this method impracticable.

Another way of increasing security and privacy is peer-to-peer (P2P), which generally has good scalability and performance in applications. These systems could be based on Distributed Hash Tables (DHT). Access control, however, must be carried out on its EPCIS, not on the data memorized in the DHT. It is reasonable that the encryption of the connection and user authentication could be carried out without great difficulty, using a common Internet connection and web security services. In particular, client authentication may be done using the emission of "shared secrets" (data items known only to the parties involved) or by using cryptography of public keys. It is important that an RFID tag, it is associated with an object, can be deactivated in a later phase, to enable the clients to decide if they wish to make use of the tag. RFID tags can be deactivated or put into a protective "Faraday cage", impenetrable by radio signals of certain frequencies. The information on ONS is eliminated to protect the privacy of the owner of the tagged object, whereas the tag can be read, and therefore, reveal further information. Furthermore, also transparency is necessary for identifiable non-personal information recovered by RFID. An active RFID may, for example, trace movements without identifying a people, who remain anonymous. However, it remains to be seen whether or not, this information not covered by privacy laws, can be collected without further restriction.

Therefore, IoT is very vulnerable to attacks for various reasons. Firstly, because it may happen that its components spend most of the time unprotected, and are, therefore, easily open to physical attack. Secondly, most communications occur via wireless systems, and this makes interception very simple. Finally, most of the components of the Internet of things are characterized by low capacities both regarding energy resources and ICT resources (an argument that is particularly valid for passive components). This means that they are unable to implement sophisticated security schemes.

The solutions for data integrity should ensure that they are not modified during a transaction without the system detecting the change. The data can be modified while they are memorized in the node or while moving through the network. To protect the data after the first attack, the memory is protected in many tag technologies. For example, both EPCglobal Class-1 Generation-2 and ISO/IEC 18000-3 (Talone

& Russo, 2008) tags protect both reading and writing operations on their memory with a password. The first solution has five areas of memory, each of which can be protected in reading or writing with an independent password. The second solution defines a pointer (a type of data, a variable that contains the address in its memory of another variable) to a "memory address" and safeguards with a password all the areas of memory with a lower "memory address". To protect the data from the second kind of attack, the messages could be protected according to the authentication of the HMAC - Keyed-Hash Message Authentication Code scheme (Krawczyk et al., 1997). This is based on a shared secret key shared between the tag and destination of the message, which is used in combination with a hash function to provide the authentication. It can be observed, however, that the solutions mentioned above have problems when we consider RFID systems. The password length supported by most tag technologies, is too short to guarantee reliable levels of protection. If the length problem can be solved, there remains the problem of management when entities belonging to different organizations are involved, as in the case of IoT.

Finally, it must be recalled that all the solutions proposed to support security consider techniques of cryptography. Also, in this case, we must face the problem of the use of significant quantities of resources regarding energy and bandwidth, both at source and destination. In fact, in IoT, elements such as RFID tags and sensor nodes are limited as regards energy, communications, and calculating capacity. Consequently, a considerable research effort is required in this field. Privacy is exposed to a more significant number of attacks because it is impossible to personally control the distribution of personal information, together with the reduction in the cost of information memorization. To this, we can add that, compared to the traditional Internet, the issues of privacy also arise for those who never use IoT services. As a consequence, individuals must be safeguarded, guaranteeing control over the data collected, and when this is done, the personal data gathered must be used only for the designated purpose authorized by the service provider and the data must be stored only for the time necessary for that purpose.

To manage the process of data collection, appropriate solutions are necessary for all the various subsystems that interact with individuals in IoT. For example, within the traditional context of Internet services, the W3C group has defined the so-called "Platform for Privacy Preference" (P3P). This is a protocol that enables websites to declare the end use destination of the information gathered. A language is established for the definition of personal data management policies which is interpreted automatically and compared with the user's preferences, considering the management of the individual's data during the rest of their browsing activity.

For sensor networks, the situation is more complicated. A possible solution in this regard could be that of limiting the capacity of the Web to gather data at such a detailed level as to jeopardize the individual's privacy (for example in the case of CCTV, surveillance images can be blurred).

In the case of RFID systems, the problem is twofold. On the one hand, the RFID tags that are usually passive respond to query readers, irrespective of the owner's own volition. On the other hand, an ill-intentioned user can intercept the response from a tag for another authorized reader. Solutions for the first kind of problem, as we have already seen, are based on the authentication of authorized readers. However, these solutions require tags that can carry out authentication procedures, which, due to their nature, would bring about an increase in costs and the need to set up an authentication infrastructure, impossible to distribute in complex systems like IoT. Solutions proposed to use a new system based on personal choices configured by the user. The decisions on privacy adopted by this system can be made by creating collisions in the wireless channel with the responses transmitted by the RFID tags, which should not be read.

The interceptions by attackers in RFID systems can be avoided through the protection of communications using cryptography, although this does not entirely solve the problem. So, there is a new family of solutions in which the signal transmitted by the reader has the form of a pseudo-noise. This signal is modulated by the RFID tags, and therefore, its transmission cannot be detected by ill-intentioned readers.

With the aim of RFID that the personal data gathered are used only to support services authorized by the same providers, solutions have been proposed which are based on a system referred to as "privacy brokering". The proxy (a server which is placed between a client and a server with the role of intermediary or interface between the two hosts) interacts with the user on the one hand and with the services on the other. Consequently, it ensures that the provider obtains only the information strictly necessary from the user. The user can set the options of the proxy. When sensor networks and RFID systems are included within the network, then the proxy operates between them and the services. However, in this case, the individual can neither configure nor monitor the policies used by the privacy brokers. Furthermore, these solutions do have a problem with scalability.

It is worth noting, finally, that in order to face problems associated with an increase in the amount of data, and due to a lowering of memorization costs, there arises the need for new software tools which can delete the information that is no longer useful for the prearranged objective (e.g., "drop.io" and "Guest Pass" on Flickr).

The Internet of Things has begun to revolutionize both the life of every single individual and the classic social-juridical schemes of companies and public institutions. However, there is still a long way to go before reaching a legislative and regulatory framework which fully satisfies the practical needs of the society.

REFERENCES

Ashton, K. (2009). That 'Internet of Things' Thing. *RFID Journal*. Retrieved June 22, 2009, from http://www.rfidjournal.com/articles/view?4986

Cranor, L.F. (2012). Necessary but not sufficient: standardized mechanisms for privacy and choice. *Journal on Telecom & High-Tech law*, 273.

FTC Report. (2012). Protecting consumer privacy in an era of rapid change: recommendations for business and policymakers. *Federal Trade Commission*. Retrieved from https://www.ftc.gov/sites/default/files/documents/reports/federal-trade-commission-report-protecting-consumer-privacy-era-rapid-change-recommendations/120326privacyreport.pdf

Krawczyk, H., Bellare, M., & Canetti, R. (1997). HMAC: Keyed-Hashing for Message Authentication. *IETF RFC*. Retrieved Feb 11, 1997, from https://www.ietf.org/rfc/rfc2104.txt

Mantelero, A. (2014). The future of consumer data protection in the E.U. Rethinking the 'notice and consent' paradigm in the new era of predictive analytics. *Computer Law & Security Report*, *30*(6), 643–660. doi:10.1016/j.clsr.2014.09.004

Narayanan, A., & Shmatikov, V. (2008). *Robust De-anonymization of Large Sparse Datasets*. IEEE Computer Society Washington. doi:10.1109/SP.2008.33

Schindler, H. R., Cave, J., Robinson, N., Horvath, V., Hackett, P., Gunashekar, S., . . . Graux, H. (2012). Examining Europe's Policy Options to Foster Development of the 'Internet of Things.' *Rand Corporation*. Retrieved October 7, 2008, from http://www.rand.org/randeurope/research/projects/internet-of-things.html

Schwartz, P. M., & Solove, D. J. (2011). *The PII problem: privacy and a new concept of personally identifiable information*. Berkeley, CA: Berkeley Law Scholarship Repository.

Scott, P. R. (2014). Regulating the Internet of Things: First steps toward Managing Discrimination, Privacy, Security, and Consent. *Texas Law Review*, *93*, 85.

Soro, A. (2016). *Privacy: "Internet delle cose", utenti poco tutelati. Garante per la protezione dei dati personali. Garante per la protezione dei dati personali*. Retrieved from http://www.garanteprivacy.it/web/guest/home/docweb/-/docweb-display/docweb/5443681

Sweeney, L. (2000). *Uniqueness of Simple Demographics in the U.S. Population*. Technical Report LIDAP-WP4. Pittsburgh, PA: Carnegie Mellon University.

Talone, P., & Russo, G. (n.d.). *Standard e protocolli di comunicazione*. Roma: Fondazione Ugo Bordoni. Retrieved Dec, 15, 2017, from http://www.rfid.fub.it/edizione_2/Parte_VI.pdf

Weber, R. H. (2015). Internet of Things: Privacy issues revisited. *Computer Law & Security Review, 31*(5), 618–627. doi:10.1016/j.clsr.2015.07.002

KEY TERMS AND DEFINITIONS

Breathometer: An application that connects to Breeze, an aethalometer which enables users to evaluate their state of drunkenness.

Ferpa: The Family Educational Rights and Privacy Act of 1974 (FERPA or the Buckley Amendment) is a United States federal law that governs the access to educational information and records.

FIPs: Federal information processing standards are a set of rules that describe the elaboration of documents, algorithms of cryptography and other standards of information technology.

FTC: The Federal Trade Commission (FTC) is an agency independent of the government of the United States, founded in 1914 by the Federal Trade Commission Act. Its main mission is the promotion of consumer protection and the elimination and prevention of anticompetitive commercial practices, such as coercive monopoly.

Nest Thermostat: An intelligent thermostat which can reprogram itself by an individual's habits.

Research Queries: Can be defined as questions that the user poses to a database.

Social Lock-In Effect: One of the consequences of the dominating position maintained by the big players, evident in the market of social networks.

Technological Lock-In Effect: Refers to technological standards and data formats that are adopted by various service providers. This effect limits data portability and the migration from one service to another even though the same functions are offered.

Chapter 11
Digital Forensics in the Context of the Internet of Things

Mariya Shafat Kirmani
University of Kashmir, India

Mohammad Tariq Banday
University of Kashmir, India

ABSTRACT

The pervasive nature of IoT, envisioned with the characteristics of diversity, heterogeneity, and complexity, is diluting the boundaries between the physical and digital worlds. IoT being widely distributed qualifies it as the breeding ground for cyber-attacks. Although remarkable work is being done to ensure security in IoT infrastructure, security vulnerabilities persist. The IoT infrastructure can either be used as a direct target in a cyber-attack or exploited as a tool to carry a cyber-attack. In either case, the security measures in IoT infrastructure is compromised. The enormous IoT data is sensitive that can act as a gold mine to both the criminals for illicit exploitation or investigators to act as digital witness. IoT forensics help the investigators to acquire intelligence from this smart infrastructure to reconstruct the historical events occurred. However, due to sophisticated IoT architecture, the digital investigators face myriad challenges in IoT-related investigations using existing investigation methodologies and, hence, demand a separate dedicated forensic framework.

DOI: 10.4018/978-1-5225-5742-5.ch011

INTRODUCTION

The gap between the physical and digital worlds is diminishing with the tremendous increase in the Internet-connected devices which is a direct result of the IoT revolution. The Internet of Things (IoT) constitutes objects or things that are seamlessly connected and possess the capabilities of more than sensing, processing, or actuating the data from their immediate environments. IoT is a remarkable convergence of Internet and sensor networks with a vision of machine-to-machine communication with least or no human intervention. However, this machine-to-machine communication is the evolution of existing technologies used by Internet with more number and types of devices connected. IoT is an extension of traditional digital devices including desktops, smartphones, laptops, etc. and takes technology one step ahead by including almost anything facilitated with a provision to connect and interact over the Internet. IoT provides a common unified infrastructure for the real-world entities, living or non-living, both of which create and share data over the Internet. The typical examples of IoT can be found in smart home appliances, automobiles, wearables, smart healthcare devices, smart cities, healthcare, smart agriculture, industrial control, etc. With IPv6 in practice, all the devices/objects in IoT are uniquely identified in the global network of things. Considering the diversity of these devices connected over the Internet, IoT is characterized by the critical features of sense, intelligence, tremendous scale, connectivity, heterogeneity, dynamic nature, etc.

The basic IoT architecture can be divided into three layers viz: perception, network, and application. The perception layer constitutes the physical devices using sensors, actuators, microcontrollers, etc. responsible for collecting information and connecting to the IoT network. The network layer is an integration of diverse devices and communication technologies required for the transmission of information and control between the perception layer and the application layer. The functional units of the network layer are hubs, switches, gateways, bridges, etc. that function using diverse technologies and protocols. The application layer constitutes the interface for the services offered to the end users and receives information from the network layer. The cloud infrastructure is integrated into the application layer. In addition to these basic functionalities offered by each layer, there are numerous other functionalities associated to these layers based on which the IoT architecture can be moulded (Lin et al., (2017).

The implementation of IoT is usually based on dealing with real-time data with the underlying things/devices being highly resource constrained. The IoT devices being small, low-powered, battery operated, is the limiting factor for hardware, software and communication functionalities that can actually be implemented. The processing or storage ability of an IoT system is limited by these physical limitations (Maple, 2017). IoT systems, hence, are designed to be minimally resource consumptive and are least immune to the burden of local storage or processing. The decision of the amount of data to be transmitted or whether to transmit the processed or unprocessed data is also affected by the limited resources available in an IoT system.

Although this seamless connection of people, devices, objects, services, etc. have a significant impact on almost all spheres of human life, the data landscape associated with IoT is enormous, the security of which is of utmost importance. The resource-constrained nature of IoT, however, makes it different from conventional Internet-connected devices, making it hard for practitioners to implement the conventional security measures (Alaba et al., 2017). To ensure adequate security in IoT devices, designers need to embed the measures of encryption and authentication at the chip or firmware level, taking into consideration the vulnerabilities in software-based security measures. However, hardware embedded security is a challengingly complex task. Remarkable work is being carried out to ensure security with an increased focus on lightweight cryptographic solutions to cater to the low-power and lossy network (LLN) needs of IoT systems (Alaba et al., 2017). Despite the security advances, the threat vector for IoT ecosystems persists at all the architectural layers due to open vulnerabilities (Rizvi et al., 2018). With the lack of regular security patches, the security risks are present not only at the system or server levels but with anything or everything that is connected. The exploited vulnerabilities lead to a wide range of attacks varying from physical to communication to application/software attacks. The cyber-attacks against IoT devices, hence, lead to the compromise of extensive data associated with IoT systems both in personal and business spaces. These attacks lead to both the security and forensic challenges in these interconnected devices that have endlessly merged in everyday life.

Hence, considering the IoT systems, they can have both the protagonist and antagonistic role in digital forensics. The contextual and humongous information generated or consumed by IoT can be used as potential evidence to prove the occurrence of any criminal event, opening a new opportunity to the solution of an investigation. However, on the other hand, the tremendously interconnected, heterogeneous and sophisticated nature of IoT systems makes it difficult to carry their forensic investigations. The cyber-crimes potentially target any vulnerability and range from stealing private information, banking credentials, phishing or spam attacks, DDoS attacks, etc. Digital forensics deals with the trails left behind in any illicit digital activity and acquisition of evidence in its most intact and correct format. This evidence related to a crime is acquired from the seized or associated digital media in a step-by-step legal procedure. Application of digital forensic procedures in IoT related crimes is underdeveloped as IoT itself is in infancy and still has a poor design and security architecture. Both the fields of IoT and digital forensics being relatively new, lack the real standards or strategies to deal with any security breaches or cyber-attacks, hence, pose a biggest challenge to forensic investigators.

Furthermore, there are remarkable limitations in IoT forensic investigation tools that face the problem of heterogeneity of infrastructure. The inseparable inclusion of cloud in IoT makes it harder for forensic investigators to extract the plethora of evidence residing there due to lack of its physical accessibility.

LITERATURE SURVEY AND RELATED WORK

The digital forensic technology, evidence management, and methodology has significantly improved since its dawn in the 1980s. The crimes committed using digital devices have increased profoundly with the proliferation of diverse technology and escalated diffusion of digital devices. In 2001, the Digital Forensics Research Workshop (DFRWS, 2001) defined digital forensic Science as:

The use of scientifically derived and proven methods toward the preservation, collection, validation, identification, analysis, interpretation, documentation and presentation of digital evidence derived from digital sources for the purpose of facilitating or furthering the reconstruction of events found to be criminal, or helping to anticipate unauthorized actions shown to be disruptive to planned operations.

Simson (Simson, 2010) has defined the years 1999-2007 as "Golden Age" of Digital Forensics making it possible to look for the residual data in case of cyber-crimes. The trend has evolved from traditional disk forensics to live investigation of physical memory and network traffic, enabling investigators to look for the potential evidence in real time. He also argued the need for a clear strategy regarding research efforts to ensure digital forensics is not left behind in oblivion considering the growth of cyber-crimes.

Hard disk and memory images hold forensically critical information and the tools for the extraction of related data structures have evolved with time. Stevens and Casey (Stevens & Casey, 2010) have dissected data structures related to command line for the reconstruction of command line history from physical memory.

Okolica and Peterson (Okolica & Peterson, 2011) have shown the importance and extraction of clipboard information to retrieve previously copied files/data/password, etc. Digital investigation of both kernel and user space metadata is possible currently. White et al. (White et al., 2012) have surveyed the userspace allocation along with the associated virtual address space. Beverly et al. (Beverly et al., 2010) proposed the techniques to recover network data from RAM that gets stored on hard disk during hibernation or swapping, giving an insight of network packets associated.

Maintenance of integrity in evidence makes it admissible before a court of law. However, cyber-criminals find their ways to compromise the evidence integrity by subverting the forensic process tools and techniques or employing other anti-forensic techniques (Rekhis & Boudriga, 2012).

Among many forensic challenges, scalability issues result in voluminous and variety of data to be examined. Substantial work has been carried out to address the issue of scalability, one such work by Marturana and Tacconi (Marturana & Tacconi, 2013), presents a solution for timely examination of enormous evidence by the method of triage using machine learning principles for automatic evidence categorization. Owen Brady et al. (Brady et al., 2015) also presented their work to address the problems of volume and variety in digital evidence by being selective of relevant evidence while ignoring rest of unapt data. This assists in a normalized and ontological evidence representation to ensure the investigator deals with the processing of limited yet relevant evidence only.

Digital objects associated with any digital incident possess the characteristics that qualify them to act as potential evidence source in the court of law. Digital evidence processing and analysis at both the higher and lower levels is carried out, after the acquisition, for the correct reconstruction of events. The event reconstruction is realized by the acquisition of diverse digital artifacts that constitute documents and files of different types and formats, log histories of devices, network traffic, browser histories, databases, hard disk and memory resident data that includes non-volatile and volatile data, banking transaction information, multimedia content including images, audio, video, mobile phone information, social networking related data, system information, information from removable media, etc. Hargreaves and Patterson (Hargreaves & Patterson, 2012) proposed a technique for the automatic reconstruction and visualization of high-level events from low-level events and vice versa. Their focus of event reconstruction includes time and date attributes of the associated artifacts.

With the advancements in technology, contemporary forensic examiners have to deal with investigations including cloud computing, wireless networks, smart devices, etc., along with the fact that cyber-criminals are minimizing the footprints of their illicit activities (Damshenas, 2014).

The increased reliance on cloud computing to deal with the overwhelming amounts of data, shifts the attack target from conventional local devices to data centers and cloud environments. In addition to the inherent security risks about the cloud, the inclusion of the cloud raises newer challenges in the path of forensic investigations. These challenges include having evidence sources distributed across different dimensions in cyberspace that adds a layer of complexity and evidence uncertainty to forensics, encryption to combat security risks in communication between the front end (client) and back-end (service provider), use of IP anonymity, etc. that can stall or slow down an investigation (David et al., 2016). Although the field has evolved a lot since its inception, there are plenty of challenging issues that exist and need to be addressed.

Internet of Things, Wireless Sensor Networks, and Ubiquitous Computing are inseparable and have much been talked about in the past decade or so. Internet of Things is gaining pace with new interesting innovations being carried in the field. The primary challenges faced in carrying IoT forensics is presented in work by Robert Hegarty et al. (Hegarty et al., 2014). These challenges span across all the major phases of digital investigation about IoT. Edewede Oriwoh et al. (Oriwoh et al., 2013) proposed a digital forensic model for IoT refered to as Next Big Thing (NBT) Model and also discusses the difference in traditional and IoT forensics. IoT forensics constitutes the consideration of all the areas that make up the IoT encompassing mobile and fixed devices, cloud and virtualization, wireless sensor networks and RFIDs, artificial intelligence and big data, etc. IoT forensics plays its role in the investigation and analysis of cyber-attacks with IoT infrastructure being the target or means. It helps the investigators in the identification of the sequence of steps used to carry an attack which involves the identification and collection of artifacts from diverse associated sources providing the insight or root cause of attacks. The process of IoT forensics, however, is limited by the challenge of dynamic nature of IoT. Perumal et al. (Perumal et al., 2015) carried forward the concept presented by Oriwoh et al. (Oriwoh et al., 2013) directing the analysis and examination in IoT related crime.

The sensors, that stream data to the cloud or remote data stores, are reliant on the network that provides connectivity between them. The network forensics, hence, is the major constituent in IoT forensics. For example., the information regarding the home environment can be acquired from the devices associated with a smart home. This network information can render or lead to the personal information of inhabitants of the smart home. Copos et al. (Copos et al., 2016) acquired the network information from the smart home network. Zawoad and Hasan (Zawoad, & Hasan, 2015) proposed a Forensic-aware IoT (FAIoT) model discussing the issues or challenges faced by IoT forensics. Their proposed model takes into account both the traditional digital forensics that can be applied to crimes involving IoT infrastructure and identification of facts that are specific to IoT only.

The IoT evidence sources are usually mobile, and the identification of such sources is a challenging task. Hence, a proper methodology or strategy needs to be employed for their identification. Rahman et al. (Rahman et al., 2016) referred to this as *mobility forensics* and have worked towards the structured collection and classification of such evidence.

The Wireless Sensor Networks being employed by IoT is itself a new field and lags behind in both security and digital forensics. The data exchanged between different IoT motes is usually broadcast and capturing these data packets in their correct form ensuring the integrity is difficult to achieve. These Wireless Sensor Networks are prone to some severe attacks, e.g., flooding attack, that needs these WSNs to be prepared for forensic investigations. Mouton and Venter (2011) presented a working prototype that demonstrates the forensic readiness in wireless sensor networks with the motive to ensure least investigation cost and time with most credible evidence.

The pace at which the IoT is expanding increases the ground for IoT related crimes, hence, follows to continuous updating of the existing digital forensics tools and techniques. IoT forensics remains the poorly studied field given the challenges of data volume, heterogeneous devices, networks and data, and other legal requirements; hence, significant efforts need to be endeavored for IoT evidence to be admissible in a court of law.

DIGITAL FORENSICS AND IOT

Digital Forensics Process Model

A unified digital forensics process model is required to cater to the needs and challenges in the path of forensic investigations. The main challenges in digital forensics include device diversity, rich media, evidence volume, distributed evidence, wireless networks, virtualization, live response, anti-forensics, encryption of static data and data in transit, cloud dependency, IoT, lack of standards, etc. Different models have been proposed so far, that more or less have the same core structure or phases. However, each new model works towards the refinement and clarity of inherited procedure.

Du et al. (Du et al., 2017) presented in their work the most prominent and remarkable digital forensic process models from the very traditional to most recent models that have more specific and precise definitions of sub-phases. These process models include Forensic Process Model (Mukasey et al., 2011), the Abstract Digital Forensics Model by Reith et al. (Reith et al., 2002) and the Integrated Digital Investigation Model by Carrier and Spafford (Carrier & Spafford, 2003). Martini and Choo (Martini & Choo, 2012) proposed an Integrated conceptual digital forensic framework with an emphasis on data preservation and acquisition of cloud-based data for digital investigations.

Since then many more models came into practice to handle the contemporary advancements in technology with Integrated Digital Forensic Process Model (IDFPM) by Kohn et al. (Kohn et al., 2013) being one of the detailed and unified standardized process models. The model includes the phases shown in Figure 1.

Figure 1. A generic digital forensic process model

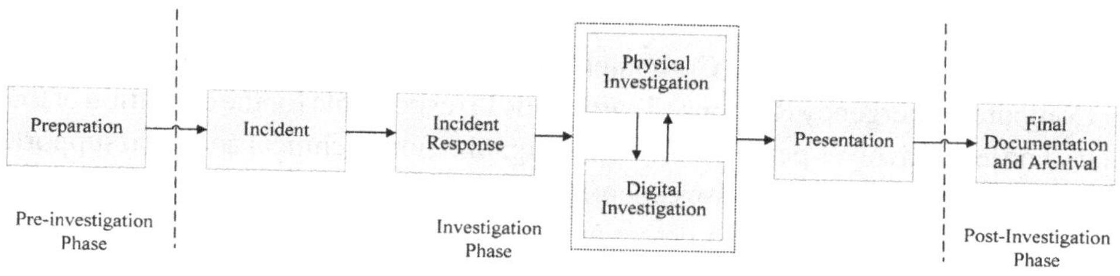

Preparation

Before carrying any forensic investigation, being prepared ahead of time is critical considering the alarming rate of cyber incidents. Lack of preparation leads to delayed investigation and loss of important artifacts that are only available immediately after an incident, e.g., volatile data. Preparation phase accounts for the selection of right personnel, tools, and methodology concerning the security incident. This stage conforms to the forensic readiness of the system which is lacking in current IoT ecosystems and is considered as the starting point of an Incident Response.

Incident

An incident or cyber-incident is an event that changes the state of a system in such a way that compromises the underlying security measures in implementation and results in disruption of normal operations of a system. Cyber-incidents mark a violation of the privacy policy of a system that results in the misuse of confidential or sensitive information, denial of services to the authentic users, unauthorized change or processing of data, hardware or software, etc. Hence, an incident affects the integrity or availability of information associated with a system. In forensic investigations, the early detection of the incident is of utmost importance and helps a great deal in determining the success of an investigation. Depending on the underlying compromised system, the appropriate approach needs to be identified before incident response initiation. Numerous parameters need to be kept in mind in an IoT related incident before any response to it.

Incident Response

All the steps performed before carrying the actual digital investigation collectively constitute an incident response. Digital forensic investigations and incident response are inseparable and always go hand-in-hand. Incident response assists in immediate containment of the situation to prevent any further potential damage and in the recovery from damage, reducing the impact on the compromised system. For any system or organization to respond to the incident immediately, proper planning is required that includes to have a Computer Security Incident Response Team (CSIRT) or Computer Emergency Response Team (CERT) responsible for the execution of the plan. The team involves personnel from the organization, technical and legal support. Incident Response involves assessment, analysis, reporting, etc. of the incident by the team of first responders to detect and separate the compromised systems and identify the available evidence artifacts. Having an instant response to an incident saves a lot of forensic investigation resources regarding cost, time and efforts. The whole digital investigation revolves around its nucleus called *digital evidence* that is presented before a court of justice in its complete, original and integrated form. The admissibility of a digital investigation is reliant on the admissibility of digital evidence. Incident Response is the best opportunity for triage to acquire all the incident-associated evidence including highly volatile evidence (physical memory, network packets, network configurations, open ports and sockets, backdoor ports, login sessions, system time, etc.) that is lost as the investigation proceeds further (Gurkok, 2013).

Physical Investigation and Digital Investigation

Figure 2 shows the steps in Digital Investigation phase of the overall digital forensic process model.

Figure 2. Steps in digital investigation

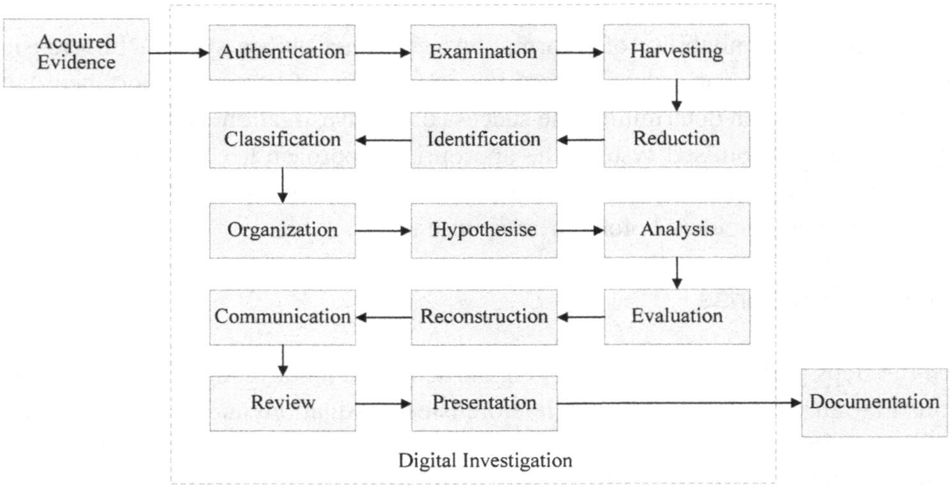

About any cyber-crime, there can be both the physical evidence and digital evidence and both need to be investigated and preserved to reach the concrete solution. The investigation process for both is different even though it needs to be done in parallel. Digital investigation is the heart of the complete Incident Response process which defines the systematic execution of various steps to reach to the solution. After the seizure of evidence media or direct evidence acquisition (in cases where there is no provision to seize or confiscate the media), the actual work starts with the creation of bit-for-bit copy or image of the evidence. This is necessary to ensure the original evidence is preserved and no changes are made to it for being admissible in the court of law. Having a separate work and original copy of evidence allows investigators to investigate the evidence with ease without the fear of accidental modification or destruction of evidence. The hash value of both the original and working copy of evidence is calculated to check its integrity, authentication, and validity. The most prominent hash algorithms are Message Digest (MD5) and Secure Hash Algorithm (SHA).

This is followed by the *examination* of evidence, checking for any prominent, hidden or deleted data, achieved by putting different forensic tools to practice. Investigators search for the remnants of the deleted data, e.g., the metadata that helps in *harvesting* or resurrecting the deleted evidence.

After this phase, to further *reduce* the content base to be analyzed and examined, some reduction techniques might be applied keeping in mind the volume and format diversity of IoT related data. Evidence reduction can also be achieved by identification of known data and software by comparing them to the National Software Reference Library (NSRL), a repository of calculated hashes of known software, hence, prevents the need to analyze them, saving forensic efforts and resources.

The acquired evidence is usually unstructured especially when it is acquired from an IoT environment. Hence, an in-depth and thorough analysis is needed to give it a structure. This leads to the extraction of facts from the collected base and the similar patterned data can be grouped during *classification*. This increases the evidence readability and assists in *organizing* the evidence in hand.

A possible *hypothesis,* regarding the possible cause of the incident, is proposed based on the understanding of available evidence. After the extraction of evidence in the examination phase, followed by other associated steps, evidence *analysis* and *evaluation* either confirms the proposed hypothesis or proves it otherwise. Once proven, the investigator can *reconstruct* the sequence of events that led to the security incident. The validated results are *communicated* to various concerned personnel for further processing including *reviewing* and validating the forensic results to proposed initial hypothesis.

Presentation

The presentation is the reporting of deduced investigation results, findings and facts in a clear and concise manner before a court of law. A detailed report of every action performed from the start of an investigation is presented, showing both the chain of custody and evidence. The final report is also complemented with the support of associated documents critical to the investigation. This might include the documents regarding any changes made to the evidence, its importance, and what it affected, etc. The final report needs to be accurate and unbiased, determining the incident root cause.

The decision regarding the case is made on the presented digital evidence that acts as the digital witness helping in the case resolution.

Documentation

Documentation is one of the essential elements of digital forensic investigation and starts right from the occurrence of a security incident. Documentation records all the critical information regarding the forensic process that assists in the decision making of investigators and the legal personnel. Forensic investigation to be admissible and acceptable in a court of law depends upon the documentation that is maintained from the inception of the case. Documentation being continuous in nature records everything that supports digital witness in the court. This includes time and date information of incident occurrence, evidence acquisition, evidence viewing, or any other operations performed, full path names of where evidence is stored, file system information, operating system information, physical media information, hurdles faced during investigation, network information, connections teared down, volatile and non-volatile evidence information, etc. This documentation assists final forensic report presented before a court of justice. Any change made to the evidence or the system during the investigation is minutely documented. The volume of digital data thwarts the digital investigation process by many folds regarding evidence collection, storage, processing, and presentation. Quick and Choo (Quick & Choo, 2014) proposed a framework to deal with the expansively extensive data by using the techniques of data reduction and data mining for immediate triage of forensic examination.

The reliance of IoT on amalgamation of devices, systems, network domains, protocols, services, applications, technologies raises the issues of blurred boundaries in networks and vague identification of devices of forensic interest. Perumal et al. (Perumal et al., 2015) proposed an approach to the forensic investigation in IoT, assisting in the identification of forensic objects in addition to the preservation of volatile data.

IOT FORENSICS

An article by Cisco presented Gartner's definition of IoT as: "*The Internet of Things (IoT) is the network of physical objects that contain embedded technology to communicate and sense or interact with their internal states or the external environment.*" Whitmore et al. (Whitmore et al., 2015) proposed that IoT technology is realized by the *hardware*, *software,* and *architecture* which are combined in a working infrastructure inseparably. Wireless Sensor Networks (WSNs), Near Field Communication (NFC), and Radio Frequency Identification (RFID) are at the heart of hardware infrastructure. The IoT devices have the sensors and actuators that aid in acquiring information from the immediate environment and interact with users. The interoperability between diverse, heterogeneous devices is achieved by software specifically written for it. The interoperability is achieved usually by a middleware layer between hardware and data and the application end. The IoT software needs to be designed to cater to the dynamic, mobile and huge nature of information. IoT architecture is both distributed and profoundly heterogeneous and involves hardware including network, software, process and general infrastructure.

However, with the rapid increase in IoT technology and the smart devices being penetrated in almost all the spheres of the physical world, new avenues to cyber-crimes are created pertinent to existing vulnerabilities. With the alarming rise in cyber incidents, IoT devices are either a direct attack target or are exploited to carry a cyber-attack. IoT forensics comes into play when malicious activities breach the security measures. These malicious activities can be carried out by the immediate user of the thing, a manufacturer who is immoral to gather sensitive user information and releases it to a third party or an external attacker or can even occur due to bad design or application programming. The attacks include ransomware attacks, frauds, malware attacks, mote/node tampering, phishing attacks, SQL injections, covert channel attacks, Denial of Service (DOS) attacks, buffer overflow, etc.

However, due to a massive difference in conventional computing and IoT, the forensic procedures and standards applied to IoT related investigations demand a different approach. For example, (Taylor et al., 2010) argued that traditional digital forensic procedures and approach need to be updated to accommodate the dynamic nature of evidence from cloud infrastructure. During a digital investigation, the devices that act as the evidence sources are usually supposed to be turned off to prevent any evidence modification. In IoT related investigations, the investigators have little or no such provision, hence, increasing the complexity of investigations.

IoT forensics is a sub-branch of digital forensics that combines different sub-branches of traditional forensics. These include device forensics, network forensics, cloud forensics, mobile/mobility forensics, live forensics, etc. and are executed together in IoT paradigm. IoT forensics has also been termed as *Smart Forensics* or *Forensics of Things.*

Each phase in the forensic model might be divided into sub-phases to bring clarity to the overall investigation, and IoT forensics is dependent on the contemporary forensic models.

ROLE OF IOT IN DIGITAL FORENSICS

IoT can be ruled out to act either as a digital witness, or a hurdle in digital investigations and is discussed below:

Role of IoT in Assisting Digital Forensics

The uniquely identifiable digital devices and digital objects in the Internet of Things (IoT) are interconnected and interoperable, transferring data between them without human intervention. With each passing day, IoT is growing in size adding more devices or things to the existing network. These digital objects collect more and more information from everyday life about their users, which in turn can be used to gain access to tremendous amounts of both personal or sensitive information. The data generated or consumed or transferred from a "thing" or "digital object" can be of prime importance to a specific investigation case, and when acquired, analyzed and presented correctly can act as a *digital witness* to solve the case within time bounds. This digital witness from these IoT devices can corroborate or contradict the occurrence of a security incident. Hence, considering the protagonist role of IoT, IoT data can act as a gold mine to investigators assisting in solving the case in a time bound manner by providing the exact time of an incident or cyber event or other log information necessary to crack the case.

This information helps investigators to extract crime-related intelligence and also encourages investigators to focus on limited suspects. This saves the forensic resources regarding cost, time, and efforts, thereby, reducing the case backlogs.

Role of IoT in Assisting Cyber-Crimes

Although IoT comes with a lot of innovative benefits and opportunities, the potential risks and dangers associated with it cannot be overlooked. The security vulnerabilities in IoT due to its vast boundaryless networks, low standards, and poor design architecture open new opportunities to cyber-criminals for IoT crime. The IoT things or objects can either be directly used as a *target* in an attack or can be used as a *tool* or *means* to carry an attack. In either case, there is a security breach and leads to the severe problem of information or services' compromise. When IoT device is used as a target, the attacks are executed directly on smart devices by exploiting their vulnerabilities. However, when an IoT device is used as a tool, it is used to commit the crime making it harder to identify the source of the attack. In the latter case, usually manufacturer-introduced security or other technical vulnerabilities are exploited.

With IoT security still in its infancy, the computing power of IoT devices can, hence, be harnessed to carry cyber-crimes that can have catastrophic consequences that can be physically tangible and real in most of the cases. These attacks include taking remote control of things, e.g., cars, light bulbs, or other connected home appliances, spying on homes, identity theft, DoS or DDoS attacks, etc. Hence, considering the antagonistic role of IoT, exploited IoT devices can act as a reason for attacks and the most significant hurdle in the digital forensic investigators.

VARIATION OF IOT FORENSICS FROM TRADITIONAL DIGITAL FORENSICS

The decision making and self-management nature of smart devices in IoT infrastructure makes it unique concerning digital forensic approach. About IoT related crimes, an investigator needs to consider all those factors in every dimension that differentiates it from the traditional digital investigations. (Oriwoh, et al., 2013) Enumerated the parameters by which IoT forensics differs from traditional digital forensics, that includes evidence sources, jurisdiction, number of devices, types of evidence, types of networks, quantity and type of data and evidence, protocols, what to seize, ownership, network boundaries, etc. Depending on these differences, IoT forensics face specific challenges that need to be addressed before starting an investigation.

Challenges in IoT Forensics

The security vulnerabilities existent in IoT environments about access control, communication, storage of information, and other privacy issues, etc., might put every IoT connected device and associated data under forensic scrutiny. Having IoT infrastructures pervasive in all spheres of life today, generates much information with forensic value.

The current conventional digital forensic tools and techniques are not explicitly designed to meet the needs of IoT related crime investigations. The investigators face prominent challenges in dealing with such cases, hence, shifting the forensic approach. Some of them are discussed below:

Diversity

IoT possesses the characteristics of high interactivity and dynamicity that escalates its complexity on each front. These characteristics are realized by the fact that "everything" is being connected over the network in almost every domain at a fast rate. This has led to the emergence of heterogeneity and diversity in IoT infrastructure on various fronts including number and types of devices, data formats, interfaces, Operating Systems, network protocols and gateways, standards, middleware, applications, services, architectures, platforms, etc. Although this level of diversity is inevitable for the deployment of IoT ecosystems, it leads to new security vulnerabilities and exploitations. The problem of diversity leads to a lack of standard procedures for data storage, data handling and management, and forensic investigations. From the forensic point of view, the investigators are burdened immensely due to the lack of any proper dedicated hardware or software support to carry forensic investigations (Zulkipli et al., 2017). The forensic tools need to have backward and forward compatibility to support all the versions of hardware and software under investigation. Not only this, investigators find it difficult to locate and identify the devices in a time-bound manner during the identification phase. Greater the time spent on device identification, higher the chances of devices being in passive or off state due to their power constrained nature. In addition to the diversity of data formats due to diverse devices, the data generated by an IoT device can be represented in a different format on the cloud, that further adds the complexity to digital investigations.

Location and Identification of IoT Devices and Data

The sheer number of smart devices or objects connected in IoT ecosystems are scattered in cyberspace that makes it difficult for forensic investigators to identify or locate the target devices. These devices hold the plethora of information that can be of forensic value. More devices refer to more information that results in better understanding of historical events. IoT based evidence is present in IoT devices, network devices, cloud infrastructure, and client application. The extraction and analysis of this data are possible only if the all the devices are identified by first responders immediately after an incident. Hence, searching and seizing (confiscating) IoT devices in case of an incident is the critical step in getting the forensic investigation started. As most of the IoT objects (nodes/motes) might be hidden from the plain sight or might be remotely located, it might be difficult to locate or detect them and is beyond the control of an investigator. The devices in IoT environments can be passive or active which pose their respective concerns to investigators. Most of the devices connected to IoT have the property of mobility, that requires investigators to have extra time, resources, expertise to locate and identify them. The nodes usually furnish a raw data sensed from their immediate environments and might lack any associated metadata while network, cloud or application holds complete and processed data along with all the necessary metadata (e.g., temporal data). However, it is practically difficult or even impossible to have the easy accessibility to network devices and cloud infrastructure. The forensic investigators, also have to face various legal and juridical issues that arise due to geographical distribution of IoT ecosystems.

The preservation of evidence throughout the investigation is one of the critical tasks of investigators, however, with IoT systems, the devices or nodes have autonomous and real-time interactivity which makes it hard to draw the crime-scene boundaries (Conti et al., 2018).

Lack of Standardization

IoT ecosystems today are highly fragmented and drastically lack to work on common grounds due to lack of standards and unified agreements that ultimately undermines the growth, security, and forensics of IoT ecosystems. This lack of standardization is a direct resultant of open design and architecture of IoT environments that is expanding at an exponential speed (Al-Qaseemi et al., 2016). The immediate repercussions of this raises the issues of lack of standard or agreed upon operating systems, programming languages, interfaces, communication protocols, etc. at different layers of IoT systems. Newman (Newman, 2016) argued about how IoT lacks a unified standardization and how the multitude of IoT ecosystems might never speak a common language.

The data generated, consumed and exchanged by the diverse components of IoT infrastructure suffer from *lack of data standards* regarding data formats or data representation, data storage, data communication protocols, etc. which hinders and plagues the IoT forensic investigations. The acquired evidence from IoT devices, e.g., logs help to build the timeline of events in forensic investigations. However, with no specific format or standard of representation of these evidence logs, the clarity in understanding and presentation of evidence suffers tremendously. The smart devices connected also suffer from a lack of wireless protocol standardization that works on different frequencies. During the device identification phase of forensics, some devices might be left out leading to incomplete evidence.

As IoT evolves towards its maturity, a standard or single platform for standardization of various IoT components, that bridges the operational and architectural gaps guaranteeing interoperability, portability, manageability needs of IoT are required at an earliest. This will ensure the evidence integrity in these complex and distributed systems.

Evidence Lifespan in IoT

The data-centric nature of IoT makes it inseparable from the fact that IoT is one of the sources of digital *big data* most talked about today. Digital forensic investigations of IoT environments rely on this data for extraction of evidential intelligence. However, for this evidence to be presented before the court the law, investigators need to ensure all the critical artifacts are acquired. However, considering the resource-constrained IoT devices, the longevity of data it holds is limited. The nodes are usually battery powered and have a limited RAM and other storage capabilities, hence, the data resident on IoT devices is short lived as it is quickly overwritten. This results in the loss of potential evidence from the device, creating gaps in the acquired evidence set. Also, as an IoT device can be active or passive, being active might result in rapid battery drain resulting in evidence loss while being passive might be a hurdle in device tracking and identification. If the device is drained of its battery power, all the volatile data may be lost. The lack of completeness, hence, questions the reliability of evidence, making it difficult to be admissible in court. Hence, it is an excellent investigation practice to have an incident response team ready to capture all the possible evidence as early as possible. Although the node data is eventually transmitted over to the cloud resource pool for storage and processing, it has its challenges and complexities associated, and volatile data will always be a missing link there.

Current Forensic Tools

The heterogeneity of IoT environments and the copious amounts of data generated by IoT environments raise new challenges that make the current digital forensics investigation tools immature to fit in. The field of digital forensics itself is not fully mature and is in the constant state of evolution, and hence, face challenges in dealing with the diversity, heterogeneity, complex architectures, and the avalanche of data volume generated by IoT. Since IoT devices are vulnerable regarding security relative to conventional digital devices, the tools need to be strong enough to acquire evidence from such devices. Otherwise, the fidelity of evidence will be questioned. Also, the available forensic tools for cloud investigations are not fully developed, while IoT requires cloud forensic tools for evidence extraction and analysis, hence, lacking the proper tool support. The reliance on cloud infrastructure implies the forensic tools have to deal with the virtual environments that add more layers of complexity to be faced by tools. Considering the limitations in current forensic tools, they are mostly immature and inappropriate for carrying investigations of IoT environments.

The accelerated growth and innovation in the Internet of Things give insufficient time to confirm on a set of unified standards, incorporate sufficient security, address the issues of privacy, inadequate testing of nodes, communication protocols, etc. IoT makes the physical world hyper-connected digitally and leaves less scope for errors, for it can bring down the whole system or will have catastrophic results due to chain reaction or propagation of errors to other components. This leads to the challenge of *chaos* in IoT environments that needs to be addressed at an earliest (Lee & Kyoochun, 2015).

While investigating an IoT-related case, if the above-mentioned challenges are not kept in consideration, serious ramifications might arise that include: delay in forensic triage and process, a misled and confounded forensic investigation, increasing privacy and security risks by not containing the incident or complicating the case rather than simplifying it (Harbawi & Varol, 2017).

IOT FORENSICS AT DIFFERENT LAYERS

The IoT forensics or *smart forensics* is still very young which lacks the enumeration and categorization of evidence into specific classes, the techniques for carrying forensic investigations comprehensively are also missing. IoT presents both the complexity as well as the potentiality to the investigators. Although the IoT infrastructure can be decomposed into several layers, currently many layered models are in practice, the IoT forensic investigators have to deal with three prominent layers.

Based on the basic IoT architecture model, the end-to-end digital investigation and procedure in IoT infrastructure are divided into three layers: device level forensics, network layer forensics, cloud layer forensics (Zawoad & Hasan, 2015). The points, worth discussing is how to proceed with the investigation at the following layers:

Perception Layer Forensics or Device Layer Forensics

With the multitude of objects/things/devices interconnected together in the IoT ecosystem, the volume of data associated with it is swarmed by endless amounts. The entry point of data into IoT environments is the perception layer. The perception layer includes devices that possess the capabilities of sensing the physical environments in a raw form. The devices at the perception layer include sensors for acquiring data reliant on some sensing technology, e.g., Radio Frequency Identification (RFID), Near Field Communication (NFC), Wireless Sensor Network (WSN), Global Positioning System (GPS), etc. and actuators for some lightweight processing. At the perception layer, the sensed data is prepared for communication over a network (internal or external) by converting it into digital form. The perception layer devices are resource constrained regarding the power supply (usually battery powered), storage (limited), range (limited), processor (low cost), security (lightweight), etc. These IoT devices can be visible or invisible, active or passive, remote or local.

During the IoT forensic investigations, for the collection or acquisition of evidence, the devices from which the evidence is to be acquired are to be identified. Since the device diversity characterizes IoT, and it is practically impossible for investigators to seize all the devices and all the data they harbor device seizure is done selectively. The goal of investigators is the selection of best evidence which is acquired keeping in mind its relevance and lifespan or longevity. Perception level forensics conceives with the identification of devices to contain and delimit the incident from propagating and to collect the potential evidence. Device and evidence identification, as proposed by (Bouchaud et al., 2018), is achieved by following the steps of device detection, localization, recognition, and check-in.

During the *detection phase*, the investigators have to deal with always-connected, semi-connected, and not-connected devices. Identification of visible devices is relatively easy, however, for hidden active devices, the frequencies emitted from them are captured and scanned for the possible device signature. This leads to the possible signal emitting source that eventually guides the investigator to device location in a local environment. In case of passive devices, investigators capture the network traffic, over a certain period, that can be force-generated by the use of wake-up commands, adding, blocking or deleting a device or a frequency in the network that forces IoT devices to communicate, that eventually leads to device discovery. This is possible because of the interdependency of devices in an IoT network. In passive devices, if signal capturing is used, it needs to be done over long periods of time which is not favorable in IoT investigations considering the evidence lifespan.

Whether the investigator uses the captured signal strength or the network traffic, the position of an IoT device is located either directly or using some analytical functions on the captured signals or data. However, the process can be limited by other objects disturbing the exchanged signals. The *localization* of one device leads to the identification, discovery, and localization of other IoT devices in the network.

In the device recognition, the investigators recognize the device by digital recognition (based on underlying sensor technology) or by physical recognition (based on the device electromagnetic signature). The recognition phase, gives the manufacturer's information, communication information, country of marketing, etc. IoT forensics requires investigators, to simultaneously create a knowledge base to keep a record of the identified heterogeneous devices, their technical information for any future references.

Proceeding with the identification, the devices and the information captured so far is cross-checked iteratively till all devices are identified. The identification of a primary node eventually guides the investigators to other connected nodes or sensor devices using MAC addresses or so. A definite relationship diagram can help investigators in better visualization of the scenario.

The device selection is made based on the acquisition of evidence that best fits the forensic case in question. This selection, hence, is done on the specific attributes of the evidence that includes case relevance, accessibility, localization, type, etc.

The sensor devices provide an entry point to the IoT system in question and are connected over a local network. The devices have limited storage and physical memory and rarely an external storage card. The acquired data from these devices is not usually in a human-readable format and dealing with it can be time-consuming delaying the forensic triage. The devices equipped with external memory card usually have the gateway component as well. The investigators need to be very careful while dealing with this evidence and the order of evidence volatility need to be followed strictly. In certain investigation cases where sensor devices are located remotely, hence, inaccessible, the investigators miss the crucial initial information and have to rely on alternate evidence sources only.

The evidence acquired at the device level includes freshly sensed data in storage or physical memory, network connections, open ports, backdoor ports, system and history logs, device boot information, temporary data, etc.

Transport Layer Forensics or Network Layer Forensics

The IoT network or transport layer comprises of technologies at various scales providing communication between smart devices (internal network), their applications and cloud services (external network). It acts as a bridge between the perception layer and the cloud layer providing a reliable interface for both.

However, in an IoT forensic investigation, the traffic that is exchanged over the network is put to scrutiny and is analyzed for any suspicious packets exchanged over the network. This helps forensic investigators to build a timeline of events occurred in IoT systems. Network forensics, most of the time, is a live process where investigators continuously capture and analyze live packets exchanged over the network. However, considering the massive traffic generated in an IoT system, it is practically impossible to capture, store and analyze all the network traffic and is often a time-consuming process. Hence, the packet capture is done selectively where packets are analyzed for suspicious behavior before being captured for further forensic investigation. The network traffic is more ephemeral that makes the investigation hard to carry. The analysis of network traffic helps investigators to trace back to the cause or source of any malicious activity affecting or attacking the IoT infrastructure. This is possible by dissecting the captured packets for the retrieval of user and control information embedded in the packets. The command information includes the source and destination addresses which help in attack traceback during investigations. The data captured from the network layer can be in different formats and might require specific conversions before being investigated or presented in a court of law. The transport or network layer forensics also captures data from the network backbone devices that enable the communication in an IoT environment. These include hubs, routers, switches, bridges, etc. The evidence resident on these devices is more persistent and structured comparatively. Also, the investigators have to deal with complexities that are inherent to IoT networks themselves including heterogeneous technologies and protocols.

The evidence acquired from the network or transport layer includes network packets, network logs, routing tables, IP addresses, etc.

Application Layer Forensics or Cloud Layer Forensics

The application layer is the frontend of an IoT infrastructure allowing users to access and interact with the IoT system. However, due to the resource-constrained nature of IoT devices, the data rendered to end users is stored on the pool of cloud resources. The analysis of devices and evidence from the user-end includes client forensics and is more or less equivalent to the conventional digital forensic procedure. The high reliance of IoT on the cloud makes these two inseparably merged and requires cloud/server forensics. The cloud infrastructure is used for data storage, data processing and data transfer in an IoT environment. However, the use of cloud resources and services poses some serious challenges that limit the forensic investigations by many folds (Pichan et al., 2015). These challenges vary from being technical to legal to organizational, adding various layers of complexities and abstractions to be resolved by investigators. The cloud environments are highly distributed geographically, making data stored there, highly decentralized. The unknown location and inaccessibility of cloud resources prevent investigators from identifying evidential artifacts stored on the cloud. This also raises the problem of legal issues as the cloud might be located in a different juridical zone. The decentralized and duplicated IoT data on the cloud is a massive problem in locking the evidence as final copy for integrity issues. Data stored at different locations with multiple copies might result in evidence contamination that renders it questionable in a court of law. The acquisition of cloud-stored data, hence, is highly dependent on Cloud Service Providers (CSP). The investigators need to request them for the possible access to restricted data with the evidential value stored there. As multiple users are sharing the cloud, acquisition of evidence about a particular user or device needs segregation of evidence so as not to disturb the data of other users.

Usually, the data transmitted over the cloud is converted to a different format and is usually encrypted for security reasons, and since most of the processing in IoT systems is performed at the cloud, the evidence acquired from it needs to be converted to a uniform format to comply to the evidence acquired from IoT devices. Meanwhile, the entire process of identifying and locating the evidence source in a cloud infrastructure needs to be done keeping in mind the preservation of evidence originality and integrity ensuring the complete chain of custody. The investigators, when dealing with cloud, encounter specific other issues including trust, dynamicity, security, volatility, virtualization, deleted data, lack of sophisticated forensic analysis tools for clouds, etc.

The evidence acquired from the cloud infrastructure includes IoT device-sent information, cloud access logs, network logs, user credentials, databases, temporary files, registry logs, memory images, etc.

DIGITAL EVIDENCE IN IOT FORENSICS

Digital Evidence is any data that is stored electronically on a digital device that is of value and serves as digital witness in forensic investigation to prove the occurrence of any historical event. The digital evidence to be analyzed or presented before a court of justice needs to be acquired securely to ensure its originality and integrity. The digital evidence often is characterized by being volatile or non-volatile, visible or hidden, persistent or deleted, structured or unstructured, etc. One of the critical aspects of digital evidence is the fact that it is highly fragile and even a minor mishandling can lead to its contamination and destruction. A digital forensic investigation should require minimum costs and make an optimal or maximum use of potential evidence ensuring minimum or no interference to evidence.

The IoT-related data can be used by investigators to solve both the physical or cyber-crimes. However, the data generated and consumed by IoT systems is tremendous and is scattered all over the IoT space which makes it difficult for investigators to capture it all. Relative to conventional digital forensics, the certainty of evidence origin is thin and faces the problem of persistence. The first responders or investigators, hence, follow the principle of *best evidence* by seizing only the particular devices while discarding the rest of irrelevant ones. During the initial triage and getting the forensic investigation started, the evidence accessibility and relevance play an essential role in best evidence selection. The relevance of evidence is defined regarding its spatial and temporal availability. The spatial relevance of evidence is based on the proximity of smart objects concerning the crime event. The temporal relevance is based on the longevity of evidence and is acquired as per the order of volatility. Furthermore, the evidence is acquired from only those devices that are directly or indirectly related to the incident. This results in reduced evidence set during the collection phase. Data present in seized devices might not be directly accessible (e.g., due to encryption) and will impact the choice of investigators to retain or discard it. The technical operation of an investigator is also determined by the data localization, whether it is acquired from a crime scene or the IoT cloud platform and choosing from diverse devices only the useful evidence. In addition to this, evidence acquired from the diverse and heterogeneous IoT environment is available in a multitude of formats or data types. The data can either be raw (sensor data) or is contextualized or modified (cloud or application data). Based on these evidence selection properties, the devices are weighted for the decision to seize. However, all the choices in device selection and selective evidence imaging should ensure that no significant piece of evidence is left out.

Importance and Need of Data Reduction of IoT Forensic Data

The overhead of the complexities and the big data in IoT makes the management and handling of evidence a challengingly difficult task during all the stages of the forensic investigation. Although the first responders make a selective acquisition of evidence, it still is not sufficient and requires further reduction in acquired evidence. Specific analytical functions are applied to the corpus of evidence imaged to decipher only the evidence that best fits the case and rules out rest of the acquired or imaged data as unnecessary noise (Quick & Choo, 2018). Although, an extra cycle for analytical execution it required, it has its benefits of removing evidence distractions, keeping investigation strictly focused, thereby, reducing wastage of forensic efforts and other resources (improving cost performance). This also impacts the overall quality of the results of an investigation. The data reduction also helps in reducing the case backlogs, that is one of the biggest challenges in digital forensic investigations in current times.

REQUIREMENTS OF FUTURE GENERATIONS OF IOT SYSTEMS

The need to deal with the exponential growth of cyber-crimes due to the rapid pace in the innovation and development of smart environment demands significant changes in both the security and the forensic disciplines. This is necessary to cut down the forensic expenses in case of a forensic incident. To bridge the gaps in security and forensics measures, the future generations of IoT ecosystems have some vital requirements uniquely dedicated to them. The existing forensic tools and techniques are premature to cater to the forensic needs of IoT investigations. The backbone standards on every front (e.g., protocols, technologies, data formats, etc.) need to be developed for the diversity and heterogeneity problems while maintaining the interoperability in the IoT ecosystem. The IoT systems need to be prepared ahead of time for any security incidents. This preparedness constitutes the forensic readiness which makes a massive impact on the forensic triage. Kebande et al. (Kebande et al., 2018) proposed in their work the importance and use of digital forensic readiness as a critical component of security. Although there is forensic preparedness in traditional digital systems, IoT infrastructure lacks this preparedness and readiness as of now.

Any functioning of an IoT infrastructure, from a forensic point of view, can be divided into three zones or processes viz: pre-incident or proactive process, IoT communication process, post-incident or reactive process. In the proactive phase, forensic readiness is acquired by management and technical readiness. Management readiness includes framing of standards, procedures, preparation of forensic tools and other infrastructure, well prepared and trained workforce, etc., while technical readiness includes preparing technically how to deal with the situation, how to proceed, what to collect, what to preserve, etc.

The IoT communication process is the normal operation of the IoT system during which an incident occurs. Zulkipli et al. (Zulkipli et al., 2017) have proposed the real-time approach to carry forensic investigations embedded in IoT system itself. This demands for live, automatic and constant forensic monitoring that is triggered automatically in case of an incident. However, this real-time approach for forensic readiness requires some advancements regarding communication, storage and synchronization. Such approaches make IoT environments all-time aware and ready for forensic investigations.

In the post-incident or reactive process, the standard digital investigation procedure is executed as described above in the digital forensic process model. Here the readiness regarding dedicated and updated tools, standards, techniques, etc. is the current requirement for future developments. This is shown in Figure 3 below:

CONCLUSION

IoT is an emerging discipline with new devices being continuously added to the existing IoT ecosystem. This exponential growth creates new opportunities for cyber-criminals resulting in a greater attack-surface. Taking into consideration the complex nature and fast growth of IoT systems, security and forensic experts face a lot of new challenges. IoT systems are heterogeneous and highly distributed with a complex architecture having constrained resources that raise new obstacles in the path of investigations. IoT systems generate and consume overwhelming amounts of data that can be used as potential evidence in forensic investigations. The first

Figure 3. IoT infrastructure and forensic zones or processes

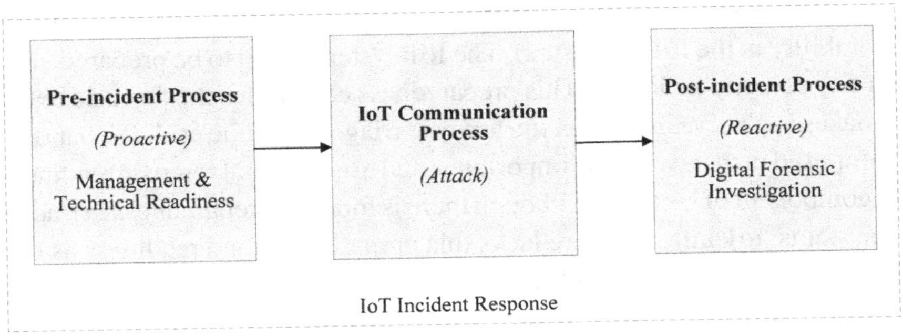

responders, however, are faced with the severe issues to collect, store or process this big data. IoT systems, to be fully deployed, are dependent on cloud services which pose their own challenges in forensic investigations. Both IoT sensors (remote or hidden) and cloud resident and network data are most of the times physically inaccessible that makes it hard to seize the media or capture the evidence. Hence, the evidence location and identification are big challenges in IoT forensics. Furthermore, a significant reduction in evidence during acquisition, examination, and analysis is needed as it is impractical to deal with the enormous amounts of data. Specific legal challenges might also arise when geographical boundaries are crossed in the case of cloud services. The mobility factor (sensors in motion) in IoT also pose hurdles in location or acquisition of evidence during the investigation. In awe of the differences between IoT and conventional systems, a separate dedicated digital forensics framework is required as the existing conventional forensic methods and the current tools are insufficient to carry the IoT investigations. The future generations of IoT are expected to have a component for forensic readiness and have thorough know-how or awareness of forensic practices. The forensic tools, standards, and entire curriculum need to be updated and revised to fit the needs of IoT systems.

ACKNOWLEDGMENT

This work has been supported by the Department of Science and Technology (DST), Ministry of Science and Technology, Government of India under its project grant no. DST/INSPIRE Fellowship/2017/IF170301.

REFERENCES

Alaba, F. A., Othman, M., Hashem, I. A. T., & Alotaibi, F. (2017). Internet of things Security: A Survey. *Journal of Network and Computer Applications, 88*, 10–28. doi:10.1016/j.jnca.2017.04.002

Beverly, R., Garfinkel, S., & Cardwell, G. (2010). Forensic carving of network packets and associated data structures. *Digital Investigation, 8*, S78-S89.

Bouchaud, F., Grimaud, G., & Vantroys, T. (2018). IoT Forensic: identification and classification of evidence in criminal investigations. *Proceedings of the 13th International Conference on Availability, Reliability and Security - ARES 2018.* 10.1145/3230833.3233257

Brady, O., Overill, R., & Keppens, J. (2015). DESO: Addressing volume and variety in large-scale criminal cases. *Digital Investigation, 15*, 72–82. doi:10.1016/j.diin.2015.10.002

Carrier, B. & Spafford, E. H. (2003). Getting Physical with the Investigative Process. *International Journal of Digital Evidence, 2*(2).

Conti, M., Dehghantanha, A., Franke, K., & Watson, S. (2018). Internet of Things security and forensics: Challenges and opportunities. *Future Generation Computer Systems, 78*, 544–546. doi:10.1016/j.future.2017.07.060

Copos, B., Levitt, K., Bishop, M., & Rowe, J. (2016). *Is Anybody Home? Inferring Activity From Smart Home Network Traffic. In 2016 IEEE Security and Privacy Workshops.* SPW. doi:10.1109pw.2016.48

Damshenas, M., Dehghantanha, A., & Mahmoud, R. (2014). A Survey on Digital Forensics Trends. *International Journal of Cyber-Security and Digital Forensics, 3*(4), 209–234.

David, L., Becker, B. A., O'Sullivan, T., & Scanlon, M. (2016). Current Challenges and Future Research Areas for Digital Forensic Investigation. *Annual ADFSL Conference on Digital Forensics, Security and Law, 6.* Retrieved from https://commons.erau.edu/adfsl/2016/tuesday/6

DFRWS. (2001). A Road Map for Digital Forensic Research. *Proceedings of The Digital Forensic Research Conference DFRWS 2001.*

Du, X., Le-Khac, N., & Scanlon, M. (2017). Evaluation of Digital Forensic Process Models with Respect to Digital Forensics as a Service. *16th European Conference on Cyber Warfare and Security (ECCWS 2017).*

Gurkok, C. (2013). Cyber Forensics and Incident Response. *Computer and Information Security Handbook*, 601–621. doi:. doi:10.1016/b978-0-12-394397-2.00034-9

Harbawi, M., & Varol, A. (2017). An Improved Digital Evidence Acquisition Model for the Internet of Things Forensic I: A Theoretical Framework. *2017 5th International Symposium on Digital Forensic and Security (ISDFS)*. 10.1109/ISDFS.2017.7916508

Hargreaves, C., & Patterson, J. (2012). An automated timeline reconstruction approach for digital forensic investigations. *Digital Investigation*, *9*, S69–S79. doi:10.1016/j.diin.2012.05.006

Hegarty, R., Lamb, D. J., & Attwood, A. (2014). Digital Evidence Challenges in the Internet of Things. *Proceedings of the Ninth International Workshop on Digital Forensics and Incident Analysis*. Retrieved from https://www.cscan.org/openaccess/?id=231

IoT Architecture Challenges and Issues. Lack of Standardization. (2016). FTC 2016 - Future Technologies Conference 2016.

Kebande, V. R., Karie, N. M., & Venter, H. S. (2018). Adding Digital Forensic Readiness as a Security Component to The IoT Domain. *International Journal on Advanced Science. Engineering and Information Technology*, *8*, 1–11. doi:10.18517/ijaseit.8.1.2115

Kohn, M. D., Eloff, M. M., & Eloff, J. H. P. (2013). Integrated Digital Forensic Process Model. *Computers & Security*, *38*, 103–115. doi:10.1016/j.cose.2013.05.001

Lee, I., & Lee, K. (2015). The Internet of Things (IoT): Applications, investments, and challenges for enterprises. *Business Horizons*, *58*(4), 431–440. doi:10.1016/j.bushor.2015.03.008

Lin, J., Yu, W., Zhang, N., Yang, X., Zhang, H., & Zhao, W. (2017). A Survey on Internet of Things: Architecture, Enabling Technologies, Security and Privacy, and Applications. *IEEE Internet of Things Journal*, *4*(5), 1125–1142. doi:10.1109/JIOT.2017.2683200

Maple, C. (2017). Security and privacy in the internet of things. *Journal of Cyber Policy*, *2*(2), 155–184. doi:10.1080/23738871.2017.1366536

Martini, B., & Choo, K. R. (2012). An integrated conceptual digital forensic framework for cloud computing. *Digital Investigation*, *9*(2), 71–80. doi:10.1016/j.diin.2012.07.001

Marturana, F., & Tacconi, S. (2013). A Machine Learning-based Triage methodology for automated categorization of digital media. *Digital Investigation, Vol., 10*(2), 193–204. doi:10.1016/j.diin.2013.01.001

Mouton, F., & Venter, H. S. (2011). A prototype for achieving digital forensic readiness on wireless sensor networks. IEEE Africon 2011 - The Falls Resort and Conference Centre.

Mukasey, M. B., Sedgwick, J. L., & Hagy, D. W. (2011). Electronic Crime Scene Investigation A Guide for First Responder. *National Institute of Justice*. Retrieved from http://www.ncjrs.org/pdffiles1/nij/187736.pdf

Newman, J. (2016). Why the Internet of things might never speak A common language. *App Economy, Fast Company, 2016*. Retrieved from http://www.fastcompany.com/3057770/why-the-internet-of-thingsmight-never-speak-a-common-language

Okolica, J., & Peterson, G. L. (2011). Extracting the windows clipboard from physical memory. *Digital Investigation, 8*, S118–S124. doi:10.1016/j.diin.2011.05.014

Oriwoh, E., Jazani, D., Epiphaniou, G., & Sant, P. (2013). Internet of Things Forensics: Challenges and approaches. *IEEE International Conference on Collaborative Computing: Networking, Applications, and Worksharing*, 608–615. DOI: 10.4108/icst.collaboratecom.2013.254159

Perumal, S., Norwawi, N. M., & Raman, V. (2015). Internet of Things (IoT) digital forensic investigation model: Top-down forensic approach methodology. *Fifth International Conference on Digital Information Processing and Communications (ICDIPC)*, 19–23. DOI: 10.1109/ICDIPC.2015.7323000

Perumal, S., Norwawi, N. M., & Raman, V. (2015). Internet of Things (IoT) Digital Forensic Investigation Model: Top-Down Forensic Approach Methodology. *2015 Fifth International Conference on Digital Information Processing and Communications (ICDIPC)*. 10.1109/ICDIPC.2015.7323000

Pichan, A., Lazarescu, M., & Soh, S. T. (2015). Cloud forensics: Technical challenges, solutions and comparative analysis. *Digital Investigation, Vol., 13*, 38–57. doi:10.1016/j.diin.2015.03.002

Quick, D., & Cho, K. R. (2018). IoT Device Forensics and Data Reduction. *IEEE Access: Practical Innovations, Open Solutions, 6*, 47566–47574. doi:10.1109/ACCESS.2018.2867466

Quick, D., & Choo, K. R. (2014). Data Reduction and Data Mining Framework for Digital Forensic Evidence: Storage, Intelligence, Review and Archive. *Trends and Issues in Crime and Criminal Justice*, *480*, 1–11.

Rahman, K. M. S., Bishop, M. & Hol, A. (2016). Internet of Things mobility forensics. *Information Security Research and Education (INSuRE) Conference*.

Reith, M., Carr, C. & Gunsch, G. (2002). An Examination of Digital Forensic Models. *International Journal of Digital Evidence*, *1*(3).

Rekhis, S., & Boudriga, N. (2012). A System for Formal Digital Forensic Investigation Aware of Anti-Forensic Attacks. *IEEE Transactions on Information Forensics and Security*, *7*(2), 635–650. doi:10.1109/TIFS.2011.2176117

Rizvi, S., Pfeffer, J., Kurtz, A., & Rizvi, M. (2018). Securing the Internet of Things (IoT): A Security Taxonomy for IoT. *2018 17th IEEE International Conference On Trust, Security And Privacy In Computing And Communications/ 12th IEEE International Conference On Big Data Science And Engineering (TrustCom/ BigDataSE)*. DOI: 10.1109/TrustCom/BigDataSE.2018.000

Simson, L. (2010). Garfinkel. Digital forensics research: The next 10 years. *Digital Investigation*, *7*, S64–S73. doi:10.1016/j.diin.2010.05.009

Stevens, R. M., & Casey, E. (2010). Extracting Windows command line details from physical memory. *Digital Investigation*, *7*, S57–S63. doi:10.1016/j.diin.2010.05.008

Taylor, M., Haggerty, J., Gresty, D., & Hegarty, R. (2010, May). Digital evidence in cloud computing systems. *Elsevier Computer Law & Security Review*, *26*(3), 304–308. doi:10.1016/j.clsr.2010.03.002

White, A., Schatz, B., & Foo, E. (2012). Surveying the user space through user allocations. *Digital Investigation*, *9*, S3–S12. doi:10.1016/j.diin.2012.05.005

Whitmore, A., Agarwal, A., & Xu, L. D. (2015). The Internet of Things—A survey of topics and trends. *Information Systems Frontiers*, *17*(2), 261–274. doi:10.100710796-014-9489-2

Zawoad, S., & Hasan, R. (2015). FAIoT: Towards Building a Forensics Aware Eco System for the Internet of Things. *2015 IEEE International Conference on Services Computing*, 279–284. DOI: 10.1109/SCC.2015.46

Zulkipli, N. H. N., Alenezi, A., & Wills, G. B. (2017). IoT Forensic: Bridging the Challenges in Digital Forensic and the Internet of Things. *Proceedings of the 2nd International Conference on Internet of Things, Big Data and Security*, 1, 315-324. 10.5220/0006308703150324

Compilation of References

Aarestad, J., Plusquellic, J., & Acharyya, D. (2013). Error-Tolerant Bit Generation Techniques for Use with a Hardware-Embedded Path Delay PUF. *IEEE Int'l Symp. Hardware- Oriented Security and Trust (HOST 13)*, 151–158. 10.1109/HST.2013.6581581

Abdul-Ghani, H. A., Konstantas, D., & Mahyoub, M. (2017). Comprehensive IoT Attacks Survey based on a Building-blocked Reference Model. *(IJACSA). International Journal of Advanced Computer Science and Applications*, *9*(3), 2018.

Abed, F., List, E., Lucks, S., & Wenzel, J. (2014, March). Differential cryptanalysis of round-reduced Simon and Speck. In *International Workshop on Fast Software Encryption* (pp. 525-545). Springer.

ABI Research. (2013). *More Than 30 Billion Devices Will Wirelessly Connect to the Internet of Everything in 2020.* ABI Research Press Release. Retrieved from https://www.abiresearch. com/press/more-than-30-billion-devices-willwirelessly-conne

Agrawal, R., Evfimievski, A., & Srikant, R. (2003). Information sharing across private databases. *Proceedings of the 2003 ACM SIGMOD international conference on Management of data*, 86-97. 10.1145/872757.872771

Ahemd, M. M., Shah, M. A., & Wahid, A. (2017). IoT Security: A layered approach for attacks & defenses. *2017 International Conference on Communication Technologies (ComTech)*, 104–110.

Ahmed, M., & Khan, K. (2013). Trust-Based Secure Gateway Discovery Mechanism for Integrated Internet and MANET. *International Conference on Distributed*. Retrieved from http://link.springer.com/chapter/10.1007/978-3-642-36071-8_7

Akter, M., Rahman, M. O., Islam, M. N., Hassan, M. M., Alsanad, A., & Sangaiah, A. K. (2018). Energy-efficient tracking and localization of objects in wireless sensor networks. *IEEE Access: Practical Innovations, Open Solutions*, *6*, 17165–17177. doi:10.1109/ACCESS.2018.2809692

Akyildiz, I. F., Su, W., Sankarasubramaniam, Y., & Cayirci, E. (2002). A survey on sensor networks. *IEEE Communications Magazine*, *40*(8), 102–114. doi:10.1109/MCOM.2002.1024422

Alaba, F. A., Othman, M., Hashem, I. A. T., & Alotaibi, F. (2017). Internet of things Security: A Survey. *Journal of Network and Computer Applications*, *88*, 10–28. doi:10.1016/j.jnca.2017.04.002

Al-Fuqaha, A., Guizani, M., Mohammadi, M., Aledhari, M., & Ayyash, M. (2015). Internet of Things: A Survey on Enabling Technologies, Protocols, and Applications. *IEEE Communications Surveys and Tutorials*, *17*(4), 2015.

Al-Gburi, A., Al-Hasnawi, A., & Lilien, L. (2018). Differentiating security from privacy in internet of things: A survey of selected threats and controls. In K. Daimi (Ed.), *Computer and network security essentials* (pp. 153–172). Springer International Publishing. doi:10.1007/978-3-319-58424-9_9

Alioto, M., Bongiovanni, S., Djukanovic, M., Scotti, G., & Trifiletti, A. (2014). Effectiveness of leakage power analysis attacks on DPA-resistant logic styles under process variations. *IEEE Transactions on Circuits and Systems. I, Regular Papers*, *61*(2), 429–442. doi:10.1109/TCSI.2013.2278350

Alioto, M., Poli, M., & Rocchi, S. (2010b). Differential power analysis attacks to pre charged buses: A general analysis for symmetric-key cryptographic algorithms. *IEEE Transactions on Dependable and Secure Computing*, *7*(3), 226–239. doi:10.1109/TDSC.2009.1

Ali, S. T., Sivaraman, V., Ostry, D., & Jha, S. (2013). Securing data provenance in body area networks using lightweight wireless link fingerprints. *Proceedings of the 3rd international workshop on Trustworthy embedded devices*. 10.1145/2517300.2517303

Alkabani, Y., Koushanfar, F., & Potkonjak, M. (2007). Remote activation of ICs for piracy prevention and digital right management. *Proc. IEEE/ACM Int'l Conf. Computer- Aided Design (ICCAD 07)*, 674–677. 10.1109/ICCAD.2007.4397343

AlKhzaimi, H., & Lauridsen, M. M. (2013). Cryptanalysis of the SIMON Family of Block Ciphers. *IACR Cryptology ePrint Archive, 2013*, 543.

All Seen Alliance. (n.d.). Retrieved from https://allseenalliance.org/

Allemang, D., & Hendler, J. (2011). *Semantic Web for the Working Ontologist: Effective modeling in RDFS and OWL*. Semantic Web for the Working Ontologist. doi:10.1016/B978-0-12-385965-5.10016-0

Alvarez, A. B., Zhao, W., & Alioto, M. (2016). Static physically unclonable functions for secure chip identification with 1.9–5.8% native bit instability at 0.6–1 V and 15fJ/bit in 65 nm. *IEEE Journal of Solid-State Circuits*, *60*(5), 1–4.

Alvarez, A., & Alioto, M. (2017). Security Down to the Hardware Level. In M. Alioto (Ed.), *Enabling the Internet of Things: From Integrated Circuits to Integrated Systems* (pp. 247–270). Singapore: Springer. doi:10.1007/978-3-319-51482-6_8

Alvarez, A., Zhao, W., & Alioto, M. (2015). 15 fJ/bit static physically unclonable functions for secure chip identification with <2% native bit instability and 140x inter/intra PUF hamming distance separation in 65 nm. *IEEE Int. Solid-State Circuits Conf. 5*, 256–258.

Aman, M. N., Chua, K. C., & Sikdar, B. (2017). Secure Data Provenance for the Internet of Things. *Proceedings of the 3rd ACM International Workshop on IoT Privacy, Trust, and Security*. 10.1145/3055245.3055255

Aman, M., Chua, K. C., & Sikdar, B. (2017). Mutual Authentication in IoT Systems using Physical Unclonable Functions. *IEEE Internet of Things Journal*, *4*(5), 1327–1340. doi:10.1109/JIOT.2017.2703088

Amin, S. A. A., Ali-Eldin, A., & Ali, H. A. (2016). A context-aware dispatcher for the Internet of Things: The case of electric power distribution systems. *Computers & Electrical Engineering*, *52*, 183–198. doi:10.1016/j.compeleceng.2015.05.012

Anderson, R. J., Biham, E., & Knudsen, L. R. (2000). *Serpent: A Proposal for the Advanced Encryption Standard*. Retrieved from https://www.cl.cam.ac.uk/~rja14/Papers/serpent.pdf

Arrowhead. (2018). *Arrowhead Framework*. Retrieved from https://forge.soa4d.org/plugins/mediawiki/wiki/arrowhead-f/index.php/Main_Page

Ashton, K. (2009). That “Internet of Things” Thing. *RFID Journal*. Retrieved from: http://www.rfidjournal.com/articles/view?4986

Ashton, K. (2009). That ‘Internet of Things’ Thing. *RFID Journal*. Retrieved June 22, 2009, from http://www.rfidjournal.com/articles/view?4986

Atzori, L., Iera, A., & Morabito, G. (2011). SIoT: Giving a social structure to the internet of things. *IEEE Communications Letters*, *15*(11), 1193–1195.

Atzori, L., Lera, A., & Morabito, G. (2010). Internet of Things: A Survey. *Computer Networks*, *54*(15), 2787–2805. doi:10.1016/j.comnet.2010.05.010

Aumasson, J. P., Henzen, L., Meier, W., & Naya-Plasencia, M. (2013). Quark: A Lightweight Hash. *Journal of Cryptology*, *26*(2), 313–339.

Awad, W. S. (Ed.). (2015). Improving Information Security Practices through Computational Intelligence. IGI Global.

Aysu, A., Gulcan, E., Moriyama, D., Schaumont, P., & Yung, M. (2015). End-To-End Design of a PUF-Based Privacy Preserving Authentication Protocol. In T. Güneysu & H. Handschuh (Eds.), *Cryptographic Hardware and Embedded Systems -- CHES 2015: 17th International Workshop, Saint-Malo, France, September 13-16, 2015, Proceedings* (pp. 556-576). Berlin: Springer Berlin Heidelberg. 10.1007/978-3-662-48324-4_28

Aysu, A., & Schaumont, P. (2016). Precomputation methods for hash-based signatures on energy-harvesting platforms. *IEEE Transactions on Computers*, *65*(9), 2925–2931. doi:10.1109/TC.2015.2500570

Azer, M., & El-Kassas, S. (2010). An innovative approach for the wormhole attack detection and prevention in wireless ad hoc networks. *Networking, Sensing and*. Retrieved from http://ieeexplore.ieee.org/abstract/document/5461523/

Babar, S., Mahalle, P., Stango, A., Prasad, N., & Prasad, R. (2010). Proposed security model and threat taxonomy for the Internet of Things (IoT). *International Conference on Network Security and Applications*, 89, 420–429.

Babbage, S., & Dodd, M. (2008). The MICKEY Stream Ciphers: 'New Stream Cipher Designs - The eSTREAM Finalists'. *LNCS*, *4986*, 191–209.

Balanis, C. A. (2005). *Antenna theory: Analysis and design*. New York: John Wiley and Sons Inc.

Baldauf, M., Dustdar, S., & Rosenberg, F. (2007). A survey on context-aware systems. *International Journal of Ad Hoc and Ubiquitous Computing*, *2*(4), 263. doi:10.1504/IJAHUC.2007.014070

Bard, G. V., Courtois, N. T., Nakahara, J., Sepehrdad, P., & Zhang, B. (2010, December). Algebraic, AIDA/cube and side channel analysis of KATAN family of block ciphers. In *International Conference on Cryptology in India* (pp. 176-196). Springer. 10.1007/978-3-642-17401-8_14

Bari, A. (2005). Relay Nodes in Wireless Sensor Networks: A Survey. University of Windsor.

Barkhuus, L., & Dey, A. K. (2003). Is Context-Aware Computing Taking Control away from the User? Three Levels of Interactivity Examined. In Ubicomp 2003: Ubiquitous Computing (Vol. 2864, pp. 149–156). Springer Berlin Heidelberg. Retrieved from doi:10.1007/978-3-540-39653-6_12

Bassi, A. (2013). Enabling things to talk – designing IoT solutions with the IoT architectural reference model. Springer.

Batina, L., Guajardo, J., Preneel, B., Tuyls, P., & Verbauwhede, I. (2008). Public-Key Cryptography for RFID Tags and Applications. In P. Kitsos & Y. Zhang (Eds.), *RFID Security: Techniques, Protocols and System-on-Chip Design* (pp. 317–348). Boston, MA: Springer US. doi:10.1007/978-0-387-76481-8_13

Bauer, K., McCoy, D., Anderson, E., Breitenbach, M., Grudic, G., Grunwald, D., & Sicker, D. (2009). The directional attack on wireless localization-or-How to spoof your location with a tin can. In *Proceedings of Global Telecommunications Conference* (pp. 1-6). Honolulu, HI: IEEE. 10.1109/GLOCOM.2009.5425737

Beaulieu, R., Shors, D., Smith, J., Treatman-Clark, S., Weeks, B., & Wingers, L. (2013). *The SIMON and SPECK Families of Lightweight Block Ciphers*. IACR Cryptology ePrint Archive.

Beaulieu, R., Treatman-Clark, S., Shors, D., Weeks, B., Smith, J., & Wingers, L. (2015, June). The SIMON and SPECK lightweight block ciphers. In *Design Automation Conference (DAC), 2015 52nd ACM/EDAC/IEEE* (pp. 1-6). IEEE. 10.1145/2744769.2747946

Bellare, M., & Rogaway, P. (1993). Random oracles are practical: A paradigm for designing efficient protocols. *Proceedings of the 1st ACM Conference on Computer and Communications Security*, 62-73.

Bellare, M., & Goldreich, O. (1993). *On defining proofs of knowledge. In Advances in Cryptology CRYPTO92* (pp. 390–420). Springer.

Bettini, C., Brdiczka, O., Henricksen, K., Indulska, J., Nicklas, D., Ranganathan, A., & Riboni, D. (2010). A survey of context modelling and reasoning techniques. *Pervasive and Mobile Computing, 6*(2), 161–180. doi:10.1016/j.pmcj.2009.06.002

Bettini, C., Wang, X. S., & Jojodia, S. (2005). Protecting privacy against location-based personal identification. In *Proceedings of the Second VDLB International Conference on Secure Data Management* (vol. 1, pp. 185-199). Trondheim, Norway: Springer. 10.1007/11552338_13

Beverly, R., Garfinkel, S., & Cardwell, G. (2010). Forensic carving of network packets and associated data structures. *Digital Investigation, 8*, S78-S89.

Bhargava, M., & Mai, K. (2013). A high reliability PUF using hot carrier injection based response reinforcement. *Proc. 15th Int'l Workshop Cryptographic Hardware and Embedded Systems (CHES 13)*, 90–106. 10.1007/978-3-642-40349-1_6

Bhargava, M., & Mai, K. (2014). An efficient reliable PUF-based cryptographic key generator in 65 nm CMOS. *Design Autom. Test Europe Conf. Exhibition, 1*, 1–6.

Biswas, R. N., Mitra, S. K. & Naskar, M. K. (2014). A robust mobile anchor based localization technique for wireless sensor networks using smart antenna. *International Journal of Ad-Hoc and Ubiquitous Computing, 15*(1/2/3), 23-37.

Bloch, M., & Barros, J. (2011). *Physical-layer security: From information theory to security engineering*. New York: Cambridge University Press. doi:10.1017/CBO9780511977985

Bloom, B. H. (1970). Space/time trade-offs in hash coding with allowable error. *Communications of the ACM, 13*(7), 422–426. doi:10.1145/362686.362692

Bogdanov, A., Knežević, M., Leander, G., Toz, D., Varıcı, K., & Verbauwhede, I. SPONGENT: A Lightweight Hash Function. *Proc. 13th International Workshop on Cryptographic Hardware and Embedded Systems (CHES 2011)*, 312-325.

Bogdanov, A., Knudsen, L. R., Leander, G., Paar, C., Poschmann, A., Robshaw, M. J. B., ... Vikkelsoe, C. (2007). PRESENT: An Ultra-Lightweight Block Cipher. *Proc. 9th International Workshop on Cryptographic Hardware and Embedded Systems (CHES 2007)*, 450-466.

Bohm, C., & Hofer, M. (2013). *Physical Unclonable Functions in Theory and Practice: Springer.* Chakraborty. doi:10.1007/978-1-4614-5040-5

Boneh, D. (1998). *The decision diffie-hellman problem. In Algorithmic number theory* (pp. 48–63). Springer.

Bonomi, F., Milito, R., Natarajan, P., & Zhu, J. (2014). *Fog computing: a platform for internet of things and analytics. In Big Data and Internet of Things: A Road Map for Smart Environments* (pp. 169–186). Berlin, Germany: Springer.

Bonomi, F., Milito, R., Zhu, J., & Addepalli, S. (2012). Fog computing and its role in the internet of things. *Proceedings of the 1st ACM MCC Workshop on Mobile Cloud Computing*, 13–16.

Bouchaud, F., Grimaud, G., & Vantroys, T. (2018). IoT Forensic: identification and classification of evidence in criminal investigations. *Proceedings of the 13th International Conference on Availability, Reliability and Security - ARES 2018*. 10.1145/3230833.3233257

Boukerche, A., Oliveira, H. A. B. F., Nakamura, E. F., & Loureiro, A. A. F. (2008). Secure localization algorithms for wireless sensor networks. *IEEE Communications Magazine*, *46*(4), 96–101. doi:10.1109/MCOM.2008.4481347

Brady, O., Overill, R., & Keppens, J. (2015). DESO: Addressing volume and variety in large-scale criminal cases. *Digital Investigation*, *15*, 72–82. doi:10.1016/j.diin.2015.10.002

Brandt, F. (2006). *Efficient cryptographic protocol design based on distributed elgamal encryption. In Information Security and Cryptology-ICISC 2005* (pp. 32–47). Springer. doi:10.1007/11734727_5

Breivold, H. P. (2017). A Survey and Analysis of Reference Architectures for the Internet-of-things. *ICSEA 2017: The Twelfth International Conference on Software Engineering Advances*.

Brier, E., Clavier, C., & Olivier, F. (2004). Correlation power analysis with a leakage model. *Cryptographic Hardware and Embedded Systems*, 16–29.

BuildItSecure. Ly. (2018). *BuildItSecure.Ly*. Retrieved from http://builditsecure.ly

Camenisch, J., & Shoup, V. (2003). Practical verifiable encryption and decryption of discrete logarithms. *Annual International Cryptology Conference*, 126-144. 10.1007/978-3-540-45146-4_8

Camenisch, J., & Stadler, M. (1997). *Efficient group signature schemes for large groups. In Advances in Cryptology CRYPTO'97* (pp. 410–424). Springer. doi:10.1007/BFb0052252

Camenisch, J., & Zaverucha, G. (2009). Private intersection of certified sets. *International Conference on Financial Cryptography and Data Security*, 108-127. 10.1007/978-3-642-03549-4_7

Cao, X., Kou, W., & Du, X. (2010). A pairing-free identity-based authenticated key agreement protocol with minimal message exchanges. *Information Sciences*. Retrieved from http://www.sciencedirect.com/science/article/pii/S0020025510001519

Carrier, B. & Spafford, E. H. (2003). Getting Physical with the Investigative Process. *International Journal of Digital Evidence*, *2*(2).

Chandra, B. T., Verma, P., & Dwivedi, A. K. (2016). Operating systems for internet of things: A comparative study. *Proceedings of the Second International Conference on Information and Communication Technology for Competitive Strategies*.

Chandramouli, R., Bapatla, S., Subbalakshmi, K. P., & Uma, R. N. (2006). Battery power-aware encryption. *ACM Transactions on Information and System Security*, *9*(2), 162–180. doi:10.1145/1151414.1151417

Chantzara, M., & Anagnostou, M. (2005). Evaluation and Selection of Context Information. *Second International Workshop on Modeling and Retrieval of Context*. Retrieved from http://ceur-ws.org/Vol-146/paper7.pdf

Chatterjee, U., Chakraborty, R. S., & Mukhopadhyay, D. (2017). A PUF-Based Secure Communication Protocol for IoT. *ACM Transactions on Embedded Computing Systems*, *16*(3), 1–25. doi:10.1145/3005715

Chauhan, A., Patle, A., & Mahajan, A. (2011). A Better Approach towards Securing Mobile Adhoc Network. *International Journal of Computer*. Retrieved from http://citeseerx.ist.psu.edu/viewdoc/download?doi=10.1.1.206.2993&rep=rep1&type=pdf

Checkpoint. (2017). *A New IoT Botnet Storm is Coming*. Retrieved from https://research.checkpoint.com/new-iot-botnet-storm-coming

Cheng, P., Chuah, C. & Liu, X. (2004). Energy-aware Node Placement in Wireless Sensor Networks. *IEEE Communications Society, Globecom 2004*.

Cheng, X., Du, D. Z., Wang. L. & Xu, B. (2001). Relay Sensor Placement in Wireless Sensor Networks. *IEEE Transactions on Computers*.

Chen, H., Finin, T., Joshi, A., Kagal, L., Perich, F., & Chakraborty, D. (2004). Intelligent agents meet the semantic Web in smart spaces. *IEEE Internet Computing*, *8*(6), 69–79. doi:10.1109/MIC.2004.66

Chen, H., & Wang, X. (2016, March). Improved linear hull attack on round-reduced Simon with dynamic key-guessing techniques. In *International Conference on Fast Software Encryption* (pp. 428-449). Springer. 10.1007/978-3-662-52993-5_22

Chen, Y., Kleisouris, K., Li, X., Trappe, W., & Martin, R. P. (2006). The robustness of localization algorithms to signal strength attacks: A comparative study. In *Proceedings of International Conference on Distributed Computing in Sensor Systems* (vol. 1, pp. 546-563). San Francisco, CA: Springer. 10.1007/11776178_33

Chen, Y., Yang, J., Trappe, W., & Martin, R. P. (2010). Detecting and localizing identity-based attacks in wireless and sensor networks. *IEEE Transactions on Vehicular Technology*, *59*(5), 2418–2434. doi:10.1109/TVT.2010.2044904

Chen, Y., Zhou, J., & Guo, M. (2016). A context-aware search system for Internet of Things based on hierarchical context model. *Telecommunication Systems*, *62*(1), 77–91. doi:10.100711235-015-9984-x

CISCO. (2014). *Internet-of-everything Reference Model*. CISCO. Retrieved from http://cdn.iotwf.com/resources/71/IoT_Reference_Model_White_Paper_June_4_2014.pdf on Nov 23, 2018.

Clerc, M., & Kennedy, J. (2002). The particle swarm: Explosion, stability, and convergence in a multidimensional complex space. *IEEE Transactions on Evolutionary Computation*, *6*(1), 58–73. doi:10.1109/4235.985692

CNET. (2018). *IoT attacks are getting worse -- and no one's listening.* CNET. Retrieved from https://www.cnet.com/news/iot-attacks-hacker-kaspersky-are-getting-worse-and-no-one-is-listening on Nov 23, 2018.

CNN. (2017). *FDA confirms that St. Jude's cardiac devices can be hacked.* Retrieved from https://money.cnn.com/2017/01/09/technology/fda-st-jude-cardiac-hack/

Collard, B., Standaert, F.-X., Wheeler, D. J., & Needham, J. (1995). *A Tiny Encryption Algorithm.* Cambridge University.

Conti, M., Dehghantanha, A., Franke, K., & Watson, S. (2018). Internet of Things security and forensics: Challenges and opportunities. *Future Generation Computer Systems, 78*, 544–546. doi:10.1016/j.future.2017.07.060

Copos, B., Levitt, K., Bishop, M., & Rowe, J. (2016). *Is Anybody Home? Inferring Activity From Smart Home Network Traffic. In 2016 IEEE Security and Privacy Workshops.* SPW. doi:10.1109pw.2016.48

Cramer, R., & Shoup, V. (1998). *A practical public key cryptosystem provably secure against adaptive chosen ciphertext attack. In Advances in Cryptology CRYPTO'98* (pp. 13–25). Springer.

Cranor, L.F. (2012). Necessary but not sufficient: standardized mechanisms for privacy and choice. *Journal on Telecom & High-Tech law*, 273.

Daemen, J. (1995). *Cipher and hash function design strategies based on linear and differential cryptanalysis* (Doctoral Dissertation). K. U. Leuven.

Daemen, J., Peeters, M., Assche, G. V. & Rijmen, V. (2000). The Noekeon block cipher. *The NESSIE Proposal.*

Damshenas, M., Dehghantanha, A., & Mahmoud, R. (2014). A Survey on Digital Forensics Trends. *International Journal of Cyber-Security and Digital Forensics, 3*(4), 209–234.

Dasgupta, K., Kukreja, M., & Kalpakis, K. (2003). Topology-Aware Placement and Role Assignment for Energy-Efficient Information Gathering in Sensor Networks. *Proceedings of the Eighth IEEE International Symposium on Computers and Communication (ISCC'03).* 10.1109/ISCC.2003.1214143

Data sheet for Crossbow MICAz mote. (n.d.). Retrieved on August 14, 2018, from http://edge.rit.edu/edge/P08208/public/Controls_Files/MICaZ-DataSheet.pdf

David, L., Becker, B. A., O'Sullivan, T., & Scanlon, M. (2016). Current Challenges and Future Research Areas for Digital Forensic Investigation. *Annual ADFSL Conference on Digital Forensics, Security and Law, 6.* Retrieved from https://commons.erau.edu/adfsl/2016/tuesday/6

De Canniere, C., Dunkelman, O., & Knežević, M. (2009). KATAN and KTANTAN—a family of small and efficient hardware-oriented block ciphers. In *Cryptographic Hardware and Embedded Systems-CHES 2009* (pp. 272–288). Berlin: Springer. doi:10.1007/978-3-642-04138-9_20

De Cannière, C., & Preneel, B. (2008). Trivium: 'New Stream Cipher Designs - The eSTREAM Finalists'. *LNCS*, *4986*, 244–266.

De Cristofaro, E., Gasti, P., & Tsudik, G. (2012). *Fast and private computation of cardinality of set intersection and union. In Cryptology and Network Security* (pp. 218–231). Springer.

Debnath, S. K. & Dutta, R. (2016). Fair mpsi and mpsi-ca: Efficient constructions in prime order groups with security in the standard model against malicious adversary. *IACR Cryptology ePrint Archive*.

Debnath, S. K., & Dutta, R. (2015). Efficient private set intersection cardinality in the presence of malicious adversaries. *International Conference on Provable Security*, 326–339. 10.1007/978-3-319-26059-4_18

Degnan, B., & Durgin, G. D. (2017). *Simontool: Simulation support for the Simon Cipher*. IEEE J. RFID.

Delvaux, J., & Verbauwhede, I. (2013). Side channel modeling attacks on 65nm arbiter PUFs exploiting CMOS device noise. In IEEE International Symposium on Hardware-Oriented Security and Trust. HOST. http://ieeexplore.ieee.org/document/6581579/

Delvaux, J., & Verbauwhede, I. (2014). Fault Injection Modeling Attacks on 65nm Arbiter and RO Sum PUFs via Environmental Changes. *IEEE Transactions on Circuits and Systems*, *61*(6), 13.

Deogirikar, J. (2017). Security Attacks in IoT: A Survey. *International conference on I-SMAC*, 32–37.

Dey, A. K., & Abowd, G. (1999). Towards a Better Understanding of Context and Context-Awareness. In *Handheld and Ubiquitous Computing* (pp. 304–307). Springer Berlin Heidelberg. doi:10.1007/3-540-48157-5_29

DFRWS. (2001). A Road Map for Digital Forensic Research. *Proceedings of The Digital Forensic Research Conference DFRWS 2001*.

Dhillon, S. S., & Chakrabarty, K. (2003). Sensor Placement for Effective Coverage and Surveillance in Distributed Sensor Networks. IEEE.

Dinur, I. (2014, August). Improved differential cryptanalysis of round-reduced speck. In *International Workshop on Selected Areas in Cryptography* (pp. 147-164). Springer.

Dong, C., Chen, L., Camenisch, J., & Russello, G. (2013a). *Fair private set intersection with a semi-trusted arbiter, Data and Applications Security and Privacy*. Springer.

Dong, C., Chen, L., & Wen, Z. (2013b). When private set intersection meets big data: An efficient and scalable protocol. *Proceedings of the 2013 ACM SIGSAC conference on Computer & communications security*, 789–800. 10.1145/2508859.2516701

Dong, C., & Loukides, G. (2017). Approximating private set union/intersection cardinality with logarithmic complexity. *IEEE Transactions on Information Forensics and Security, 12*(11), 2792–2806. doi:10.1109/TIFS.2017.2721360

Dorri, A., Kamel, S. R., & Kheirkhah, E. (2015). *Security challenges in mobile ad hoc networks: a survey*. doi:10.5121/ijcses.2015.6102

Dorri, A., Kanhere, S. S., Jurdak, R., & Gauravaram, P. (2017). Blockchain for IoT security and privacy: the case study of a smart home. *2017 IEEE International Conference on Pervasive Computing and Communications Workshops (PerCom Workshops)*, 618-623.

Dorsemaine, B., Gaulier, J. P., Wary, J. P., Kheir, N., & Urien, P. (2016). A new approach to investigate IoT threats based on a four layer model. *IEEE Transactions on Emerging Topics in Computing*.

Dragomir, D., Gheorghe, L., Costeal, S., & Radovici, A. (2016). A survey on secure communication protocols for IoT systems. *International Workshop on Secure Internet of Things*, 47-62. 10.1109/SIoT.2016.012

Du, P., Putra, P., Yamamoto, S., & Nakao, A. (2016). A context-aware IoT architecture through software-defined data plane. In *Proceedings - 2016 IEEE Region 10 Symposium, TENSYMP 2016* (pp. 315–320). IEEE. 10.1109/TENCONSpring.2016.7519425

Du, X., Le-Khac, N., & Scanlon, M. (2017). Evaluation of Digital Forensic Process Models with Respect to Digital Forensics as a Service. *16th European Conference on Cyber Warfare and Security (ECCWS 2017)*.

Dyn. (2016). *Dyn Status Update*. Retrieved from https://www.dynstatus.com/incidents/nlr4yrr162t8

Ejigu, D., Scuturici, M., & Brunie, L. (2007). An ontology-based approach to context modeling and reasoning in pervasive computing. In *Proceedings - Fifth Annual IEEE International Conference on Pervasive Computing and Communications Workshops, PerCom Workshops 2007* (pp. 14–19). IEEE. 10.1109/PERCOMW.2007.22

El-badry, R., Sultan, A., & Youssef, M. (2010). HyberLoc: Providing physical layer location privacy in hybrid sensor networks. In *Proceedings of International Conference on Communications* (pp. 1-5). Cape Town, South Africa: IEEE. 10.1109/ICC.2010.5502104

Engels, D., Fan, X., Gong, G., Hu, H., & Smith, E. M. (2010). Hummingbird: Ultra-Lightweight Cryptography for Resource-Constrained Devices. In FC 2010 Workshops, LNCS 6054, (pp. 3–18). IFCA/Springer-Verlag Berlin Heidelberg.

Ergen, S. C. & Varaiya, P. (2006). Optimal Placement of Relay Nodes for Energy Efficiency in Sensor Networks. *IEEE ICC*.

Fang, S., Xu, L. I., Zhu, Y., Ahati, J., Pei, H., Yan, J., & Liu, Z. (2014). An integrated system for regional environmental monitoring and management based on Internet of things. *IEEE Transactions on Industrial Informatics, 10*(2), 1596–1605. doi:10.1109/TII.2014.2302638

Farooq, H. & Jung, L. T. (2013). Energy, Traffic Load, and Link Quality Aware Ad Hoc Routing Protocol for Wireless Sensor Network, Based Smart Metering Infrastructure. *International Journal of Distributed Sensor Networks.*

FBI. (2015). *Internet of Things Poses Opportunities for Cyber Crime.* FBI, Alert Number: I-091015-PSA. Retrieved from https://www.ic3.gov/media/2015/150910.aspx

Ferdous, R., & Muthukkumarasamy, V. (2010). A node-based trust management scheme for mobile ad-hoc networks. *Network and System.* Retrieved from http://ieeexplore.ieee.org/abstract/document/5635570/

Ferscha, A., Vogl, S., & Beer, W. (2005). Context Sensing, Aggregation, Representation and Exploitation in Wireless Networks. *Scalable Computing: Practice and Experience, 6*(2), 71–81. Retrieved from http://scpe.org/index.php/scpe/article/view/327

FIPS. (1999). *FIPS Publication 46-3. Data Encryption Standard (DES).* U. S. Department of Commerce / National Institute of Standards and Technology. *Reaffirmed, 1999.*

FIT. (2018). IoT experimentation at a larger scale. *FIT IoT Lab.* Retrieved from https://www.iot-lab.info/

Flajolet, P., & Martin, G. N. (1985). Probabilistic counting algorithms for data base Applications. *Journal of Computer and System Sciences, 31*(2), 182–209. doi:10.1016/0022-0000(85)90041-8

Forrester. (2017). *Internet of Things Security Report.* Author.

Forrester. (2018). *Predictions 2019: The Internet of Things.* Retrieved from https://www.forrester.com

Fraden, J. (2010). *Handbook of Modern Sensors: Physics, Design and Applications* (4th ed.). Springer.

Freedman, M. J., Hazay, C., Nissim, K., & Pinkas, B. (2016). Efficient set intersection with simulation-based security. *Journal of Cryptology, 29*(1), 115–155. doi:10.100700145-014-9190-0

Freedman, M. J., Nissim, K., & Pinkas, B. (2004). *Efficient private matching and set intersection. In Advances in Cryptology-EUROCRYPT 2004* (pp. 1–19). Springer.

Fremantle, P. (2015). *A reference architecture for the Internet of things.* WSO2 white paper, version 0.9.0, 2015.

Frikken, K. B., Blanton, M., & Atallah, M. J. (2009). Robust Authentication Using Physically Unclonable Functions. *Proceedings of the 12th International Conference on Information Security.*

FTC Report. (2012). Protecting consumer privacy in an era of rapid change: recommendations for business and policymakers. *Federal Trade Commission.* Retrieved from https://www.ftc.gov/sites/default/files/documents/reports/federal-trade-commission-report-protecting-consumer-privacy-era-rapid-change-recommendations/120326privacyreport.pdf

Fuhr, T., & Minaud, B. (2014, March). Match box meet-in-the-middle attack against KATAN. In *International Workshop on Fast Software Encryption* (pp. 61-81). Springer.

Furukawa, J. (2005). Efficient and verifiable shuffling and shuffle-decryption. *IEICE Transactions on Fundamentals of Electronics, Communications and Computer Science*, *88*(1), 172–188. doi:10.1093/ietfec/E88-A.1.172

Gartner. (2015). *Gartner Says 6.4 Billion Connected "Things" Will Be in Use in 2016, Up 30 Percent From 2015* [Press release]. Retrieved from http://www.gartner.com/newsroom/id/3165317

Gassend, B., Clarke, D., Dijk, M. v., & Devadas, S. (2002). Silicon physical random functions. *Proceedings of the 9th ACM conference on Computer and communications security*.

Gaur, P., & Mohit, P. T. (2015). Operating systems for IoT devices: A critical survey. In *Region 10 Symposium (TENSYMP)*. IEEE.

Gezici, S. (2008). A survey on wireless position estimation. *Wireless Personal Communications*, *44*(3), 263–282. doi:10.100711277-007-9375-z

Gil, D., Ferrández, A., Mora-Mora, H., & Peral, J. (2016). Internet of things: A review of surveys based on context aware intelligent services. *Sensors (Switzerland)*, *16*(7), 1069. doi:10.339016071069 PMID:27409623

Gill, A. Q., Phennel, N., Lane, D., & Phung, V. L. (2016). IoT-enabled emergency information supply chain architecture for elderly people: The Australian context. *Information Systems*, *58*, 75–86. doi:10.1016/j.is.2016.02.004

Godara, L. C. (1997). Application of antenna arrays to mobile communications, part II: Beam-forming and direction-of-arrival considerations. *Proceedings of the IEEE*, *85*(8), 1195–1245. doi:10.1109/5.622504

Godara, L. C. (2004). *Smart antennas*. Boca Raton, FL: CRC Press LLC. doi:10.1201/9780203496770

Goldreich, O. (2009). Foundations of cryptography: Volume 2, basic applications. Cambridge University Press.

Goldwasser, S., & Micali, S. (1984). Probabilistic encryption. *Journal of Computer and System Sciences*, *28*(2), 270–299. doi:10.1016/0022-0000(84)90070-9

Granjal, J., Monteiro, E., & Sá Silva, J. (2015). Security for the Internet of Things: A Survey of Existing Protocols and Open Research Issues. *IEEE Communications Surveys and Tutorials*, *17*(3), 2015.

Grau, A. (2015). Can you trust your fridge? *IEEE Spectrum*, *52*(3), 7. doi:10.1109/MSPEC.2015.7049440

Greenberg, A. (2015). *Hackers Remotely Kill a Jeep on the Highway—With Me in It*. Retrieved from https://www.wired.com/2015/07/hackers-remotely-kill-jeep-highway/

Gross, F. B. (2005). *Smart antennas for wireless communications*. New York: McGraw-Hill Companies, Inc.

Guan, D., Yuan, W., Lee, S., & Lee, Y. K. (2007). Context selection and reasoning in ubiquitous computing. In *Proceedings The 2007 International Conference on Intelligent Pervasive Computing, IPC 2007* (pp. 184–187). Academic Press. 10.1109/IPC.2007.102

Gubbi, J., Buyya, R., Marusic, S., & Palaniswami, M. (2013). Internet of Things (IoT): A vision, architectural elements, and future directions. *Future Generation Computer Systems*, *29*(7), 1645–1660. doi:10.1016/j.future.2013.01.010

Guo, J., & Chen, I. R. (2015). A Classification of Trust Computation Models for Service-Oriented Internet of Things Systems. *Proceedings - 2015 IEEE International Conference on Services Computing, SCC 2015*, 324–331.

Guo, J., Peyrin, T., & Poschmann, A. (2011). The PHOTON Family of Lightweight Hash Functions. *Proc. 31st Annual International Cryptology Conference (CRYPTO 2011)*, 222-239.

Guo, J., Thomas, P., Axel, P., & Matt, R. (2011). The led block cipher. *Proceedings of the 13th International Conference on Cryptographic Hardware and Embedded Systems, CHES'11* (pp 326-341). Springer.

Gupta, A., Kumar, R., & Gupta, N. (2014). A trust based secure gateway selection and authentication scheme in MANET. *Contemporary Computing and*. Retrieved from http://ieeexplore.ieee.org/abstract/document/7019816/

Gupta, G., & Younis, M. (2003). Performance Evaluation of Load Balanced Clustering of Wireless Sensor Networks. IEEE.

Gurkok, C. (2013). Cyber Forensics and Incident Response. *Computer and Information Security Handbook*, 601–621. doi:. doi:10.1016/b978-0-12-394397-2.00034-9

Halder, S., & Ghosal, A. (2016). A survey on mobile anchor assisted localization techniques in wireless sensor networks. *Wireless Networks*, *22*(7), 2317–2336. doi:10.100711276-015-1101-2

Hall, M., Frank, E., Holmes, G., Pfahringer, B., Reutemann, P., & Witten, I. H. (2009). The WEKA data mining software. *SIGKDD Explorations Newsletter*, *11*(1), 10. doi:10.1145/1656274.1656278

Hamlet, J. R., Bauer, T. M., & Pierson, L. G. (2014). *Deterrence of device counterfeiting, cloning, and subversion by substitution using hardware fingerprinting*. US patent 8,848,905, Sandia Corporation.

Hammouri, G., & Sunar, B. (2008). PUF-HB: A Tamper-Resilient HB Based Authentication Protocol. In S. M. Bellovin, R. Gennaro, A. Keromytis, & M. Yung (Eds.), *Applied Cryptography and Network Security: 6th International Conference, ACNS 2008, New York, NY, USA, June 3-6, 2008. Proceedings* (pp. 346-365). Berlin: Springer Berlin Heidelberg. 10.1007/978-3-540-68914-0_21

Hankel, M., & Rexroth, B. (2015). *Industrie 4.0: The Reference Architectural Model Industrie 4.0 (RAMI 4.0)*. ZVEI - German Electrical and Electronic Manufacturers' Association. Retrieved from https://www.zvei.org

Harbawi, M., & Varol, A. (2017). An Improved Digital Evidence Acquisition Model for the Internet of Things Forensic I: A Theoretical Framework. *2017 5th International Symposium on Digital Forensic and Security (ISDFS)*. 10.1109/ISDFS.2017.7916508

Hargreaves, C., & Patterson, J. (2012). An automated timeline reconstruction approach for digital forensic investigations. *Digital Investigation*, *9*, S69–S79. doi:10.1016/j.diin.2012.05.006

HealthData. (2016). Medical devices pose weak link in preventing cyber-attacks. *Health Data Management*. Retrieved from https://www.healthdatamanagement.com/news/medical-devices-pose-weak-link-in-preventing-cyber-attacks?issue=00000158-7951-dff3-a1db-fb7b29000000

Hegarty, R., Lamb, D. J., & Attwood, A. (2014). Digital Evidence Challenges in the Internet of Things. *Proceedings of the Ninth International Workshop on Digital Forensics and Incident Analysis*. Retrieved from https://www.cscan.org/openaccess/?id=231

Helfmeier, C., Boit, C., Nedospasov, D., & Seifert, J. P. (2013). Cloning Physically Unclonable Functions. *IEEE Int'l Symp. Hardware-Oriented Security and Trust (HOST 13)*, 1–6.

Helinski, R., Acharyya, D., & Plusquellic, J. (2009). A physical unclonable function defined using power distribution system equivalent resistance variations. *ACM/IEEE Design Automation Conference*, 676–681. 10.1145/1629911.1630089

Henricksen, K. (2003). *A framework for context-aware pervasive computing applications*. The School of Information Technology and Electrical Engineering, The University of Queensland. Retrieved from http://henricksen.id.au/publications/phd-thesis.pdf

Henricksen, K., & Indulska, J. (2004). Modelling and using imperfect context information. In *Proceedings - Second IEEE Annual Conference on Pervasive Computing and Communications, Workshops, PerCom* (pp. 33–37). IEEE. 10.1109/PERCOMW.2004.1276901

Henry, P., Williams, J., & Wright, B. (2013). The SANS Survey of Digital Forensics and Incident Response. In Tech Rep.

Hirose, S., Ideguchi, K., Kuwakado, H., Owada, T., Preneel, B., & Yoshida, H. (2010). A Lightweight 256-Bit Hash Function for Hardware and Low-End Devices: Lesamnta-LW. *Proc. 13th International Conference on Information Security and Cryptology (ICISC 2010)*, 151-168.

Hohenberger, S., & Weis, S. A. (2006). *Honest-verifier private disjointness testing without random oracles. In Privacy Enhancing Technologies* (pp. 277–294). Springer.

Holdowsky, J., Mahto, M., Raynor, M. E., & Cotteleer, M. (2015). Inside the Internet of Things (IoT): A primer on the technologies building the IoT. *Deloitte Insights*. Retrieved from http://dupress.com/articles/iot-primer-iot-technologies-applications

Hong, D., Sung, J., Hong, S., Lim, J., Lee, S., Koo, B., ... Chee, S. (2006). HIGHT: A new block cipher suitable for low-resource device. In L. Goubin & M. Matsui (Eds.), *Cryptographic Hardware and Embedded Systems – CHES 2006, Vol. LNCS 4249* (pp. 46–59). Springer. doi:10.1007/11894063_4

HP. (2014). *Internet of Things Research Study.* Retrieved from https://www.intel.com/content/www/us/en/internet-of-things/infographics/guide-to-iot.html

Huang, L., Matsuura, K., Yamane, H., & Sezaki, K. (2005). Enhancing wireless location privacy using silent period. In *Proceedings of Wireless Communications and Networking Conference* (vol. 2, pp. 1187–1192). New Orleans, LA: IEEE.

Hynes, G., Reynolds, V., & Hauswirth, M. (2009). A context lifecycle for web-based context management services. In Lecture Notes in Computer Science (including subseries Lecture Notes in Artificial Intelligence and Lecture Notes in Bioinformatics) (Vol. 5741, pp. 51–65). Springer Berlin Heidelberg. doi:10.1007/978-3-642-04471-7_5

IIC. (2018). Reference Architecture. *IIC Security Working Group Reference Guide.* Retrieved from http://www. iiconsortium.org/wc-security.htm

Indulska, J., & Sutton, P. (2003). Location management in pervasive systems. In *Proceedings of the Australasian information security workshop conference on ACSW frontiers* (Vol. 34, pp. 143–151). Retrieved from http://dl.acm.org/citation.cfm?id=828003

Infineon. (2018). The right security for the Internet of Things (IoT). *Infineon.* Retrieved from http://www.infineon.com/cms/en/applications/smart-card-and-security/internet-of-things-security

Intel. (2014). The Intel IoT Platform. *Intel Corporation.* Retrieved from https://www.intel.com/content/dam/www/public/us/en/documents/white-papers/iot-platform-reference-architecture-paper.pdf

Internet Live Stats. (2014). *Number of Internet Users (2014) - Internet Live Stats.* Retrieved February 9, 2017, from http://www.Internetlivestats.com/Internet-users/

IoT Architecture Challenges and Issues. Lack of Standardization. (2016). FTC 2016 - Future Technologies Conference 2016.

IoTSC-16001. (2016). *Embedded Hardware Security for IoT Applications.* Retrieved from https://www.securetechalliance.org/downloads/Embedded-HW-Security-for-IoT-WP-FINAL-December-2016.pdf

Isobe, T., Sasaki, Y., & Chen, J. (2013, July). Related-key boomerang attacks on KATAN32/48/64. In *Australasian Conference on Information Security and Privacy* (pp. 268-285). Springer. 10.1007/978-3-642-39059-3_19

Isobe, T., & Shibutani, K. (2012, July). Security analysis of the lightweight block ciphers XTEA, LED and Piccolo. In *Australasian Conference on Information Security and Privacy* (pp. 71-86). Springer. 10.1007/978-3-642-31448-3_6

ITU. (2015, November). *The Internet of Things*. ITU Internet Reports.

Jeyanthi, N. (2016). Internet of things (IoT) as interconnection of threats (IoT). In F. Hu (Ed.), *Security and privacy in internet of things (IoTs): Models, algorithms, and implementations* (pp. 1–19). Boca Raton, FL: Taylor & Francis Group, LLC. doi:10.1201/b19516-3

Jha, A., & Sunil, M. C. (n.d.). Security considerations for Internet of Things. *L&T Technology Services*.

Jia, J., Zhang, G., Wu, X., Chen, J., Wang, X., & Yan, X. (2013). On the Problem of Energy Balanced Relay Sensor Placement in Wireless Sensor Networks. *International Journal of Distributed Sensor Networks*.

Jiang, T., Wang, H. J., & Hu, Y.-C. (2007). Preserving location privacy in wireless LANs. In *Proceedings of the 5th International Conference on Mobile Systems, Applications and Services* (pp. 246-257). San Juan, Puerto Rico: ACM.

Jie, S., & ZhaoHui, W. (2006). Context Reasoning Technologies in Ubiquitous Computing Environment. *Embedded and Ubiquitous Computing. Proceedings*, *4096*, 1027–1036. doi:10.1007/11802167_103

Jing, Q., Vasilakos, A. V., Wan, J., Lu, J., & Qiu, D. (2014). Security of the Internet of Things: Perspectives and challenges. *Wireless Netw. Springer*, *2014*. doi:10.100711276-014-0761-7

Jin, Y., & Makris, Y. (2008). Hardware Trojan detection using path delay fingerprint. *IEEE International Workshop on Hardware-Oriented Security and Trust*.

Juels, A. (2006). RFID security and privacy: A research survey. *IEEE Journal on Selected Areas in Communications*, *24*(2), 14. doi:10.1109/JSAC.2005.861395

Jung, S. W., & Jung, S. (2013). *HRP: A HMAC-based RFID mutual authentication protocol using PUF*. Paper presented at the International Conference on Information Networking. Retrieved from http://ieeexplore.ieee.org/document/6496690/

Jungo, C. (2015). Integrity and trust in the Internet of Things. *Swisscom Ltd*. Retrieved from https://www.swisscom.ch/content/dam/swisscom/en/about/responsibility/digital-switzerland/security/documents/integrity-and-trust-in-the-internet-of-things.pdf.res/integrity-and-trust-in-the-internet-of-things.pdf

Kajaree, D., & Behera, R. (2017). A Survey on IoT Security Threats and Solutions. *International Journal of Innovative Research in Computer and Communication Engineering*, *5*(2), 1302–1309.

Kamienski, C., Jentsch, M., Eisenhauer, M., Kiljander, J., Ferrera, E., & Rosengren, P. ... Sadok, D. (2016). Application development for the Internet of Things: A context-aware mixed criticality systems development platform. *Computer Communications*. doi:10.1016/j.comcom.2016.09.014

Kang, L. (2009). Protecting location privacy in large-scale wireless sensor networks. In *Proceedings of the International Conference on Communications* (pp. 603-608). Dresden, Germany: IEEE. 10.1109/ICC.2009.5199372

Kanuparthi, A., Karri, R., & Addepalli, S. (2013). Hardware and embedded security in the context of internet of things. *Proceedings of the 2013 ACM workshop on Security, privacy & dependability for cyber vehicles.* 10.1145/2517968.2517976

Karakoyunlu, D., & Sunar, B. (2010). Differential template attacks on PUF enabled cryptographic devices. *IEEE Int'l Workshop Information Forensics and Security (WIFS 10)*, 1–6. 10.1109/WIFS.2010.5711445

Kazmierski. C. (2011). *SIA president testifies at Senate Armed Services Committee on dangers of counterfeit chips.* Retrieved from www.semiconductors.org/news/2011/11/08/news_2011/sia_president_testifies_at_senate_armed_services_committee_on_dangers_of_counterfeit_chips

Kebande, V. R., Karie, N. M., & Venter, H. S. (2018). Adding Digital Forensic Readiness as a Security Component to The IoT Domain. *International Journal on Advanced Science. Engineering and Information Technology, 8*, 1–11. doi:10.18517/ijaseit.8.1.2115

Khan, M., Din, S., Jabbar, S., Gohar, M., Ghayvat, H., & Mukhopadhyay, S. C. (2016). Context-aware low power intelligent SmartHome based on the Internet of things. *Computers & Electrical Engineering, 52*, 208–222. doi:10.1016/j.compeleceng.2016.04.014

Kirkpatrick. M. S, & Bertino. E. (2010). Software techniques to combat drift in PUF-based authentication systems. *Secure Component and System Identification (SECSI 10).*

Kissner, L., & Song, D. (2005). *Privacy-preserving set operations. In Advances in Cryptology–CRYPTO 2005* (pp. 241–257). Springer. doi:10.1007/11535218_15

Knappmeyer, M., Kiani, S. L., Frà, C., Moltchanov, B., & Baker, N. (2010). ContextML: A light-weight context representation and context management schema. In *ISWPC 2010 - IEEE 5th International Symposium on Wireless Pervasive Computing 2010* (pp. 367–372). IEEE. 10.1109/ISWPC.2010.5483753

Koblitz, N. (1987). Elliptic curve cryptosystems. *Mathematics of Computation.* Retrieved from http://www.ams.org/mcom/1987-48-177/S0025-5718-1987-0866109-5/

Kocher, P., Ja, J., & Jun, B. (1999). Differential power analysis. *Lecture Notes in Computer Science, 1666*, 388–397. doi:10.1007/3-540-48405-1_25

Kohn, M. D., Eloff, M. M., & Eloff, J. H. P. (2013). Integrated Digital Forensic Process Model. *Computers & Security, 38*, 103–115. doi:10.1016/j.cose.2013.05.001

Kortuem, G., Kawsar, F., Fitton, D., & Sundramoorthy, V. (2010). Smart Objects as Building Blocks for the Internet of Things. *IEEE Computer Society, 10*, 1089–7801. doi:10.1109/MIC.2009.143

Krawczyk, H., Bellare, M., & Canetti, R. (1997). HMAC: Keyed-Hashing for Message Authentication. *IETF RFC.* Retrieved Feb 11, 1997, from https://www.ietf.org/rfc/rfc2104.txt

Kulau, U., Busching, F., & Wolf, L. (2015). Undervolting in WSNs—Theory and practice. *IEEE Internet Things J., 2*(3), 190–198. doi:10.1109/JIOT.2014.2384207

Kumar, J. S., & Patel, D. R. (2014). A Survey on Internet of Things: Security and Privacy Issues. *International Journal of Computers and Applications*, *90*(11), 20–26.

Kumar, R., & Burleson, W. (2014). On design of a highly secure PUF based on non-linear current mirrors. *IEEE Int'l Symp. Hardware-Oriented Security and Trust (HOST 14)*, 38–43. 10.1109/HST.2014.6855565

Kumar, S. S., Guajardo, J., Maes, R., Schrijen, G., & Tuyls, P. (2008). The butterfly PUF protecting IP on every FPGA. *IEEE International Workshop on Hardware-Oriented Security and Trust (HOST)*, 67–70.

Kushwaha, P., Singh, M., & Kumar, P. (2014, June). A Survey on Lightweight Block Ciphers. *International Journal of Computers and Applications*.

Leander, G., Paar, C., Poschmann, A., & Schramm, K. (2007). New lightweight des variants. In *Fast Software Encryption* (pp. 196–210). Springer. doi:10.1007/978-3-540-74619-5_13

Leander, G., Paar, C., Poschmann, A., & Schramm, K. (2007). New Lightweight DES Variants. *Proc. 14th International Workshop on Fast Software Encryption (FSE 2007)*, 196-210.

Lee, J. W., Lim, D., Gassend, B., Suh, G. E., Dijk, M. v., & Devadas, S. (2004). *A Technique to Build a Secret Key in Integrated Circuits for Identification and Authentication Applications*. Academic Press.

Lee, I., & Lee, K. (2015). The Internet of Things (IoT): Applications, investments, and challenges for enterprises. *Business Horizons*, *58*(4), 431–440. doi:10.1016/j.bushor.2015.03.008

Li, Y., & Ren, J. (2010). Source-location privacy through dynamic routing in wireless sensor networks. In *Proceedings of 29th IEEE Conference on Computer Communications* (pp. 1-9). San Diego, CA: IEEE. 10.1109/INFCOM.2010.5462096

Liberti, J. C., & Rappaport, T. S. (1999). *Smart antennas for wireless communications: IS-95 and third generation CDMA applications*. Englewood Cliffs, NJ: Prentice-Hall.

Li, J., & Seok, M. (2015). A 3.07 μm^2/bitcell physically Unclonable function with 3.5% and 1% bit-instability across 0 to 80 _C and 0.6 to 1.2 V in a 65 nm CMOS. *IEEE Symposium on VLSI Circuits, Digest of Technical Papers*, 250–251.

Lin, S., Miller, B., Durand, J., Bleakley, G., Chigani, A., Martin, R., . . . Crawford, M. (2017). *The Industrial Internet of Things Volume G1: Reference Architecture*. Industrial Internet Consortium, white paper.

Lin, C.-F., Chi, K.-H., Hsu, Y.-Y., & Liu, C.-Y. (2017). Mobile anchor-assisted localization over android. *Wireless Networks*, *23*(8), 2379–2394. doi:10.100711276-016-1295-y

Lin, J., Yu, W., Zhang, N., Yang, X., Zhang, H., & Zhao, W. (2017). A Survey on Internet of Things: Architecture, Enabling Technologies, Security and Privacy, and Applications. *IEEE Internet of Things Journal*, *4*(5), 1125–1142. doi:10.1109/JIOT.2017.2683200

Lin, K., Rodrigues, J., Ge, H., Xiong, N., & Liang, X. (2011). Energy efficiency QoS assurance routing in wireless multimedia sensor networks. *IEEE Systems Journal*, *5*(4), 495–505. doi:10.1109/JSYST.2011.2165599

Li, S., Tryfonas, T., & Li, H. (2016). The Internet of Things: A security point of view. *Internet Research*, *26*(2), 337–359.

Liu, X., & Baiocchi, O. (2016). A comparison of the definitions for smart sensors, smart objects and Things in IoT. In *2016 IEEE 7th Annual Information Technology, Electronics and Mobile Communication Conference (IEMCON)* (pp. 1–4). IEEE. 10.1109/IEMCON.2016.7746311

Lloyd, E. L., & Xue, G. (2007). Relay Node Placement in Wireless Sensor Networks. *IEEE Transactions on Computers*, *56*(1), 134–138. doi:10.1109/TC.2007.250629

Lu, C. C., & Tseng, S. Y. (2002). Integrated design of AES (Advanced Encryption Standard) encrypter and decrypter. *Application-Specific Systems, Architectures and Processors, 2002. Proceedings. The IEEE International Conference*, 277-285.

Maes, R. (2012). *Physically unclonable functions: Constructions, properties and applications*. Leuven: Katholieke Universiteit.

Maes, R. (2013). *Physically Unclonable Functions: Construction, properties and applications*. London: Springer. doi:10.1007/978-3-642-41395-7

Mahalle, N., & Railkar, P. N. (2015). *Identity management for Internet of Things*. Rivers Publishers.

Mahmoud, A., Rührmair, U., Majzoobi, M., & Koushanfar, F. (2013). Combined Modeling and Side Channel Attacks on Strong PUFs. *IACR Cryptology ePrint Archive, 2013*, 632.

Maiti, A., McDougall, L., & Schaumont, P. (2011). The impact of aging on an FPGA-based Physical Unclonable Function. *Int'l Conf. Field Programmable Logic and Applications (FPL 11)*, 151–156. 10.1109/FPL.2011.35

Maiti, A., Nagesh, R., Reddy, A., & Schaumont, P. (2009). Physical Unclonable Function and True Random Number Generator: A compact and scalable implementation. *Proc. ACM Great Lakes Symp. VLSI (GLSVLSI 09)*, 425–428. 10.1145/1531542.1531639

Mangard, S., Oswald, E., & Popp, T. (2007). *Power analysis attacks: Revealing the Secrets of smart cards*. New York: Springer.

Manifavas, C., Hatzivasilis, G., Fysarakis, K., & Rantos, K. (2014). Lightweight cryptography for embedded systems–A comparative analysis. In *Data Privacy Management and Autonomous Spontaneous Security* (pp. 333–349). Berlin: Springer. doi:10.1007/978-3-642-54568-9_21

Manoharan, R. (2011). A trust based gateway selection scheme for integration of MANET with Internet. *Recent Trends in*. Retrieved from http://ieeexplore.ieee.org/abstract/document/5972415/

Mantelero, A. (2014). The future of consumer data protection in the E.U. Rethinking the 'notice and consent' paradigm in the new era of predictive analytics. *Computer Law & Security Report*, *30*(6), 643–660. doi:10.1016/j.clsr.2014.09.004

Maple, C. (2017). Security and privacy in the internet of things. *Journal of Cyber Policy*, *2*(2), 155–184. doi:10.1080/23738871.2017.1366536

Martini, B., & Choo, K. R. (2012). An integrated conceptual digital forensic framework for cloud computing. *Digital Investigation*, *9*(2), 71–80. doi:10.1016/j.diin.2012.07.001

Marturana, F., & Tacconi, S. (2013). A Machine Learning-based Triage methodology for automated categorization of digital media. *Digital Investigation, Vol.*, *10*(2), 193–204. doi:10.1016/j.diin.2013.01.001

Mashal, I., Alsaryrah, O., Chung, T.-Y., Yang, C.-Z., Kuo, W.-H., & Agrawal, D. P. (2015). Choices for interaction with things on Internet and underlying issues. *Ad Hoc Networks*, *28*, 68–90.

Mathew. S. K, Satpathy. S. K, Anders. M. A, Kaul. H, Hsu. S. K, Agarwal. A, … De. V. (2014). A 0.19pJ/b PVT-variation- tolerant hybrid physically unclonable function circuit for 100% stable secure key generation in 22 nm CMOS. *Digest Tech. Pap. - IEEE Int. Solid-State Circuits Conf.*, *2*, 278 280.

Mathew, S., Satpathy, S., Suresh, S., Anders, M., Kaul, H., Agarwal, A., ... De, V. (2016). A 4fJ/bit delay-hardened Physically unclonable function circuit with selective bit destabilization in 14 nm trti-gate CMOS. *Symposium on VLSI Circuits*, 248–249.

Matsuda, T., Nakayama, H., Shen, X., & Nemoto, Y. (2010). Gateway selection protocol in hybrid manet using dymo routing. *Mobile Networks and*. Retrieved from http://link.springer.com/article/10.1007/s11036-009-0173-6

Mehta, K., Liu, D., & Wright, M. (2012). Protecting location privacy in sensor networks against a global eavesdropper. *IEEE Transactions on Mobile Computing*, *11*(2), 320–336. doi:10.1109/TMC.2011.32

Mendel, F., Rijmen, V., Toz, D., & Varıcı, K. (2012, December). Differential analysis of the LED block cipher. In *International Conference on the Theory and Application of Cryptology and Information Security* (pp. 190-207). Springer. 10.1007/978-3-642-34961-4_13

Meyerowitz, J., & Roy Choudhury, R. (2009). Hiding stars with fireworks: location privacy through camouflage. In *Proceedings of the 15th Annual International Conference on Mobile Computing and Networking* (pp. 345–356). Beijing, China: ACM. 10.1145/1614320.1614358

Micro, T. (2018). Threats to Voice-Based IoT and IIoT Devices. *Trend Micro*. Retrieved from https://www.trendmicro.com/vinfo/us/security/news/internet-of-things/threats-to-voice-based-iot-and-iiot-devices

Microsoft. (2018). *Microsoft Azure IoT Reference Architecture*. Microsoft Corporation. Retrieved from https://aka.ms/iotrefarchitecture

Miller, V. (1998). Use of elliptic curves in cryptography. *Exploratory Computer Science*. Retrieved from https://www.researchgate.net/profile/Victor_Miller/publication/227128293_Use_of_Elliptic_Curves_in_Cryptography/links/0c96052e065c94b47c000000.pdf

Miorandi, D., Sicari, S., De Pellegrini, F., & Chlamtac, I. (2012). Internet of things: Vision, applications and research challenges. *Ad Hoc Networks*, *10*(7), 1497–1516. doi:10.1016/j.adhoc.2012.02.016

Misra, S., Maheswaran, M., & Hashmi, S. (2017). *Security challenges and approaches in internet of things*. Springer International Publishing. doi:10.1007/978-3-319-44230-3

Mohsen-Nia, A., & Jha, N. K. (2016). A Comprehensive Study of Security of Internet-of-Things. *IEEE Transactions on Emerging Topics in Computing*. doi:10.1109/TETC.2016.2606384

Mouton, F., & Venter, H. S. (2011). A prototype for achieving digital forensic readiness on wireless sensor networks. IEEE Africon 2011 - The Falls Resort and Conference Centre.

Moyer, J. W. (2015). Hacker Chris Roberts told FBI he took control of United plane, FBI claims. *Washington Post*. Retrieved from https://www.washingtonpost.com/news/morning-mix/wp/2015/05/18/hacker-chris-roberts-told-fbi-he-took-control-of-united-plane-fbi-claims/

Mukasey, M. B., Sedgwick, J. L., & Hagy, D. W. (2011). Electronic Crime Scene Investigation A Guide for First Responder. *National Institute of Justice*. Retrieved from http://www.ncjrs.org/pdffiles1/nij/187736.pdf

Myeong, H., Chang, J. Y., & Lee, K. M. (2012). Learning object relationships via graph-based context model. In *Proceedings of the IEEE Computer Society Conference on Computer Vision and Pattern Recognition* (pp. 2727–2734). IEEE. 10.1109/CVPR.2012.6247995

Myles, G., Friday, A., & Davies, N. (2003). Preserving privacy in environments with location-based applications. *IEEE Pervasive Computing*, *2*(1), 56–64. doi:10.1109/MPRV.2003.1186726

Myoung, G. L., Park, J., Kong, N., Crespi, N., & Chong, Y. (2012). *The Internet of Things - Concept and Problem Statement*. Internet Research Task Force.

Nakahara, J., Sepehrdad, P., Zhang, B., & Wang, M. (2009, December). Linear (hull) and algebraic cryptanalysis of the block cipher PRESENT. In *International Conference on Cryptology and Network Security* (pp. 58-75). Springer. 10.1007/978-3-642-10433-6_5

Naraghi-Pour, M., & Rojas, G. C. (2014). A novel algorithm for distributed localization in wireless sensor networks. *ACM Transactions on Sensor Networks*, *11*(1), 1–25. doi:10.1145/2632150

Narasimhan, S., & Bhunia, S. (2009). Hardware Trojan: Threats and emerging solutions. *IEEE High Level Design Validation and Test Workshop*.

Narayanan, A., & Shmatikov, V. (2008). *Robust De-anonymization of Large Sparse Datasets*. IEEE Computer Society Washington. doi:10.1109/SP.2008.33

Nedospasov, D., Seifert, J. P., Helfmeier, C., & Boit, C. (2014). Invasive PUF analysis. *Workshop on Fault Diagnosis and Tolerance in Cryptography (FDTC)*, 30–38.

Needham, R. M., & Wheeler, D. J. (1997). Tea extensions. Technical Report, Computer Laboratory, University of Cambridge.

Newman, J. (2016). Why the Internet of things might never speak A common language. *App Economy, Fast Company, 2016*. Retrieved from http://www.fastcompany.com/3057770/why-the-internet-of-thingsmight-never-speak-a-common-language

Nikolić, I., Wang, L., & Wu, S. (2013, March). Cryptanalysis of Round-Reduced $$\mathtt {LED} $$. In *International Workshop on Fast Software Encryption* (pp. 112-129). Springer.

Ning, H., & Wang, Z. (2011). Future internet of things architecture: Like mankind neural system or social organization framework. *IEEE Communications Letters*, *15*(4), 461–463.

NIST. (1998). *Skipjack and kea algorithm specifications (version 2.0)*. National Institute of Standards and Technology. Retrieved from http://csrc.nist.gov/groups/ST/toolkit/documents/skipjack/s kipjack.pdf

NS. (n.d.). *Network Simulator-2*. Retrieved from http://www.isi.edu/nsnamlnsl

NYTimes. (2016). Cyberattacks on Iran — Stuxnet and Flame. *New York Times*. Retrieved from https://www.nytimes.com/2011/01/16/world/middleeast/16stuxnet.html

Ocenasek, P., & Sveda, M. (2009). AVISPA: Towards Practical Verification of Communication Properties. *IFAC Proceedings Volumes*. Retrieved from http://www.sciencedirect.com/science/article/pii/S1474667016324624

Oh, S., & Gruteser, M. (2011). Multi-node coordinated jamming for location privacy protection. In *Proceedings of the Military Communications Conference* (pp.1243-1249). Baltimore, MD: IEEE.

Okolica, J., & Peterson, G. L. (2011). Extracting the windows clipboard from physical memory. *Digital Investigation*, *8*, S118–S124. doi:10.1016/j.diin.2011.05.014

Oriwoh, E., Jazani, D., Epiphaniou, G., & Sant, P. (2013). Internet of Things Forensics: Challenges and approaches. *IEEE International Conference on Collaborative Computing: Networking, Applications, and Worksharing*, 608–615. DOI: 10.4108/icst.collaboratecom.2013.254159

Ou, C.-H. (2011). A localization scheme for wireless sensor networks using mobile anchors with directional antennas. *IEEE Sensors Journal*, *11*(7), 1607–1616. doi:10.1109/JSEN.2010.2102748

OWASP. (2018). *Open Web Application Security Project (OWASP) Top 10 IoT Issues, OWASP Internet of Things Project, 11 Nov, 2018*. Retrieved from http://www.owasp.org /index.php/OWASP_Internet_of_Things_Top_Ten_Project

Pan, J., Hou, T., Cai, L., Shi, Y. & Shen, S. X. (2003). Topology Control for Wireless Sensor Networks. *MobiCom'03*.

Pappu, R., Recht, B., Taylor, J., & Gershenfeld, N. (2002). Physical one-way functions. *Science*, *297*(5589), 2026–2030. doi:10.1126cience.1074376 PMID:12242435

Part 11: Wireless LAN medium access control (MAC) and physical layer (PHY) specifications. (n.d.). Retrieved on August 14, 2018, from http://www.di-srv.unisa.it/~vitsca/RC-0809I/IEEE-802-11.pdf

Pascoe, J. (n.d.). Adding generic contextual capabilities to wearable computers. In *Digest of Papers. Second International Symposium on Wearable Computers (Cat. No.98EX215)* (pp. 92–99). IEEE Comput. Soc. 10.1109/ISWC.1998.729534

Patel, M., Chandrasekaran, R., & Venkatesan, S. (2005). Energy Efficient Sensor, Relay and Base Station Placements for Coverage, Connectivity and Routing. IEEE.

Patwari, N., Ash, J. N., Kyperountas, S., Hero, A. O., Moses, R. L., & Correal, N. S. (2005). Locating the nodes: Cooperative localization in wireless sensor networks. *IEEE Signal Processing Magazine*, *22*(4), 54–69. doi:10.1109/MSP.2005.1458287

Paula, M., Durand, F. R., & Abrao, T. (2016). WDM/OCDM energy-efficient networks based on heuristic ant colony optimization. *IEEE Systems Journal.*

Pazzi, R. W. N., & Boukerche, A. (2008). Mobile data collector strategy for delay-sensitive applications over wireless sensor network. *Computer Communications*, *31*(5), 1028–1039. doi:10.1016/j.comcom.2007.12.024

Perera, C., Zaslavsky, A., Christen, P., & Georgakopoulos, D. (2014). Context aware computing for the Internet of things: A survey. *IEEE Communications Surveys and Tutorials*, *16*(1), 414–454. doi:10.1109/SURV.2013.042313.00197

Perttunen, M., Riekki, J., & Lassila, O. (2009). Context Representation and Reasoning in Pervasive Computing.pdf. *International Journal of Multimedia and Ubiquitous Engineering*, *4*(4), 1–28.

Perumal, S., Norwawi, N. M., & Raman, V. (2015). Internet of Things (IoT) digital forensic investigation model: Top-down forensic approach methodology. *Fifth International Conference on Digital Information Processing and Communications (ICDIPC)*, 19–23. DOI: 10.1109/ICDIPC.2015.7323000

Pichan, A., Lazarescu, M., & Soh, S. T. (2015). Cloud forensics: Technical challenges, solutions and comparative analysis. *Digital Investigation, Vol.*, *13*, 38–57. doi:10.1016/j.diin.2015.03.002

Pietschmann, S., Mitschick, A., Winkler, R., & Meißner, K. (2008). CROCO: Ontology-based, cross-application context management. In *Proceedings - 3rd International Workshop on Semantic Media Adaptation and Personalization, SMAP 2008* (pp. 88–93). Academic Press. 10.1109/SMAP.2008.10

Pinkas, B., Schneider, T., & Zohner, M. (2014). Faster private set intersection based on ot extension. *USENIX Security*, *14*, 797–812.

Pwnieexpress. (2017). *The IoT Attacks Everyone Should Know About.* Retrieved from https://www.pwnieexpress.com/blog/the-iot-attacks-everyone-should-know-about

Pytbull. (2017). Retrieved August 20, 2017, from http://pytbull.sourceforge.net

Quedenfeld, F. M. (2015). *Modellbildung in der algebraischen Kryptoanalyse* (Doctoral dissertation). Universitätsbibliothek Kassel.

Quick, D., & Cho, K. R. (2018). IoT Device Forensics and Data Reduction. *IEEE Access: Practical Innovations, Open Solutions*, *6*, 47566–47574. doi:10.1109/ACCESS.2018.2867466

Quick, D., & Choo, K. R. (2014). Data Reduction and Data Mining Framework for Digital Forensic Evidence: Storage, Intelligence, Review and Archive. *Trends and Issues in Crime and Criminal Justice*, *480*, 1–11.

Radware. (2017). *'BrickerBot' Results In PDoS Attack.* Retrieved from https://security.radware.com/ddos-threats-attacks/brickerbot-pdos-permanent-denial-of-service

Rahman, K. M. S., Bishop, M. & Hol, A. (2016). Internet of Things mobility forensics. *Information Security Research and Education (INSuRE) Conference.*

Rakocevic, G. (2004). *Overview of Sensors for Wireless Sensor Networks.* Internet Journals.

Rawat, D. B., White, T., Parwez, M. S., Bajracharya, C., & Song, M. (2017). Evaluating secrecy outage of physical layer security in large-scale MIMO wireless communications for cyber-physical systems. *IEEE Internet of Things Journal*, *4*(6), 1987–1993. doi:10.1109/JIOT.2017.2691352

Red Hat and August Schell run world's largest PKI installation on Red Hat Enterprise Linux. Red Hat government team. (2007). Retrieved from www.redhat.com/ about/news/archive/2007/6/red-hat-and-august-schell-run -worlds-largest-pki-installation-on -red-hat-enterprise-linux

Reith, M., Carr, C. & Gunsch, G. (2002). An Examination of Digital Forensic Models. *International Journal of Digital Evidence*, *1*(3).

Rekhis, S., & Boudriga, N. (2012). A System for Formal Digital Forensic Investigation Aware of Anti-Forensic Attacks. *IEEE Transactions on Information Forensics and Security*, *7*(2), 635–650. doi:10.1109/TIFS.2011.2176117

Rios, R., & Lopez, J. (2011). Analysis of location privacy solutions in wireless sensor networks. *IET Communications*, *5*(17), 2518–2532. doi:10.1049/iet-com.2010.0825

Rivest, R. L. (1994). The RC5 Encryption Algorithm. *Proc. Second International Workshop on Fast Software Encryption (FSE 1994)*, 86-96.

Rizvi, S., Pfeffer, J., Kurtz, A., & Rizvi, M. (2018). Securing the Internet of Things (IoT): A Security Taxonomy for IoT. *2018 17th IEEE International Conference On Trust, Security And Privacy In Computing And Communications/ 12th IEEE International Conference On Big Data Science And Engineering (TrustCom/BigDataSE)*. DOI: 10.1109/TrustCom/BigDataSE.2018.000

Robinson, J., & Rahmat-Samii, Y. (2004). Particle swarm optimization in electromagnetics. *IEEE Transactions on Antennas and Propagation, 52*(2), 397–402. doi:10.1109/TAP.2004.823969

Rokni, S. A., & Ghasemzadeh, H. (2016). Autonomous sensor-context learning in dynamic human-centered Internet-of-things environments. In *Proceedings of the 35th International Conference on Computer-Aided Design - ICCAD '16* (pp. 1–6). New York: ACM Press. 10.1145/2966986.2967008

Rosenblatt, S., Fainstein, D., Cestero, A., Safran, J., Robson, N., Kirihata, T., & Iyer, S. S. (2013). Field tolerant dynamic intrinsic chip ID using 32 nm high-K/metal gate SOI embedded DRAM. *IEEE Journal of Solid-State Circuits, 48*(4), 940–947. doi:10.1109/JSSC.2013.2239134

Rosenfeld, K., Gavas, E., & Karri, R. (2010). Sensor physical unclonable functions. IEEE International Symposium on Hardware-Oriented Security and Trust. HOST. http://ieeexplore.ieee.org/document/5513103/

Roy, R., & Kailath, T. (1989). Esprit - estimation of signal parameters via rotational invariance techniques. *IEEE Transactions on Acoustics, Speech, and Signal Processing, 37*(7), 984–995. doi:10.1109/29.32276

Ruangchaijatupon, N., & Krishnamurthy, P. (2001). Encryption and Power Consumption in Wireless LANs-N. *Third IEEE workshop on wireless LANS 2001*, 148-152.

Rührmair, U., S€olter, J., Sehnke, F., Xu, X., Mahmoud, A., Stoyanova, V., … Devadas, S. (2013). PUF modeling attacks on simulated and silicon data. *IEEE Trans. Inf. Forensics Secur., 8*(11), 1876–1891.

Rührmair, U., Sehnke, F., S€olter, J., Dror, G., Devadas, S., & Ürgen Schmidhuber, J. (2010). Modeling attacks on physical unclonable functions. *Proceedings of ACM Conference on Computer and Communications Security*, 237–249.

Ruhrmair, U., Xu, X., Solter, J., Mahmoud, A., Majzoobi, M., Koushanfar, F., & Burleson, W. (2014). Efficient Power and Timing Side Channels for Physical Unclonable Functions. *Proceedings of the 16th International Workshop on Cryptographic Hardware and Embedded Systems, 8731*. 10.1007/978-3-662-44709-3_26

Rukhin, A., Soto, J., Nechvatal, J., Smid, M., Barker, E., Leigh, S., … Vo, S. (2010). A statistical test suite for random and pseudorandom number generators for cryptographic applications. *Natl. Inst. Stand. Technol. 800–22(Rev 1a)*, 131.

Russell, B., & Van-Duren, D. (2016). Practical internet of things security. *Packt Publishing Ltd.*

Sachdeva, N., Dhir, R., & Kumar, A. (2016). Empirical analysis of Machine Learning Techniques for context aware Recommender Systems in the environment of IoT. In *Proceedings of the International Conference on Advances in Information Communication Technology & Computing - AICTC '16* (pp. 1–7). New York: ACM Press. 10.1145/2979779.2979818

Sadeghi, A. R., & Naccache, D. (2010). *Towards hardware-intrinsic security: Foundations and practice*. Berlin: Springer. doi:10.1007/978-3-642-14452-3

Sadeghi, A.-R., Visconti, I., & Wachsmann, C. (2010). Enhancing RFID Security and Privacy by Physically Unclonable Functions. In A.-R. Sadeghi & D. Naccache (Eds.), *Towards Hardware-Intrinsic Security: Foundations and Practice* (pp. 281–305). Berlin: Springer Berlin Heidelberg. doi:10.1007/978-3-642-14452-3_13

Sai, V., & Mickle, M. H. (2014). Exploring energy efficient architectures in passive wireless nodes for IoT applications. IEEE Circuits Syst. Mag., 14(2), 48–54.

Said, O., & Masud, M. (2013). Towards internet of things: Survey and future vision. *International Journal of Computer Networks*, *5*(1), 1–17.

Sain, M., Kang, Y. J., & Lee, H. J. (2017). Survey on Security in Internet of things: state of the art and challenges. *2017 19th International Conference on Advanced Communication Technology (ICACT)*, 699-704.

Sandhu, R., & Sood, S. K. (2016). A stochastic game net-based model for effective decision-making in smart environments. *Concurrency and Computation*. doi:10.1002/cpe.3843

Sarika, S., Pravin, A., & Vijayakumar, A. (2016). Security Issues in Mobile Ad Hoc Networks. *Procedia Computer*. Retrieved from http://www.sciencedirect.com/science/article/pii/S1877050916316106

Schatsky, D., Muraskin, C., & Gurumurthy, R. (2014). Demystifying Artificial Intelligence: What business leaders need to know about cognitive technologies. Deloitte University Press.

Schilit, B., Adams, N., & Want, R. (1994). Context-aware computing applications. In Wmcsa (pp. 85–90). IEEE Comput. Soc. Press. doi:10.1109/WMCSA.1994.16

Schindler, H. R., Cave, J., Robinson, N., Horvath, V., Hackett, P., Gunashekar, S., . . . Graux, H. (2012). Examining Europe's Policy Options to Foster Development of the 'Internet of Things.' *Rand Corporation*. Retrieved October 7, 2008, from http://www.rand.org/randeurope/research/projects/internet-of-things.html

Schlangen, R., Rainer, L., Lundquist, T. R., Egger, P., & Boit, C. (2009). RF performance increase allowing IC timing adjustments by use of backside FIB processing. *IEEE Int'l Symp. Physical and Failure Analysis of Integrated Circuits (IPFA 09)*, 33–36. 10.1109/IPFA.2009.5232703

Schmidt, A., & Van Laerhoven, K. (2001). How to build smart appliances? *IEEE Personal Communications*, *8*(4), 66–71. doi:10.1109/98.944006

Schrijen. G. J, & Van Der Leest. V. (2012). Comparative analysis of SRAM memories used as PUF primitives. *Design, Automation & Test in Europe Conference & Exhibition (DATE)*, 1319–1324.

Schulz, S., Sadeghi, A. R., & Wachsmann, C. (2011). Short paper: Lightweight remote attestation using physical functions. *Proc. ACM Conf. Wireless Network Security (ACM WiSec)*, 109–114. 10.1145/1998412.1998432

Schwartz, P. M., & Solove, D. J. (2011). *The PII problem: privacy and a new concept of personally identifiable information*. Berkeley, CA: Berkeley Law Scholarship Repository.

Scott, P. R. (2014). Regulating the Internet of Things: First steps toward Managing Discrimination, Privacy, Security, and Consent. *Texas Law Review*, *93*, 85.

Security Intelligence. (2015). *Eight Crazy Hacks: The Worst and Weirdest Data Breaches of 2015*. Retrieved from https://securityintelligence.com/eight-crazy-hacks-the-worst-and-weirdest-data-breaches-of-2015

Selimis, G., Konijnenburg, M., Ashouei, M., Huisken, J., De Groot, H., Van Der Leest, V., ... Tuyls, P. (2011). Evaluation of 90nm 6T-SRAM as physical unclonable function for secure key generation in wireless sensor nodes. *Proceedings of IEEE International Symposium on Circuits Systems*, 567–570. 10.1109/ISCAS.2011.5937628

Shanmugam, D., Selvam, R., & Annadurai, S. (2014, October). Differential power analysis attack on SIMON and LED block ciphers. In *International Conference on Security, Privacy, and Applied Cryptography Engineering* (pp. 110-125). Springer. 10.1007/978-3-319-12060-7_8

Sheth, A., Henson, C., & Sahoo, S. S. (2008). Semantic sensor web. *IEEE Internet Computing*, *12*(4), 78–83. doi:10.1109/MIC.2008.87

Shiozaki, M., Kubota, T., Nakai, T., Takeuchi, A., Nishimura, T., & Fujino, T. (2015). Tamper-resistant authentication system with side-channel attack resistant AES and PUF using MDR-ROM. *IEEE International Symposium on Circuits and Systems (ISCAS)*, 1462–1465. 10.1109/ISCAS.2015.7168920

Shi, R., Mu, Y., Zhong, H., Zhang, S., & Cui, J. (2016). Quantum private set intersection cardinality and its application to anonymous authentication. *Information Sciences*, *370*, 147–158. doi:10.1016/j.ins.2016.07.071

Shiu, Y.-S., Chang, S. Y., Wu, H.-C., Huang, S. C.-H., & Chen, H.-H. (2011). Physical layer security in wireless networks: A tutorial. *IEEE Wireless Communications*, *18*(2), 66–74. doi:10.1109/MWC.2011.5751298

Silberschatz, A., Galvin, P. B., & Gagne, G. (2009). *Operating System Concepts* (8th ed.). New Delhi, India: Wiley.

Simpson, L., & Lamb, R. (2010, February 20). IoT: Looking at sensors. Jefferies Equity Research, 4.

Simson, L. (2010). Garfinkel. Digital forensics research: The next 10 years. *Digital Investigation*, *7*, S64–S73. doi:10.1016/j.diin.2010.05.009

Smith, S. W., & Weingart, S. (1999). Building a high-performance, programmable secure coprocessor. *Computer Networks*, *31*(8), 831–860. doi:10.1016/S1389-1286(98)00019-X

Soosahabi, R., & Naraghi-Pour, M. (2012). Scalable PHY-Layer security for distributed detection in wireless sensor networks. *IEEE Transactions on Information Forensics and Security*, *7*(4), 1118–1126. doi:10.1109/TIFS.2012.2194704

Soro, A. (2016). *Privacy: "Internet delle cose", utenti poco tutelati. Garante per la protezione dei dati personali. Garante per la protezione dei dati personali.* Retrieved from http://www.garanteprivacy.it/web/guest/home/docweb/-/docweb-display/docweb/5443681

Srinivasan, A., & Wu, J. (2008). *A survey on secure localization in wireless sensor networks. In Encyclopedia of Wireless and Mobile Communications.* Taylor and Francis Group.

Ssu, K.-F., Ou, C.-H., & Jiau, H. C. (2005). Localization with mobile anchor points in wireless sensor networks. *IEEE Transactions on Vehicular Technology*, *54*(3), 1187–1197. doi:10.1109/TVT.2005.844642

Standaert, F. X., Piret, G., Gershenfeld, N., & Quisquater, J. J. (2006, April). SEA: A scalable encryption algorithm for small embedded applications. In *International Conference on Smart Card Research and Advanced Applications* (pp. 222-236). Springer. 10.1007/11733447_16

Stephen, L. (2014). IEEE standards group wants to bring order to IoT. *Computerworld*. Retrieved from https://www.computerworld.com/article/2686714/networking-hardware/ieee-standards-group-wants-to-bring-order-to-internet-of-things.html

Stevens, R. M., & Casey, E. (2010). Extracting Windows command line details from physical memory. *Digital Investigation*, *7*, S57–S63. doi:10.1016/j.diin.2010.05.008

Stojmenovic, I., & Wen, S. (2014). The fog computing paradigm: scenarios and security issues. *Proceedings of the Federated Conference on Computer Science and Information Systems (FedCSIS '14)*, 1–8, IEEE.

Suh, G. E., & Devadas, S. (2007). *Pysical Unclonable Functions for Device Authentication and Secret Key Generation.* Paper presented at the IEEE/ACM DAC.

Sundmaeker, H., Guillemin, P., & Friess, P. (2010). *Vision and challenges for realising the Internet of Things. ... the Internet of Things*. doi:10.2759/26127

Sun, G., Anand, V., Liao, D., Lu, C., Zhang, X., & Bao, N. (2015, June). Power-Efficient Provisioning for Online Virtual Network Requests in Cloud-Based Data Centers. *IEEE Systems Journal*, *9*(2), 427–441. doi:10.1109/JSYST.2013.2289584

Sutherland, I., Read, H., & Xynos, K. (2014). Forensic Analysis of Smart TV: A Current Issue and Call to Arms. *Digital Investigation*, *11*(3), 175–178.

Suzaki, T., Minematsu, K., Morioka, S., & Kobayashi, E. (2012). TWINE: A Lightweight, Versatile Block Cipher. *Pre-proceeding of SAC 2012*.

Sweeney, L. (2000). *Uniqueness of Simple Demographics in the U.S. Population.* Technical Report LIDAP-WP4. Pittsburgh, PA: Carnegie Mellon University.

Sweeney, L. (2002). k- Anonymity: A model for protecting privacy. *International Journal of Uncertainty, Fuzziness and Knowledge-based Systems*, *10*(5), 557–570. doi:10.1142/S0218488502001648

Symantec. (2018). Internet Security Threat Report. *Symantec*. Retrieved from https://www.symantec.com/content/dam/symantec/docs/reports/istr-23-2018-en.pdf

Talone, P., & Russo, G. (n.d.). *Standard e protocolli di comunicazione*. Roma: Fondazione Ugo Bordoni. Retrieved Dec, 15, 2017, from http://www.rfid.fub.it/edizione_2/Parte_VI.pdf

Tang, J., Hao, B., & Sen, A. (2005). Relay node placement in large scale wireless sensor networks. In Computer Communications. Elsevier.

Tang, J., Hao, B., & Sen, A. (2005). Relay node placement in large scale wireless sensor networks. *Computer Communications*.

Tao, F., Zuo, Y., Xu, L. D., & Zhang, L. (2014). IoT-based intelligent perception and access of manufacturing resource toward cloud manufacturing. *IEEE Transactions on Industrial Informatics*, *10*(2), 1547–1557. doi:10.1109/TII.2014.2306397

Taylor, M., Haggerty, J., Gresty, D., & Hegarty, R. (2010, May). Digital evidence in cloud computing systems. *Elsevier Computer Law & Security Review*, *26*(3), 304–308. doi:10.1016/j.clsr.2010.03.002

Tehranipoor, M., Salmani, H., Zhang, Z., Wang, M., Karri, R., Rajendran, J., & Rosenfeld, K. (2011). Trustworthy Hardware: Trojan Detection and Design-for-Trust Challenges. *IEEE Computer*, *44*(7), 9. doi:10.1109/MC.2010.369

The Register. (2016). Finns chilling as DDoS knocks out building control system. *The Register*. Retrieved from https://www.theregister.co.uk/2016/11/09/finns_chilling_as_ddos_knocks_out_building_ control_ system

The Register. (2017). Reaper IoT botnet ain't so scary, contains fewer than 20,000 drones. *The Register*. Retrieved from https://www.theregister.co.uk/2017/10/27/reaper_iot_botnet_follow_up

Theodorakopoulos, G., & Baras, J. (2006). On trust models and trust evaluation metrics for ad hoc networks. *IEEE Journal on Selected*. Retrieved from http://ieeexplore.ieee.org/abstract/document/1589111/

Triantafyllou, A., Sarigiannidis, P., & Lagkas, T.D. (2018). Network Protocols, Schemes, and Mechanisms for Internet of Things (IoT): Features, Open Challenges, and Trends. *Wireless Communications and Mobile Computing*. . doi:10.1155/2018/5349894

Tuyls, P., & Batina, L. (2006). RFID-Tags for Anti-counterfeiting. In D. Pointcheval (Ed.), *Topics in Cryptology – CT-RSA 2006: The Cryptographers' Track at the RSA Conference 2006, San Jose, CA, USA, February 13-17, 2005. Proceedings* (pp. 115-131). Berlin: Springer Berlin Heidelberg.

Ukil, A., Sen, J., & Koilakonda, S. (2011). Embedded Security for Internet of Things. In *2011 2nd National Conference on Emerging Trends and Applications in Computer Science* (pp. 1–6). IEEE.

Vallimayil, A., Karthick, R. K. M., Sarmam V. R. D., & Chandrasekaran, R. M. (2011). *Role of Relay Node in Wireless Sensor Network: A Survey*. IEEE.

Van Bunningen, A. H., Feng, L., & Apers, F. M. G. (2005). Context for ubiquitous data management. In *Proceedings of the International Workshop on Ubiquitous Data Management, UDM 2005* (pp. 17–24). IEEE. 10.1109/UDM.2005.7

Van Nguyen, T., Lim, W., Nguyen, H. A., & Choi, D. (2008). Context awareness framework based on contextual graph. *5th IEEE and IFIP International Conference on Wireless and Optical Communications Networks, WOCN 2008*. 10.1109/WOCN.2008.4542542

Vermesan, O., Friess, P., Guillemin, P., Gusmeroli, S., Sundmaeker, H., Bassi, A., … Pat, D. (2009). Internet of Things Strategic Research Roadmap. *Internet of Things Strategic Research Roadmap*, 9–52.

Wang, X., Salmani, H., Tehranipoor, M., & Plusquellic, J. (2008). *Hardware Trojan Detection and Isolation Using Current Integration and Localized Current Analysis - IEEE Conference Publication.* Paper presented at the IEEE International Symposium on Defect and Fault Tolerance of VLSI Systems.

Wang, N., Li, W., Jiang, T., & Lv, S. (2017). Physical layer spoofing detection based on sparse signal processing and fuzzy recognition. *IET Signal Processing*, *11*(5), 640–646. doi:10.1049/iet-spr.2016.0378

Wang, T., & Yang, Y. (2011). Location privacy protection from RSS localization system using antenna pattern synthesis. In *Proceedings of International Conference on Computer Communications* (pp. 2408-2416). Shanghai, China: IEEE. 10.1109/INFCOM.2011.5935061

Wan, M., He, Z., Han, S., Dai, K., & Zou, X. (2015). An invasive attack- resistant PUF based on switched-capacitor circuit. *IEEE Trans. Circuits Syst. I*, *62*(8), 2024–2034. doi:10.1109/TCSI.2015.2440739

Weber, R. H. (2015). Internet of Things: Privacy issues revisited. *Computer Law & Security Review*, *31*(5), 618–627. doi:10.1016/j.clsr.2015.07.002

Wheeler, D. J., & Needham, R. M. (1994). TEA, A Tiny Encryption Algorithm. *Proc. Second International Workshop on Fast Software Encryption (FSE 1994)*, 363-366.

Wheeler, D. J., & Needham, R. M. (1994, December). TEA, a tiny encryption algorithm. In *International Workshop on Fast Software Encryption* (pp. 363-366). Springer.

White, A., Schatz, B., & Foo, E. (2012). Surveying the user space through user allocations. *Digital Investigation*, *9*, S3–S12. doi:10.1016/j.diin.2012.05.005

Whitmore, A., Agarwal, A., & Xu, L. D. (2015). The Internet of Things—A survey of topics and trends. *Information Systems Frontiers*, *17*(2), 261–274. doi:10.100710796-014-9489-2

Winters, J. H. (2006). Smart antenna techniques and their application to wireless ad hoc networks. *IEEE Wireless Communications*, *13*(4), 77–83. doi:10.1109/MWC.2006.1678168

Wong, F. L., Lin, M., Nagaraja, S., Wassell, I., & Stajano, F. (2007). Evaluation framework of location privacy of wireless mobile systems with arbitrary beam pattern. In *Proceedings of Fifth Annual Conference on Communication Networks and Services Research* (vol. 2, pp. 157-165). Fredericton, Canada: IEEE. 10.1109/CNSR.2007.30

Wrona, K., & Gomez, L. (2005). Context-aware security and secure context-awareness in ubiquitous computing environments. In *Proceedings of the XXI Autumn Meeting of Polish Information Processing Society* (pp. 255–265). Academic Press.

WSJ. (2017). WikiLeaks Dumps Trove of Purported CIA Hacking Tools. *The Wall Street Journal*. Retrieved from https://www.wsj.com/articles/wikileaks-posts-thousands-of-purported-cia-cyberhacking-documents-1488905823 on Nov 23, 2018.

Wu, B., Chen, J., Wu, J., & Cardei, M. (2007). A survey of attacks and countermeasures in mobile ad hoc networks. *Wireless Network Security*. Retrieved from http://link.springer.com/chapter/10.1007/978-0-387-33112-6_5

Wu, M., Lu, T.-J., Ling, F.-Y., Sun, J., & Du, H.-Y. (2010). Research on the architecture of internet of things. *Proceedings of the 3rd International Conference on Advanced Computer Theory and Engineering (ICACTE '10)*, 5, V5-484–V5-487.

Wurm, J., Hoang, K., Arias, A., Sadeghi, A. R., & Jin, Y. (2016). Security analysis on consumer and industrial IoT devices. *2016 21st Asia and South Pacific Design Automation Conference (ASP-DAC)*, 519-524.

Xie, L., Wang, W., Shi, X., & Qin, T. (2017). *Lightweight mutual authentication among sensors in body area networks through Physical Unclonable Functions.* Paper presented at the 2017 IEEE International Conference on Communications (ICC), Paris, France. 10.1109/ICC.2017.7996735

Yang, K., Dong, Q., Blaauw, D., & Sylvester, D. (2015). A physically unclonable function with BER < 10^-8 for robust chip authentication using oscillator collapse in 40 nm CMOS. *IEEE International Solid-State Circuits Conference (ISSCC)*, 254–256.

Yanwei, S., Guangzhou, Z., & Haitao, P. (2011). Research on the context model of intelligent interaction system in the Internet of Things. In *IT in Medicine and Education (ITME), 2011 International Symposium on* (Vol. 2, pp. 379–382). IEEE. 10.1109/ITiME.2011.6132129

Yao, Y., Zou, K., Chen, X., & Xu, X. (2016). A distributed range-free correction vector based localization refinement algorithm. *Wireless Networks*, *22*(8), 2667–2680. doi:10.100711276-015-1129-3

Yilmaz, M. H., & Arslan, H. (2015). A survey: Spoofing attacks in physical layer security. In *Proceedings of 40th Annual IEEE Conference on Local Computer Networks* (pp. 812-817). Clearwater Beach, FL: IEEE. 10.1109/LCNW.2015.7365932

Yu, M. M., Sowell, R., Singh, A., Raihi, D. M., & Devadas, S. (2012). Performance metrics and empirical results of a PUF cryptographic key generation ASIC. *IEEE International Symposium on Hardware-Oriented Security and Trust (HOST)*, 108–115.

Yu, M., M'Raïhi, D., Verbauwhede, I., & Devadas, S. (2014). A noise bifurcation architecture for linear additive physical functions. *IEEE Int'l Symp. Hardware-Oriented Security and Trust (HOST 14)*, 124–129.

Yu, C., Yao, D., Yang, L. T., & Jin, H. (2017). Energy Conservation in Progressive Decentralized Single-Hop Wireless Sensor Networks for Pervasive Computing Environment. *IEEE Systems Journal*, *11*(2), 823–834. doi:10.1109/JSYST.2014.2339311

Yu, L. (2011). *A Developer's Guide to the Semantic Web. Language*. Berlin: Springer Berlin Heidelberg. doi:10.1007/978-3-642-15970-1

Zawoad, S., & Hasan, R. (2015). FAIoT: Towards Building a Forensics Aware Eco System for the Internet of Things. *2015 IEEE International Conference on Services Computing*, 279–284. DOI: 10.1109/SCC.2015.46

Zawoad, S., & Hasan, R. (n.d.). FAIoT. *Towards Building a Forensics Aware Eco System for the Internet of Things.*

Zetter, K. (2015). *A Cyberattack Has Caused Confirmed Physical Damage for the Second Time Ever*. Retrieved from https://www.wired.com/2015/01/german-steel-mill-hack-destruction/

Zetter, K. (2016). *Everything We Know About Ukraine's Power Plant Hack*. Retrieved from https://www.wired.com/2016/01/everything-we-know-about-ukraines-power-plant-hack/

Zhang, D., Yang, L. T., Chen, M., Zhao, S., Guo, M., & Zhang, Y. (2014). Real-time locating systems using active RFID for Internet of things. *IEEE Systems Journal*. doi:10.1109/JSYST.2014.2346625

Zhang, X., Seo, S. H., & Wang, C. (2018). A Lightweight Encryption Method for Privacy Protection in Surveillance Videos. *IEEE Access: Practical Innovations, Open Solutions*, *6*, 18074–18087. doi:10.1109/ACCESS.2018.2820724

Zhao, K. & Ge, G. (2013). A Survey on the Internet of Things Security. *2013 Ninth International Conference on Computational Intelligence and Security.*

Zhao, W., Ha, Y., & Alioto, M. (2015). Novel self-body-biasing and statistical design for near-threshold circuits with ultra-energy-efficient AES as case study. *IEEE Trans. VLSI Systems*, *23*(8), 1390–1401. doi:10.1109/TVLSI.2014.2342932

Zheng, Y., Matsumoto, T., & Imai, H. (1990). On the construction of block ciphers provably secure and not relying on any unproved hypotheses. Advances in Cryptology CRYPTO 89 Proceedings, 461–480.

Zhou, X., Song, L., & Zhang, Y. (Eds.). (2014). *Physical layer security in wireless communications*. Boca Raton, FL: Taylor & Francis Group, LLC.

Zhu, J. (2016). *Physical layer security in massive MIMO systems* (Unpublished doctoral dissertation). The University of British Columbia, Vancouver, Canada.

Zou, Y., Zhu, J., Wang, X., & Hanzo, L. (2016). A survey on wireless security: Technical challenges, recent advances, and future trends. *Proceedings of the IEEE, 104*(9), 1727–1765. doi:10.1109/JPROC.2016.2558521

Zoyama, A. Y. (Ed.). (2008). Algorithms and Protocols for Wireless Sensor Networks. Wiley-IEEE Press.

Zulkipli, N. H. N., Alenezi, A., & Wills, G. B. (2017). IoT Forensic: Bridging the Challenges in Digital Forensic and the Internet of Things. *Proceedings of the 2nd International Conference on Internet of Things, Big Data and Security*, 1, 315-324. 10.5220/0006308703150324

Zurita, L. N. R. (2014). *Optimising multiple antenna techniques for physical layer security* (Unpublished doctoral dissertation). The University of Leeds, Leeds, UK.

About the Contributors

M. Tariq Banday was born in Srinagar, India. He obtained hisM. Sc., M. Phil. and Ph. D. degrees in Electronics (Network Security) from the Department of Electronics and Instrumentation Technology, University of Kashmir, Srinagar, India in 1996, 2008, and 2010 respectively. At present, he is working as Associate Professor in the same department. He is a senior member of IEEE, ACM, and CSI. He currently investigates a few government-sponsored research projects in network security. He has to his credit over 100 research publications in reputed journals and conference proceedings. His teaching and research interests include microprocessors & microcontrollers: architecture, programming, and interfacing; programming and problem solving, computer organization, design & architecture, network, internet, e-mail and web security, Internet of Things, data structures and database management systems.

* * *

Laura Abba graduated in mathematics in 1979, Technical Executive of the Institute of Informatics and Telematics of the Italian National Research Council (CNR) . She is committed in the field of Global Internet Governance as a new interdisciplinary research field. Her main activity is in supporting the process of interaction between the Research networks and the Internet in Italy. She has participated in projects introducing the Internet in Italy at CNR-CNUCE, collaborating, within the GARR Italian Academic and Research Network framework, in the establishment of research networks and in the development of the information society. Since 2003 she is a member of the Board of ISOC Italy, the Italian Chapter of Internet Society. She is a member of the promoting committee of IGF Italy. She participated, since the beginning, in the Internet Governance Forums promoted by the United Nations. She has continuously worked for the dissemination of the Internet culture and technologies (training, conventions, editorials).

Muhammad Naveed Aman received a B.Sc. degree in Computer Systems Engineering from KPK UET, Peshawar, Pakistan, M.Sc. degree in Computer Engineering from the Center for Advanced Studies in Engineering, Islamabad, Pakistan, M.Sc. degree in Industrial and Management Engineering and Ph.D. in Electrical Engineering from Rensselaer Polytechnic Institute, Troy, NY, USA in 2006, 2008, and 2012 respectively. He is currently working as a Senior Research Fellow with the Department of Computer Science of National University of Singapore, Singapore. Dr. Aman previously served on the faculty of National University of Computer and Emerging Sciences Pakistan as an Assistant Professor. His research interests include IoT and network security, wireless and mobile networks, and secure embedded systems.

Valentina Amenta is a Researcher in Public Law and Economics and Research Assistant at the Institute of Computer Science and Telematics of the National Research Council for Internet governance issues.

Rathindra Nath Biswas received his B.E and M.E degree in Electronics and Telecommunication Engineering from Bengal Engineering College (Deemed University) and Jadavpur University, India in the year of 2002 and 2008 respectively. He is associated as a lecturer in the Department of Electronics and Telecommunication Engineering at Acharya Jagadish Chandra Bose Polytechnic, India since 2008. He has more than 14 years of teaching experience and his research interests include network security, sensor localization, adaptive antenna arrays design and FPGA based implementation etc.

Kee Chaing Chua received a Ph.D. in electrical engineering from the University of Auckland, New Zealand, in 1990 and joined the Department of Electrical Engineering at the National University of Singapore (NUS) as a Lecturer. He is now a Professor in the Department of Electrical & Computer Engineering at NUS. He served as the Faculty of Engineering, Vice Dean for Research twice, from 2003 to 2006 and from 2008 to 2009. From 1995 to 2000, he was seconded to the Center for Wireless Communications (now the Institute for Infocomm Research), a national telecommunication R&D center funded by the Singapore Agency for Science, Technology, and Research as its Deputy Director. From 2001 to 2003, he was on leave of absence from NUS to work at Siemens Singapore where he was the Founding Head of the Mobile Core R&D Department funded by Siemens ICM Group. From 2006 to 2008, he was seconded to the National Research Foundation as a Director. He was appointed Head of the Department of Electrical & Computer Engineering at NUS in 2009. He chaired the World Economic Forums Global Agenda Council on Robotics and Smart Devices in 2011 and spoke on the role of robotics and smart devices in shaping new models of development at the World Economic Forum in Davos in January 2012. He is a Fellow of the Singapore Academy of Engineering.

Sumit Kumar Debnath is working as Assistant Professor in the Department of Mathematics at National Institute of Technology, Jamshedpur, India. He has received his M.Sc. in Mathematics from Indian Institute of Technology Kharagpur, India in 2012 and PhD from Indian Institute of Technology, Kharagpur, India in 2017. His research interests include Private Set Intersection Protocols, Lattice-based Cryptography, Multivariate Cryptosystem, Functional Encryption and Attribute-Based Cryptosystems, Elliptic Curve Cryptography, Multilinear maps and their applications, Obfuscation: constructions and applications, etc.

Harsuminder Kaur Gill is Ph.D. scholar at Jaypee University of Information technology, Solan. She has a gold medal in her Master of Engineering from Guru Nanak Dev University. She has published papers in reputed journals. Her research areas are recommender systems and deep learning.

Bisma Javid received her B.Tech degree in Computer Science Engineering from Islamic University of Science and Technology, India and M.Tech. degree in Communication and Information Technology from National Institute of Technology, Srinagar, India in 2015 and 2018 respectively. She is currently working as a Project Associate at the Department of Electronics and Instrumentation Technology, University of Kashmir, India. Bisma has served as a faculty member at Islamic University of Science and Technology, India. Her research interests include Network Security, Cryptography and Internet of Things.

Malathi Jesudason is presently working as Professor of Electronics and Telecommunications Engineering and Vice Principal of D. Y. Patil College of Engineering, Akurdi, Pune. She holds bachelor's degree in Electronics and Communication from Government College of Engineering, Tirunelveli, Tamil Nadu, India, Master's degree and Ph.D. from the University of Pune. She has published 40 research papers in International Journals, 35 research papers in International Conferences. She has received Bharat Vidya Shiromani award, Best Teacher Award, and National Mahila award. She has received recognition of leadership by skify labs. She has robustly accomplished research project sponsored by ISRO-DRDO-UOP interaction cell and area of interest is in wireless communication, digital signal processing, and mobile communication. She is also a member of ISTE, IETE, and IEEE.

Mariya Shafat Kirmani received her B.Sc. degree in Information Technology from S. P. College, Srinagar, India, M.Sc. degree in Information Technology from University of Kashmir, India in 2013 and 2015 respectively. She is an INSPIRE fellow of Department of Science and Technology, Govt. of India and is currently pursuing her Ph.D. in Information Technology (Digital Forensics) from the Department of Electronics and Instrumentation Technology, University of Kashmir, Srinagar. Her research interests include Network Security and Digital Forensics particularly Forensics of Physical Memory, File Systems, Operating Systems and Internet of Things.

Adriana Lazzaroni graduated with honors in Political Sciences at the University of Pisa. Expert in international relations, she begins working in the network environment in 1992. She starts her career at the CNR-CNUCE Institute, working on projects for the development of computer infrastructures in developing countries and on pilot projects for the Information Society. In this context, she gives her contribution to the evolution of the Internet in Italy, increasing her expertise in the field of network services for CNR users, in technology transfer and in promoting scientific data by means of web technologies. From 2001 to 2003 she is a member of the board of directors of ISOC Italy, the Italian Chapter of Internet Society, contributing to the start-up activities of the Chapter. Since 2002 she is head of the Scientific Affairs Unit of the Institute for Informatics and Telematics (IIT) of the Italian National Research Council and vice-manager of the Secretariat for the Internet Governance. She dedicates herself to communication activities, scientific dissemination, and exploitation of the results achieved in the ICT research sector and she is the organizer of national and international scientific events in the field of the Internet. Since 2009 she has promoted IIT CNR international relations, and the participation of CNR, IIT, .it Registry, in international scientific organizations and research consortia dealing in information technology and applied mathematics, DNS and Internet governance (ERCIM, EFICST, ICANN, IGF, EDA, etc.). She teaches at the second level University Master in "Internet Ecosystem: governance and rights" of the Law Department of the University of Pisa and she is the author of a number of publications on Internet Governance topics.

Issmat Shah Masoodi received his B. Tech degree in Electronics and Communication Engineering from Jammu University, India, and M.Tech. degree in Electronics and Communication Engineering from the Shri Mata Vaishno Devi University, Katra, India. He is currently working as a Junior Research Fellow at the Department of Electronics and Instrumentation Technology, University of Kashmir, Srinagar, India. He has served as a faculty member at the Institute of Technology, Zakura,

University of Kashmir, Srinagar, India. His research interests include Internet of Things and network security, wireless and mobile networks and energy efficiency in WSN, and secure embedded systems.

Swarup Kumar Mitra received his B.Tech in Electronics and Telecommunication Engineering from Kalyani University, India in the year of 2000. He also obtained his M.Tech and PhD (Engg) degrees from Electronics and Telecommunication Engineering Department of Jadavpur University, India in the year of 2007 and 2012 respectively. He has more than 16 years of teaching experience. Currently, he is engaged as an Associate Professor in Electronics and Communication Engineering Department at MCKV Institute of Engineering, India. His research areas include wireless sensor networks, soft computing and FPGA based system design etc.

Mrinal Kanti Naskar received his B.Tech (Hons) and M.Tech in Electrical and Electronics Communication Engineering from Indian Institute of Technology, Kharagpur, India in 1987 and 1989 respectively. He also obtained his Ph.D. (Engg.) degree from Electronics and Telecommunication Engineering Department of Jadavpur University, India in the year of 2006. He has more than 27 years of teaching and research experience. Currently, he is a Professor of Electronics and Telecommunication Engineering Department, Jadavpur University, India. His research interests include wireless sensor networks, computer architectures and embedded system design, etc.

Rajinder Sandhu is currently working as Assistant Professor (Senior Grade) in the Department of Computer Science & Engineering at Jaypee University of Information Technology (JUIT) Waknaghat, Solan, Himachal Pradesh-India since November, 2016. He has obtained his Ph.D. from Guru Nanak Dev University, Amritsar in 2017 and M.E. with honours from Thapar University, Patiala in 2013. He was research fellow in CLOUDs Laboratory, University of Melbourne, Australia in 2016-17. He has published his research work in Scientific Citation Index journals of Elsevier, John Wiley and Springer. He also filed two patents in Indian Patent Office. He is also consultant to Gigabyte Pvt. Ltd. and Nihon Communication, Bangalore for Cloud Computing and Big Data. He is reviewer of many reputed SCI journals of Elsevier, Wiley and Springer. Starting from his M.E., he has delivered multiple expert talks on cloud computing for various workshops and FDPs of reputed universities like JNU-Delhi, PEC-Chandigarh and IIT-Kharakpur. His current working research areas are cloud computing, Big Data and Internet of Things (IoT). Currently, He is working with Prof. Rajkumar Buyya from Australia and Dr. Victor Chang from China on various projects and research papers.

Kundankumar R. Saraf is presently working as Assistant Professor in Electronics and Telecommunication Engineering department of D. Y. Patil College of Engineering, Pune, Maharashtra. He received B.E. degree in Electronics Engineering from North Maharashtra University, Jalgaon, Maharashtra in 2010. He has received M.E. degree in Electronics and Telecommunication Engineering from Savitribai Phule Pune University, Pune, Maharashtra in 2013. He has published 2 Indian patents and filed an Indian patent. He is currently a Ph.D. candidate in Savitribai Phule Pune University, Pune, Maharashtra, India. His area of interest includes cryptography and light fidelity communication.

Biplab Sikdar received a B. Tech. degree in electronics and communication engineering from North Eastern Hill University, Shillong, India, in 1996, the M. Tech. degree in electrical engineering from the Indian Institute of Technology, Kanpur, India, in 1998, and the Ph.D. degree in electrical engineering from the Rensselaer Polytechnic Institute, Troy, NY, USA, in 2001. He was on the faculty of Rensselaer Polytechnic Institute from 2001 to 2013, first as an Assistant and then as an Associate Professor. He is currently an Associate Professor with the Department of Electrical and Computer Engineering, National University of Singapore, Singapore. His research interests include wireless network and security for IoT and cyber physical systems. Dr. Sikdar is a member of Eta Kappa Nu and Tau Beta Pi. He served as an Associate Editor for the IEEE Transactions on Communications from 2007 to 2012. He currently serves as an Associate Editor for the IEEE Transactions on Mobile Computing.

Ishfaq Sultan received his B.Sc. from S.P. College, Srinagar and M.Sc degree in Electronics from University of Kashmir in 2011 and 2014, respectively. He is currently working towards completion of his Ph.D. degree in Electronics from the Department of Electronics and Instrumentation Technology, University of Kashmir, Srinagar. His research interests include Microprocessors and Microcontrollers, Computer Networking, Computer Architecture, and Security of the Internet of Things.

A. K. Verma is currently working as Professor in the department of Computer Science and Engineering at Thapar University, Patiala in Punjab (INDIA). He received his B.E., M.E. and PhD. in 1991, 2001 and 2008 respectively, majoring in Computer Science and Engineering. He has worked as Lecturer at M.M.M. Engg. College, Gorakhpur from 1991 to 1996. From 1996 he is associated with the same University. He has been a visiting faculty to many institutions. He has published over 150 papers in refereed journals and conferences. He is a member of various program committees for different International/National Conferences and is on the review board of various International journals. He has visited – USA (2005),

South Korea (2012), Japan (2013), Ireland (2015) and Bahrain (2017) for academic purpose. He is a MISCI (Turkey), LMCSI (Mumbai), GMAIMA (New Delhi). He is a certified software quality auditor by MoCIT, Govt. of India. He is a MISCI (Turkey), LMCSI (Mumbai), GMAIMA (New Delhi). He is a certified software quality auditor by MoCIT, Govt. of India.

Pooja Verma obtained her Bachelor degree in Computer Science and Engineering from Babu Banarasi Das Northern India Institute of Technology, Lucknow in 2013, and completed her Master degree in Computer Science and Engineering from Madan Mohan Malaviya University of Technology in May 2017. She has been awarded Gold medal at Post graduation level. She has 2-year teaching experience at UG level and is currently working as Assistant Professor in REC Ambedkarnagar. Her area of Interest is Security in Network such as: MANET and Internet of Things, Cloud Computing.

Index

T

W